IT'S ABOUT ETERNAL LIFE AFTER ALL

REVISITING CATHOLIC BELIEFS

Edward Jeremy Miller

Divina Press
an imprint of Lectio Publishing, LLC
Hobe Sound, Fla.

Appendix A is an article extract from Miller, E. J. "John Henry Newman's Idea of Alma Mater." *Newman Studies Journal* 8, no. 2 (Fall 2011): 19-28 (at pp. 21-22). © 2021 National Institute for Newman Studies, reprinted with permission, www.newmanstudies.org.

Appendix C (*Rome Reviews Remarriage*) is an Opinion originally published in *The Philadelphia Inquirer*, Thursday, October 22, 2015, Section A, page 19; (title chosen by newspaper editors). Reprinted with permission. https://www.inquirer.com/philly/opinion/currents/20151022_Rome_reviews_remarriage.html

Third Impression (September 2021)

Cover image: © Photos by AdobeStock. Used with Permission.

Cover and Book Design: Linda Wolf

ISBN 978-1-943901-98-2
Library of Congress Control Number: 2021908918

Published by Divina Press
an imprint of Lectio Publishing, LLC
Hobe Sound, Florida 33455
www.divinapress.com

Dedication

To my mother and father,
Mary Collins Miller and Edward Preston Miller,
who first taught me by words and especially behavior what faith means,
and to Kieran Hogue Duffy,
who became the brother I never had
and who prospered this book.

ENDORSEMENTS

A refreshingly different approach. Being a Christian is for Miller, as it was for his mentor Saint John Henry Newman, not just a matter of *believing* but of openness and receptivity in the indwelling presence of God. He argues his case with wisdom and scholarship, but also with great modesty, and with clarity and simplicity of expression.

Keith Beaumont
honorary president of Association francophone des Amis de Newman,
author of *Dieu Interieur: La théologie spirituelle de J. H. Newman*

John Henry Newman distinguished between notional apprehension and real apprehension, between dry, abstract thinking and vivid, concrete experiencing. In his thoughtful new book, Newman scholar E. J. Miller employs this distinction, along with other Newmanian devices, to help Catholic laity both think through their faith with greater precision and aspire to transform it through real, prayerful experiencing of God, who is the present, though invisible, reality of Eternal Life within us all.

Walter E. Conn
Professor Emeritus of Ethics
Villanova University

Ed Miller has drawn upon a long and rich experience as a professor, thinker, and author to create a thoughtful understanding of key Catholic dimensions of how the life of a believer now and forever changes by remaining rooted in God. This fresh articulation of the ancient tradition carefully separates the wheat from the chaff, opening the way for a rich and thoughtful presentation of Catholicism. Aimed at a lay readership, it is as accessible as it is enlightening.

James L. Heft, S.M.,
Alton Professor of Religion,
University of Southern California

Acknowledgments

Professors Carol Breslin and Marilyn Monaghan, mentioned in the Foreword, proofed and critiqued chapters as I produced them, as did my wife Kathleen. Marilyn died before this book appeared. Kieran Healy of the Western Dominican Province has ministered to laity lifelong and was another early reader. His words of encouragement still ring in my ears: "Our Catholic laity need to hear these ideas." Another Kieran in my life, mentioned in the Dedication, Kieran Duffy, has been equally encouraging from the start. Dr. Sandra Estanek (Canisius College) brought the eyes of an educated layperson to the text and offered many needed suggestions. Fr. Don Goergen of the Central Dominican Province, one of our nation's finest theologians, contributed suggestions from his unique perspective. Others read portions of the manuscript aligned to their interests, such as John Burchill of the Eastern Dominican Province in the field of Bible, Sr. Patricia Talone, RSM, in moral theology, Professor John Groppe in Newman studies, and my friend from high school days, Ken Woodring, who became sufficiently adept in philosophy that I tried out on him some of my stranger ideas. Bro. John Mahon, FSC, and Bruce Williams, OP, shared early life experiences with me, as did Sr. Mary Ellen Sheehan, IHM. They reviewed my recollections of life in Philadelphia, in the Dominicans, and in Louvain. Other readers agreed to contribute endorsements for the book. To all these fine people I am grateful, and I hereby remove them from accountability for my ideas about Catholic beliefs for which I alone am responsible. A special thanks to Linda Wolf (Divina Press, Hobe Sound, Fla.) who had confidence in this book and guided its production.

CONTENTS

Preface: Topics And Style Of Writing

TOPICS

In recent years I arrived at the conviction that Eternal Life is a reality I possess now, one that is not essentially different from the Eternal Life awaiting me in heaven. Eager to share with others my journey toward this conviction, I have written this book to explore topics that I hope may serve others as stepping stones along their personal faith journeys. I readily admit that there is obviously a difference between being a resurrected reality in heaven and lacking it on earth. But bear with me for now. I promise to return to this topic in its proper place.

I've chosen to begin with a chapter entitled "How the Bible Works," which explains how Catholic biblical understanding, as taught at the Second Vatican Council, avoids the literalism of Christian fundamentalists on the one hand and the *reductionism* of those biblical scholars these days who claim that there is very little one can know of what Jesus actually said and did. The Bible, and especially the New Testament, is called upon in later chapters to explain convictions about Eternal Life that I am proposing. For this reason, chapter one provides a sort of orientation to the entire Bible that many Catholic laity may lack. Growing up Catholic, I certainly lacked it.

Following this description of how the Bible works, I move in the next chapter, "Having, Losing, And Regaining More," to some advice on how the Bible might be read most advantageously. This chapter addresses a clear instance of the tendency to read the Bible literally and thereby mistake it. The two creation stories at the beginning of the *Book of Genesis*, the story of creation in six days, and the story of Adam and Eve in the Garden, contain profound religious truths that are obscured by the customary literal reading of them. I elaborate, then, the two stories using principles of how the Bible works. Other stories in the Bible could have been chosen for this exercise in interpretation. But these two stories, and particularly that of Adam and Eve, bear on the doctrine of Original Sin, and Original Sin bears heavily on understanding Eternal Life, especially if misconstrued. Binding teachings on Original Sin issued from the sixteenth-century Council of Trent. The Council also read the Adam and Eve story quite literally. Therefore, I needed to sort out which aspects of the Council's teachings are binding on Catholic faith and which no longer are. These, then, are the two subdivisions of chapter two: the creation stories and the teachings of Trent.

Since a running motif of this book is what my Catholic faith has come to mean to me, something I wish to share with readers as clearly as I can, then writing about God—what we can know about God and what we cannot know—needs to be addressed, and addressed early in the book after some groundwork on the Bible. Thus, chapter three, "So What Is God Like?" raises a question coming naturally to mind if I propose to write about my conviction concerning Eternal Life. Because Eternal Life is based on the indwelling presence of God in us, whether now or in heavenly life, you cannot avoid asking what God is like if you wish to talk about how Eternal Life is experienced, or gained, or lost.

For me, chapter four, "On Prayer," is a logical next step. Some could argue, as prominent theologians do, that God's nature is incomprehensible, but Jesus is the visible expression of the invisible God and to know him is to know God his Father. Therefore, a chapter about Jesus should come next. There is some truth to this thought. I am struck, however, by the nature of God as a person and that I am a person. Persons talk; they communicate. In reference to God, such human talk is called prayer. In reference to me, God's talking is called inspiration and causing discernments. Besides, whatever is to be known about God, about Jesus, and about Eternal Life, if not nourished by a prayerful life, runs the danger of being sterile knowledge.

Chapter five, "The Life, Death, And Resurrection of Jesus," accepts the insight that Jesus is the revelation of God. "If you have seen me, you have seen the Father," Jesus said to Philip the Apostle. Information about Jesus' life, death, and resurrection can fill thick volumes—just take biblical scholar Raymond E. Brown's *Birth of the Messiah*, and *Death of the Messiah*, as examples—but I approach these features of Jesus differently. I am wishing to share features of my faith in the mystery of the Incarnation: in his birth (*Christmas* feature), in his temptations and suffering (*Lenten* feature), in his resurrection (*Easter* feature), in his glorification (*Ascension* feature), and in his Spirit-dispensing role (*Pentecost* feature). My angle to all these features is presenting how redemption should be understood. Redemption has to do with Original Sin and with the reality of Eternal Life. The chapter also contains a brief survey of early church councils. In sharing my faith insights with readers, I am persuaded that Catholics need to know more about the history of our church, especially as it bears upon our beliefs, such as the church's ecumenical councils do.

Because Jesus' resurrection is really an inexhaustible topic, I've chosen to extend it in the next chapter, "Other Features of Resurrection Belief." All along, in thinking about Eternal Life, the philosophical notion of eternity has possessed my mind and imagination. The wrong way to think about eternity is as perpetuity, as endless duration, as forever and ever as if the clock never stops ticking. Instead, eternity is an all-at-once reality, and therefore so is heaven. There is no passage of time because there is no reality called time. We can think about eternity but we cannot imagine it because our imaginations are locked into the temporality of earthly existence. Jesus resurrected into eternal immortality. Struggling against the time tilt of our imaginations, this chapter treats questions such as: What does Jesus' descent into hell mean? What happens to us at the moment of death? What is purgatory? What is the end of the world like? Do angels and devils exist? I conclude with my surmise regarding whether there are very bad people damned to hell for eternity.

Chapter seven, "Eternal Life In The Church On Earth," treats the Christian experience closest to our own experience, hence in our imaginations: our Catholic Church here and now. What is it like in terms of its sacramental life? What is it like in terms of scandalous behavior? The former is selected because sacraments are the places of encounter with Eternal Life, whether meeting it or being nourished in it. The latter is mentioned because it is a present-day reality driving people out of the church.

The last chapter, "Faith & Science Plus Some Unfinished Promises," is quite personal. Although I went on to graduate studies in philosophy and theology, I was a physics major as an undergraduate and I never abandoned my affection for science. I realize that many scientists think that belief in God makes no sense; in fact, a scientific view of life and a theistic view of life are incompatible. I do not think so. I begin this chapter making the case why not, taking as instances human origins, planetary origins, and evolutionary theory. In the earlier chapters topics arose to which I promised I would return. As one who works at keeping promises, I turn to them after the opening science segment and after mentioning positive aspects of using imagination, having spoken negatively about imagination when describing eternity. I conclude with thoughts on popes and on dying.

Some short extensions of a few features in the chapters above are treated in appendices.

WRITING STYLE

I am writing this book for Catholic laity with whom I hope to share my faith insights in an accessible and useful way. Thus, I have dispensed with the more formal style and detailed documentation that characterize academic publishing. I will have achieved my purpose if what I have come to understand as my Catholic faith, which for me has become simpler and uncluttered with extraneous features, speaks to them in a similar and nourishing manner.

I am taking a clue for a style of writing from John Henry Newman (1801–

xii PREFACE: TOPICS AND STYLE OF WRITING

1890). He was an Oxford professor and Anglican until 1845 before becoming a Roman Catholic. For many, his name resonates as Cardinal Newman, but he only became a cardinal in his last years after having had a controversial Catholic life. He published many books and sermons, and some literary critics consider him the finest prose writer of Victorian England.

He wrote on matters of faith and religion that resounded with many types of readers, both the highly educated and the less versed. What was his knack for communicating so successfully with so broad a sweep of people? It came down to this: He wrote on religious matters out of his experience that he thought mirrored that of others. He described himself. Many readers and listeners mentioned that Newman seemed to be describing them to themselves whenever he wrote or preached. "He was reading my own soul" was a common refrain. This, then, became my clue. I want to share my faith and share the experiences throughout my life that shaped it. The faith features are met in the book's eight chapters. The experiences are related in the *Foreword: My Story*, which brought me to realize what's key and what is not.

I just used the word *realize*. And I have introduced Newman's name. They are connected. Two of Newman's ideas concerning religious matters have become part of my lexicon because I think they size up so usefully our religious experiences. I explain them now because I want to call upon them later without pausing to elaborate.

Each idea amounts to a distinction. One of them is the distinction Newman draws between something being *real* (hence, to realize) and something else being *notional*. Take the sentence "My father loves me." In saying that it is true, the person is grasping all the words of the sentence in a very concrete fashion. The phrase lives in one's imagination. The daughter's or son's memories are flooded with concrete instances of the father's love being true beyond doubt and would resist anyone claiming that it is not true. Newman terms such grasping of a sentence like "My father loves me" a *real apprehension* of it, and the stating of its truthfulness a *real assent*. The son or daughter *realizes* the loving person captured by the words of the assertion. On the other hand, take the sentence, "Parents are duty bound to love their children." This sentence is as equally true as the other sentence, but notice that there is something very abstract about it. It is a *concept*, not a concrete picture in one's imagination. The concept may have been built up from individual experiences of watching parents perform or fail to perform, and someone then draws the conclusion about parental duties; still, it is a piece of generalized knowledge. It may even have been read out of a book or a catechism and memorized for a test. The grasping of this sentence Newman terms *notional* apprehension.

Here is a contemporary example of real vs. notional apprehension without the phrases ever being used or known. Bob Beckel was campaign manager for Walter Mondale when Mondale lost 49 states in the 1984 presidential reelection of Ronald Reagan. Beckel was also a drug addict, an alcoholic, and frequenter of brothels, all of which he kept under wraps while working in Washington political circles. After experiencing God, he removed all the covers when he came to write an autobiography, *I Should Be Dead: My Life Surviving Politics, TV, and Addiction.* He had had several moments when he thought his life had bottomed out, but lower levels remained. AA failed him because he never accepted the reality of a "higher power" of Step Two. Such was the impasse until the day he sat in a field crying, with car keys in his hand and his truck pointed in the direction of the nearest bar. But something was stopping him. As his autobiography describes it,

> As I sat there on that rock, the tears began to flow. In that moment I knew, without a shred of doubt…it would have been the signature on my death warrant. And I knew there was a force that had wanted me not to do that, a force that loved me enough to stop me in my tracks and redirect my steps. That loved *me*? Me? If there is one moment I can point to, a moment when the idea of God's grace shifted from being some kind of abstract concept to being something flesh and blood, something meaty and rich, something *real*, that was it.[1]

The application of the real *vs.* notional distinction for describing a person's faith is clear. Someone can have only a notional sense of God or of Jesus Christ. If the idea of God was bookish from the beginning, and it never got nurtured by prayer, and the idea became, as it were, "tabled" due to other personal interests, then it began and remains a notional apprehension of God. The person uses the *God* word now and then, may even answer in a poll, "Yes, I believe in God," but there is nothing vivid corresponding to the word, nothing real, nothing realized about the being of God like Bob Beckel realized. True religious life is about real apprehensions. So is secular life for that matter. When someone gets energized in playing the stock market, the whole fiscal marketplace is real to the person, the ebb and flow of one's money is realized by being imagined constantly and vividly. The adrenalin flows. Certain rules of financial investing may be notional but the notional is feeding what's real, and the real feeds back and may modify the notional rules. I will be using the words *real* and *notional* in the way Newman does.

Newman's second idea involves the distinction between *visible* and *invisible* realities. The difference is easier to explain because the two adjectives are just as we use them. The visible world is the world we know through our bodily senses. It is the world we hear and see and feel, and by that same token it also includes the far-flung cosmos, which we experience with the help of telescopes. God, the workings of grace, Eternal Life itself, and the members

---

1. (New York: Hachette Books, 2015), p. 241.

of the Kingdom (the saints) make up the invisible world. We do not see them the way we see trees and animals and people and stars. But both realms of the visible and invisible worlds can be real in the way the phrase, *real apprehension*, was described. The invisible world is met here, in the visible world we inhabit. When someone believes in God as more than a mere concept but rather as a real person, he or she is led to affirm, "God truly exists as much as this tree right in front of me truly exists." I will be using this type of language later, and further explanation of its applications can wait. For the moment, I am suggesting an advantage that is provided by the vocabulary of visible and invisible. It is better than the vocabulary of *earthly* life and *heavenly* life because the latter language makes heaven seem to be a place where people "go." Earth is here, heaven is elsewhere. But heaven is not *where* you exist but *how* you exist.

As mentioned, there will not be detailed documentation (i.e., academic footnotes) save for two exceptions: (a) to clarify or elaborate an issue without interrupting the flow of the narrative, and (b) to provide for more trained readers a warrant, usually in Latin, for how I translate a pivotal source lest it be thought gratuitous. Good examples of unreferenced material will be quotations from early Christian writings, from the period in church history called the Patristic Period or the era of the Fathers of the Church, a period from approximately AD 150 to 600. Their writings are not scripture but they are as close to the beating soul of scripture as is possible in our Catholic tradition.[2] From reading Patristic sources for many years, these writings have come to shape my faith, just as they captured in almost a providential manner in their own day the essence of the scriptural testimony of the Apostolic Age.

This book shares my faith with readers but avoids the organized format of a catechism; instead, it follows the logic of the topics described above. Two catechisms, however, have exercised an influence on my thinking. The first was St. Augustine's (AD 354–430) *Enchiridion*, his handbook on faith, hope and charity that was organized around an early church creed. From it I derived clear notions of evil and grace and the role of Christ. (Later I will share how a remark from Augustine in this book came to shape the basis of my thoughts on the meaning of Original Sin.) Another was the 1994 *Catechism of the Catholic Church*. It treated just about every topic of Catholic doctrine and was a good reminder of matters for me. It was meant as a guide for writers who produce catechisms aimed at their own culture and people, but it was also intended, something like a meter stick, to be a watchman or warden measuring such efforts. Where I perceive any of my reflections going beyond or against its parameters, I will indicate it.

---

2. Often they will use a biblical text from a Greek or Latin version they possessed. For the most part I am using the *New American Bible* translation, especially for book name abbreviations. Their words can differ from the NAB.

My choice of topics might raise objections to some readers. I'll use an illustration. Take someone who is very concerned, and rightly so, about the environment, such as the loss of the oxygen-producing and carbon dioxide-absorbing Amazon Rain Forest. For this reader, a central portion of Catholic faith is about protecting the earth from humanly caused destruction, which is a matter not unconnected with Eternal Life. This reader might indeed brandish the encyclical from Pope Francis, *Laudato Si'*, to contend that I am remiss in not making environmental matters sufficiently central. It's true that I am not treating the environment with the same care and attention I give other topics. My only defense is that to treat every important topic with the attention it deserves is to finally give up the project and treat nothing well.

An expectation that I cannot meet is avoiding altogether masculine language referring to God for there are some, mostly within theological circles, who wish entirely genderless words in writing about God.[3] God is a person, and the absence of gender language for God reduces references to "it" language, at least in English, leaving God depersonalized. But God communicates to us and has willed self-disclosure. It is called revelation. It describes a relationship between persons. To be sure, God by nature is without gender, and the scriptural imagery of God-as-mother accompanies the God-as-father imagery in the Old Testament in order to preserve in balance the personhood of God. One of the authors I've used in a medieval seminar is St. Anselm of Canterbury (AD 1033–1109), a writer as masculine in his usual style as any medieval author I know. Yet here is one of his texts about the Son of God: "But you, Jesus, good lord, are you not also a mother? Are you not the mother who, like a hen, collects her chickens under her wings? Truly, master, you are a mother. For what others have conceived and given birth to, they have received from you....You are the author, others are ministers. It is then you, above all, Lord God, who are mother." Overly masculine or exclusively masculine language for God is wrong for two reasons: It's incorrect for a genderless God and it's hurtful for women when it implies their exclusion or inferiority. I strive to achieve a rightful balance on this sensitive matter.

From time to time I will be mentioning things from the history of Christianity and from Catholic Church history in particular. This is not a deviation from discussing matters of personal belief because the faith of people, mine and others and especially others of long ago, is played out in this community we call the church. Thus the history of the church is not accidental to the story of faith's doctrines. I will refer to some ecumenical councils of the church or to this individual or that event. I will mention various Fathers of the Church from whose writings an explanation of our faith is given. It will

---

3. Inclusive language is another matter. I champion it, and I was perturbed when the inclusive language text for the new Lectionary for Mass was rejected by Rome and replaced by a text containing mandated *he's, him's, mankind's.*

reflect what I have come to accept for myself but it is expressed in their words, so much better put to use than I could muster. And I will share some incidents in church history that are hardly matters for boasting. A sanitized view of church without sinners amounts to a notional apprehension of church. A sanitized church never existed in the concrete.

The words *conservative* and *progressive* have come to describe American Catholics today. The profiles did not exist in the Catholic Philadelphia world in which I grew up. The Catholic use of these words originated during the Second Vatican Council to describe two sorts of bishops, the progressive bishops who were open to changes in church life and thinking, such as putting Mass in vernacular languages, and conservative bishops arguing to maintain traditions.

Vatican II was a progressive triumph mainly, although its final documents show the fingerprints of both orientations in the promulgated texts. The division between progressive and conservative Catholics continues today and has become contentious, even politicized, which for the unity of my church I regret to see. My own inclinations tend to be more progressive, yet there are certain faith convictions I have that someone else could call conservative. In the *My Story* segment that follows, I make the case that for someone living before and after Vatican II, as I have, a sense of balance is possible. I think that the Catholic Church, here in America and worldwide, is a big enough tent to embrace both types of orientation, provided each side can listen to the other side respectfully and in openness.

A codicil of sorts about the title of the book: Following a knee joint replacement, I was confined to the first floor of our home for some weeks. In the long hours and days of lying only on my back, I was thinking of the fact that you don't wait to go to heaven to have Eternal Life. You have it now. I was thinking of early Christian texts like "God became human so that humans could become gods." One afternoon the two Gwynedd University professors mentioned in *My Story* came to visit me in my bedridden state. One of them asked, "What have you been up to, Ed?" I said that I am thinking about writing a book, and if I do, I already have mused about the title. "It's About Eternal Life After All."[4]

---

4. That master of spiritual writing, Romano Guardini, wrote that Eternal Life "is not the opposite of transitory life. Perhaps we come closest to the truth when we define it as the life which participates in the life of God....This eternal life does not wait till after death to begin. It already exists." *The Lord* (ET of his *Der Herr*), Gateway, 1996, p. 277. Much of this book attempts to describe Eternal Life in this manner.

Foreword: My Story

"I have written this to you to make you realize that you possess eternal life, you who believe in the name of the Son of God" 1 John 5:13

In wanting to share what my Catholic faith has come to mean to me, after many years thinking about it, I need to tell you my story. It won't be a biography nor even a memoir. It will be more like a chronicle of faith-forming events in my life, and of the people, including authors, who influenced me, who shaped me. I'd like to think that God was using these events and persons, and that God was really doing the shaping.

An observation about the book you are holding in your hand: To say clearly what got me started on it, it was three women. Some books begin intriguingly, like "Call me Ishmael" (*Moby Dick*), or "Happy families are all alike; each unhappy family is unhappy in its own way" (*Anna Karenina*). I am beginning with this acknowledgment of the roles of three women, without whose encouragement I may not have ever written what is contained in your hand.

Foremost of the three is my wife, Kathleen, and a custom we have each Easter is the setting. When it is warm enough, and Easter days usually are when Ash Wednesday does not happen too close to Christmas, we gather on our outdoor deck with a glass of wine and talk about what resurrection means. More than once Kathleen observed that I ought to write up some of the ideas I had about how Jesus "appeared" to this or that disciple or to many at once, about how I thought our own resurrected bodies after death would function, or about what it means to exist in eternity. Ours was a conversation, not a lecture from her professor husband to his wife the nurse, and so her own strands of thought over several Easters worked their way into the fabric of my own thinking and at this point cannot be unraveled for separate attribution.

The other two women who urged me to put to paper my ideas about religious topics were professors at Gwynedd Mercy University where I taught till recently. The situation with each was similar: team-taught courses in Gwynedd's Honors Program. I team taught an honors course with Professor Marilyn Monaghan on the American experience in literature and religion from the Civil War period to mid-twentieth century, which for the religious component meant until the dawn of Vatican Council Two. I learned much from Marilyn about Twain, Upton Sinclair, Stephen Crane, Hemingway, Scott Fitzgerald, and some others. I presented on nineteenth-century American religion (read: the varieties of Protestantism that practically defied counting), Tom Merton's *Seven Storey Mountain* (and what undergraduate could not identify with college-age Merton's extracurricular escapades), and John Courtney Murray's essays on being a consensus-seeking citizen in multi-denominational America, not to mention living in an increasingly secular America. There were many occasions to talk religion, and these honors students were keen to engage religious topics. Mark Twain's poking fun at the traditional Protestant ideas of heaven in "Letters from the Earth" was as much occasion for me to frame religious issues as were Merton's reflections on what brought him around from idle dissipations and fathering a child to firm religious commitments, and entry into an austere monastery no less. I don't think a fall semester with Prof. Monaghan ended without her asking me to record my observations. They were Catholic insights, and she said things like, "You added such interesting angles to topics I've met all through my life as a Catholic." So, with her encouragement I began thinking about this book.

It was a similar experience with Professor Carol Breslin. From the very inception of Gwynedd's honors program, I have team taught the Middle Ages seminar with her. The medieval period was dear to both of us and tapped into our respective expertise, she in its history and literature, especially Chaucer, and I in its theology and philosophy. Catholic Christianity pervaded the entire period as a cohesive glue that gave common language and fundamental principles to everything medieval. The "religious question," if I may so call it, was close to the surface in all the primary documents we read with our students. The familiar names were met: Augustine, Boethius, Hildegard (proclaimed a Doctor of the Church in 2012), Aquinas and Chaucer. We introduced the students to other, lesser known, voices, particularly female voices such as Hrotsvitha of tenth-century Lower Saxony, Heloise whose twelfth-century story unfolded with that of Abelard, and Christine de Pizan at the turn of the fifteenth century. As a consequence, the religious features of life, both then and today, came into play somewhat spontaneously. And not to be overlooked, there were observations and challenging queries from our inquisitive honors students. Like Marilyn Monaghan, Carol Breslin encouraged me to elaborate, at some future point, on certain theological insights I offered in the spontaneity of the seminar that she, also a life-long educated Catholic, found personally instructive.

If any of these motivations makes me sound as if I think I am a religious guru of sorts, it would be alien to why I began this writing effort in the first place. I had a theological training in a very illustrious place, but I am not one of the University of Louvain's star graduates. Nor do I think I enjoy special luster among the theologians of my own country. All I can confess with a sense of honesty is that as I have grown older and been informed especially by my experiences in being married and being a parent, I have come to see my Catholic Christianity in a richer and simpler way and cleaned of clutter. I think some of this directness got communicated to my two esteemed team teachers. I hope one senses that I am not talking about bookish religious knowledge because I do not want to make a book out of bookish ideas about Christian faith.

Here is another curiosity. This book was not meant to be the next piece of writing on my work horizon. As I approached retirement from Gwynedd Mercy University in May 2014, I had spent my last two university years on a half-time schedule in order to edit a collection of essays on Cardinal John Henry Newman's teachings on the nature of conscience. That book came into being not long after those released-time years ended.[1] The plan was then to undertake another book on Newman, this one fully from myself. It was to treat Newman's educational philosophy in dialogue with the issues of Catholic higher education in the United States today, especially the matter of the required *mandatum* from the local bishop for Catholic theology professors. In the lead up to the 1990 papal document *Ex Corde Ecclesiae*, which introduced the *mandatum* idea—a kind of church recognition and tasking of Catholic professors teaching theology—and in the follow-up strategy how the American bishops were to bestow it, there were all varieties of articles and books published on American Catholic higher education, some of them fearful that the *mandatum* was a threat to academic freedom. To this mix I contributed a few articles. But there did not appear to be any book-length integration of Newman's ideas into the animated discussions going on among bishops, Catholic college presidents, and professors in the United States, whereas Newman after all carried the image of the Catholic university educator par excellence.

What happened to my grand intention for this kind of a book? It got pushed off the "next-thing-to-do" list. I was closing in on being 75 years old. A wish had been growing within me to write down, while I still could, things I have been pondering about God, about Catholic faith, about the end of my own life and the nature of resurrection, and about living in a church to which I remain fully committed while continuing to be unnerved by its scandals. On the other hand, it was going to take some years to shape a cohesive and hopefully persuasive story of Newman and contemporary Catholic higher

---

1. *Conscience the Path to Holiness: Walking with Newman*, edited with introduction by Edward Jeremy Miller, (Newcastle upon Tyne: Cambridge Scholars Press, 2014).

education. I feared starting the effort and getting bogged down. I also feared letting the chance slip to write a book that would not be geared to university academics, as the Newman book would necessarily have been. I wanted to write a book about the Catholic faith geared to non-academics, to Catholic laity in general.

Even though I am in good health, the approach of my 75th birthday had a lot to do with switching the agenda. The death in 2013 of one of my best friends from childhood played a subconscious role, I think. A year before he died, he asked me to deliver his eulogy. I directed the following remarks to our grade and high school classmates at his October funeral service: "These funerals for friends our own age are increasingly autobiographical. When you are 73, as John Glaser was and as we are, his Holy Child Grade School and LaSalle High School classmates, these funerals are sober moments, moments made for introspection and self-appraisal. To be seventy-something is not aged, but it is to be old. With each passing year, the funeral of someone else our age becomes increasingly autobiographical, a foretaste of our earthly life closing down." A sober thought, yes, and an agenda switcher.

I now need to turn the calendar pages backward from being seventy something to years earlier. My story then unfolds in three segments. These stages of life capture who I was and who I have become. Some of the experiences remain defining of my religious thinking, some no longer do.

STAGE ONE

The first twenty years of my life were spent in Philadelphia of the World-War-Two years and its peacetime aftermath. My father returned from naval service in the Pacific at war's end when I was five. One of my earliest memories was of globs of crude oil looking like very large pancakes on the sandy beach of North Wildwood, NJ, the evidence of German submarine torpedoes and dead merchant mariners in the summer of 1943. When the war ended, it became a peaceful and uncomplicated time to grow up, even as a teenager, on the streets of North Philadelphia, and the same goes for growing up in the Catholicism of those years. Both city life and church life reflected, at least for me and my friends, an ordered and unchallenged structure in which to navigate.

My experiences of being a Catholic by the end of this period—John F. Kennedy was just about to become the first Catholic president, *our* president—reflected order and stability. Catholicism was a very large but not unruly affair. Our parish church had ten Masses each Sunday, one each hour from 6 to 11 am, and four "overflow" Masses—*liturgies* we now call them—running simultaneously in a school annex. For everyone, Catholic life seemed to run like clockwork. Mirroring Sunday Masses beginning precisely on the hour, Catholic events unfolded with predicable regularity. The season of Christmas services was followed by "Little Christmas" because we at that moment knew nothing of how Orthodox Christians celebrated Jesus' birth. We simply called January 6th the Epiphany feast, and it meant Christmas decorations could come down. Soon after Epiphany came Candlemas Day, the Feast of the Presentation, when the parish school children, at least the older ones—no small number back then—were brought into church for a procession carrying candles. The next day, February 3rd, was the Feast of St. Blaise, when Catholics gathered for the annual blessing of throats. And these regular Catholic "events" I've just narrated reached only into February.

Devotional events punctuated the entire year and even claimed use of city streets, as when the parochial school children in white suits and dresses on "May Procession Day" circled the parish neighborhood to honor the Virgin Mary, with police officers (mostly Irish men then) stopping traffic. Catholicism was the "biggest player" in city life, representing almost 50% of the population. Its wide impress was such that folks, including many non-Catholics, would not say "I live in the Philly's Olney neighborhood," but rather "I live near Holy Child Church."

In using language I acquired later, I would say that the *institutional model* or face of Catholicism played very strongly in our lives, from the young to the old. It engulfed us in its institutional girth. Catholicism possessed another feature that shaped us all, again from young to old. None of us living in mid-twentieth-century Philadelphia thought of being Catholic as other than that this was the way Catholicism had always been. I suspect that most of the parish clergy shared in this same timeless version of what Catholicism was about because there was never a sermon that gave any inkling that Catholicism had evolved over time. Everything seemed timeless: the importance and centrality of the pope, the catechism answers, the priests dressed in ankle-length black soutanes and biretta hats, the way sacraments were done, to name just a few of the unchanging identifiable features molding our imaginations of Catholicism. The result was that many laity had a crisis of conscience when changes in Catholic devotions happened in the 1960s. When the language of the Mass switched from Latin to English, I remember one of my uncles, an educated man working for the Pennsylvania Railroad, asking me, "How can this be? Jesus prayed in Latin at the Last Supper, didn't he?"

Once again, in a language and viewpoint I acquired later, we in 1950s American Catholicism that we imagined as timeless and enduring were but experiencing Baroque Catholicism, a Catholicism that took shape after the sixteenth-century Council of Trent that had bucked the Protestant challenges to Roman Catholicism. Baroque Catholicism was an internal renewal movement in the Roman Catholic Church from the late 1500s all through the 1600s that stressed emotions and the role of actual graces to do this and avoid offending in that, and, consequently, produced its own Catholic art; for example, the Jesuit-style churches and the graphic statues of weeping saints and a Jesus brutalized by his Passion and Crucifixion. But normal Catholics had no awareness that this was just a phase in Christian art. We lived as Catholics engulfed by Baroque Catholicism, totally unaware of that strange word and thinking that this style of being Catholic went back very early in church history, if not to Jesus.

Unawares, we were children of Baroque Catholicism. We meditated on emotion-laden church statues in order to make our "examination of conscience" to determine how we were not measuring up to being "perfect," and to prepare ourselves for going to Saturday Confession to confess our sins. This Baroque tradition also produced a "certain mechanization in prayer and liturgy," as a later theologian friend of mine put it. People had prayer books or stacks of holy cards from which they said "their prayers" every day, many even using them while Sunday Mass was going on.

Our individualized faith and emotions—Jesus and I, not Jesus and we— was buoyed up by the testimony of apparitions from heaven given to certain saints, including many saints from the recent nineteenth century. We had no idea that the first fourteen-hundred years of the Catholic Church did not report apparitions of Mary or of other saints. To repeat, we thought that the Catholic style we knew went back to Christianity's beginnings. I should rather say that we assumed it did because we didn't think in the categories of a historical sweep. We just pondered the present in its seemingly enduring aspect. And this impression was not restricted to my city or my country. When later I lived in Belgium and came to know Flemish families, new friends my age said that they grew up thinking the same about the Catholicism they experienced in West Flanders or Brabant.

In sharing these memories of my earliest Catholic years, I want to be clear about two intentions. In later years it became great sport for writers or TV comedians to burlesque this old-time Catholic piety for laughs that made its practitioners seem silly. On the contrary, I am not dismissive in any way of what might be called pre-Vatican II Catholicism because those people using Mass time to read holy cards or finger rosaries—my mother was one—were holy people and close to God. There were things of this period that do merit critique. For example, the service of Benediction had become a more emotionally satisfying experience for many people than the Mass was; in retrospect this seems upside-down. But again, it was the influence of the Baroque stress on feelings and having Benediction conducted in English as opposed to a Latin Mass that no one understood. Also meriting critique was the constant focus from preachers on the possibility of committing mortal sins and the need for going frequently to Confession. This was a great disservice to people of tender conscience, and especially to the scrupulous.

My second intention is to indicate with sufficient examples that I experienced a pre-Vatican II Catholicism whose activities were real apprehensions to me then, even as now recalled. We of that era are a disappearing bunch, but we are able to bring to an assessment of Vatican Council II itself and to the post-conciliar church of the last fifty years advantages younger critics lack. We know, and not just from readings, what went on before: what was good about it and what wasn't, what were improvements due to the Council and what were missteps. We of this earlier era bring a balanced assessment, I think, to the debate going on today whether Popes John Paul II and Benedict XVI represented a retrenchment from legitimate developments in the post-conciliar church or were a return to the Council's true spirit.

STAGE TWO

I began at LaSalle University in this pre-Vatican II period as a physics major, with no particular interest in religion other than practicing it in a slightly lower and suitable-for-college key, someone who liked to play sports a lot and to date young coeds even more and intending to marry one of them after getting a job out of college. But this kind of carefree college life came to an end after a couple of years. I found myself not only departing the experience of being a loosely involved Catholic in the manner described above but also swapping my layman's identity for a clerical one. I requested and was accepted into a monastic life style, a community of Dominican priests and brothers that had its beginnings in the early thirteenth century. For the reader to understand how my experiences have shaped my present faith insights, this second stage of my life, if I may so call it, is as important as my first formative period in sturdily Catholic Philadelphia. But because I want this book to avoid drifting into a full-fledged memoir, there is no need to recount the many elements leading to this decision to undertake monastic living other than mentioning the quiet and gentle influence on me from LaSalle chaplain and Dominican, Fr. Mark Heath. But losing any attraction to being married was not one of the influences. I accepted the celibacy features of monastic life but never with an acquired ease and peace.

I knew hardly anything about what I was getting into. I knew Dominicans wore white habits (monastic-speak for robes) because the three Dominicans teaching at LaSalle walked around campus in their white robes while I was there. In Ohio, I got my own habit at the start of the trial year, called a novitiate. I was informed a few days before getting the garment that I needed to adopt a "religious name" for the future. Others of my entrance group, arriving more prepared than I and knowing a lot more about the Dominicans, had famous old Dominican names in mind, such as Albert, Vincent Ferrer, and Aquinas. My mind latched onto *Jeremy* because Brother Jeremy McNamara at a Christian Brothers high school in Philadelphia had influenced me through his own character and inner spirit. The impression stuck and the name sounded nice besides, so I became Brother Jeremy, a Dominican in process. To this day the religious name functions as my middle name.

Dominican life from the start introduced me to community prayer. The vocal praying was something you did with others, and this felt very new, even strange at first. But you might say, "Well, that is what the Mass is, so what seemed so new to you?" It is true. The Mass is a community prayer in its very essence, but my family, my friends, and I in Philadelphia never thought of the Mass like that. We went to Mass and we observed it from afar. The priest said its Latin prayers under his breath. Or you went to a Baptism and observed it. There were some things we said in common, as if by rote, but the priest did all the praying, it seemed. But now, in a monastic praying style that went back to the first Benedictines fifteen hundred years earlier, the white-robed assembly came together five times a day into choir (monastic-speak for chapel), dividing ourselves into rows of seats facing each other, a large center aisle interposing. We chanted psalms and other prayers back and forth. One side of the choir would sing a verse of a psalm, then the other side would sing the next verse, and so it went. It was like feeding each other pieces of prayers. After a week of doing this, the community would have sung its way through almost all 150 psalms.

There was lots of singing in the many forms of monastic praying that I began experiencing, and our teachers of Gregorian chant would remind us of St. Augustine's famous "he who sings prays twice." Thus it was that the essentially communal nature of Christian prayer entered my experience, and it has never left me. The beauty of the Gregorian chant melodies, going back over a thousand years, has never left either. Some more recent church hymns pale in comparison. Private praying during the monastic silences still counted, and it would have been a desiccated Christian life without it.

Monastic life introduced me to meditation, which may sound more mysterious than it is. Following early morning pre-breakfast psalm chanting in choir, the group turned to silent reflection for a half hour or more. It was not unlike what happens in a quiet Quaker Meetinghouse where the members sit in silence. Meditation's purpose is to foster a sense of inner recollection and an ability to listen for God. The Dominican tradition encouraged "silent time" to happen elsewhere: in one's room, in a private visit to chapel, on a solitary walk. Meditation at an earlier stage of practicing it might begin with mulling over some passage of Scripture or some poignant experience, such as someone's death or severe illness. The reflections are not meant to be analyzed in a rational manner as if mentally preparing a talk on them. Activity may start in the mind, but movement to the heart, to the source of loving, is sought. Blaise Pascal, a seventeenth-century French mathematician and spiritual writer, captured its essence in a few words that have become famous: *Le coeur a ses raisons, que la raison ne connaît point* [The heart has its reasons that reasoning hardly knows]. Cardinal Newman's motto comes close to it: *cor ad cor loquitur* [Heart speaks to heart, God's and ours]. Meditative silence awaits God's breaking it with inspirations to our hearts.

Thus it was that community prayer and meditative prayer shaped how I had begun to grasp what Christian faith, at least my own, consisted in. I am referring to an appreciation of the nature of faith that continues into my present lifestyle but retains the imprint of these earlier years. Creating space for meditation became ingrained, and a place and time happen for Kathleen and me to this day in our home. Once, in the early morning, is enough, with cups of coffee at the ready, and the day's latter distractions held at bay. To anticipate some later discussions on prayer, I think meditative prayer provided me what to expect, and what not to expect, about how God "answers our praying." It also explains why the *Gospel of John*, the most meditative of the four gospels, became my favorite.

I retain another legacy from this Dominican period. The community is like a scaled-down church in many respects. The experience of living in a religious community, both in its moments of praying in common, and in the daily living of the so-called "common life," has enabled me to view the *church* as essentially a single spiritual reality and not just a collection of people. Such a concept of the church is a hard one to achieve. I never had it all through college, and it helps me understand now why others lack this sense of the church. The church, externally, is an assemblage of those who can be seen and touched and spoken to, but this collective reality has a soul, as it were. Call it the Mystical Body. Call it the animating spirit of the Risen Christ. Whatever you call it, it is hard to come to appreciate. It is like saying each person has a physical body (skin, organs, etc.) and each person has a soul, an animating principle that makes all the physical stuff to be *human* stuff. It's true but is it easy to grasp?

When later as a university professor I taught theology classes on the church, I wanted to present the church as the Mystical Body of the Risen Jesus. But I found it too hard to explain the idea of the soul of the church to undergraduates. They knew in an institutional sense who the individuals were and how they functioned; for example, "Our pastor preaches too long;" "Today's newspaper reports more church scandals;" "Some saint's relic is coming to our parish." They had little idea what the church as Jesus' Mystical Body meant no matter how many analogies I tried to draw. Still, this idea of the church is true, and my experience of religious community life prepared me to appreciate it. I was less successful teaching it to others. The idea of *church* for students remained too *notional*, in Newman's sense. It was simply descriptive.

During this monastic period, I acquired something important that remained with me as an intellectual value. I acquired an extensive knowledge of, and a fondness for, the teachings of St. Thomas Aquinas (AD 1225–1274). The Dominicans are rather bullish about his teachings because he became one of them in the early 1200s and went on to have a celebrated career in the university world of the High Middle Ages. The University of Paris, during Thomas's two periods there in the 1250s and the late 1260s, was the center of theological debate and influence in Western Christendom. In subsequent

centuries, there were ways in which some of his devotees hurt his heritage by
repeating in rote fashion his teachings on this or that topic, with little concern
for how their own contemporary issues differed from his thirteenth-century
concerns. In making Aquinas seem timeless and ever applicable, this subsequent tradition calcified Thomas Aquinas into Thomistic mantras, practically jargon. His theological formulas were used like ammunition to combat
the enemies of the church.

This was not my Dominican experience. We studied Aquinas as a primary text in his original Latin and in his historical context. Still, it was not until
I was sent later to Belgium's University of Louvain as a priest to do doctoral
studies that I met Dominicans whose Thomism engaged the modern world
in a sympathetic and non-hostile manner. Like some other Jesuit theologians,
they were silenced by Vatican authorities in the 1940s and 1950s for their
forward thinking that drifted from the *status quo* theology being taught in the
Roman seminaries. Fr. Yves Congar, O.P., was one of them, for he dared to
try to understand Protestant Christianity and Eastern Orthodox Christianity sympathetically. Another "silenced" Dominican was Congar's Parisian
confrère, Dominique Chenu, who proposed a Thomistic theology engaging contemporary thought in increasingly atheistic France, using a dialogical
manner rather than condemnations. John XXIII exonerated them after he
became pope, and they played crucial roles at Vatican II. Fr. Jan Walgrave
was another Dominican, eventually my Louvain mentor par excellence,
whose work in theology engaged the philosophies of modernity in an open
fashion. It was from people like these three that I continued my immersion
into the thought of Thomas Aquinas.

During this part of my life, which I am calling its second period, attending the University of Louvain was as paramount an influence on my thinking
as anything else that happened. Fr. Mark Heath entered my life once again
in a providential way as he had earlier at LaSalle University. As I was near to
concluding my second and congenial year of undergraduate theology teaching at Ohio Dominican College (now University) in Columbus that was a
foretaste of what I was meant to do lifelong, my superiors in New York asked
me to undertake doctoral studies anywhere I wanted. I am forever grateful to
Provincial Terence Quinn for having such confidence in me to make a good
choice. By happenstance, Mark came to visit me, and after I told him I was
looking into this or that American university, he asked, "Why don't you go
study with Prof. Jan Walgrave in Louvain?" To show how ill-read I was in
1970, I did not know, as Mark Heath did, that the Katholieke Universiteit te
Leuven (Walgrave, being Flemish, taught in its Dutch language division) was
the preeminent university to study theology after the Second Vatican Council. Louvain had supplied more theological experts (called *periti*) to the Council commissions and to individual bishops than any other university, even
those in Rome itself. Nor did I then know that Walgrave was an esteemed

theologian in philosophical theology and a renowned expert on the thought of John Henry Newman.

And so Louvain happened by good fortune. I wrote Walgrave asking him to mentor me. He accepted because he respected Mark Heath's referral. I began doctoral studies in Fall semester, 1971. I even lived in the same religious community as Prof. Walgrave, with the Flemish Dominicans in Leuven. Those years of studying with other Louvain professors, visiting with Congar and Chenu in Paris, and conducting research under Walgrave on Newman's theology had a richness I am unable to describe without seeming to exaggerate. If alma mater means a university that's like a "nourishing mother," Louvain's mine. (See Appendix A.)

I mention one more influence from Dominican life, and it derives from the experience of living together in a community. I refer to the friendships, many still in force from a lifestyle that ended for me almost forty years ago. The prescribed closeness of that kind of life, such as eating together daily, relaxing together—called *recreating* together in the language of a monastery—studying together, gave me firsthand experiences of what makes living together work well and what makes it difficult. It is not unlike forging a married life together. And just as with marriage some people don't fit so well together, so in monastic community life there are unfit people, or at least people who make the fit uneasy for themselves and others. But in religious community life it is easier to tune out someone, to avoid talking to him, and keep going on in the community activities; quite the contrary with a marriage where such continual rubbing-the-wrong-way behavior already predicts the inevitable breakup of the marriage. On the whole, however, I experienced religious community life to be populated by good people, people keen on living with others in a supportive and kindly manner. Monastic life became a school for learning how to live well and in a growthful manner with others. When I departed this community, I left behind daily living with a lot of good people whom I knew I would miss, and they me. With many I keep in contact.

STAGE THREE

The third period of my life finds me both a married person and a parent. What are its lines of influence? I want to mention three of them: Emory University, transitioning from cleric to spouse and parent, and coming to Gwynedd Mercy University.

Teaching at Emory University in Atlanta is the first influence to relate, and my professor's role there straddles the second and third periods of my life. I was the first Roman Catholic theologian and priest to be appointed to the Divinity School of Emory, the Candler School of Theology. (A divinity school is a Protestant seminary within a larger university, such as the Schools of Divinity at Yale or Harvard.) The students came to Candler from almost every mainline denomination (Lutheran, Methodist, Episcopal, etc.) except from strict evangelical groups such as the Assembly of God, who thought Candler not sufficiently conservative or correctly biblical.

Our students came seeking the academic credentials to qualify for ordination by their respective churches, and our studies led to master's or doctoral degrees in ministry. I arrived fairly well read in Protestant theology, but this was my first experience collaborating alongside Protestant professors, teaching Protestant students wanting to serve the church in ministry, and praying with them. We had chapel services mid-morning every Tuesday and Thursday.

Since then, I have rarely heard such good preaching and hymn singing, well-known characteristics of Protestantism. The dozen years I spent at Emory gave me the experience of Protestant life up close and personal. It did not make me less of a Catholic. In fact, I came to appreciate my Catholic tradition even more, but I also came to value how much Protestants and Catholics share. Ecumenism became real for the first time in my life.

Candler had a student structure that Catholic seminaries ought to adopt and perhaps by now some have. Entering seminarians were divided into clusters, about a dozen students to each, and assigned a Candler professor for their three years of studies at Emory. The professor was more than a course advisor, although that was part of the responsibility. The professor was to help each of his or her students prepare for the academic and the personal expectations of future ministry. A distinctive contribution I made to my triennial groups was to introduce students to meditative prayer and "quiet time."

Twenty miles east of Atlanta in Conyers, GA, is a wonderful Cistercian monastery, the Monastery of the Holy Spirit. I taught its younger monks one morning a week every spring. This haven of reflective silence fed my contemplative bent. Conyers has a guest house where visitors can stay overnight, and a cafeteria with three fine but simple meals a day. Visitors are allowed into the back of the abbey church when the monks gather five times a day to chant the psalms.

To this tranquil place I brought my Candler students once each semester. "Bring your Bible and any other spiritual book, but no theology books, no radios, and try to leave your wristwatches at home. If you get silent enough this weekend, you might hear God speaking to you in a way you have never heard before." The first visit was unnerving for them but by their second and third years going to Conyers, they looked forward to this unique "time at the monastery." Protestant worship services tend to be very vocal. There isn't much quiet time. My aim was to provide these seminarians with the experience of silence because I was convinced it is the great antidote to ministerial burnout, which I knew would challenge them years later.

The second influence, in a sense, constitutes the heart of this third period of my life. It is the influence on my Catholicism of being married and being a parent to two fine sons. The story began while a professor at Emory University, and I need tell just enough of it because it involved so much about discerning God's will, about the nature of commitment, and the reality of honesty.

The longer I was at Emory, the more I became acquainted with the priests of the Archdiocese of Atlanta. Four of them invited a Jesuit and me to join in forming a support group based on the spirituality of Blessed Charles de Foucauld and the Little Brothers of Jesus that he founded before being martyred in Algeria. All six of us were living very busy lives. Joining this group required the commitment of carving out a full half day each month, no matter what. We would meet at the rural home of one of the Atlanta priests, have a simple breakfast and then a short reading from the Little Brothers booklet. At least 90 minutes to ourselves in silence wandering the woods followed. Then came a sharing in the group of "what's going on in my life." It took a while for this last feature to become honest-from-the-heart sharing, but it did eventually. I was already overextended: teaching full time at Emory and heading a Ph.D. program in its Graduate School, teaching monks periodically at Conyers, writing columns for the *Georgia Catholic Bulletin*, chaplain every Monday evening to a Cursillo group on the north side of Atlanta, helping the Marriage Tribunal with foreign language translations when testimonies required it, and, not to be overlooked, helping with ministry in the Dominican parish in suburban Chamblee Tucker where I lived. All this is not meant as a brag. It describes covering up a serious problem that led to a tough decision.

I came up for a year-long sabbatical from Emory, and I took it at the University of Chicago. It was to write a book on Newman's ideas about the church, and this did happen.[2] But I also decided I would not return to the grind mentioned above because I thought it was hiding my unease with the celibate life. When I returned to Atlanta, I cut back on an incessant work life. All too quickly, I came to feel lost, without moorings. And to the Charles de Foucauld group I brought this honest talk. This group, and a psychologist working for the archdiocese recommended by the group, led me to the very hard conclusion that celibacy put me in a false position, both with God and with my own self. I then took steps to depart the Dominicans and apply for the dispensation that would enable marriage and family life in the Catholic Church.

My Dominican confreres were wonderful to me during this tender time. For example, the worldwide leader of Dominicans in Rome, Master General Vincent de Couesnongle, wrote a letter thanking me for my theological work and hoping I could continue in it. The same support came from the Southern Dominicans USA, where I served as one of their officers. It must be added that the celibate life had been a false position for me even after ordination

2. *John Henry Newman on the Idea of Church*, with a Foreword by J. H. Walgrave, (Patmos Press, 1987).

in Washington. My spiritual director in seminary, Tom Heath, brother of Mark Heath, continued to serve that function after I left Washington to teach and preach. We exchanged lengthy letters at least twice a year for the next dozen years, I saying how nothing gets peaceful and he encouraging me to dig deeper in prayer for peace.

I share these personal features because a crisis of faith was never an issue, a dislike of Dominican spirituality or people was never an issue, and my correspondence with Fr. Tom Heath turned out to be providential. My request to receive a Vatican dispensation from Dominican life happened and in surprisingly short fashion, something unheard of in the 1980s under Pope John Paul II. A Vatican Dominican later told me why: "Tom Heath saved all your letters and submitted them as honest testimony to support your petition." I have always interpreted the quick approval to undertake a married and parenting life to be a sign of God's providence and a warrant for making the right decision in conscience, however tough. The woman I came to marry, and the two healthy and fine sons we had, have only enhanced the sense I have that God's providence has been guiding my life from earliest years to where it is now. I have related enough of my transition from cleric to spouse and parent, as befits a chronicle and not a memoir, to indicate how I experience God as shepherd of my life. What God does for me, he does for others who walk by faith. God's Providence figures in my faith in ways I cannot overstate. To deny the truth of it would mean tossing aside most of my life.

When I told my father, a WWII naval officer, that I was leaving Dominican life and hoping to marry eventually and have a family, he simply said, "You did good service and now it is time to leave the service." This is not theological language from him but it is insightful and true language from one whose support I have always felt and whose own sense of service was to enlist in the Navy the day after Pearl Harbor and return to his family when the "service" after the war was done.

Marriage and parenting made my thoughts about Catholic faith and practice more real, more engaged. When I was single and teaching theology at the university level, my thinking was more abstract. It was the difference between notional apprehension and real apprehension, using that distinction from Cardinal Newman described in the Preface. I moved in a world of notions, notions teaching students and notions from book reading. Responsibilities to a wife and children, as the children develop from infancy to young adults, are very concrete, unavoidable, exacting, and occasions of personal growth. It is as if I had dealt with concepts and notions before, and only now with what was real and concrete. Don't over-read my contrast. I dealt with real people in my Dominican days in ministry and classroom, and they were not abstractions. But a gulf remained also. I was always "the professor" to the students and "the cleric" to the laity. On the other hand, the intimacy of family wants always to erode gulfs.

The third line influencing my current thinking on religious matters comes from teaching undergraduates in the university from which I recently retired, Gwynedd Mercy University outside Philadelphia. In a sequence that does not require elaboration, I left Emory to take a position in the National Endowment for the Humanities, left that for a graduate school deanship in New York, and then left full-time campus administration so that I could return to teaching students theology. I missed the classroom.

How different Gwynedd's teaching was to be from Emory's. In the latter I taught theology to graduate students (for the Master of Divinity, the Doctor of Divinity or for the Ph.D.) Gwynedd lacked an undergraduate major in religion or theology. I taught students who majored in other areas and who were keen on those subjects (nursing, business, education certifications), not at all keen about curriculum-mandated religion courses. It was then up to me to make students feel engaged with religious topics. I had to unlearn Emory-style lofty language and learn how to express matters in simpler and clearer cadences. One great exception to this experience was Gwynedd's Honors Program where the undergraduates were among our best, and their intellectual curiosity was to me like sipping cool water on a parched day. The line of influence on my thinking from years teaching Gwynedd undergraduates can be simply put: I devised ways to present more imaginatively and simply what I thought religion in general and Catholicism in particular was about. And I put to great use chalk and blackboard—called today PowerPoint presentations—that I first used doing math back in college. I used to say, with not much exaggeration, that if you were first trained in math or physics, it was hard to teach any subject without a piece of chalk in your hand. And so, in the chapters to follow, you will sense my recourse to imaginative description and to analogies to describe what I believe and why.

CHAPTER ONE

How The Bible Works

"Your word is a lamp for my feet, a light for my path" Ps 119:105

Where to begin the story about what my Christian faith has come to mean? Here is its boiled-down essence lest it get lost behind the unfolding of the story: God exists without doubt and God is benevolent, a benevolent shepherd to me and, I'm convinced, to everyone, even if many reject God-talk as simply silly. Whether these two convictions frame someone's hopes, fears, sufferings or blessings, that is to say, one's concrete life, depends on that distinction from Cardinal Newman whether the convictions are being grasped and affirmed as notions or as concretely real apprehensions. If real, then God's existence is as real as my spouse, my children, and my parents are real to me and, equally, His ever-present guidance when I suffer or feel adrift. But if notions, they are just ideas I mull over from time to time. They might as well lurk at a distance from my everyday life. To God's reality and shepherding I return later. They are mentioned at the start to stress their centrality to everything.

INTRODUCTION

My starting point is the Bible for two reasons: First, in the words of the psalm above, reading the Bible has become real nourishment, like a light and warmth to my spirit in this world of conflicts and shadows. I identify with the words that St. Augustine spoke to his people as their bishop: "When that day [of heaven's arrival] has come, the prophet will not be read to us, the book of Paul will not be opened, we shall have no need of the Gospel itself. All scriptures will be removed, those scriptures that in the night of this world burned like lamps so that we not walk in darkness...that ray of light sent through slanting and winding ways into the heart of our darkness." Because many Catholic readers, for whom I envision this book, may possess scant knowledge of how the Bible works, I am including in this chapter reflections on the natures of the Old and New Testaments. I draw upon commonly accepted Catholic biblical scholarship. It will be a measure of success if readers conclude that Catholics are not wedded, and ought not to be wedded, to a *literal-only* understanding of all sacred texts. Full-blown biblical literalism is a hallmark of certain Protestant fundamentalist sects. It has never been the Roman Catholic benchmark.

Second, in relationship to the Bible, my own upbringing reflected the experience of the wider church of which I was part. As a young Catholic in a Philadelphia parochial school, I was nurtured on the *Baltimore Catechism*. The Catechism was a listing of Catholic doctrines in Q & A format. Some were and still are immensely and enduringly profound. Why did God make me? "God made me to know Him, to love Him, and to serve Him in this world and to live happily with Him when this earthly life ends." Who can claim to grasp fully the answer in all its important implications? But there it is, and it arrived long ago like a delivery package into my mind as a doctrine, a church teaching.

The Bible played a limited role in the Catechism I learned. The Bible, of course, was the object of a teaching as when the Catechism taught that God's revelation is contained in the Bible. But it was as proof texts that the Bible served the Catechism. By proof texts I mean that the Catechism taught a doctrine and listed a scriptural text as proving it, such as "the Anointing of the Sick is one of the seven sacraments" and its scriptural proof was the text from the *Letter of James* 5:14: "Is anyone among you sick? He should summon the presbyters of the church, and they should pray over him and anoint him with oil in the name of the Lord." And likewise with marriage as one of the seven sacraments; its proof text was the *Letter to the Ephesians* 5:32. This passage drew the parallel between the oneness of Christ and the church and the bond of husband and wife "becoming one flesh." St. Paul's words seemed straightforward proof: "...and the two shall become one flesh. This is a great sacrament, but I speak in reference to Christ and the Church."

A couple of issues make problematic the falling back on proof texts, like this one for marriage. Christians married each other in the first centuries of the church in the secular fashion everyone else used for marrying; there was not a church sacramental ritual. In fact, marriage was not taught as a sacrament until the twelfth century. Further, the writers of my Catechism used the English translation of the Latin Vulgate Bible. The Vulgate in those days of my youth was *the* authorized version of the Bible for Roman Catholics. The Latin version of *Ephesians* has the word *sacramentum* in verse 32, having it very convenient for making the case that marriage is a sacrament, and claiming that St. Paul taught its sacramentality. But in the original Greek text of *Ephesians*, the word is more properly translated into English as *mystery*, which is saying something profound about the Christ/church, man/woman parallel but it is not an instance of St. Paul calling marriage a sacrament. Marriage indeed is a sacrament based on other warrants. But such was how the Baltimore Catechism mediated the Bible to the young me in a series of proof texts.

The opposite was happening with Protestant youths at the same moment. Their main informant of religious doctrine was the Bible, even more than the catechisms that serviced some of them, Lutherans for example. Protestant youths came to know Bible stories early on and well. Protestants could say with some confidence, "This Jesus story is from *Matthew* and that one is from *Luke*," something Catholics, youths or adults, could not do. However, it was on doctrines that Protestantism as a whole wobbled; the Bible itself seemed to partition them into different churches. Methodists baptized babies and Baptists did not, save for young adults. Quakers baptized no one. Lutherans believed that Jesus was really present in the ritualized bread and wine and Presbyterians did not. The Bible was well known in Protestantism but interpretations of its stories caused divided denominations.

Catholicism was quite different on this score. Its doctrines were uniformly taught and practiced, and Catechism instruction ensured that it remained so with each generation. The enduring oneness of the Catholic Church was an impressive effect of it. The Bible itself was never to become an instrument of divisions in Catholicism because a further Catholic doctrine, readily accepted by everyone, was that biblical interpretations rested with the pope and bishops, and from them a consistent teaching voice was heard. As to the doctrines being taught us, they were learned in the sense of being memorized. Were they grasped in Newman's phrase of a *real apprehension* of them? I think not, and I use myself as illustration of being a docile student but hardly a comprehending student of Catholic teachings. I knew a lot of Catholic teachings and could verbalize them when tested. Memory is a wonderful thing. Such is why this book aims to share what this or that aspect of Catholic faith has come to mean in terms of a real grasp affecting how I live and act on it.

Since those early days much has happened to my church and to me. An awareness of the fuller richness of the Bible and how the Bible is meant "to work" have come into view. Besides understanding *church* in terms of official teachings concerning scripture, a matter to which I will return, I am here envisioning the church as the laity, the people implied in the answer Newman once gave the Bishop of Birmingham when asked, "Well, who are the laity?" Newman simply responded, "Well, the church would look funny without them." Since the Second Vatican Council of the 1960s, the laity have become much more biblically literate or, perhaps better stated, more biblically immersed. Some Catholic critics of post-Vatican II developments grouse that the laity no longer know our church's doctrines. There is some truth to the criticism, which I attribute to the depopulation of the Catholic parochial school system and not to the laity's slacking off. But Catholic laity today, at least those who are still practicing Catholics, are enveloped in a biblical milieu that was lacking before the 1962–1965 Second Vatican Council happened.

Let me illustrate the matter with Mass. Most Roman Catholics hear their Bible stories at Sunday Mass, and this was also the case years earlier but with a very different look. The scriptural readings after Vatican II undergo substantial change. Two readings are increased to three. The gospel reading is preceded by an Old Testament reading and the third reading, between these two, comes from elsewhere in the New Testament. Moreover, the readings vary over a three-year cycle. The result of this innovation is that laity now hear many more portions of the Bible than previously.

What went on previous to Vatican II? The question might seem archaic because it is likely remembered only by Catholics of an advanced age. There were only two readings at each Sunday Mass. The readings, devised by Pope St. Pius V in 1570, were the same year after year, save for a very few tweaks to the arrangement over the 400-year span. (Pius V was the source of white papal vestments; a Dominican cardinal when elected, he didn't want to give up his white Dominican habit.) So entrenched was this unchanging biblical cycle that Catholics going to weekday Masses heard the previous Sunday readings repeated unless the weekday Mass happened to fall on the feast day of a saint that had its own Bible readings. Many of the pre-Vatican II Sundays took on the name of the designate gospel reading. The Second Sunday after Easter was simply called "Good Shepherd Sunday." The Twelfth Sunday after Pentecost was "Good Samaritan Sunday." Yes, it was a familiar way to name the Sundays, but it also meant that Catholic laity were not hearing much of the Bible. To overcome the lack of exposure, one might wonder if parishes conducted Bible study groups as some parishes today do. For sure, no, because that would have smacked of Protestantism in those days.

It is one thing for Catholics today to be more biblically immersed but it is quite another thing for them to know how the Bible works, and most may not. I can think of no better phrase to use than *how does the Bible work* to describe the official Catholic approach to the Bible and how it differs from the literalism of Evangelical fundamentalists on the one hand and from a "reductionism" found among some non-Catholic biblical scholars on the other. The latter so interpret passages about Jesus that hardly anything historical about him is left over. The problem these days is that Catholic laity watch TV programs on the Bible but the producers of the documentaries like to pit fundamentalist "experts" against the *au courant* scholarship of the reductionist "experts." Balanced middle positions on how the Bible works, such as the voices of recognized Catholic experts on the Bible, are absent from such documentaries. Balanced positions don't sell on TV and take too long to elaborate. Documentaries like stark contrasts and pithy observations. Balanced nuances are thought to bore.

How the Bible works is therefore the focus of this opening chapter, and it provides a necessary foundation for teachings to be addressed later. For some laity the ideas may appear novel but, I hope, not unsettling should the feeling arise, "I've never heard that before about the Bible," or "I always took this or that to be literally true and you're saying it isn't." I shall be sharing principles on how the Bible works that come from official Catholic teaching on these matters. Catholics very familiar with the Bible will find commonplace what I'm about to say, and college-educated laity may have learned beforehand many of my observations, but it is better to assume too little than too much in explaining so important a matter as how the Bible, from a Catholic perspective, works.

SOME COMMON PRINCIPLES

I begin with a few principles regarding nomenclature and languages. The Bible is a collection of books, which is what *Bible* in Greek (*ta biblia*) literally means, "the books." Catholics accept as inspired scriptures 46 books in the Old Testament and 27 books in the New Testament. All Christian bodies accept these same 27 and use them in worship. As sacred writings about Jesus, Mormons add other books, but Mormons stand alone in having a larger official list of such scriptures about Jesus.

Inspiration simply means that God is the chief sacred author of the books, working through the human authorship of people who were not unlike you and me save for our differing historical situations. God used them to reveal Himself and His purposes through the inspired text they produced, *if read properly*. These human authors are also called sacred or inspired writers, some of whose personal names are known, such as St. Paul of Tarsus, but most others are anonymous, such as the person(s) who wrote the Old Testament *Book of Job*. I think the best definition of inspiration comes from the Vatican II document on divine revelation, *Dei Verbum*, in its eleventh section. "Since everything asserted by the inspired authors or sacred writers must be held to be asserted by the Holy Spirit, it follows that the books of Scripture must be acknowledged as teaching firmly, faithfully, and without error that truth which God wanted put into the sacred writings *for the sake of our salvation*" (italics mine).

It's a superb definition because it is properly restrictive. Does God reveal science or political history for our salvation? No. Is it revealed for our salvation that Jesus attacked the Temple money changers at the start of his public ministry? No, and good thing it isn't because *John* puts it at the beginning of the Lord's work while the gospels of *Matthew*, *Mark*, and *Luke* put it toward the end of Jesus' remaining days in Palestine. What is "for the sake of our salvation" is what is truly revealed, and it enjoys the inerrancy that a message from God must have. It claims our faith in it. "The Word (the Son) of God became flesh and dwelt among us." Its paraphrase by the early church bishops into "God became human so that humans could become gods" shows how salvation-infused this short line from *Jn* 1:14 is.

Rembrandt van Rijn has a famous painting of St. Matthew writing his gospel. Standing behind him is an angel whispering into his ear. The accurate part of the painting is the truth that God is the principal sacred author, revelation's source. The painting's fault is that Rembrandt makes Matthew to be a passive recording secretary, writing what is whispered him. I do not think any sacred writer was aware of being divinely inspired when the writer was putting down words on paper. I think all the sacred writers felt "called" to record oral religious traditions that were part of the religious community to which the writers belonged. The writer of *Job* recorded a story of maintaining steadfast faith in God in spite of life's evils, an uplifting oral story that circulated somewhere within Judaism until it achieved a longer life by becoming a written story. The evangelist of the *Gospel of Matthew* lived in a Christian community—many scholars think it was Antioch in Syria—whose retention of the teachings of Jesus became part of a gospel he felt called to compose. How he felt called to do so or whether the Christian community's leadership played a role, we do not know. But the evangelist did not experience some inner spiritualizing vibration.

Nor did St. Paul when he wrote letters to Christian communities here and there. He just perceived or heard about a need, and he dashed off a letter to address it. In fact, if Paul were to be told that his letters would be recognized retroactively by the universal church as divinely inspired and were to be saved and read forever, he would probably say, "Let me have back for rephrasing my letter to the Galatian church. I expressed my feelings too harshly." To sum up, an inspired sacred writer is not a passive recording secretary nor is he feeling "caught up in the Holy Spirit" when writing, the author of the *Book of Revelation* being a possible exception. But the person is the human instrument of inspiration, writing in his own language, with his own cultural viewpoints, and with a framework shaping what he inherits, all of which God uses to communicate truths *for our salvation*. I'm even led to suggest that the better understanding of biblical inspiration is to perceive the Holy Spirit's guidance acting in the earliest local churches. Some of these churches were preserving, with faithfulness due to the Spirit, teachings and memories of Jesus. The four evangelists, under the imperceptible guidance of the Spirit, utilized these memories and shaped them into the narratives we now know as gospels.

Canonical is another word needing elaboration. Its opposite is *apocryphal*. A biblical book is canonical if it has been officially accepted as inspired. It requires more difficult explaining to answer who or what does the official accepting, how long did it take to get decided, and were some books at first wrongly accepted or wrongly rejected as inspired. When all the dust had settled by the fourth century, regarding the New Testament books at least, there was a canonical collection, called a *canon*, of 27 books. All these books were written originally in Greek.

The books can be divided into four writing styles or genres: the gospel genre (four books), letter writing (twenty-one books), a historical genre but in the style of how the Holy Spirit is guiding history (one book, called *Acts of the Apostles*), and a strange—some might say exotic—writing style inherited from Judaism called apocalyptic (one book, called the *Book of Revelation*, or in older Catholic Bibles, the *Book of Apocalypse*). There are other ancient writings about Jesus called apocryphal books, such as the *Gospel of Thomas* and the *Letter to the Laodiceans*. For one reason or another, they were not accepted into the final canonical listing. There are discomforting teachings in many of them—for example, the *Gospel of Thomas* records Jesus as saying that women must become male in order to go to heaven—which is likely why it and others were judged to be lacking God's inspiration when the canon was achieving its final arrangement of 27 books.

THE OLD TESTAMENT

Suppose it is asked, as I used to ask undergraduates, "How many canonical books in the Old Testament, and the answer is not a number?" After the students puzzled long enough, I would say, "The answer is that it depends on whom you ask." If you ask a Protestant, it is 39 canonical books. If you ask a Jew, it is also 39 although the Jewish tradition lumps together many of these books so as to come up with 22 books, the same number as the consonants in a Hebrew alphabet lacking vowels. If you ask a Catholic, the answer is 46 canonical books. The reasons behind this difference, 39 versus 46, get fairly complicated, but I want to relate a story, with risk of oversimplification, that caused the difference in order to introduce another important word, the *Septuagint*, to which important Catholic doctrines are connected. I want also to introduce the idea of ongoing divine revelation. The story involves Israelite history, itself the backdrop for Christianity's emergence from Judaism.

The story involves knowing something about languages and having a sense of Israelite history that a rough timeline allows. Abraham lived about 1750 BC.[1] Moses was at Mt. Sinai (also called Mt. Horeb) about 1250. King David ruled about 1000. After his son and successor, Solomon, the one kingdom split into two kingdoms, the north called Israel and the south called Judah, each with its own succession of kings. About 725 BC, the Assyrian Empire attacked the Northern Kingdom and deported most of the people, resettling other conquered peoples in their place. (The so-called "ten lost

---

1. Because of perceived sensitivities, there is a tendency today to use BCE (before the common era) in place of BC (before Christ) and to use CE (common era) to replace AD (anno Domini = year of the Lord). Besides the fact that the pivot of numbering years in either system doesn't change—Jesus' reckoned birth remains the transition point—I perceive that BC and AD have long been secularized and function without prejudices. This seems the case for my envisioned audience of Catholic laity.

tribes of [northern] Israel" is no deep mystery; they were simply deported.) The Babylonians, who defeated the Assyrians, attacked the Southern Kingdom, which practically identified itself with the tribal land of Judah. Most of the Judeans were exiled to Babylon for a period of almost 70 years. In rounded-off numbers, think of the Exilic Period as from 600 to 530. When the Persians defeated the Babylonians, they let these Judean captives, henceforth to be called Jews, return home if they wished. Some stayed in Babylon, some returned to Palestine, and some kept going farther west, to places like Egypt and Asia Minor (present-day Turkey). Jews living outside the Holy Land, then and today, are called *diaspora* Jews.

Next in the timeline comes a non-Jew, a Macedonian general, Alexander the Great, leading a Greek army. He and his army created a vast empire, stretching from Greece to the Indus River of present-day Pakistan, and including the lands stretching south to Egypt. 325 BC roughly locates him. The lands he conquered comprised a vast Greek Empire, and Greek language and customs, what is called Hellenistic culture, arrived with him and remained after he departed.

Regarding the languages, Moses spoke Hebrew and so did all the other Israelites on the timeline, save for Greek-speaking Alexander. (How Moses came to learn Hebrew has always puzzled me because he was given as an infant to Pharaoh's daughter and raised in an Egyptian milieu, supposedly speaking its ancient Coptic. At a certain point he killed an Egyptian and fled to Midian in the central Sinai Peninsula where he lived for some years and married Zipporah, a non-Hebrew. What language did he speak in Midian? But he came to speak Hebrew and for our story that is what matters.) With this brief background of dates and languages, the origin of the Septuagint and its 46 books can be described.

Israelite religion begins with Moses and Mt. Sinai as recounted in the *Book of Exodus*. The *Book of Genesis* is more the preface to *Exodus* than it is Israel's central originating event. *Genesis* explains how a Hebrew-speaking people migrated from Canaan to Egypt and got caught there as slaves. And so it explains who Joseph was and his eleven brothers, and who was their father (Jacob aka Israel), and their grandfather (Isaac), and finally Isaac's own father (Abraham). This backward look takes a reader from chapter 50 to the "call of Abram=Abraham" in chapter 12 of *Genesis*, whose first eleven chapters are a kind of crafted world history meant to situate the patriarch Abraham in time and place. But the central originating event of Israelite religion comes centuries later, Moses atop Mt. Sinai and Israelites encircling its base. Moses led the Hebrew slaves out of Egypt to this mountain where he and they experienced a "being claimed" by God. It goes by the name *covenant* in English, *berith* in Hebrew. "I will be your God if you will be my people" is the marriage-like formula of the covenanting and approaches the sense of a deal between God and the Israelites. But, above all, the covenant is to be thought of as a blessing that God initiated on behalf of a people God first decided to bless. And God's name, Yahweh, the name he revealed earlier to Moses on this same mountain when tasking Moses to lead the Israelites from Egypt, means "I am in your midst as who I am."[2]

It is from this *divine presence within* that God continued to reveal himself and his will to these covenanted people, and the people came more and more to discern and to articulate God's reality and their responsibilities to God (maintaining faith in the one God and obeying his laws). God also inspired individuals to preach what believing and obeying God meant as the context of Israelite covenanted life underwent changes in history. We call them *prophets*—first Moses, then Joshua, Elijah, Jeremiah and others. Their words shaped the religious traditions of the people. The point not to be lost is that revelation continued to occur as the years unfolded. Stories were repeated generation after generation in an oral tradition and captured by sacred repeated actions such as celebrating Passover and the Day of Atonement. The ability to write down the revealed traditions was not possible at first. The people lived by what was passed down in oral fashion, that is, by their traditions.

The Israelites, like other cultures, spoke a language long before they devised an alphabet to capture the sound of words and a grammar to write the words together coherently. (Scholars of Semitic languages think that the Hebrew language achieved this transition about the tenth century BC.) Thus began the possibility of biblical texts capturing God's revelations. Among the earliest such texts was the "Song of Deborah" in chapter five of *Judges*, some of its Hebrew being so ancient that portions are difficult to translate. As the centuries unfolded up to the period of the Exile in Babylon and thereafter, biblical books came into existence in Hebrew. Think of the books as welling up out of the oral traditions bearing God's revelations but also think of God's hand sifting the oral traditions because elements unworthy of scripture are also being swept along in the oral retellings. If God was inspiring the process, as Christians and Jews think, then the emerging books are the word of God, worthy to be read in church and synagogue. Without going into the complexities involved, approximately 39 Hebrew writings emerged eventually, some of them originating as late as the second century BC, such as the *Book of Daniel*. (Other writings appeared that took questionable matter from

---

2. "I am who am" is too philosophical a translation of the Hebrew *'ehyeh 'asher 'ehyeh* that God out of the burning bush spoke to Moses. Ancient Israelites were a relationship-oriented people. Someone is a son of X, a member of tribe Y. "I am the one in your midst as who I am" best captures God's self-designation as a relationship without ever locking God down into human concepts. When later texts refer to God in the third person, "He is the one in your midst," the Hebrew word lacking vowels is YHWH ("Yahweh"), *Lord* in most English Bibles. Without intending bookishness, this relational description of God's revealed name sets the stage for the notion of ongoing revelations to the Israelites that I need to utilize.

the oral traditions; they were classified apocryphal, such as *The Assumption of Moses*, but my focus is the 39 canonical books.)

There is one further element to add for the Septuagint story. Following the Babylonian Exile, many Jews resettled in Gentile lands, living in what is called the diaspora. They, like their co-religionists living in Palestine, continued receiving the effect of "Yahweh in their midst as who He is," which meant that ongoing revelation was experienced by them, too. To this covenanted experience in the diaspora one must add the cultural effect of Alexander the Great. His military conquests delivered a Hellenistic culture that shaded diaspora areas like an umbrella. Diaspora Jews began thinking and speaking in Greek. At one point, Alexandria in Egypt—General Alexander claimed naming privileges for this and many other cities—had more Jews than Jerusalem did. And from diaspora oral traditions there emerged biblical writings too, but in Greek, of course. Approximately 7 books emerged.[3]

There came a time when rabbis in the diaspora had synagogue congregations who understood Greek but not Hebrew. And so a translation effort was begun in Alexandria to translate the 39 Hebrew books into Greek, to which canonical collection were added the 7 others. This canonical collection of 46 books is called the Septuagint, a word suggesting seventy, hence using LXX as its abbreviation. Its popularity was such that its usage spread to other parts of the diaspora, even to portions of the Holy Land. All this was happening before Jesus was born.

The Septuagint was used as Israel's sacred scriptures by the first Christians and by all Christians up to the rise of Protestantism. Among the first Christians using the Septuagint were Paul and the four gospel writers. Take, for example, the well-known prophecy met at Christmas time from *The Gospel of Matthew*. It quotes the Septuagint version of *Isaiah* 7:14 for Jesus' virginal conception where the prophecy[4] in the LXX reads, "a virgin [*parthenos*] shall conceive." The Hebrew text reads that an *almah* shall conceive, which in Hebrew could mean either a young married woman (e.g., the wife of Judean King Ahaz) shall conceive or could mean that a virgin shall conceive. Therefore, in the message of the New Testament, the Septuagint version of the Old Testament, plays often a crucial role for Catholic doctrines.

But what about Protestants and Jews having only 39 canonical books? Those 7 books that entered the Septuagint (*Judith, Tobit, Baruch, 1* and *2 Maccabees, Wisdom*, and *Ben Sirach* or *Ecclesiasticus* in its Greek title) have very strong

---

3. This is intended oversimplification. Some of the 7 likely arose in Aramaic, thence into Greek. It was a complex process.

4. Old Testament prophecies are not like predictions, akin to predicting future weather. Isaiah was not foreseeing Jesus' virginal birth 700 years in the future. His words, in the LXX version, are used by Matthew as applicable to a true statement about Jesus' origins that Matthew was inspired to state. As grounded in *Is* 7:14, the "prophecy" expresses how Divine Providence (salvation history) unfolds.

teachings on life after death and on resurrection. The first Christian preachers asserted the resurrection of Jesus, and since Christianity did not have its
own unique scriptures at first, scriptural support for the possibility of resurrection was often drawn from these books. (Note that in Catholic funeral services, a reading about life after death from one of these seven books is likely.)

In the aftermath of the Roman destruction of Jerusalem's Temple and
the extermination of Judaism's priests and leading Pharisees in AD 70, the
remaining rabbinical leaders salvaged what was left of a crippled Judaism by
expelling deviant groups from the synagogue as if to purify itself of contami-
nations. One of these expelled groups was Jesus-believing Jews preaching his
resurrection as Messiah. (Read *Jn* 9:22 between the lines to see it described.)
The rabbis, accordingly, reverted to the Old Testament original canon of 39
books and made a condition that the canon was restricted to books written
in Hebrew. This decision happened about AD 90, and Judaism from then on
refused canonicity to *Judith* and the others. One of the most popular Jewish
festivals today is Hanukkah, which celebrates the purification of the Temple
after Gentile occupiers of Jerusalem had profaned it. A curiosity is that the
event is described in the two books of *Maccabees*, no longer part of the Jewish
canon.

Christianity from the outset maintained the 46 canonical books of the
Septuagint, since Christianity grew out of Judaism and the Septuagint came
with it. This situation remained unchanged until the time when Luther was
translating the Old Testament into German. He prioritized the 39 books
and considered the 7 others useful but not inspired. Given Luther's stature,
other Protestant translations followed suit, including the English translation
of the King James Version. The KJV became the staple of English-speaking
Protestantism, and most Protestants have Bibles lacking these seven books
and likely never heard of them. Why Luther downgraded the seven books
continues to puzzle scholars although some portions of them, e.g., offering
sacrifices for the dead, went against positions he held (e.g., his objection to
Masses for the dead).

Although lengthy, this description of the Septuagint's origin portrays another and even more important element of Catholic faith about the nature
of God's revelation that would have been difficult to describe otherwise. Revelation is remembered and repeated orally by the people receiving it before
the revelation is captured by the transcribed words of the sacred texts. Thus
revelation has an unfolding aspect to it. It grows. More and more is seen into
it, and new convictions arise about God's will as the historical circumstances
of Israelites change. It is not an all-at-once phenomenon before achieving
finality in the writings of a sacred author.

Even more difficult to appreciate is another feature of the sequence having oral traditions coming first and written expressions of them coming later.
It is the technique of the later sacred writers to project onto an earlier situa-

tion or religious figure a revelation that emerged later on. The case of Moses, the famous lawgiver of Mt. Sinai, offers a clear case in point. After the full written story of the Sinai covenant came into existence, as recounted in the *Book of Exodus*, a reader gets the impression that Moses spoke all 600-plus commandments of God's law to the people gathered at the base of Mt. Sinai. But some of the commandments clearly reflect the living situation after the Israelites settled in the Promised Land years later and long after the death of Moses.

One of the commandments directs Israelites to care for the poor by leaving uncollected for hungry people some of the grain harvest and some of the orchard fruit. This is a religious insight of the Israelites that is expressing God's will for the covenant. It could only have come into awareness after Israelites possessed a land capable of agriculture. This is a case of unfolding revelation, a "revealed commandment" not foreseen back at Mt. Sinai. But the sacred writer projects it and other specifications of covenant life backwards onto the lips of Moses because it is binding covenant law nonetheless. Moses is the remembered great lawgiver and therefore the warrant for any binding law. The retrojection of later religious insights onto Moses, as if he were their original source, is not falsification if the essence of any commandment is kept in view: This commandment is God's will for how He wants His people to act. In terms of how the Bible works, this technique used by inspired writers of projecting certain insights into an earlier situation will be very important in grasping how the New Testament gospels work. Some important examples will be considered soon.

A final nomenclature issue involving the Old Testament is the word *Tanak* or *Tanakh*. The meaning of Old Testament is clear enough, and it usage by Catholics has been common. But Jews do not call their sacred scriptures by this phrase because the phrase is somewhat insulting. To them there is nothing "old" about their scriptures, nothing "former" about them. Some Christian writers today used the term the *Hebrew Bible*. But Jews themselves do not use this term for their sacred writings either. They use Tanak. There is a very functional reason why Jews call the Old Testament the Tanak and did so even before Jesus was born. These biblical books, 39 for Jews and 46 for Catholics, can be divided conveniently into three sections: one section involving the Sinai covenant and its context, a second section having books about or by prophets, and a third section containing books of an uplifting nature in general. Because a listing of covenant laws is major portion of the Sinai experience, the Hebrew word for law, *Torah*, is applied to the first five books of the Bible. The term for the second section is the Hebrew word for prophets, *Neviim*. The many other books of the third section, the many uplifting stories as it were, are simply called "the Writings," *Kethuvim* in Hebrew. TNK is derived from the first letter of the three Hebrew words. Because vowels are needed to pronounce TNK, one gets *tanak*. Jews call their Bible the Law, the Prophets, and the Writings and how logical this is. Jesus himself used the phrase when he asked, "What do the Law and Prophets tell you?" It stood in shorter form for "what do our scriptures tell you?" I suggest that it is properly sensitive to substitute Tanak for Old Testament in our speech and in our writing, unless we are talking to someone who has no idea of the derivation related above. But a Jew would not be such a person.[5] (See Appendix F.)

Before turning to some foundational principles about the New Testament and how it works, I wish to draw, as an example, a conclusion from one of the words introduced above: *Bible*. As we saw, it means "the books." The Bible is a collection of many books. Connect with this fact the popular kindergarten Bible song, "Jesus loves me, this I know, for the Bible tells me so." Switch the opening phrase to "Angels exist, this I know, for the Bible tells me so." Pose the question in a more adult fashion to the Tanak: Does it teach that angels exist? In the earliest composed books of the Tanak, such as its first five books (the Torah), the answer is no. (Where the word *angel* does appear in the Torah, the context makes clear it is Yahweh.) But the last books coming into the Tanak assume the existence of angels and even talk about individual angels, e.g., Raphael with *Tobit*, Gabriel with *Daniel*. Does the Tanak teach that angels exist? The truer answer is, it depends which books you have in mind. Did the Israelites conquer the land of Canaan in a blitzkrieg, killing off everyone (*Book of Joshua*)? Or did settlement entail a more peaceful infiltration (*Book of Judges*)? The same principle holds for the New Testament about biblical books differing in their teaching aims. Did Jesus perform exorcisms? *Mark*, practically an exorcism-centered gospel, says yes; John says no, or at least does not report them when they would have been important to that gospel's notion of signs Jesus performs to display his identity. Rather than saying, "The Bible teaches so and so," it is more accurate to say that certain books of the Bible teach this or that. The Bible is a collection of books and while all of them are inspired, the Bible is not a uniform treatise.

THE NEW TESTAMENT

With the New Testament, and keeping in view my envisioned readership, I am on more tender territory regarding principles on how the Bible works. The material is more sensitive because for most laity this is the portion of the Bible vastly more familiar than the Tanak is. And, of course, the New Testament describes the life of Jesus, the focus of the laity's faith. Thus, any comment on how the New Testament works might seem to dislodge convictions or assumptions fondly held and perhaps held since childhood. I must proceed carefully, and to do so I wish to enlist some authoritative directions from the Catholic Church about New Testament materials, leading to what I judge to

5. In printed versions of the Tanak and in Christian Bibles, the section on prophets comes after the Torah and the "Writings." *Genesis* comes first and the prophet *Malachi* comes last.

be the richest insight into how the four gospels work. It is striking that this insight became the official teaching of the Catholic Church in the Vatican II Dogmatic Constitution on Divine Revelation, *Dei Verbum.*

But first, a caution. In terms of how the Bible works, the Catholic Church seems in agreement with Cardinal Newman's observation that the Bible is not geared to be teaching doctrines. The church teaches doctrines certainly; for example, it teaches the real presence of the Risen Christ in the consecrated bread and wine of Mass, but it does not teach the meaning of biblical verses as such, with the possible exception at the Council of Trent of texts in *Romans* about sharing in the sin of Adam. Doctrines, of course, spring from the Bible as from a font of truth, but a discernment process is needed to craft a doctrine from biblical verses. A ready experience why the Bible does not teach doctrines is that, as Newman once remarked, "A Unitarian sits down and reads the Bible and gets up a Unitarian, and the same for a Trinitarian."

On the other hand, there have been some directives from the Catholic Church, not initially at the level of solemn teachings but still of a serious import, which have framed the approach to understanding the Bible and how it works. I am referring to papal encyclicals. These are letters from popes carrying a type of authority eliciting respect. They are usually sent to Catholic bishops worldwide or even to people of good will worldwide, as was Pope John XXIII's *Pacem in Terris* in 1963 about human rights. Encyclicals are of recent vintage in the long history of the church. There were not many before Pope Leo XIII (AD 1878-1903). The earliest appears to be from Benedict XIV in 1740. Leo wrote more than any other pope before or after him, 85 in fact, his *Rerum Novarum* on the rights of laborers for a just wage and the right to unionize being the most famous.[6]

Leo's encyclical *Providentissimus Deus* (1893) was the church's first foray into biblical debates. It was occasioned by Protestant archaeological and textual discoveries questioning the historical reliability of some biblical passages. Leo's encyclical spared Catholics a problem that bedeviled pious Protestants who felt their Bible faith undermined by this new German scholarship. Many Protestants banded together to assert the "fundamentals" (Jesus' resurrection, his miracles, God's creation of the world from scratch), which these fundamentalists protected by insisting on the literal historicity of every line in the Old and New Testaments. Leo taught that biblical authors shared in the scientific outlooks of their times, described things "in more or less figurative language," and that the Bible was not teaching science or political history. The debate between human evolution and creationism (i.e., the present world came into existence all at once) was never the problem for Catholicism as it was for Protestants in the early twentieth century, save for those

6. Leo's predecessor, Pius IX, wrote 38. Pius XII wrote 41. After him, the number of encyclicals fall off. John XXIII wrote 8, Paul VI wrote 6, John Paul II wrote 14, and Benedict XVI wrote 3.

creationist Catholics who never read or had explained to them the teachings of *Providentissimus*. (See chapter eight.)

Leo set up a biblical commission to encourage Catholic biblical scholarship, but under the next pope, Pius X, who did not share Leo's trust in Catholic biblical scholars, the Pontifical Biblical Commission (PBC) began issuing cautionary directives and admonitions to Catholic scholars, some of whom lost their university teaching positions. The PBC and Pius X feared Protestant scholarship's infecting the church and its laity through the unsupervised work of Catholic professors of the Bible. New insights, such as Moses could not have been the writer of the Torah, were declared dangerous. These Vatican watchdogs, known as the *Sapinière* or papal heresy hunters, suffocated Catholic research.[7] As a result, Catholic biblical studies were stagnant for decades.

A pope noted for his doctrinal conservativism changed everything. Pope Pius XII published a groundbreaking encyclical on the Bible in 1943, *Divino Afflante Spiritu*. He was personally convinced that reading the Bible was enriching, and he wanted more Catholic laity to do it. So he opened the door for Catholic scholars to utilize methods previously forbidden them in order to produce translations of the Bible that were as faithful to the original texts as possible. To do so, they needed to become adept in the original languages, Hebrew, Greek for the Septuagint and the New Testament, and to learn other ancient languages such as Aramaic.[8] They needed expertise in allied sciences like archeology and comparative religions of the ancient world. Until this time Bibles in Catholic homes were handicapped. The Council of Trent (1545-1563) insisted on the Latin Vulgate text (being itself a translation of the Hebrew and Greek texts) as "the authentic edition" for Catholic usage. English translations were made from the Vulgate. So Catholic Bibles were a not-so-smooth translation into English of a not-so-smooth translation into Latin of a gospel written in Greek.

Divino Afflante also steered Catholics away from any biblical fundamentalism. Pope Pius taught that the Bible contains many different genres or liter-

---

7. During this period of the Vatican as a suspicious watchdog, proponents of human evolution came under fire in spite of *Providentissimus*. Fr. John Augustine Zahm, a priest-scientist at the University of Notre Dame, was brought to the brink of public condemnation, and he ceased writing on the subject. The best brief study of the sorry period of heresy hunters, and the good scholars they reviled, is Louis Janssens, "The Non-infallible Magisterium and Theologians," *Louvain Studies* 14 (1989), 195-259.

8. Jesus spoke Aramaic but he would have known how to read Hebrew passages from the Tanak in synagogue. Like Hebrew, Aramaic is a Semitic language and quite akin. By the seventh century before Christ, it became the common language of the Middle East, save for Palestine where Hebrew held out. The Aramaic of international dealings then became the language of local governance (after the Exile), then the language of the marketplace, and finally the language of the home. Mary and Joseph would have taught Jesus Aramaic, and with a Galilean accent. Biblical texts in Aramaic translation are called targums.

ary forms, such as poetry, embellished drama, parables, "idioms peculiar to Semitic languages," and forms of history of different sorts. Finally, the pope offered an admonition, not to the Catholic scholars whom he was encouraging, but to closed-minded clergy and laity prone to criticize anything new. It is one of the most striking papal statements of the twentieth century: "Let all other sons [and daughters] of the church bear in mind that the efforts of these resolute laborers in the vineyard of the Lord [viz., scholars seeking solutions to "difficult problems"] should be judged not only with equity and justice, but also with the greatest charity; all moreover should abhor that intemperate zeal which imagines that whatever is new should for that very reason be opposed or suspected" (§ 47). The great champion of openness at Vatican II, Cardinal Augustin Bea, S.J., is thought to be one of the biblical experts in 1943 on whom Pius XII relied.

In 1955, the secretary—Vatican language for chief executive—of the Pontifical Biblical Commission wrote that Catholic scholars had now complete freedom regarding the 1905–15 decrees of the Commission, which had insisted, for example, besides the Mosaic authorship matter, that all of *Isaiah* was written prior to the Exile, that Jesus' apostle Matthew wrote the gospel bearing his name and that it appeared before any other gospel. Then Pius XII died in 1958 and things changed.

In preparation for the Vatican Council that was to begin in September 1962, a document prepared for the discussion on the sources of revelation was sent to the worldwide episcopate. It stated that Catholic doctrines could be sourced either to scripture or to tradition, as if there were two fonts of revelation covering different doctrines. In the scripture portion, the preparatory text appealed to positions advocated by the Pontifical Biblical Commission at the beginning of the century. Some Vatican insiders, who obviously chafed under Pius XII, were trying to turn the clock back. When the bishops assembled in 1962 in Rome, a handout from the Italian episcopate was distributed to them listing a series of biblical proposals with the statement, "What good Catholic could accept these proposals?" A French journalist got hold of a copy, sensed some of the proposals sounded familiar, and he found them verbatim in the encyclical of Pope Pius XII! Not only did the two-font theory for doctrines alarm many arriving bishops and their theologians, such as Yves Congar mentioned in the Foreword, the journalist's exposé insured the rejection of the preparatory document. (The vote of the bishops to reject it and send it back was just under the rule for needing a two-thirds majority. Pope John XXIII moved into action and requested a more suitable document be formulated by a new drafting committee, this time including the input of Cardinal Bea and biblical scholars from his Secretariat for Christian Unity.)

It was at this time that the Pontifical Biblical Commission (PBC) produced for the work of the new drafting committee an extraordinary document concerning the gospels, *Instruction on the Historical Truth of the Gospels*. The

PBC held that the gospels retain the truth of the sayings of Jesus without implying that his words are verbatim. The truth and the historicity of the words and deeds of Jesus must be judged on the basis that they were remembered after his death for the purpose of preaching them and not for the purpose of preserving the words and deeds inviolate, as if they were the product of an audio/video recording. To explain this principle, the *Instruction* described how the gospels, without being verbatim accounts, reflect truly what Jesus said and did if the first century is seen within three stages. So important were these stages to how the gospels work that the bishops of Vatican II voted to incorporate their conclusions into the Dogmatic Constitution on Divine Revelation, *Dei Verbum*.[9]

My story above, which began with Leo XIII in 1893, might seem too long and unnecessary. But for a Catholic to understand his or her faith and penetrate it more deeply, it is also necessary to understand how the church works. There are forces that contend with each other. Good people get hurt and some never recover their prominence. Others get silenced by Vatican authorities, only to be rehabilitated by a later pope, as happened with Congar by John XXIII. Some popes (Pius XII) undo what others (Pius X) mandated. Christian faith lives in swirling waters, something like Peter getting out of a boat to walk toward Jesus on choppy seas.

Before undertaking to outline the three stages of how the gospels came to be the realities they are, it must be noted that this is official Catholic teaching from an Ecumenical Council on understanding how the gospels work. Nearly all New Testament scholars of every persuasion—Catholic, Protestant, Eastern Orthodox—accept the three stages as a commonly possessed insight, but the Catholic Church is the only church of which I am aware that advances this insight as official church teaching about the Bible.

FIRST THIRD OF THE FIRST CENTURY

Imagine the first century as divided into three equal periods. Period I would embrace the years from Jesus' birth in Bethlehem to his crucifixion in Jerusalem. I follow those scholars who date his death to be about AD 33. Others place it earlier, around 30, with plausible reasons. We do know that death was in the spring, around Passover, and that it was on a Friday,[10] just before Sabbath began that evening. Jesus' death is his immediate entry into resurrected life. (In a later chapter I will consider the meaning of something happening

9. The official title of the PBC *Instruction* comes from its opening Latin words, *Sancta Mater Ecclesia*, and §19 of Vatican II's *Dei Verbum* adopts these very words and other phrases from the Instruction. Although *Dei Verbum* was one of only two "dogmatic constitutions" from Vatican II, hence an extremely high-level teaching, nothing at Vatican II was solemnly proclaimed as an infallible teaching, as did happen at Councils centuries earlier.

10. The Jews followed a seven-day week, with the day of Sabbath concluding the week. Note the format of the famous creation story in *Genesis* where the Creator God "rests" on the seventh day.

"on the third day," such as Jesus was raised on the third day.) Period II, then, begins with his resurrection appearances to his followers. Leave to the side, for now, how many had appearances and who got them. Make AD 70, when Rome sacked Jerusalem, or a couple years earlier, the transition from Period II to III, the last third of the century. The three periods can be understood as the three stages of tradition by which God's revelation in Jesus has come to be contained in the gospels.

The description of three stages or periods is an inference drawn by the scholars of the PBC, as well as most other scholars, working backwards. All that we possess of the Jesus of Period I and the events of Period II come from the four gospels, which are from Period III. From a proper study of the four gospels, the PBC experts were able to "look through" them into the events lying behind our gospels. Lest anyone be unsettled by this reconstruction because it does not match ideas always assumed to be true, recall for ease of mind that the PBC findings were given approval by Pope Paul VI on 21 April 1964 and incorporated in 1965 into the Vatican Council document of highest authority, *Dei Verbum*. The teaching authority of the church stands behind this reconstruction.

Are there other documents from secular sources describing the life of Jesus corresponding to Period I and the activities of his disciples in Period II? Unfortunately, no! There are Roman documents written in the early second century about crazed followers of Jesus who sang hymns "to Christ as God" (Pliny the Younger, about AD 110). The secular references, scarce as they are, describe the impact of Jesus on second-century followers, which these writers liken to a "pernicious superstition" (the historian Tacitus, about AD 115).

Period I describes the life of the Jesus of Palestine, sometimes called the period of "the Historical Jesus." There are items that can be readily surmised, not from the gospels but from common sense, about the Palestinian Jesus. For example, he was of a certain height, certain weight, certain color of hair, and if he happened to be walking in the hills barefooted and stepped full weight on a small stone, he would have limped for a while. But the PBC and the Vatican II document on revelation describe Period I from another angle. They are concerned with the words and deeds of Jesus involved in announcing that the Kingdom of God is at hand. How tall Jesus was is irrelevant. That he did miracles and exorcisms is quite relevant. Furthermore, the concern is with the ministry of an adult Jesus. With all four gospels, Period I can be thought as beginning with Jesus' baptism by John the Baptist. This is where *Mark* begins. The other three gospels can be reckoned also as beginning at the baptismal scene, after their respective inclusions of material—Infancy stories in *Matthew* and *Luke*, and Jesus' eternal existence in *John* before becoming human—that serve as important prefaces to the gospels that follow. It is as if these three evangelists are telling their readers, before they get to the baptismal scene, answers to the question, "Just who is this who is being baptized and whose story unfolds thereafter?"

The words and deeds of the Jesus of Period I are the foundations of Christian faith and salvation. Leaving to the side, until Period II is described, whether the disciples of Jesus during Period I fully understood the salvific meaning of his words and deeds up to and including Crucifixion, official church teaching is at pains to assert "the historical character" of the gospels regarding the Jesus of Period I. It opposes whatever contemporary writings that would reduce the Jesus story to a bunch of myths or to some emaciated figure who was only a prophet of the end of the world or to a Jesus having no real connection to a "heavenly Father" or to anything supernatural. All that said, church teaching asserts that Jesus was a fully embodied inhabitant of first-century Palestine. His thinking involved current thought forms, just as our thinking does today. His language used the idioms and vocabulary limitations of the Aramaic that he and everyone else spoke. His outlook was of the specific time, location, and circumstances in which he lived. If the culture then thought that the sun moved and the earth did not, so did Jesus. If the general Jewish sense at that time was that King David composed almost every psalm in the Tanak, then Jesus would have thought the same as apparently he does (*Mt* 22:43). Matters such as these do not bear on the definitive revelation Jesus embodies *for our salvation*. Such mistakes in Jesus' human awareness (e.g., the sun moves in the sky) do not undermine his divinity nor threaten the fact that he bears God's revelation in full integrity.

If one aspect of the Incarnation of Jesus as the enfleshed Word—"and the Word became flesh" of *Jn* 1:14—means his immersion into human life and Jewish society in the manner in which everyone else was immersed, this does not preclude the manner in which his human life and consciousness "outdistanced" others. His intimacy with God reflected a personhood that the later church, with the help of better language tools in Greek, came to describe as an at-one-ness with God: Jesus fully human, fully divine, and one in personhood. Jesus' self-consciousness would have engaged his unique personhood, a personhood the rest of us do not have. From this self-consciousness springs the words of the Jesus of Period I, remembered and preached in Period II, and preserved in Period III. His words describe his relationship with God as his Father—think of this as a revelation to his human consciousness arising from within himself—that impels Jesus to invite others into similar intimacy with God as their Father, or their Mother if you will. Think of this invitation by Jesus being extended to us as a revelation proceeding outward from him to us, proceeding into the world, not unlike Yahweh's revelation in the Tanak as a revelation to covenanted Israelites from the *God-in-their-midst*. The invitation to let God be our own Father is spoken by Jesus in Period I, remembered and preached in Period II, and preserved in the gospels of Period III as "honest truth" from the actual Jesus, to quote the Vatican Council document.

SECOND THIRD OF THE FIRST CENTURY

Period II can be called the period of apostolic preaching. The foundation and impetus for the preaching are the resurrection appearances of the now-transformed and glorified status of Jesus of Nazareth. Using the Greek words in *Acts* 2:36 of Peter's Pentecost-day sermon, by resurrecting him God has constituted Jesus as Lord (*Kyrios*) and Messiah (*Christos*). "I have seen the Lord" and "Christ appeared" can be shorthand formulae for resurrection appearances of Jesus. The effect of these appearances on the first disciples leads to a most important assertion by the PBC, and it deserves to be quoted in full: "After Jesus has risen from the dead, and *when His divinity was clearly perceived*, the faith of the disciples, far from blotting out the remembrance of the events that had happened, rather consolidated it" (italics mine). When the disciples followed Jesus in Period I, they were unable to grasp that he was divine. Remember that they were monotheistic Jews. Yahweh alone is God. There are indeed gospel passages portraying the disciples as understanding Jesus' identity fully, but these are examples of post-resurrection insights projected back into Period I that had come only into their awareness in Period II. Some examples will be considered later. The PBC is concerned to raise the question of what was *actually* understood by disciples during Period I and what came later to be understood due to a resurrection appearance.

Christ's resurrection appearances cannot be underestimated. In Period I, all the disciples fled when Jesus was captured, their hopes quashed in whatever they had been expecting of him, their fears sky-high lest they be drawn into the turmoil that awaited Jesus. But a resurrection appearance undid fears and disappointments in sudden fashion, like an instantaneous conversion experience. Think of a resurrection appearance as revelatory to the disciple receiving it and not just a proof that Jesus is back from the dead for those who had seen, or heard as they fled Jerusalem, that he died violently. The appearances open the minds of disciples to the deeper meanings behind the words and deeds of Jesus in Period I. Above all, as the PBC text states, an appearance enables the disciples to perceive his divine status, a perception that eluded them during his Palestinian days. In a resurrection appearance they perceive him, the same person they had known, but now his human nature is glorified, transformed, and fully transparent to the divine status that Jesus had possessed all along. What before was opaque or even hidden to the disciples is now revealed. (I shall use later the phrase *post-resurrectional faith*, and this is what is being described here.) Such is the transformative effect of resurrection appearances on those receiving them. To use the language of the definition of inspiration given earlier, the truths that God wished for our salvation are embedded in their minds and memory by resurrection appearances. It is this enhancement of understanding that the first disciples then preached in Period II.

These first Jewish disciples proceeded to do something Jews then and now do not do. They evangelized. In the first century Jews did not go around preaching to non-Jews or to fellow Jews. Jews came to synagogue and a rabbi preached to them; the same situation prevails today.[11] But these first preachers about Christ felt impelled to proclaim Jesus and his message, and they travelled afar doing it. We call them *apostolic* preachers because they experienced themselves as *sent forth* [*apostellein* in Greek] by the risen Christ.

Some important matters are to be noted about their preaching. At some point the resurrection appearances of the Risen Christ stopped, and it is impossible when in Period II to date the termination. St. Paul had a resurrection appearance that might be dated to AD 36, some 3-4 years after the Crucifixion. (I will return to this issue later when discussing the meaning of "forty days.") The inspiration of the Holy Spirit can be thought, as it should, as applying to protecting from error the first preachers, for such an idea would be embedded in the experience of a resurrection appearance, and protecting from error those other preachers shaped and informed by the initial generation of preachers. It is therefore not crucial to date the termination of the resurrection appearances during Period II and determine who did and who did not get them. The term *apostolic preachers* can apply to very many preachers of the Period. The phrase is not to be restricted to the Twelve Apostles, as if those twelve and they alone enjoyed the resurrection appearances. Besides Paul, who was not a member of the Twelve, there were others beyond these few, as we read of information Paul had gotten and passed on to the Corinthians: "After the Twelve, [the Risen Lord] appeared to more than five hundred brethren at once, most still alive but some dead; then he appeared to James, and then to all the apostles" (1 Cor 15:6-7). Who were these others? James's identity is clear. He is a blood relative of Jesus—see Mk 6:3 for the male relatives of Jesus—and head of the Jerusalem church in the 30s and 40s. The five hundred and also the other apostles? It's anyone's guess. I think Apollos must have been included, the preacher described as "learned in the Scriptures" (Acts 18:24).

It is not wise to try to extract factual detail from sources unsuitable to such fact hunting, and often the scriptures are unsuitable to knowing just who received an appearance. But here is a theological detail, not a factual detail, that sums up the where and when of resurrection appearances. It is a phrase from the Baltimore Catechism of my earlier memories. "The appearances ended with the death of the last apostle." I am sure my grade school teacher and I understood it to refer to the last member of the Twelve, whoever he may have been. But the phrase reports an important truth in itself. At some point during Period II the appearances ended, and this means that there are

11. To avoid oversimplifying, there is today some Jewish outreach to "fallen away" Jews, especially on college campuses via the Hillel establishments on them.

no new revelations about the mystery of God and of Jesus Christ. If anyone claims to have received a brand new revelation from Jesus, such as exactly when the world may end or some other "new religious information," the person is not to be given hearing. Understanding of existing and once-for-all revelations can be deepened and probed further, but this is another and very important matter called development of doctrine. With the human life of the Incarnate One and his Resurrection, which is illuminated through appearances that the Lord bestows, the revelation in Christ is unsurpassable. It is essentially full and complete. Mormons do not think so and neither do Muslims, but the catechism formula draws a line in the sand between Catholics and them. (Mainline Protestants believe identically with Catholics on the matter.)

Other characteristics of Period II stand out. The PBC document states that the apostolic preachers "interpreted his words and deeds according to the needs of their hearers." There is a gospel story of the ninety-nine sheep and the one straying sheep. The preaching that *Mt* 18 picked up has the story preached to leaders in the early church: Get up and go after strays, because "it is never the will of the Father that any little one be lost." *Lk* 15 picked up preaching addressed to anyone feeling so discouraged by sinfulness that he or she may be dreading the never-to-be-regained love of God. In Luke's stray sheep story, the shepherd carries back on his shoulders to the flock (church) the lost sheep with the truth that "there is more rejoicing in heaven [in the heart of God as it were] over even one lost sheep than over the ninth-nine who did not stray." No sin suffocates forever God's love of someone.

One more example of accommodating a Jesus event. There's a story of Jesus in Capernaum and people bring him a paralytic to heal. When the story is retold by preachers in Palestine of letting the man down through a hole in the roof, it is a Palestinian village-style roof being described (*Mk* 2:4); they cut a hole through the pressed clay and branches. When the story is retold in Gentile lands closer to Greece, the house has a customary tile roof that is breached (*Lk* 5:19).

The preachers of Period II used "various forms of speech as were adapted to their purposes or to the mentality of their hearers," in the words of the PBC. It can be seen that the words and deeds of Jesus underwent change by the apostolic preachers in order to present the "true and enduring" message of Jesus for the purpose of bringing listeners to conversion and faith. The words and deeds of Period I are modified (i.e., no longer verbatim), under the inspiration of the Holy Spirit, without loss of their essential historical truthfulness. Jesus himself preached the kingdom of God, and the apostolic era preached the kingdom that the life, death, and resurrection of Jesus brought about. It is continuity without needing to be verbatim.

Period II witnessed a very large adaptation of language. Jesus spoke Aramaic. The first apostolic preachers spoke Aramaic to Aramaic-understanding fellow Jews in Palestine. Jesus' words from Period I resonated in their ears in Aramaic tones. At some point in Period II, probably in the mid-40s, preaching began happening to Jews in the diaspora or those who visited Jerusalem. They spoke Greek, of course, and therefore the preaching about Jesus was in Greek. Soon thereafter, preaching was directed to Greek-speaking Gentiles. Familiar words and titles describing Jesus, such as being the Messiah needed to be put into Greek for listeners to understand. It was an easy task for *Messiah*. Its meaning is "anointed one." The Greek word for anointed one is *Christos*. In Greek-speaking areas, then, Jesus was preached as the Christ. In the Aramaic period Jesus was preached as *mar* (Lord). In the Greek period Jesus was the *Kyrios* (Lord), and Catholics remembering or now attending Latin Masses hear and say this Greek word at the "Lord, have mercy" invocation (*Kyrie, eleison*). A few times in the Greek New Testament Aramaic words push through untranslated. Mar in the formulaic expression *marana-tha* (Do come, Lord) is how Paul ends *I Corinthians*, expressing his normal hope for the quick Second Coming of the Lord and reflecting his bi-lingual abilities. He spoke both languages and surely understood the Tanak in Hebrew because he was, as I interpret his life, trained as an orthodox rabbi. Great importance attaches to this language transition from Aramaic to Greek in the late 40s and early 50s. By the time the gospels were composed some decades later, the preponderant preaching was being done in Greek and therefore the gospels were written in Greek.[12]

Some final characteristics of Period II preaching: (1) The earliest followers of Christ expected a quick return of the Risen Lord to end the world. Therefore they had no pressure to write documents. They were about preaching with urgency the Kingdom that Jesus' death and resurrection begot. (2) But did they possess sacred scriptures? Indeed they did because they were believing Jews. They possessed the Tanak, and if they were preaching in the Greek-speaking diaspora, it would have been the Septuagint expression of the Tanak. Their preaching was often against the background of Old Testament prophecies, so that God's providence in preparation for Jesus and achieving fulfillment in his words and deeds was pressed home to listeners. The "Four Servant Prophecies" from *Isaiah* were most important to early preachers because there are no prophecies that the Messiah would suffer or die, but this mysterious servant figure does die that others may be healed. (3) Like effective sermons today that make a single point, the early sermons about Jesus circulated orally in communities of converts in a somewhat free-floating form. They did not exist in a framework of a cohesive life story of

12. There is one reference, questionable in its historical accuracy, from Papias in the second century that a gospel in Aramaic set the stage for Greek *Matthew*. There's no other confirmation, and biblical scholars adopt the position that all four gospels first appeared in Greek. That other written documents could have predated the four gospels, such as a collection of Jesus teachings that *Matthew* and *Luke* independently used, is quite probable.

Jesus, with the possible exception of preaching on the passion of Jesus. The passion topic required a sequence of arrest, trial, torture, and crucifixion to which allied issues could be attached, such as Peter's denial in one kind of sermon, or the women standing at a distance from the Crucifixion hill in another, or the flight of his intimates in a third kind of sermon. Bringing isolated and free-floating sermon topics into a cohesive story about Jesus is the work of the last third of the century, the work of a gospel writer. Let this idea introduce Period III.

LAST THIRD OF THE FIRST CENTURY

The Age of the Evangelists is a suitable title for Period III beginning in the late 60s of the first century. This is the period of time during which the four evangelists wrote their gospels. Why this happened, and only after many years since the death of Jesus, is another important implication of those resurrection appearances happening early in Period II. Those recipients of the appearances can be called eyewitness apostolic preachers. Most knew the pre-Crucified Jesus—Paul did not—but they now knew him in his glorified appearances and the revelations that accompanied appearances. In Peter's first recorded preaching, meant to be prototypical of earliest preaching, is the customary warrant, "and of this we are all witnesses" (Acts 2:32). All these details of Jesus' life became the substance of their preaching, and the warrant for their message was their stature as eyewitnesses. But by the 60s of the first century these disciples, approximately the same in age as Jesus, had begun dying out. Some died naturally. Others were put to death, like Peter. But the importance of their preaching message, called the *apostolic kerygma*, cannot die with them lest the Lord's intention for an enduring church be undone. An impossible prospect! And thus it was, under the inspiration of the Holy Spirit who insures a lasting church built on "revelation in Christ," that certain individuals were led—call it inspired—to write down the apostolic preaching about the Lord lest it fade and become lost. This they did, not in the haphazard manner of piling sermon atop sermon, but as organizing a narrative, as providing a cohesive story of the words and deeds of Jesus, including death and resurrection. Cohesion was supplied by each one of the four, and each in his own inspired manner. The formatting of the story, if it may be so called, is their work as inspired sacred writers. Their four gospels and their cohesive narratives have become *canonical* for us.

A teaching about the church, which came to expression years later in the creed of the Council of Nicea (AD 325), is best explained here in light of what I've just written. The church is one, holy, catholic, and apostolic. This is to say, it is not splintered, it embodies the holiness of Christ its head, it is universal and not localized or ethnic, and it is apostolic, meaning that its message and self-understanding is based on the apostolic eyewitness preaching. If that first group of disciples receiving appearances got it wrong, the church collapses like a house of cards. But they were protected from getting it wrong because the resurrection appearances had imbedded in them the inspiration that protects from error. The Risen Lord revealing himself through the appearances ensures truthful apprehension within the disciples. The language of the *Gospel of John* calls this protection from error the work of the Paraclete (Holy Spirit).

The Christians of the last third of the first century represent the second generation of believers. The disciples who walked with Jesus, who preached him as Lord and Messiah after his Resurrection, were the first generation of the church. This places the four evangelists in the second generation and removed in time from experiencing the Jesus of Palestine as adults or of meeting him at all as children. This claim may jar someone long accustomed to accepting the writer of one gospel being a tax collector named Matthew and another gospel writer being John, son of Zebedee, both called by Jesus as disciples and hence his contemporaries. But again let the PBC document issued by Pope Paul VI provide the assurance that the four evangelists are truly second generation.

> The sacred authors, for the benefit of the churches, took this earliest body of instruction [the apostolic eyewitness preaching], which had been handed on orally at first and then in writing [some individual teachings of Jesus were likely transcribed][13] and set it down in four gospels. In doing this each of them followed a method suitable to the special purpose which he had in view. They selected certain things out of the many which had been handed on; some they synthesized, some they explained with an eye to the situation of the churches…[being] adapted to the varied circumstances of the faithful as well as to the end which they themselves wished to attain.

Think of the four evangelists as standing on the shoulders of the first generation of eyewitness preachers and drawing from them an inherited oral tradition of revelation that divine inspiration led them to select "for us and our salvation."

The beginning of one of the four gospels reflects exactly this process: "Of events that have been fulfilled among us, just as those who were eyewitnesses

13. Although it is no longer in existence to be displayed, a written document of many individualized teachings of Jesus is thought to have existed prior to the existence of the four gospels. This is an inference, but the scholarly arguments for the document's existence are very strong. The sacred authors of *Matthew* and *Luke*, writing independently of each other, seemed to have copied teachings from it; otherwise it is difficult to explain why certain teachings of Jesus in both gospels are practically verbatim in the Greek. The document is called Q, from the German word *Quelle* for "source." It's possible other pre-gospel written materials existed that we no longer have.

from the beginning and ministers of the word have handed them down to us, I too have decided, after investigating everything accurately anew, to write it down in an orderly sequence" (Lk 1:2-3). The above passage also indicates a creativity the gospel writer brings to his task. He is not slavish to what he inherits but imposes a sequence, adapts it "to the situation of the churches" in the words of the PBC. Apropos this creative writing role of each evangelist that divine inspiration both causes and protects, consider these concluding words of the PBC document concerning the four gospel writers.

> For this reason the exegete [the Catholic biblical schol-ar] must ask himself[14] what the Evangelist intended by re-counting a saying or a fact in a certain way, or placing it in a certain context. For the truth of the narrative is not affected in the slightest by the fact that the Evangelists report the say-ings or doings of our Lord in a different order, and that they use different words to express what he said, not keeping to the very letter, but nevertheless preserving the sense.

Let me offer a clear example of a gospel writer making a decision about placement "in a certain context." In composing an organized account of the *salvific meaning* of the life of Jesus, an evangelist needs to figure where to posi-tion the teachings of Jesus within the narrative of his life. Luke's decision is striking. He writes the ominous words, "When the days for his being taken up were fulfilled, he resolutely determined to journey to Jerusalem" (9:51). Why ominous? At the end of the journey, Jesus will be crucified in Jerusalem. But Jesus is resolved to start off. (Another freer translation captures it better: Jesus set his face like steel toward Jerusalem.) It takes ten chapters to get there, and this is where Luke inserts most of the teachings he, as gospel writer, wishes to preserve. (In *Mark*, the journey to Jerusalem takes one chapter.) To capture the poignancy of this situation, I used to ask my Gwynedd Mercy undergraduates to imagine being summoned by an elderly grandmother on hospice so that "I can share some important early family history with you be-fore I die." Then I ask the students, "Can you think of anything to which you would listen more attentively?" I continue, "In such a similar situation, the evangelist Luke puts Jesus' teachings. He wants the disciples 100% attentive and, of course, he wants the future readers of his gospel equally attentive to what Jesus is teaching."

By the last third of the century, Christians are living in small communi-ties, called *churches*, as in the church of Antioch and the church of Ephesus. The church in Jerusalem is itself something of a mother church whose evan-gelizing begot other enclaves of believers. Some churches are more heavily

---

14. Applying the PBC *Instruction* to the present, as it is meant to be, "and herself" needs to be inserted. In 1964 there were hardly any women in Catholic biblical scholarship. When I studied in Louvain in 1971, women were taking scripture courses at the highest level and later became recognized scholars.

Jewish in background, meaning that the baptized people who believe in Jesus were raised Jewish and likely preserve Jewish sensitivities to the Torah. Other churches reflect a majority of converted Gentiles. In all these churches the apostolic preaching of Period II is being preserved as oral traditions. In some churches important apostolic figures may have labored and died there. Peter seems connected with the Christian community in Rome. He certainly died there about AD 64 in the massacre of Christians caused by Emperor Nero when he blamed them for the fire destroying most of the city, a fire Nero himself started that leapt out of control. It seems that the Jewish enclave in Rome—Rome seems to have had twelve synagogues and about 50,000 Jews—was evangelized by preachers from Jerusalem before Peter would have arrived there for the first time. (It was never evangelized by St. Paul although he wrote a letter to them in the mid-50s of the first century, and he was put to death there sometime in the 60s.[15])

In these localized churches of Period III an evangelist would have lived. It is among fellow believers that he would have heard the preaching about Jesus. The preaching would have been passing on the remembered stories of Jesus, cherished as they were, as well as making ongoing applications of the words and life of the Lord to pastoral situations that local church was facing. Recall the two different applications of the ninety-nine sheep and one that strayed off. The evangelist we call Mark is an illustration of the situation of his local church. His gospel, when read carefully between the lines, seems to be reflecting a church suffering persecution or having recently done so. If the *Gospel of Mark* originated in Rome, as many scholars think it did, it would make sense. Roman Christians suffered greatly under Nero. Mark would seem to fulfill writing "with an eye to the situation" of the local church, the PBC phrase. All evangelists did. *Luke* reflects the imprint of a Gentile local church.

Among that first generation of believers who lived during Period II, the conviction was strong that the Risen Jesus would return very soon to bring the consummation of all things. To bring about the end of the world is another way of stating it. This generation thought Jesus would return in its lifetime. With this sense of immediacy, there was no need for them to produce what might be termed a permanent literature of their beliefs. St. Paul thought the same of the soon-to-be-ended world when he was writing in the year 50 to the church in Thessalonica: "We can tell you this from the Lord's own teaching, that we who are still alive for the Lord's coming [i.e., return] will not have any advantage over those who have fallen asleep [died]" (*1 Thes* 4:15).

By the time the last third of the century is reached, that first generation

---

15. The end of *Acts* (28: 17ff) describes Paul the prisoner arriving under house arrest and speaking to local Jews, making the case for Jesus with mixed results. This scene is crafted two decades later by the sacred writer, whom we call Luke, to list the real meaning of *Acts*: "You Jews have refused to listen but the Gentiles will" (28:28).

is nearly gone and with it the idea that the Second Coming of Christ was to be imminent. So the gospels represent permanent literature because Christianity begins to see itself as enduring for however long, as seen in the end of *Matthew*, "Go out into the whole world preaching and...I will be with you all days, even to the end of the world." Gospels are preserving for an unknown future the heritage of the apostolic faith. Letter writing is another matter. Letters were written to a particular group or person about a particular matter relevant at that moment; they could have happened at any time in Period II or III. A consequence is that a number of letters in the New Testament were written before any of the gospels were written.

With the possible exception of the first written gospel that is judged to have appeared just before the destruction of Jerusalem in AD 70, the other gospels and the later writings of the New Testament reflect the view that the Return of Christ will indeed happen but at an unknown future time. The first generation was mistaken about the return of Jesus, based on what they concluded his words meant, but they ought not to be blamed for a mistake. On their behalf I have told students, "If you or I had received in that first age a resurrection appearance of Jesus whose risen humanity revealed the end-time reality that God has decreed for all the saved, we would have been so overwhelmed and we, too, would have been inclined to think that the fulfillment of God's plans won't delay for long."

Another consequence of the church's teaching that three stages were involved in the formation of the gospels is that the personal identity of each evangelist is unknown. The four writers are anonymous. The PBC document and the Council's *Constitution on Divine Revelation* support the anonymity by carefully using the generic phrase, *sacred author*, for each writer. But names do come to be attached to each gospel. How did this happen?

The answer lies partially in the nature of paper and the role of copyists. The *autograph* is the technical name given to the original document that an evangelist wrote. It was written on *papyrus*, which is a paper-like product made from the stems of a swamp plant. Papyrus is not nearly as good as our paper today. The papyrus doesn't hold up well, especially if it is fingered frequently when reading it. But the gospel message on the paper was considered too precious to lose out to illegibility. As the text of a gospel got worn, it was copied. Copies of a gospel were also made for other local churches. Since few could write Greek clearly in a small space on flimsy paper,[16] being a copyist was a very important trade in that era. Years pass. Copies of copies abound.

By mid-second century the autograph is long gone, replaced by copies. There is no author's name associated with a gospel until an *apostolic* name comes to be associated. The text, after all, transmits as a precious bequest the

16. The Greek New Testament papyri had small letters with no spaces between the words and no grammar markings.

life of Jesus first preached by the apostolic eyewitnesses. About the middle of the second century copyists begin introducing a gospel with the stark phrase in Greek capitals, KATA MAPKON, "According to Mark," for instance. No contemporary document tells us why the names Matthew, Mark, Luke and John begin to be associated with the respective gospels. We are left to educated and plausible guesses, but it can be noted that the understandable tendency to associate an illustrious name with a sacred document was common practice in the biblical world.

Take the *Book of Proverbs*, for example, which is attributed to King Solomon, known traditionally for his wisdom. The book was composed in the sixth century BC, more than two hundred years after Solomon died. And the same for the *Psalms of David*. David was known to sing religious hymns, but many psalms are clearly from the period of the Exile or thereafter. It is understandable, and likely enhancing prestige to a psalm, that David's name was later identified with psalms, as if their author. A last example comes from usage in the Catholic Church and is an example of a name being removed recently from the sacred text. For centuries St. Paul was reckoned to write the *Letter to the Hebrews*, and in this way he was acknowledged in the Vulgate Bible read in Catholic churches for centuries: "A Reading from the Epistle of Blessed Paul Apostle to the *Hebrews*." Paul's authorship of Hebrews had long been suspect; even St. Thomas Aquinas in the thirteenth century puzzled over authorship before bowing to St. Jerome's authority that Paul wrote it. When the Catholic Church, known to esteem the wisdom of tradition and therefore cautious to change its ritual, somewhat recently removed Paul's name before the *Letter to the Hebrews* in the Lectionary read in church, it must have startled a Catholic who listens carefully at Mass. But it underlines a deeper truth that is the point to retain. It is the inspired text that is important, not the title listing its presumptive author.

Here is a short illustration why the anonymity of the gospels removes a trouble spot. If Jesus' disciple Matthew wrote *Matthew*, and if the disciple John wrote *John*, then why does one gospel have Jesus confronting the Temple money changers at the outset of his ministry and the other gospel have the event at the end of his ministry, *if both men were present for it?* But if, as said above, each sacred author, whoever he was, was free to arrange the order of Jesus material to achieve some deeper aim, then we are left to probe the respective aims for our deeper gospel nourishment and not to explain why two disciples of Jesus seem to be at loggerheads.

Some gospel nomenclature is called for. "Matthew," for example, can have two senses. If the sacred writer himself is being referenced, writers will just say Matthew, and it will only mean the anonymous sacred author of that gospel to which the name of the apostle was affixed later. If the text of that gospel is being referenced, then *Matthew* with italics is used, as in *Matthew* has twenty-eight chapters. But another sentence would properly read: "There is strong evidence that Matthew had rabbinical training."

Synoptic (synoptics) is an important word, very frequently used in writings about the New Testament. Three of the gospels have great similarities as if they can be "seen all together" (syn + ophthē in Greek). They are *Matthew*, *Mark*, and *Luke*. To undergraduates I liken them to being cousins. *John* is very different from the three synoptic gospels. I liken *John* to a quite distant relative. Its Jesus stories are different. The manner in which Jesus speaks in John is different. Ninety percent of the material in *John* is not found elsewhere in the synoptic gospels. The underlying connection, of course, is that all four writings are "good news" proclamations about the one and same Jesus.

When the four gospels are compared and contrasted in the most general way, some conclusions about them have become generally accepted and in no way violate any Catholic doctrine. *Mark* is the earliest written gospel, perhaps a year or two before the Roman destruction of Jerusalem. *Matthew* and *Luke* were composed independently of each other sometime in the mid-80s. Each sacred writer knew of the existence of *Mark* because the text had begun being shared with other local churches in somewhat close fellowship with the Jerusalem mother church. Matthew and Luke incorporated into their narratives a great deal of the Lord's teachings, and some of these short teachings, in the Greek, are verbatim or almost so. Because the two evangelists were not copying from each other, they must have been copying from a written source of teachings. (See above footnote about the *Q* source.)

Mark has very little of Jesus' teaching. It is a gospel of action and deeds, especially exorcisms. The evangelist wanted to bring to central attention the Passion of Jesus and the necessity of suffering for the followers of Jesus. The good news arrived through the Cross. It is guessed that Mark thought that this focus was being clouded by circulating writings restricted to Jesus' impressive and arresting teachings. I used to suggest the following image of *Mark* to students. In a darkened room, if you shine a flashlight behind a crucifix that you hold in your hand, a shadow of the cross will fall on the floor. *Mark* is like that. The shadow of the Passion and Cross pervades this gospel, and *Mark* became the consecrated account of Jesus whose suffering and death brought redemption. Matthew and Luke adopt Mark's orientation, outline if you will, to which each sacred writer enhances the passion portrait by adding Jesus' teachings, each in his characteristic manner.

On some very plausible evidence, it is surmised that a small number of Jesus' disciples, along with someone called "the disciple Jesus loved," departed the Jerusalem community in its earliest years. Among them, of course, were disciples who had resurrection appearances. They were eyewitnesses as were others who stayed in Jerusalem and evangelized various cities from that base. There is some thought that this departing group eventually settled in western Asia Minor. However speculative the geography may be, what is certain is that an evangelist among them is inspired to compose a gospel based on how the Risen Christ was being remembered and proclaimed. It is thought that this happened in the mid-90s. Thus it is the last gospel to be written and is sometimes called "the Fourth Gospel" in later church history. The others never get a first, second, third designation in official nomenclature.

The preaching in this community recalls some events in Jesus' life that the Jerusalem-influenced churches did not, like a certain wedding feast in Cana of Galilee, or a visit to Jesus from someone named Nicodemus, and these stories enter the gospel we know today as *John*. The community, or cluster of small communities, in this orbit becomes termed the *Johannine* Community. In fact, this group produces five books in the New Testament that have very similar motifs: *John*, the *Book of Revelation*, and the three letters, *1 John*, *2 John*, and *3 John*. (When different biblical books have the same common title, prefix numbers are used to distinguish them, for example, *1 Kings* and *2 Kings* in the Tanak.)

A brief proof that the four personal names became affixed by the middle of the second century to the four hitherto anonymous gospels comes from well-known Christian writings from the turn of the century. St. Clement of Rome, writing in the mid-90s, and the letters of St. Ignatius of Antioch, written about AD 100, used quotations of Jesus from the gospels but simply called them words of the Lord or words of scripture. There is no mention of the name of a sacred writer. Clement and Ignatius were using anonymous gospels but to them and others of this period it did not matter. They were in possession of gospels conveying the words and deeds of their Lord and Master. After mid-century, writers such as St. Irenaeus (about AD 180) were referring to *Matthew*, *Mark*, etc. Conclusion: Only by mid-second century did gospel copyists begin adding "According to Matthew...Mark...Luke...John."

There will be other things to share about the New Testament and the Tanak, as sacred writings, when I consider other topics of Catholic faith. In the Foreword I mentioned certain people who influenced my thinking. And this is true in my New Testament reading. I want to acknowledge particularly the influence of Raymond E. Brown, a Sulpician priest who served on the Pontifical Biblical Commission in later years. He was frequently asked by the American bishops to lecture to them on various biblical issues. And to complete his *bona fides*, Pope Benedict XVI once remarked, "I wish we had more exegetes like Fr. Brown." He died of cardiac arrest on August 8, 1998 at the Sulpician seminary in Menlo Park, CA. I've learned biblical insights from many sources, beginning in Louvain, but Brown has been special.[17]

---

17. Ray Brown's books and articles are many. Although the book is not for absolute beginners, I would recommend his *An Introduction to the New Testament* (New York: Doubleday, 1997).

CHAPTER TWO

Having, Losing, and Regaining More

*"Yet you have made him little less than a God,
crowned him with glory and honor"* Psalm 8:6

In recent years I've come to the judgment that the single most profound verse in the entire Bible is found in the six-days-of-creation story in *Genesis*, where on the sixth day is the verse, "God created humans ['ādām in the Hebrew text] in his image, in the image of God he created them; male and female he created them." Shortly I will examine the two creation stories found in the beginning of *Genesis*, the one with the world being created in six days and the Creator "resting" on the seventh, the other happening in a garden with Adam and Eve and their sin of disobedience. Both stories do not contradict each other but they are quite different. Being created in God's image is the apex of six-day story and what an apex! That all human beings, all men and women, owe their human lives to God and carry about in themselves God's image, God's likeness. Later tradition, and especially our Catholic theologians in it, call this feature of being human the *imago Dei* [image of God]. In the most general sense, everything else in the Bible is a derivation of God's generosity in creating human lives to reflect features of Himself.

Something negative happened to the image reality. In the Catholic tradition, it became obscured, and in the Protestant tradition it was eradicated, a difference to be addressed later when proposing how our redemption comes about. But God was not content with the negative turn of events, a situation that can be called Original Sin and its effects. God refashioned the image, and this was achieved by the Christmas and Easter stories. God took on the likeness of wounded—in the sense of vulnerable, not in the sense of sinful—human life by becoming fully and vulnerably human. In this human existence, Jesus suffers and dies in obedience to carrying out the Father's mission to him of preaching the "kingdom of God" (Mk 1:14), and the Father raises him from being dead so that his resurrected human nature is now fully transparent to the divine nature that always was his fundamental identity. Men and women are "redeemed," that is, their human natures become shaped by the human nature of Christ by being absorbed into it. Since Christ images the very nature of God, they in consequence are refashioned into God's image. But the refashioning achieves more than the original *imago Dei* possessed by simply being created human. Human beings in the *Genesis* story *reflect* God, just as the angels are described as doing in later tradition. Humans are not God but they mirror features of God in simply being human, as in possessing freedom and power of reflection. But human beings in the Jesus story *share* in God's nature itself. They become like unto God. Merely *reflecting* is elevated into *being*.

All of the very highly compacted account above is a derivative of that single verse in *Genesis*. As unfolding within history, human life is being directed under God's Providence. Its story begins with an exalted view of being human and concludes with God's design to share with his human creatures his very nature, his very self. This is why I've come to see that brief and awesome verse in *Genesis* as foundational. It is another question, for other parts of the human story and of theology reflecting on it, whether and how individuals come to bear in themselves the likeness of Christ. This involves matters like the nature of Baptism, the roles of faith and conversion, the process of how people living in parts of the world oblivious of Jesus can nevertheless be redeemed in Christ, and the same possibility for atheists and agnostics living in the Christian West. The teaching of the Second Vatican Council on these latter situations is clear: The possibility of salvation in Christ is denied by God to no human person who at his or her inception had become an image of God. These beliefs await further elaboration.

What is needed now is a better understanding of the two creations stories that begin the *Book of Genesis*. As an immediate application of principles from chapter one, the two accounts offer a clear illustration that the *Genesis* texts ought not to be understood literally, even though too many people read them in this manner. Consequently, many readers never get to the more profound religious teachings of the creation stories. After my analysis of the stories, there follows an examination of the church's teaching on Original Sin, and this for two reasons: The stories, along with New Testament texts, especially Paul's *Letter to the Romans*, shaped official Catholic teaching about Original Sin at the Council of Trent. But what is permanently binding on Catholic belief from Trent and what no longer is, because bishops at Trent worked from literal understandings of the creation stories then commonly accepted but not so today? Second, the doctrine of Original Sin affects other beliefs, such as: Are humans who lived a hundred thousand years ago saved or did they die with an inherited sinfulness and, if so, from whom? What happens to a Catholic baby who tragically dies before the Baptismal ceremony? And if Christ is called Redeemer, from what are we redeemed?

AVOIDING THE DILEMMA

The Adam and Eve story presents a dilemma that enables getting to a deeper level of what is actually being taught in Genesis. For the moment, let *Adam and Eve* be the phrase that means the first human beings, the first instances of *homo sapiens*. The story is familiar to most Catholics, and without rehearsing its details for the moment, note that it is a story, an account that this thing happened followed by that thing happening. Here's the dilemma: Either the first humans came into existence 5781 years ago (that is, about 3760 BC) or they came into existence hundreds of thousands years ago. I take 5781 from the Jewish New Year of Rosh Hashanah that began 9/18/2020. (This represents rabbinical calculations of when the world began, gotten by adding up the generations mentioned in the Bible reaching back to Adam. There were Christian generation counters, too. Anglican Archbishop James Ussher in the seventeenth century claimed the world began in 4004 BC.) Setting the emergence of *homo sapiens* to 200,000 years or more ago—recent archeological digs push the date further back—is the testimony of the scientific community dating bone fossils. To sense how untenable 4004 BC is, there is direct evidence of human *activity* 30,000 years ago (the Chauvet Cave drawings in southern France) and 45,000 years ago (the discovery of animals in the Russian Arctic that had been butchered with tools). So how did the story of Adam and Eve get all the way down to the people who finally wrote it in our Bible, since Adam and Eve were the only humans around to pass down their own story?

If the Adam and Eve story happened about 6,000 years ago, then a transmission of their story through the centuries could be possible because we have access today to similarly ancient Sumerian stories from Mesopotamia that passed from an oral transmission to cuneiform-written clay tablets we can access. If Adam and Eve lived 200,000+ years ago, then no oral transmission of a story could make it down the millennia, let alone be trusted, let alone flipping from one human language to others. The dilemma is that if you want an oral transmission of a story from the first humans meant for the Bible, you have to claim humans began only 6,000 years ago. But this cannot be true. If humans are very much older, then you have to give up on the Adam and Eve story's being orally transmitted. Jettisoning it creates a dilemma because the Adam and Eve story is biblical, and that means it is inspired, and that means God is revealing in the story *truths for our salvation*.

The way out of the dilemma is the notion of a religious story and its crucial teaching role. A story can be true but it can also be a crafted story, that is to say, a made-up story. Jesus provides a wonderful example of such a story in *Luke* 15 where he tells the story of a man having two sons. The younger wants early access to his share of inheritance, and the father, who is presented as caring to a fault, divides things between the two sons. Off goes the younger to a distant country where he squanders his money on idle dissipations and ends up hiring himself out as a laborer working with pigs—note the Jewish irony. Remembering that his father's farm laborers were far better off than he, he decides to crawl back home as it were and say to his father words of contrition that he has practiced: "I have sinned against heaven and against you and no longer deserve to be thought your son. Just hire me on as one of your laborers." But the father sees him coming from a distance, runs out to him, and before the son can get out his confession formula, his father embraces him as a lost and returned son. The son does get out his words but it's as if the father never hears them. The father orders that proper clothing be given him and orders a special feast to celebrate his return home. The story continues with the older son, the one who stayed by his father and supported him, being disgruntled over the seeming unfairness of the treatment toward his younger brother. Without retelling this concluding portion, I simply point out how powerful the story is in revealing God's compassion and forgiveness because Jesus intends the father of the story to image God.

My own most powerful experience of this story happens every time I view the 1977 Franco Zeffirelli film, *Jesus of Nazareth*, often replayed on television near Easter. Jesus (played by Shakespearean actor Robert Powell) tells the story to Matthew, the hated tax collector, but it is within the hearing of Simon Peter, hitherto Matthew's sworn enemy. The story causes Matthew to return home to his Judaism and causes Peter (the "older son" who never left Jewish practice) to embrace Matthew as a lost brother. I went at some length into this story to show how powerful its religious teaching is, but Jesus made up the story. This is my point about the value of religious storytelling even if it is a manufactured story.

The door out of the dilemma is that the Adam and Eve account was crafted into an oral story by early Israelites sometime after Mount Sinai (± 1250 BC). So was the six-days-of-creation account. But being crafted, that is, being made up, does not mean that the stories do not teach profound religious truths any more than thinking that Jesus' story about the caring father and his two sons lacks revelatory insight into the nature of God just because Jesus invented the story as a teaching device. Elaboration of the *religious* teachings of these two stories is soon to follow.

To be noted at the outset is the fact that there are two stories. Something already treated in the last chapter makes this fact plausible, even likely. Written texts arise from a pre-existing oral tradition. An oral tradition is hardly ever a single stream flowing through decades or centuries toward its written expression. Like a river itself, sometimes the oral tradition branches into tributaries. Another motif is that there are different sources flowing aside each other, like the Tigris and Euphrates rivers flowing to a common junction in southern Iraq. The oral tradition behind our two creations stories in *Genesis* partakes likely of both motifs.

Beginning in the nineteenth century among German Protestant scholars and continuing into the twentieth centuries among Protestant and Catholics biblical experts was the insight that the five books of the Torah (*Genesis,*[1] *Exodus, Leviticus, Numbers, Deuteronomy*), also called the Pentateuch or "five scrolls," showed evidence of four different oral traditions lying behind the present texts. The scholarly detective work was not unlike a person today, with a keen ear for music and voices, hearing a song and saying "Frank Sinatra is singing it," and hearing the same song later and saying "It's Dean Martin." (The example resonates with readers of a certain age.) At some point after the possibility of putting spoken words to paper,[2] an editor wove the four traditions into a single composite text that we now call the Torah. (Debated among scholars is whether the editor worked directly from oral stories or from pre-existing written units; the latter is more likely but the debate is unimportant for our purposes.) Two of the oral traditions regarding creation stories concern us. One tradition is given the letter J, standing for the German word for Yahweh, *Jahve*. This tradition has unique characteristics, one of them being the preponderant name Yahweh for God, the name met in the story of Moses at the Burning Bush. Another oral tradition, originating later in time than J, is the P tradition, from the German word for priest, *Priester*. This oral tradition reflects a great concern with cultic matters associated later with the Jerusalem Temple and also a concern with order and structure that one would associate with the record keeping by temple priests.

Recall that the dilemma described above was avoided by suggesting that the Adam and Eve story came neither from 4000 BC nor from about 200,000 BC; the story, which is essentially dependent upon the Hebrew language for meaningfulness, was crafted sometime after Mount Sinai. Let me elaborate both stories, under this supposition, and leave you, the reader, to answer for yourself whether the stories thus elaborated make more religious sense, and whether they avoid dilemmas and clashes with modern science, and whether they provide more enlightenment to various Catholic doctrines about human life than if the two stories are *taken literally*.

GOD SAID, "LET THERE BE LIGHT"

The six-day creation story is from the P oral tradition, and even though P originated later than J did, the Israelite editor of the Torah (Pentateuch) books, as scholars call the unknown writer, placed it first in *Genesis*, going

1. Notice that the five names echo a Greek-language background because they are book titles from the Greek Septuagint. The Hebrew text titles biblical books from the books' opening words in the same manner the Vatican titles Catholic documents from the opening Latin words. The Tanak and rabbis today call the first book of the Torah *Bereshith*, meaning "In the beginning." See Appendix F.

2. Near Eastern language scholars think that the ancient Semitic Hebrew language only achieved an alphabet and written possibilities in the tenth century BC.

from chapter one, verse one to chapter two, verse 4a. This place tagging of chapter and verse sounds strange, and let me explain it before proceeding. Until about AD 1220, the Bible was differentiated only by the name of its books. Archbishop of Canterbury Stephen Langton, the same person on the side of the barons against the King John in the Magna Carta event at Runnymede, undertook a division of the entire Bible into chapters. It was a job of great common sense and achievement, breaking up incidents and stories into chapters, with only a few puzzling exceptions, and this is one of them. Chapter two should have begun the Adam and Eve story. It was not until 1551 that chapters were subdivided into verses by a Calvinist printer in Geneva, Stephanus. Stephanus made good decisions for the most part except for a few puzzling subdivisions, such as concluding the six-day story half way through verse four and beginning the Garden of Eden story at that point.[3] In most Bibles, the J story goes from *Gen* 2:4b to the end of chapter three.

It is an easier path to clarity if we begin with the P story of God creating the world in six days and resting on the seventh than to begin with the Adam and Eve Garden story. Why would the Israelites have crafted a creation story along P lines because they seemingly had all that was needed from their Mt. Sinai experience? They had the experience that the one and only God had chosen them in a kind of embrace and that they were to acknowledge and worship this one God and obey his commandments as these commandments continued to come into their awareness. "You are a people sacred to Yahweh. He has chosen you from all the people on earth to be a people especially his own" *(Dt 7:6)*. However, they crafted the P story for the same reason that parents today wish to protect their growing children from influences in the wider culture judged to sully and corrupt. One strategy is to provide parameters or to provide alternative stories (instructions) that run counter to the corrupting influence.

Here's an easy example that my wife and I used in conversation with our younger sons: "Boys, it is very easy to lie your way out of an embarrassing situation even though other kids do it to escape being caught. But don't choose that way because lying will become a habit that in later life will hurt you more. Besides, it's wrong itself." After the Israelites began living in Canaan, what they called their Promised Land, they became ever more aware that they were surrounded by pagan cultures, older than they by centuries, more powerful than they, and with a power to entice Israelites away from monotheism and other covenant values.

Encircling Israel were the imposing cultures of the Egyptians, the Hittites of Anatolia (present-day Turkey), and the Babylonians of Mesopotamia,

---

3. The Old Testament of the *New American Bible* (1970) retained the traditional division between 2:4a and 2:4b. The Old Testament of the *New American Bible Revised Edition* (2010) eliminated it, having the phrase "This is the story of the heavens and the earth at their creation" (2:4a) introduce the Garden Story *(Gen* 2:4-3:24).

the latter especially. Babylonian culture had generated a few creation stories that circulated in the Ancient Near East that had the very real prospect
of subverting Israelite faith. Their teachings about the world of competing
gods, the reason for human death and evil, and the nature of being human,
all these features undermined the beliefs of Israel. But how to combat the
pagan influences? The answer was to replace the Babylonian creation stories
with their own stories about "origins" that conveyed truthful views of God's
nature, of human nature, and why people are mortal. The replacement happened in the cleverest of ways: They adopted elements of a pagan story,
neutral enough in themselves, and fashioned them into a teaching vehicle
about the true nature of reality. The story's construction was calculated to be
readily repeated generation after generation. By recasting familiar elements,
Israel was able to avoid having competing creation stories side by side, a pagan one and theirs, vying for allegiance. The P story of creation in six days
was fashioned to replace the allure of the Babylonian *Enuma Elish* (hereafter
EE) creation story.

What does *EE* teach? Within the format of a six-day working week, a
motif found elsewhere in the ancient world, *EE* uses a sexual image to describe the creation of the world. Apsu, the male principle, commingles with
Tiamat, the female principle "as a single body." This is the union of the
primeval fresh and salt waters, undoubted suggested by Mesopotamia's great
river flowing into the Arabian Sea. The fresh water flows into the salty as if
impregnating it. All other gods spring from this union of the primal two gods.
But there is discord among the divine children, and the parents decide to kill
all of them. One of the children, Ea, learns the plan and kills Apsu instead.
Fearing Tiamat's revenge, the gods choose a warrior god, Marduk, to kill
their mother. Out of one half her body, Markuk makes the earth; the heavenly bodies are made out of the rest of Tiamat. This is the heavenly chaotic
lead up to Day One, on which Light emanates from the gods. On Day Two
the sky dome or firmament—think of an upside-down bowl—is created. Dry
land (part of Tiamat's body) comes about on Day Three, heavenly bodies
(rest of Tiamat) on Day Four. Without the element of warring gods, the
"days of creation" should be sounding familiar to a reader of *Genesis* 1. Day
Six deserves quoting in full to show why Israelite leadership would detest this
story. Marduk proposes to create humans by having Ea fashion them from
the blood of an executed god:

> *Blood I will mass and cause bones to be.*
> *I will establish a savage, man shall be his name.*
> *Truly, a savage man I will create*
> *His role in life shall be as a man-servant to the gods*
> *That they may be at ease.*[4]

4. James B. Pritchard, *Ancient Near Eastern Texts* (Princeton Univ. Press, 1955), § 68.

The crafters of the P story adopt the format of a six-day creation but notice what kind of teachings their format serves. Day One: "In the beginning" all was without form and shape and darkness hovered over the abyss. Ancient Israelites were not philosophical. They had no conception of *nothingness*. They could no more say that God creates out of nothing than saying God creates the matter that causes gravitational and magnetic fields. Nothingness thinking is beyond them. On the other hand, they did have conceptions of order and purpose, and the experience that God *spoke* to them through Moses. To express the equivalent of "nothing preexisted God's act of creation," they say that "God begot order." The opposite of order is chaos, so this is how verse one begins with a backdrop of chaos. And then God *speaks*, "Let there be light." And on the following days God speaks things into existence, and what's created is described as being good.

The "opening week of the world," as it were, unfolds in an orderly manner. God's word creates. We today might say, God wills things into existence. They say that God spoke things into existence. After all, God spoke them into being a covenanted people. "I will be your God if you will be my people." And notice the order of 1-4, 2-5, and 3-6: On Day One light is created; on Day Four appear the heavenly bodies of light like the sun, moon and stars. How misplaced is it to raise the scientific objection, "How can you have light on Day One when the sun is created on Day Four? On Day Two a dome is created separating waters above from those below, thus opening up sky; on Day Five the creatures of sky and sea are created. On Day Three God creates dry land; on Day Six the occupiers of dry land are created, animals and humans. Don't think in taxonomy fashion as if looking for a listing of *everything* in support of the doctrine that "God creates everything." In having familiar but neutral elements from the *EE* days of creation, the items listed in days 1-6 are the Israelite equivalent of teaching that whatever exists anywhere has its existence due to God Creator and there is nothing of evil in it.

Day Six of the P story pertains to human beings and deserves mention in full:

> Then God said: Let us make human beings [*'ādām* in Hebrew] in our image, after our likeness. Let them have dominion over the fish of the sea, the birds of the air, the tame animals, all the wild animals, and all the creatures that crawl on the earth. God created mankind in his image; in the image of God he created them; male and female he created them. God blessed them and God said to them: Be fertile and multiply; fill the earth and subdue it....And it happened. God looked at everything he had made, and found it very good.

P's difference from *EE* is striking. The *EE* human being is created as a savage who provides menial service to the gods. The human beings of the priestly account have as high a nobility as imaginable, being like God. Notice also that no distinction is made between men and women; there's no preference or temporal precedence for the male. Both are created in the divine image, both have equal stature. God is portrayed as creating heterosexuality because a divine commandment is given to men and women to be fertile and propagate. And as with all that God creates in the P account, this teaching of gender equality and fecundity is pronounced *good*. The same teaching of gender equality is found in the J story, but it is not as immediately obvious.

Psalm 8 was composed centuries after the P story appeared and captures the nobility men and women enjoy. Translations use the word man, but in the Hebrew inclusive sense of *'ādām*, the human being without gender distinction is meant.

> *O Lord, our Lord,*
> *how awesome is your name through all the earth....*
> *When I see the heavens, the work of your hands,*
> *the moon and the stars that you set in place,*
> *"What is man that you are mindful of him....*
> *Yet you have made him little less than a God*
> *crowned him with glory and honor.*
> *You have given him dominion over the works of your hands."*

God Creator rests on the seventh day and this diverges from *EE*, too. In doing so it is attacking *EE*'s paganism. When the six-day format of creation in *EE* is run through, culminating in a menial human savage, the gods enjoyed themselves on Day Seven with feasting. But the banquet is in the nature of a bacchanal and orgy. In the P account, God *rests* [*shabat* in Hebrew] on the seventh day. Obviously, there is no implication in this Israelite story or in Christian piety that God gets fatigued in creating. What is implied is the Sinai commandment of Sabbath [*Shabbat*] rest. The crafters of the P account were already observing Sabbath rest when the story was being fashioned in their religious imaginations. They could not insert it into the P story as a commandment because that would have been an anachronism, but they could present God "at the beginning" doing what the Sinai revelation commanded Israel to do in the time of Moses. Think of it as a strategy of clever prediction that God Creator even observes Sabbath rest.

Before itemizing the doctrinal teachings of the P creation story, the use of the word *God* bears scrutiny. The normal word for God is *El*, and it is met in many biblical names: Daniel [God is my judge], Ezekiel [God strengthens], Nathanael [God has given]. The P story uses Elohim, the plural form of El, in the six-day story. The plural form intensifies what the singular means. Elohim does not mean many gods but rather god to the utmost. But once the plural form for God is chosen, the grammatical rules have to follow. Thus Elohim said, "let us make human beings...." Some overly devout Bible readers try to see the "let us" text as the earliest reference to the Trinity, but this is misplaced piety. It is a plausible argument, though not one I follow, to claim that the ancient world imagined a heavenly court, that is, a single god or many gods with the members of the court in attendance, hence the use of the phrase "let us."

The ancient Israelites had several names for the one God. *Psalm* 91:1-2 has a poetic quatrain that captures, in Hebrew, four divine names together.

You who dwell in the shadow of Elyon [the Most High],
who abide in the shadow of Shaddai [the Almighty].
say to Yahweh, "my refuge, my fortress,
my Elohim in whom I trust."

The name *Yahweh* for God has already been met. Hebrew being an alphabet of consonants, its letters are simply YHWH, with the vowel sounds being a rabbinical estimation in order to say the name aloud. It is the most frequently used name for God in the Tanak, perhaps reaching 7000 times, translated as *Lord* and often printed in English Bibles in a different font form.

It is one thing for YHWH to be written in the Hebrew texts, it is another to be pronounced aloud. Some centuries after the Sinai experience, Israelites stopped pronouncing the name out of deep reverence for its sacredness. They used the circumlocution *Adonai* for Yahweh in their speech and prayers. The practice continues to this day when Jews say the daily Shema prayer in Hebrew, "Hear, O Israel, the Lord is God, the Lord alone." Behind the English *Lord* is YHWH in the text (*Dt* 6:4) but it is vocalized as Adonai.[5] However, the beginning sound of Yahweh (Yah or ah) is allowed, being vocalized in the ending of biblical names: Isaiah [Yahweh is salvation], Jeremiah [Yahweh will raise up] and Jesus' name in Hebrew, Yēšûa [Yahweh saves], which is Joshua in modern English. Our familiar word *Alleluia* is merely the Hebrew *Hallĕlû yāh*, meaning Praise Yahweh. We shall see that the name for God in the Adam and Eve story is Yahweh.

RELIGIOUS TEACHINGS OF THE SIX-DAYS-OF-CREATION STORY

Some religious teachings from the P creation story are discernable. (1) There is only one God who is creator and lacks sexual gender. God alone creates, and this is done effortlessly. This is a direct negation of the role of many gods, begetting in a sexual manner, and involved in strife in order to create, which are met in *EE*.

(2) Creation proceeds from the goodness of God, and instances of cre-

---

5. Other circumlocutions abounded for avoiding addressing God directly. God is "the Blessed One" (words of High Priest to Jesus in *Mk* 14:61), God is called "Jehovah" (arrived at by inserting vowel sounds of Adonai into YHWH), and God is called "the name" [*Hashem*]. The King James Bible used Jehovah to stand for God. Jehovah's Witnesses learned it from the KJB and thereafter insist upon it as alone correct for addressing God.

ation evidence this goodness as in the mantra, "and God saw that it was good." Although *EE* was not based on a philosophical dualism, later ideologies will be dualistic, maintaining an inherent evil in matter itself, such as Gnosticism in the early years of Christianity. P teaches that nothing, including sexuality, is fundamentally evil. If evil is experienced, it cannot be from God.

(3) The God of order and purpose creates an ordered and purposeful world. The story is not making the case that our world resembles the *Genesis* description, save for the commonsensical statements that fish and birds (Day Five) inhabit the waters and the sky (Day Two) and that animals and humans (Day Six) inhabit the dry land (Day Three). But the Israelite story language does express a truth about God that is as central to Israelite belief as it is to Catholic thought. Behind God's activity lies a wisdom that may escape our grasp in this or that situation yet remains a wisdom inviting our trust. God's will is not outdone by randomness. Furthermore, a rational proof for God's existence is not to be drawn from these orderly six days any more than drawing the conclusion that the world was created in 144 hours (six days) or its seemingly nuanced variant, that the world was created in six geological epochs (e.g., the Mesozoic, the Cenozoic, and the like). As Pope Leo XIII taught long ago, *Genesis* is not teaching geology or biology or physical science of any sort. This also means that any theory of evolution cannot be addressed to *Genesis* for answers.

(4) The Catholic teaching on how God creates the world locates the answer in God's will and avoids guessing at any scientific procedure. There are many who are prone to bring science into play and talk about the "Big Bang" event of 13.8 billion years ago as if it is the moment of creation. Creation is not a science question because science is restricted to material phenomena and their laws. The realm of science is like having all the phenomena and their governing laws within a cosmic bubble, and escape from the bubble to look at all of it from outside the bubble is by definition impossible. All that science can do is project back in time to the earliest moments of an expanding cosmos, even to milliseconds of its start. Science cannot answer why matter began expanding after however long that it had not been happening, and what caused the Big Bang to erupt. (These matters are more fully explored in chapter eight.)

The Catholic doctrine of creation describes why things (phenomena) exist at all, not at how they behave, which is the realm of science. The answer to the *why* is that God wills everything other than God's self into existence because God's identity is his underived existence. But the existence of everything else is a derived existence. Things are in existence and remain in existence because God continually sustains them in being. If God stopped sustaining, things would not simply degenerate; they would stop and would be as nothingness.

The P story teaches conferral of existence in its own concrete way. God *speaks*, and it comes to be. The Israelites can describe God only by the way they have experienced God. They experienced God speaking variously: out of the Burning Bush to Moses; to them at Sinai where Moses carried down the mountain to them the words making them a special people, "I will be your God..."; to them through the later prophets who themselves heard God speaking and tasking them. Implicit in speaking to Israel is the divine motive, "I have loved you with an everlasting love" (Jer 31:3). The Catholic doctrine on creation combines the why of creation—in freedom God wills bestowing existence—with the why behind the why—God creates everything because God's nature is love, and it is the nature of love to spread out, to diffuse itself, to express itself in "the other," as the Catholic tradition says. Some sobriety of thought is required. Avoid imagining that "God loves stones," or "God loves subatomic particles." The motive of God's love behind his bestowal of existence to creation is properly applied to human beings, because loving essentially is an interpersonal reality.

(5) Humans are gifted with the ability to propagate and are tasked to do so. This is readily seen in the P story but it needs to be joined to the fundamental assertion that God alone creates human beings. Therefore God *creates* and couples *procreate*; God brings human couples into the very act of creation, partners in a fashion. The crafters of the P story and their listeners took for granted that Israelite couples procreated within the context of a marriage. What was a common marriage experience for these earliest Israelites was thus receiving from the P creation story the support that marital fecundity was God's will for them from the very beginning. Parenting, along with God's role in it, was viewed as a most noble task of the covenanted life lived by Israelites.

With the useful knowledge that biological science affords today, most people focus on the scientific aspect of how human beings come to be: A single sperm fertilizes a female egg with its genetic code producing the zygote where all prenatal development begins. After some days it implants in the endometrium of the woman's uterus as an embryo (blastocyst) and further development ensues. So important is the study of these matters in order to help couples conceive and to protect a developing embryo that the complexity of this process can easily obscure the fundamental aspect of the P creation story that God creates human beings. God's role can easily be put aside, soon forgotten, eventually denied. This seems to be a feature of contemporary culture. But consider couples who see their married lives being shepherded by God. For them the newborn baby is a breathtaking mystery of their own biological contribution and of God's "making." So many small behaviors perceived in the developing youngster remind such couples that "we ourselves and just our contributions" cannot explain the wondrous reality that our youngster is. Our youngster is also from God.

As much as Catholic doctrine champions the nobility of parenting, which the P story proclaims, some cautions against the exaggeration of its *nobility* should be noted. Examples make the cautions clear. Not everyone is called by God to the married life. I am not simply referring to those who become clerics or vowed religious. I refer to single people who never marry and not because selfish motives dictated it. People can remain single to perform an altruistic purpose in life. There should be no temptation to look askance at the single life or at people in it. Given the nobility of married and parenting life in Catholic teaching, it is easy to slight the single life, and this happens. Here's a test question: How many times does one hear "singles" being prayed for in the Sunday liturgy petitions in comparison to prayers for families or for people in religious life?

Another misuse of the nobility-of-parenting idea is the assumption, especially in years past, that a Catholic couple should be having as many children as possible. (No criticism of large families and the sacrifices of these parents is meant. I'm from a large family, and my wife of even larger, and so the prospect is unsettling that any sibling might never have been.) The advocacy of *responsible parenthood* came into Catholic thinking at the time of the Second Vatican Council. The idea is sometimes written off as "contraceptive behavior" but this is not true. There is a rightful and legitimate role for married couples to decide on how many children they judge in conscience God calls them to raise, and that they be open, in a loving and generous manner, to what may be termed "unintended" conceptions. I return to notion of responsible parenting in chapter seven; for now it suffices to say that the nobility of parenting does not require irresponsible procreating.

(6) Jews and Christians, in observing Sabbath to whatever extent they observe it, have been influenced more by the Ten Commandments than by the P story account of God resting on Day Seven. Furthermore, observation of Sabbath—Sunday for Christians, Friday sundown to Saturday sundown for Jews, Friday for Muslims—has become more heavily influenced by our secular culture than by religious prompts, which is to say, our modern American approach to weekends has eroded Sabbath expectations. There are exceptions, of course: Roman Catholicism retains the obligation for Sunday Eucharistic worship although church attendance numbers have plummeted; Orthodox Jewish neighborhoods slow down to a walking pace within the *eruv* (a wire encircling the neighborhood); Muslims congregate on Friday noon to pray.

I've come to see Sabbath as an important corrective to the fast-paced American life and its unending preoccupations. Just as a marriage relationship, or any important personal relationship such as parent to offspring, requires attentiveness and convincing conversation for its lifeblood, lest the relationship slip into a taken-for-grantedness, so does the cultivation of a relationship with God. Some married couples have resorted to the strategy of "scheduling dates with each other" to achieve what they call quality marriage time. Periodically, I used to take our young sons, not together but separately, out for breakfast to an IHOP to just talk, all the while devouring the buttermilk pancakes we loved. Sometimes getting a good "let's just talk" talk with youngsters underway at home is tricky. Whatever the strategy, interpersonal relationships require attentiveness. It is the purpose of Sabbath to avoid taking God for granted, to avoid putting God aside because of life's "real" preoccupations. Treating inattentively anyone like this—spouse, child, God—is a step toward losing the richness of the relationship. The rationale behind *Sabbath* makes rich sense.

Perhaps the reader will have noticed that these half dozen identifications of religious teachings from the six-days-of-creation story are truths for today and for the future, as they were truths in time's past. God creates men and women in God's image is a truth about every human being who has ever been born. Although the P story seems to be describing the "long ago and far away," it is not a teaching of a time long past. It is not an archival story. It is better called an existential story, that is, it teaches the fundamental and enduring features of human existence at any time by its use of primordial language. It is crafted in the format of how things began *in the very beginning* in order to achieve its existential import of teaching things that are essential at any time and in any place. This is a feature of what is called *myth* in the literary sense. Using primordial language, a myth offers the justification of why things yesterday, today, and tomorrow are as they are.

Hinduism provides a clear example of it in how it warrants the fourfold caste system that has operated in India for centuries. In its myth of the *Cosmic Man*, recounted in the *Rig Veda* 10.90, Hindus see their ranking of brahmins, kshatriyas, vaishyas, and shudras based on this primeval story:

> The cosmic Man [*purusha* in Sanskrit] has a thousand heads, a thousand eyes, a thousand feet. He spread out over the earth....When they divided the Man, into how many parts did they divide Him? What do they call his mouth, his two arms, his thighs and his feet? His mouth became the Brahmin. His arms were made into the Warrior (kshatriya). His thighs became the People (vaishyas). His feet became the Servant (shudra).

The two creations stories, P and J, are myths in this same sense. Primeval language is not attempting to be historical but to be existential. Notice its application to God being creator. God creates by sustaining in existence whatever "things" we identify as existing. This means that God never stops being creator, in the past, now, or ever. It does not mean that God created at the very beginning, and everything took off on its own from there. If God as ever-ongoing creator did stop sustaining, nothing other than God would be. But such a drastic picture seems to me an impossible happening. If God

creates out of love, and all humans are made in God's image, for these are
the revelations to us in the P story, how could God undo what is the essential
makeup of reality and founded on God's nature as love. It seems to me that
being creator is of the very essence of how God is God in His freedom and
in His eternal nature.

The above religious teachings of the P creation story are, in my judgment, what God is revealing *for the sake of our salvation*, to recall chapter one's
definition of biblical inspiration. The other story features, such as the six-day
format, or a literalism that seems to be teaching science or ancient history,
are not part of revelation. A concluding observation about the P story reiter-
ates an earlier proposal I made. The P story was meant to be apologetical.
This means that it was fashioned as an argument against the allure of a false
vision of the world and of people. That false vision, the *Enuma Elish*, exercised a strong attraction in the Ancient World, coming as it did from a vast
and powerful culture. The P story was crafted to combat a subversive myth.

"DO NOT EAT FROM THAT PARTICULAR TREE"

Much of what has been said about the six-days-of-creation story applies to
the Adam and Eve story in the Garden of Paradise. It is a creation story
crafted by Israelites after the Mount Sinai experience around 1250 BC. It is
directed against a different Babylonian myth at variance with Israelite faith.
The Adam and Eve text comes from another of the four oral traditions lying behind the Pentateuch. It utilizes some common elements from the myth
in order to remove that primeval story of origins from the imaginations of
Israelites. The Garden story, invented like the first story, teaches profound
religious truths about human existence and about God in the manner that
Jesus' made-up story about a forgiving father and his two sons did. While the
crafters of the Garden story inject into it convictions of religious faith using
some of the borrowed pagan framework, the source of Israelite faith is the
self-revealing God of the covenant relationship. Although the story is made
up, the faith imbedded in it is not. It is a revealed faith received and passed
on to future generations in story format.

Without contradicting it, the Adam and Eve story differs in significant
respects from the six-days-of-creation story. It is an older story in the oral
tradition and comes from that stream in the tradition called the Yahwist or
J source. That it is placed second in the opening of the *Book of Genesis* was a
decision of the editor of the Pentateuch, upon whose motive one can only
speculate. It does not matter for us because the religious teachings of the
story are unaffected by its location coming second in the Bible. It was crafted
first and it functioned independently as a teaching tool.

Several features reflect its older status. It is a more concrete story. Its elements are easier to imagine. Compared to it, the P story seems abstract such
as "God speaks and light is created." Read both stories to youngsters, and

they will repeat back more accurately the J story than the P story because it clings to their imaginations. In human storytelling in all cultures, the older the story, the more concrete and imaginative its elements tend to be. In another sign of age, the J story is also anthropomorphic, a large word to mean simply that God and God's activities are described in human fashion. Ask a child, even ask anyone, to draw a picture of God after reading the P story. It's just too difficult. But not so with the J story. God will be drawn to look as we humans look.

If a creation story is intended to describe how things are as they are, the P story leaves a reader with puzzles. If human beings are made in God's image, and God is the living God, why do people die? And why do people do evil things? It would seem that the P story ends with a description of human life today too good to be true. What P says is true in itself. What it leaves untreated requires another explanation and from a different direction. The J story provides it, and the story utilizes different tools to achieve it. The first of those tools is the Hebrew language itself. The story will use plays on words. The story will use metaphors that exist only in the Hebrew language. The story will employ the technique of etiology, a somewhat fancy word to describe the reason for something existing today in terms of a historical or mythical explanation, as we will see with God's punishment of the snake for its role in deceiving Adam and Eve.

The unique word for God in the Adam and Eve story is Yahweh.[6] In all other sections of the Pentateuch or Torah, where the J oral tradition is being reflected, Yahweh is God's name. For reasons not readily apparent, the word for God in this creation story is the combination Yahweh Elohim (*Lord God* in English Bibles) and the rare combination is found only in *The Book of Ezekiel*. There are other technical features to the story, but it is to its religious teachings we turn.

Potters need damp clay to work, and this is how the J story begins. Water wells from the ground, moistening it. Then "the Lord God shaped man [*ādām*] from the ground [*ādāmah*] and blew into his nostrils the breath [*ruah*] of life and the man became a living being [*nephesh*]" (2:7). This is not science, not biology, not anti-evolution. It's just a crafted story, capturing deep truths in simplistic description. Yahweh is a potter who shapes a clay figure and makes it into a living human by injecting his own breath into it. There are two plays on words. *Ruah* cannot be pronounced in Hebrew without pushing out air from your mouth. It is a simply way of saying that God's bestowed spirit [*ruah*] makes something material to be fully human. The other play on words concerns matter. Adam is made from the adamah. How obvious these word plays were to ancient Israelites. When people die, their "spirit" departs them and their corpse decays into ground matter. "When You take back your

6. YHWH in its four only Hebrew letters, to be read right to left: י ה ו ה

spirit, they die and return to the dust from which they came" (Ps 104:29).

In the famous "dry bones" (skeletons strewn in a field) prophecy when Israel was stuck in Babylonian Exile, "the Lord God says to these bones, 'I will make breath enter you so you may come to life'" (Ez 37:5). The reception of ashes in Lent echoes the same image: "Remember that you are dust [adamah] and unto dust you shall return." The Israelites did not have the Greek concept of body and soul. But their teaching on the nature of being human amounts to the same insight that *body and soul* have afforded Christian thought. Every person has a material component and a spiritual component. It is the spiritual component, the soul in later language, which is directly from God, and it is the essential cause of being human. This is quite compatible with accepting a material evolution through lower organisms to primates, with the transition to human life being caused by God's infusion of a person's soul, *ruah* in Israelite story language. (When human evolution is considered in chapter eight, we shall see John Paul II's teachings on evolution reflected.)

The J story continues in its characteristic anthropomorphic fashion. Yahweh plants a Garden in Eden to the east. (The suggested location is unknown but likely Sumeria in present-day Iraq, from the Sumerian word *eden* for "fertile plain." The Hebrew word for *Garden* became *paradise* in the Septuagint translation, leading to the Garden of Paradise/Garden of Eden being synonymous.) There Yahweh places Adam (now representing the first human being). From the soil of the Garden Yahweh causes (fruit) trees of all kinds to spring up, and two special kinds of trees: the tree "of life" and the tree "of the knowledge of good and evil." Yahweh gives Adam directions and a Do Not commandment. (Recall that the Israelites who crafted this story lived by the Do and Do Not commandments of the Torah where rabbis have counted 613 *mitzvahs*.) Adam can eat from all the trees but of the "knowledge of good and evil" tree, "Do not, or you will die," commands Yahweh.

It is necessary at this point to mention the Babylonian creation myth against which the J story is directed. The *Epic of Gilgamesh* recounts the adventures of Gilgamesh, king of Uruk in ancient Mesopotamia, to achieve immortality. The death of his friend Enkidu and the prospect of his own death lead him on a journey to learn about the days before the flood when the gods decided to terminate all humanity except Utnapishtim, a sort of Sumerian Noah. He lived through the flood and the gods awarded him the immortality they have. Gilgamesh finds Utnapishtim at the end of the earth and demands the secret for immortality. He's told that the gods withhold immortality from humans out of jealousy but he can have it if he passes a test to stay awake for a week. It turns out that Gilgamesh cannot. On departing, Utnapishtim gives him a miraculous plant/branch that on eating restores youthfulness. A snake steals it on his return to Uruk while Gilgamesh sleeps. As a result, Gilgamesh is fated to die and without an elixir to renew youthfulness. Notice the echo: Snakes shed their skins and seem to keep on living. Note some other elements: The gods are jealous of humans and decree death for them. There is a tree branch or plant that bestows renewal of life. There is a devious snake. These become elements in the J story to teach a very different reason why humans die.

Returning to the Garden of Eden or Garden of Paradise story, the rationale is given: "It is not good that Adam should be alone." From the soil, Yahweh the potter fashions all the animals and birds. They are brought before Adam to name; naming rights in this J story and "having dominion over" from the P story are identical teachings. Note that the animals potted from clay never receive God's breath; they are essentially different from human beings, and this feature, too, comports with the P story where only "men and women" are made in God's image.

Next in the story comes what I think is a subtle teaching against bestiality but employing the insight that the new human being is meant for companionship. None of the animals that are led before Adam are found to be a suitable mate for him. Sexual expression with animals is a plausible taboo couched in this text. In *Leviticus* 18, which lists many prohibitions against sexual intercourse (e.g., with your sister, with your daughter-in-law, with another man), is found this commandment: Do not have intercourse with any kind of animal (18:23). Why would there be a *mitzvah* like this unless sodomy happened occasionally among Israelites? On the other hand, it was a not infrequent practice in nearby pagan cultures. (Eric Berkowitz points out in *The Boundaries of Desire* that the Hittites and the Babylonians legislated what constituted acceptable sex with animals and what did not; copulating with pigs was allowed but not with cows.) The J story provides additional strength to the Levitical prohibition of bestiality by locating it in the creation story as unnatural to being human since "Adam found none of the animals suitable."

Adam's need for companionship—modern thought terms it the social nature of being human—remains the focus as the story continues. It is leading to the creation of a woman, the most remembered portion of the story as well as the most misunderstood. Yahweh casts Adam—the Hebrew *'ādām* still means the generic "the human being from the clay" but becoming more and more the male in connotation—into a deep sleep and takes one of his ribs to which Yahweh adds flesh. (Hebrew has no word for *body*, only for flesh [*basar*].) The man [*ish*] and the woman [*ishsha*] are now given almost identical Hebrew words that express gender and imply gender differentiation. And, of course, there is a play on words: the ishsha derives from the ish. When Yahweh leads the woman to the man, note what the man says: "This one, at last, is bone of my bones and flesh of my flesh."

My flesh and my bone is a metaphor in Hebrew; its meaning would have had immediate resonance for Israelites. It means you and I are alike, you are my kin, you are my equal. Two biblical incidents suffice. When Rebecca, the wife of the patriarch Isaac, wished her son Jacob to marry "a proper woman," she sent him to her ancestral land for a wife to avoid taking a local Hittite spouse. He travels, meets by accident his future wife Rachel at a well and tells her that Laban, her father, is his uncle. When Laban meets Jacob for the first time, he says, "You are indeed my bone and flesh" (Gen 29:14). When David (tribe of Judah) was replacing Saul (tribe of Benjamin) as king of Israel, the transition was contested by partisans of Saul's people until the military might of David made the outcome obvious. Tribes who have resisted David's succession and feared reprisal came to him in suppliant fashion using the Hebrew metaphor for we are kin, we are identical to you: "They said, 'Look, we are your flesh and bone'" (2 Sam 5:1).

To create a story teaching that a woman is essentially like a man and not his inferior—as pagan creation myths maintained—and wanting to use the Hebrew metaphor "flesh and bone" to assert it, then the anthropomorphic manner to do it in a crafted story is have Yahweh take Adam's rib (bone) and encase it with flesh. Because Yahweh does it, the story is teaching that gender equality is God's will. Because the woman is like the man, then the woman bears also the mark of the clay—she is material and on death her corpse decays—and the mark of God's breath is within her, too. She is as much a wonder of being created human as Adam is. This teaching of the J story is the same as the teaching in P. Women and men are created by God and carry a dignity that elevates them above the nature of any other creature. Both are made in God's image (P story); both bear God's spirit, God's *ruah*, within them (J story). And since the aim of the two stories, told in the genre of long ago and far away, is meant to teach what is fundamental to human beings at any time in history, the origins of Adam and Eve (from clay, having God's breath or spirit) describe the bodily and spiritual features of every human life whenever it comes to be. The story asserts gender equality; neither is meant to dominate the other. And it asserts gender complementarity; both are needed to procreate offspring.

How misplaced have been those interpretations of the "Adam's rib" story that claimed women are inferior because the woman was created afterwards or because she came from a piece of the man, or because women lack the rib structure men have—hard to believe but I have read such claims about rib difference. In a later portion of the Garden story, the male domination of women will be attributed to a consequence of sin. Male domination and female inferiority are describing life in a post-Garden world, our world, but they are presented as no longer reflecting what the Creator intended.

Just as being created in God's image leads to "be fruitful and multiply" for men and women in the P story, the gender difference of the J story leads to lifelong marriage in it. The story assumes the context of married life because it was crafted by Israelites who practiced monogamous marriage. And it assumes a lifelong union. The verse in the J story is famous, especially because Jesus quoted it in a later situation of misused divorce rules. "This is why a man leaves his father and mother and becomes attached to his wife, and they become one flesh [basar]" (2:24). To grasp its poignancy, recall how tribal the crafters of the J story were. To say that a man must be ready to prioritize wife-connectedness over his own family/tribe identity is an exceedingly strong statement. While some incline to interpret the becoming "one flesh" as marital intercourse, I think its primary meaning is describing men and women intent on "becoming one life together," as in forging a common life. To this end many elements contribute, including coitus to be sure, but especially the opening up of a common life to children. Children enrich the husband/wife connectedness, and it is unfortunate when children are thought to be an intrusion to it.

Later in the story (3:20), the woman gets named Eve [hawwah in Hebrew] because she is "the mother of everybody else who lives," the name echoing a Hebrew word, "to live [hayah]." My listing of Hebrew words is not meant to seem pretentious but only to underline the earlier contention that the creation story, and its plays on words, had to have been crafted by Hebrew-speaking people subsequent to Mt. Sinai.

Eden or Paradise seems idyllic for the moment. Adam and Eve have unruffled consciences, symbolically described by being naked. They live fulfilled by each other. They lack hunger because Yahweh provided trees delightful to behold and eat. And they are not meant to die. How is their immortality taught? God has provided a "tree of life" from which they eat. In story language it is as if "you are what you eat." To be in the Garden is to have access to the tree of life. By nature they are not immortal but freedom from death is God's gift (i.e., God provides a special tree from which to eat). This is all taught anthropomorphically. But to this sunny picture in the story a storm erupts, and it begins with echoes of the Gilgamesh epic.

A devious talking serpent is introduced into the story who voices to the woman a very clever temptation about Yahweh's only Do Not commandment in the story: "Of the tree of the knowledge of good and evil do not eat or you will die." The snake cajoles, "You will not die. God knows that the moment you eat from it, your eyes will be open and you will be like gods, knowing good from evil." The woman is persuaded, eats, and gives some to Adam, who himself eats. Adam and Eve disobey a Torah-like command. They immediately sense they are naked and so they make clothing to cover up. (It was a taboo and most reprehensible among the Israelite crafters of the story to be naked publicly.)

RELIGIOUS INSIGHTS & PUNISHMENT TEACHINGS

(1) Adam and Eve are hiding in the Garden when Yahweh comes walking through it, but they are discovered and questioned about the one and only Do Not commandment: "Why did you do it, Adam?" "She coaxed me." "Why did you do it, Eve?" "The snake made me." This is a keen insight into

a sinner wanting to flee from ethical accountability. The modern version is, "The devil made me do it." Or, blame the other person with me.

Do not focus on Eve sinning first and inducing Adam, as some in Christianity have done and still do, teaching such bunk as "women are the weaker sex," or "women are the downfall of men." In order to craft a story about flight from ethical accountability, there needs to be a sequence of actors in the story. It could as easily have been first Adam and then a coaxed Eve, and the story would still work. Even in the sequence we have in the J story, Adam chooses to break the commandment. He is not less at fault. The positive teaching from this crafted sequencing about accountability is that forgiveness comes only if the sinner says, "I did it. It's my own fault." Read the wonderful confessional *Psalm* 51, and its "against You, Yahweh, have I sinned."[7]

(2) The sequence is teaching in indirect fashion the social nature of sin. Of this the Israelites were very conscious. The sins of a larger group, such as by members of a tribe, affect everyone and can draw others into the culpable mix. Adam and Eve are together in sinning. One individual corrupts another. The latter is at no less fault than the former for freely choosing to be swayed.

(3) One insight into the nature of sin is disobedience to God's will or to God's commands. The insight is easy to grasp, whether the command comes from the written Torah or from the law written on one's heart, the conscience. It was how Israelites first instructed their children about sin, and it is how Christian parents still do today. The other insight into sin from the J story is deeper and would not come readily to young people, or even to many older ones. To sin is to claim autonomy from God, to deny God's greater wisdom and claims on moral behavior; in short, it is to want to become like God and to adjudicate for oneself what's right and what's wrong. These were the very words of the serpent's temptation, and because they are true human motivations, the temptation is all the more insidious. Don't disobey; that's simple to grasp. Don't set yourself up to adjudicate and rationalize your own behavior; that's harder, and the more adult people become, the more they are prone to doing it.

(4) More as a cultural aside than as another religious insight is what the tree of the knowledge of good and evil might look like as we imagine the story, other than simply being placed in the category of forbidden fruit to be avoided. The story never mentions that it is an apple tree any more than *Matthew* says it was *three* Magi who came to visit the baby Jesus. It's only a

7. Psalm numbering runs "one off" between older Catholic Bibles and more recent Bibles. Current Bibles, Catholic and Protestant, follow the numbering in the Hebrew Tanak. When the Hebrew text was translated into the Greek Septuagint, *Psalms* 9 and 10 were joined to become *Psalm* 9 in it, and the Latin Vulgate translation followed the Septuagint. Older Catholic Bibles use the Vulgate numbers; newer ones use the Hebrew. The famous "Miserere" is *Ps* 51 in newer Bibles, *Ps* 50 in older ones. *Ps* 147 Hebrew = 146 + 147 Vulgate. The last three psalms dovetail.

guess it was three, probably going on the mention of three gifts and assuming one gift per visitor. The apple connection has clearer footing. Most religious art comes from the Middle Ages, and those artists spoke Latin. The Latin word for evil is *malum*. The Latin word for apple is *malum*. So any enterprising medieval artist will paint an apple tree for the tree that is to be the occasion for the primordial sin. (The Venetian Renaissance painter Titian paints the apple tree, of course, but he also makes the tempting serpent to be the devil in the form of a baby leaning from the tree.)

The story moves to its conclusion by teaching the consequences of sinning as punishments imposed by Yahweh. (Later in the book I will propose that God does not send punishments or will evil things on people.)

(1) The first consequence is the snake's punishment. This is pure etiology, that is, providing an ancient cause behind effects we see today. The snake is condemned to crawl on its belly, feeding on the earth's dirt. Cultures associate qualities with animals: the wise owl, the cunning weasel, the devious (slithering) snake that in the later Judeo-Christian tradition is a stand-in for the Adversary (s-t-n in Hebrew, pronounced Satan). The story makers inserted the snake into the story as the devil who works against God's plans. Already being an animal that crawls on its belly, this behavior is retrojected into the J story as Yahweh's punishment. Belly crawling is not to be understood as a divine punishment on this species of animal. It's just etiology.

(2) Eve, standing for womankind, is given two punishments. One is quite existential, the other etiological. Eve is told she is to be at her husband's will and pleasure and that he will "dominate you." This describes social behavior in Ancient Israel and still did in Jesus' time. This behavior bears the socially constructed effects of sinfulness. Jewish women had very few rights in the customs of evolving Israelite covenant life; women in the Roman Empire enjoyed more rights. Jewish women could not divorce their husbands, but husbands could put away their wives by drafting a letter of dismissal, and for trivial reasons such as being unattractive. This practice raised Jesus' ire against divorce, and he quoted the J story marriage text against it, as we saw above. The J story teaches that the originally-willed equality between the sexes suffered fracture due to sin and that such domination by men was wrong and not as God intended male and female human life together to be.

The other punishment is merely etiological and not really a punishment. Eve is told she will bear children in pain. I think it is wrong to connect labor pains with sinfulness, and I believe this was not the intent of the crafters of the J story. Labor pains are as natural as the given anatomy of the narrow vaginal birth canal. Before, during, and after the crafting of the J story, Israelite women endured labor pains. Their cries announced a new human being entering into this world, a world no longer like the Garden of Eden. Any Israelite hearing the cries is reminded of the rest of the story of why there is sin and death and the seeming absence of God. The reality of labor pains is just like the Noah story later in the *Book of Genesis* and the reality of rainbows. After water destroys the world, save for Noah and his companions, God promises Noah there will never be a flood again, and the rainbow in the skies after a rain is to be the constant reminder of the promise. (Remember once more: It's a story; it is not meteorology.) Another common sense reason why labor pains have no connection with sin is that many birthing mothers are helped with epidurals to mollify or avoid the pain. What a strange theology of sin we would have if medicine could undo consequences of sin.

(3) The consequences of sin for Adam make more sense if we, like the Israelites, lived by farming the land or raising animals. Yahweh curses the soil so that living by the soil is difficult and frustrating, demanding the farmer's "full sweat of the brow" to tame it if he can. Our image of the 1930s Dust Bowl says it all. I think the contemporary name for this consequence of sin is the fragility of making a living, or living with the constant fear of getting a "pink slip." Tell me there is no presence of sin when corporate raiders take over control of a large manufacturing company, break it into smaller units and close down some of them, transfer production offshore, and do other outsourcing with the result that many people, struggling to pay mortgages or put children through school, lose their jobs and later lose their homes. And the justification offered for this shakeup is "increasing shareholder returns." The J story of Yahweh cursing the soil remains in the realm of notional apprehension, but the real apprehension of the story's teaching for people today requires an elaboration similar to mine.

(4) With the expulsion of Adam and Eve from the Garden we come to the central question behind the crafting of the J story. Why do people die? We come to the story's direct attack on the *Epic of Gilgamesh*. It taught that human mortality is due to the jealousy of the gods who for selfish reasons withhold immortality from humans. The J story teaches that mortality is a consequence of human sinfulness, as are the other consequences listed above. The J story taught the loss of the gift of immortality in a most graphic way. The Garden possesses the tree of life. Adam and Eve sin and are expelled from the Garden. Adam and Eve now lack access to the tree of life. Apart from the language of Yahweh tossing them out of the Garden, which I see as driven by story dynamics, human beings are the cause of their post-Paradise mortality.

I realize that a scientific mentality can call this teaching bunk, as above I termed bunk those teachings about women's inferiority. Thinking from a purely biological perspective, one can say that humans have a heart muscle needed to pump blood and that any muscle eventually gives out if something else doesn't kill the person beforehand. This is true. Our present bodies remind us of our limited lifespan. Could things have been different? Of course. How can one limit a gift from God by saying that this doesn't square with what I learned in biology. But was there ever a time on planet Earth when things were different? I do not think so.

Let me be clear and direct. Was there ever a paradisiacal Garden in which two humans (or possibly more) lived in a state of bestowed immortality for a certain amount of time and then lost it? I think not, nor was the Garden located in Jackson County, Missouri, as Mormon leader Brigham Young thought, or in Mesopotamia where some people still search for its vestiges. It was a crafted story, written by people sometime close to the first millennium BC, who were as mortality-bound as I am. And in order to say what is it that besets us in life, due to our own individual or collective faults, the story crafters write a "what if" situation. This is the Garden of Eden and its tree of immortality. What for them was not a "what if" was the false allure of pagan stories teaching that there are many gods who deny to humans the unending life that the gods possess and want only for themselves. J teaches that God has unending life and it is not God's fault that we do not. It's ours.

A final observation on the genre of creation stories. What is taught in them is meant for the entire human race. While the insights arise from within Israelite experience and are inserted into story frameworks, they are meant for everyone, Jew and Gentile. The word *Eve* is the code word for this global applicability. Eve is the "mother of all the living" who come after her. What pertains to Eve and Adam pertains to everyone else. What is taught at Mount Sinai, on the contrary, is meant for Israelites, like the food laws and laws describing cultic worship or Sabbath rest. The J teaching on a man leaving family roots and joining with his wife in lifelong marriage obligates everyone. This is reflected in Catholic marriage laws. Two unbaptized persons who marry, two Hindus for instance, are seen as having a "natural bond" of marriage. While it differs from what is called a sacramental bond between two baptized Christians, it is judged by the Catholic Church to be a lasting bond, not readily dissolved. Thus, an unmarried Catholic is not free, on the surface, to marry a divorced Hindu even though various Hindu religions may see no obstacles in divorced Hindus remarrying.

With expulsion from the Garden and the posting of cherubim—winged creatures borrowed from Babylonian imagery—holding fiery swords "at the gates of paradise" to block access to the tree of life, this very anthropomorphic creation story and chapter three end.[8] Other effects of human sinfulness are met in the following chapters of *Genesis*, such as fratricide (Cain kills his brother Abel) and social disintegration (the "Tower of Babel" being an etiological explanation of the diversity of languages but due to the sin of pride trying to reach heaven).

The P and J creation stories suffice to provide the biblical backdrop to important Catholic doctrines such as the meaning of creation from nothing-

---

8. The New Testament reprises the imagery of the tree of life in heaven where the baptized will feed on the tree of life once again. See *Rev* 22:14.

ness, called *creatio ex nihilo*, the meaning of God as Creator, the meaning of Original Sin, and what these and other things might mean in the context of evolution.

It was important to present how the two stories ought to be interpreted for their religious content, that is, how the Bible works in these three beginning chapters of it, in order to remove obstacles for understanding properly other Catholic doctrines. It becomes clearly an obstacle if these two creation stories are assumed to be teaching an actual history of events not that far in the past or are teaching geology about planetary formation or are teaching how *homo sapiens* emerged on earth. Furthermore, insisting on a literal interpretation of the creation stories, as some Christian groups and TV evangelists do, becomes a real stumbling block for scientific-minded people drawn otherwise toward Christianity or considering a return to a Christianity abandoned in their youth. But with a proper understanding how the two creation stories work, this need not be.

WHAT DOES ORIGINAL SIN MEAN?

Sharing my faith on a very thorny topic is now required. An understanding of Original Sin follows from the consideration above about the meaning of the Garden of Eden story.[9] Interpreted literally, this story describes the fall of a heterosexual couple, Adam and Eve, from innocence into sinfulness, and the penalty for their sin is borne not only by them but also by every other human stemming from them.

How ought Catholic faith today restate the traditional teachings about Original Sin? Sorting it out becomes complicated because the doctrine was taught by the Council of Trent (AD 1545–1563) during its initial phase in 1546. Many teachings from Ecumenical Councils are considered to be infallible teachings, therefore free from error, henceforth binding. The matter is complicated because the bishops at Trent understood the Garden of Eden story in a literal manner whereas my treatment above, reflecting contemporary Catholic scholarship, presented the meaning of that invented story in its religious sense but not in a literal sense. As with any infallible teaching of an Ecumenical Council, what is forever binding in the teaching and what isn't needs to be determined. Because the thinking of the bishops was governed by a literal reading of Adam and Eve, such as the two of them being the very first instances in history of *homo sapiens* and that they lived a blissful life before transgressing against God, the bishops' literal assumptions affect our interpretation today of the Council's teachings.

9. Neither the Jewish rabbinical tradition nor the theology of Eastern Orthodox churches draw from the story of Adam's sin the notion of a guilt inherited by all Adam's descendants in simply being born. It is a teaching in Western Christianity, that is, in Roman Catholicism and Protestantism.

THE PLACE OF ECUMENICAL COUNCILS

Councils figure significantly in what Catholics believe, so this is an opportune moment to review their place in the church's history. Councils are like the architecture of a home, setting in proper perspective the home's furnishings; in our case, the furnishings are doctrines of faith housed in the edifice called the Church. Older Catholics today have some sense of the 1962–1965 Second Vatican Council—a sense, unfortunately but understandably, evaporating more and more with each younger generation of Catholics. Vatican II was the 21st church council accepted by the Roman Catholicism with the heightened importance of being termed *ecumenical*. The descriptor does not refer to the interchurch relationships of Catholics and Protestants that sponsor joint efforts (e.g., for the homeless or for peace in society) or work toward possible church reunion, all of which are embraced in the modern phrase, "the ecumenical movement." Applied to church councils, however, the word ecumenical harkens to its Greek root, meaning worldwide.

These twenty-one councils were for the most part gatherings of bishops; the Fourth Lateran Council in 1215 was something of an exception, with 400 bishops and 800 voting abbots in attendance. Vatican II with its 2500 bishops and Vatican I in 1869–1870 with its 800 bishops were the only two councils that gathered successfully bishops from around the entire (Catholic) world. For the other nineteen councils *worldwide* is a misnomer. The Council of Trent, mentioned above, began its first session in December, 1545, with 34 bishops, and they were mostly Italian, a number that never grew beyond 80 in the next two years after some Spanish and Portuguese bishops arrived.

The first eight ecumenical councils took place in Asia Minor (present-day Turkey). They were convoked by the Byzantine emperors—in one case (Nicea II in AD 787) by a woman, Empress Irene—and popes never attended any of them. The sessions were conducted in Greek, and the bishops with few exceptions were from the Greek-speaking Eastern Roman Empire. During these early centuries there were about 1000 bishops in the East and 800 in the Latin-speaking West. The first ecumenical council, Nicea I (AD 325), convoked by the Emperor Constantine and meeting in his own residence, had about 250 bishops from the East and 10 from the West, with two priest-legates to represent Pope Sylvester I. Invitations to attend councils may have been sent widely, but the actual participants were hardly worldwide. And this enables the first point to be made about ecumenical councils. They take on heightened importance because they and their teachings are *recognized* as supremely important by the church, sometimes at the very first, sometimes years afterward.

In Christianity's first millennium the Church was united in its Eastern Greek portion and its Western Latin portion. Eight ecumenical councils occurred in this period in Asia Minor, but only the first seven are recognized as ecumenical by Eastern Orthodox churches today. The eighth council, Constantinople IV in 870, involved a political squabble (the disputed election of the patriarch of Constantinople in which Pope Nicholas influenced the council to decide in favor of one faction, an outside intervention that the Eastern Orthodox to this day resent).

A second point about ecumenical councils can be drawn: Some councils have issued infallible proclamations of doctrines judged to have been divinely revealed. The doctrines were deliberated because they were under attack or being denied. But political or purely administrative matters preoccupied other ecumenical councils, such as the disputed election of the patriarch of Constantinople just mentioned, or the Council of Constance (1414–1418) that met to solve the scandal of three persons claiming to be pope; the council deposed John XXIII and Benedict XIII (both of them later termed antipopes), forced Gregory XII to abdicate, and then it elected Martin V to be the one and only pope.

After the official split between Eastern and Western Christianity in 1054, when each side excommunicated the other—a mutual hardening of animosity recently overturned by Pope Paul VI and Patriarch Athenagoras I on 7 December 1965 rescinding the excommunications—the ecumenical councils moved to the West and became papal councils in both name and control. Regarding Christian churches today, the tally is easily made: Roman Catholicism recognizes twenty-one ecumenical councils, the Orthodox recognize the first seven of them, mainline Protestantism such as Lutheranism and Methodism recognize the first four of them, and evangelical Christianity, such as Pentecostal churches that are committed to the "Bible and nothing but the Bible," recognize none. The first four councils (Nicea I in 325, Constantinople I in 381, Ephesus in 431, and Chalcedon in 451) enjoy a particular gravity. They produced the dogmas about the divinity and full humanity of Jesus Christ and the Trinitarian dogma that the Father, Son and Holy Spirit are equally divine and constitute but one God. It is easy to perceive that early heresies about the nature of Jesus and about the meaning of the phrase *Holy Spirit* led to the need to formulate binding teachings (dogmas) on these crucial matters.

ORIGINAL SIN AND THE COUNCIL OF TRENT

I might have begun this section with the title "Original Sin and Saint Augustine" because some people blame him for elaborating a dismal doctrine on Original Sin from his interpretation of St. Paul's *Letter to the Romans*. I admit that he has a severe cast of mind about it; for example, he thinks that most human beings will end up damned due to unhealed Original Sin. But from Augustine's other writings I have drawn a better understanding of Original Sin that is far more positive about its nature and about the generous reach of the grace of salvation, which I treat below.

I do not think that Catholic laity busy themselves much with thinking about Original Sin, except for the wish to have their infants baptized soon after birth to avoid having the children die with Original Sin. (I treat this unfounded fear in chapter seven.) I would rank the topic of Original Sin with something like the doctrine of "Jesus' Second Coming" at the end of time as being at the periphery of Catholic concerns and religious attention.

Besides being at the edge of the laity's consciousness, the very notion of Original Sin, as commonly presented, seems incredulous to the general public. How is it possible that a first human being, or a first human couple, committed some kind of transgression for which everyone coming after them is saddled with a penalty for it? Or even saddled with sharing in the personal guilt of the original perpetrators? And ought we to be talking about the first humans who were little more than hunter-gatherers from several hundred thousand years ago and whose lack of ethical sophistication matched their barely developed mental life? These are the perplexities that cause many contemporaries to scoff at the very proposal of an inherited sin.[10] Still, there is a sense other people have had that there is something so skewed in our experience of human nature that some truth about Original Sin makes sense. The French writer mentioned earlier, Blaise Pascal, gives expression to this sentiment in his famous journal, the *Pensées*:

> It is, however, an astonishing thing that the mystery furthest removed from our knowledge, that of the transmission of sin, should be a fact without which we can have no knowledge of ourselves. For it is beyond doubt that there is nothing which more shocks our reason than to say that the sin of the first man has rendered guilty those who, being so removed from this source, seem incapable of participation in it. This transmission does not only seem to us impossible, it seems also very unjust.... Certainly nothing offends us more rudely than this doctrine; and yet without this mystery, the most incomprehensible of all, we are incomprehensible to ourselves. The knot of our condition takes its twists and turns in this abyss, so that man is more inconceivable without this mystery than this mystery is inconceivable to man. § 434

Additional derision met today results from proposing a literal interpretation of the Garden of Eden story that pictured a very definite *before* and *after* with a defining moment of a cataclysmic sin, called "the Fall," separating the two periods. Stemming from the Latin word for Fall (*lapsus*), the *before* aspect is the blissful *prelapsarian* lives of Adam and Eve, and the *after* aspect is their (and our) *postlapsarian* period, that is, a life outside the Garden played out on Earth where everyone is saddled with the effects of the Fall by simply being born.

---

10. The German word for Original Sin, *die Erbsünde*, literally means inherited sin, not a primordial sin.

In the prelapsarian period, humans are said to have lived without Original Sin, whatever that condition might have meant. So goes the explanation. It is this explanation that our contemporaries trip over, and so do I.

COUNCIL OF TRENT

These remarks, by way of preface, bring us to the nineteenth Ecumenical Council in Roman Catholic reckoning. The Protestant Reformation had recently erupted, and challenges to Catholic teachings were widespread. The topic of Original Sin was not one of them; if anything, the Reformers overstressed its negative nature. For Luther and Calvin, Original Sin so deformed human nature that it was entirely vitiated, rendered worthless, rendered unable to accomplish anything of good on its own. Possessing human freedom to choose the good was a charade. Under attack, however, were the Catholic teachings about justification (that is, the process of being saved) and about the number and nature of the sacraments. Protestants were teaching that Baptism removed nothing of the sinfulness that saddled humanity from the first. Moreover, some Protestant sects, such as the Anabaptists (Mennonites, etc.) restricted being baptized to already-believing adults. Infant Baptism availed nothing.

In the late spring of 1546, during Trent's first period, the bishops deliberated the topic of Original Sin and produced on June 17th five sternly worded declarations, called canons, each ending with the threatening *anathema sit*: "Whoever denies this teaching comes under the harshest of penalties." Small wonder that these teachings shaped Roman Catholic thinking thereafter. But what is binding among them and what is not? Against what are they to be measured?

Some measures derive from a more proper understanding of the Garden story, treated earlier, and from the accepted science of human origins. "Adam and Eve" stand for *homo sapiens*, and humans emerged many thousands of years ago. Nor did they emerge suddenly in full stature, as the Garden story portrays; rather, they were born from primates. (I treat evolutionary theory in chapter eight). A prelapsarian period of bliss makes little sense if *homo sapiens* emerged 200,000 years ago, nor can a "Fall," a breaking of a divine commandment, be readily imagined for them, and especially if it becomes a penalty passed on to all human descendants. Another measure is the Greek language. The text of *Rom* 5:12 has underpinned the connection between Adam's sin and our own. As read in Latin, as the bishops at Trent did, one derives a causal connection between Adam's guilt and ours. As read in Greek, which is the inspired text, the connection is otherwise. (This measure becomes easily esoteric and so I am rendering it in footnote 11 for more interested readers.)

Canon I describes a prelapsarian Adam sinning and losing blissfulness. Canon II teaches the penalty of death, both bodily death and the spiritual death of damnation, that Adam brought on himself and passed on to the rest of humanity, an inheritance Canon III calls "our personal sin." I perceive these declarations so tied into a literal acceptance of the Garden story that they are not binding features of an infallible teaching.

Matters stand quite differently with the other features of these canons. I find them binding. However one construes the human natures with which we and the very first humans were born, our common natures do not act in harmony with the reality that applies to every human being without exception: each human was created to image the very nature of God (Gn 1:26). But things are less than perfect with us. Something needs healing, and the healing cannot come from our efforts alone. It must come from God's goodness. Canons III, IV, and V utilize the language of Christ's redemption to describe divine healing. Because inherited sinfulness had been the context in these canons, redemption is presented "for the remission of sins," and this happens especially in the Sacrament of Baptism. But if the context of inherited sin is removed, one is still left with shared human natures that do not operate with an innate goodness one would desire. From Trent's teaching, one is left with the goodness of God as healer, as Redeemer. From a Church Father whose name I cannot now recall, these words ring: God is in such great debt to us, not because we have given him so much but because he has promised us so much. I perceive an implied promise in being created in God's own image.[11]

INSIGHTS FROM AUGUSTINE ON ORIGINAL SIN

The following insights derive from reading St. Augustine's little handbook on *Faith, Hope, and Charity* that is a synopsis of his vast theology. The reading changed just about everything for me.[12] His answers to three of its questions, when considered together, forged the insight for me that Original Sin is a "what if" situation that never, purely as such, existed. Let me explain it very carefully because the reality behind Original Sin is not being denied, and I take the Council of Trent as requiring that it not be denied.

Augustine's question 11 asks, "Just what is the nature of evil?" I paraphrase his answer: In our experience, what we call *evils* underscore very

---

11. The other measure against which Trent's teachings are to be measured is the proper reading of *Rom* 5:12. The text begins, "Through one man sin entered the world, and through sin death entered. Thus death spread to everyone...." The verse in Latin ends "in quo omnes peccaverunt" and *in quo* can mean either *in whom* or *in what* sin everyone else has sinned. In either case Adam passes on the penalty of sin and death, that is, it's inherited. In the inspired Greek text, and putting the Greek letters into English ones, the verse ends "*eph' hō pantes hēmarton.*" The meaning of this phrase is "because of the fact that everyone, himself or herself, has sinned." There is therefore a cause/effect connection between everyone being a transgressor and the entry of death into the world. It's not an inherited penalty. The bishops at Trent followed the Latin. The NABRE version, used today by the Catholic Church, follows the Greek: "...and thus death came to all, inasmuch as all sinned."

12. It is Augustine's *Enchiridion*, and it is a catechism of 122 questions with short answers.

graphically what are good realities. He illustrates the point with the example of disease. It is an evil thing to be diseased. Abstracting from the nature of this or that particular disease, disease is the absence of health; it is the lacking of something that ought to be present. Anyone growing old knows this connection. I'll add an example to Augustine's. Deafness is the absence of the power of hearing. People ought to be able to hear, and most do. But some, through no fault of their own, cannot hear sounds. Our experience of deaf persons who have never experienced music, or laughter, is a graphic reminder to us of the goodness of hearing. Deafness is a physical evil, not a moral evil. Hence Augustine's point: An evil is the absence of a corresponding good that ought to be present, and the evil makes us appreciate the absent good all the more. Although not developed in question 11, moral evils also fulfill the definition of lacking what ought to be present in human behavior. Take our experience of persons disposed to lying. They cannot be trusted. Not only are we wary of them, they make us appreciate the goodness that is veracity. They make us appreciate the goodness of someone "whose word is golden."

To this philosophical definition of what is an evil, Augustine adds a theological truth that he will incorporate later. God is omnipotent and full of goodness; even the pagan writers whom Augustine studied admitted such. Therefore, God would not *tolerate* evils in the world unless He could draw goodness from the evil, which basically means restoring what was lacking. (Much language about evils tends to say that God *permits* or *allows* evils, which makes no sense to me. As a parent I never allowed an evil to harm my son but things happened that needed to be tolerated until a "way out" or a "way through" could be devised or strategized. Nor does God permit evils to hurt us, or to teach us by them, as if God devised and intended them for us, although some texts in scripture have this tone.)

In subsequent questions in his *Enchiridion*, Augustine elaborates the nature of Original Sin, and it is a dire picture he sketches. It is a state of slavery to sinning. People cannot not sin, but the sin remains their fault because they freely sin, even if inevitably. Everyone stands "under condemnation and tossed from one form of evil to another." Infected with Original Sin, all "are being drawn through diverse errors and sufferings into that last and endless punishment which they suffer in common with the fallen angels, their corrupters and masters and partakers of their doom." They're meant for hell. Bodily death foreshadows the death of the soul, the latter being a code word for damnation. A dire picture indeed! Let us call this picture Augustine's elaboration of "Pure Original Sin," describing an envisioned environment of Original Sin that alone existed, devoid of any grace to heal it. It's a hellish life bent on ending up in hell.

The all-too-easy interpretation of this morbid picture is to think that the state of Original Sin existed for some lengthy period of time in human history and then there appeared the healing graces of the Lord's redemption on behalf of sinners. But would this not mean that many people were automatically damned before the time grace intervened? Before springing to this (wrong) conclusion, let's look at question 118 in the *Enchiridion* wherein Augustine draws the parallel between four stages in a Christian's life with the four stages in the history of salvation. A person may begin living "according to the flesh" and beset by ignorance. Then comes a stage of being aware of God's laws, and now one is simply more conscious of transgressing. But one can begin to be led by the spirit of God in the next stage, and the stronger power of God's love counters the attraction to sin. And if someone perseveres until the end, heavenly peace awaits in the final stage of a Christian's life. (I think Augustine writes autobiographically.)

To these four stages in an individual's life corresponds the story of "the People of God" (*Sic est Dei populus*). Initially, God's people existed before Moses received the Sinai commandments. In Stage Two, God's people lived under the Mosaic laws. After that, they lived under the grace revealed in the life of Christ. The fourth stage, heavenly life for God's People, is assumed to follow but goes unmentioned; however, Augustine writes the following words to describe Christ's grace from Stage Three: "Indeed, this grace was not lacking beforehand to those to whom it behooved God to bestow grace, although grace was veiled and hidden in God's temporal plan." The grace of Christ, though *veiled*, was therefore present in Stage One of the history of humanity and in Stage Two. It is quite remarkable that Augustine describes Stage One human beings as being "God's People."

What does this mean? It means that the grace of the Lord's redemption is retroactive. Retroactive to when? To the very beginning of the human race! With biblical imagery, numerous Fathers of the Church speak of salvation offered from Adam's son Abel to the last just person living. Pope Gregory the Great (540–604), in a sermon on the parable comparing the Kingdom of Heaven to the owner of a vineyard, put it very eloquently: "The owner represents God Creator, who cares for all His creatures. The vineyard is the universal church which includes everyone from the righteous Abel to the last member of the elect awaiting to be born at the end of the world. The landowner secured workers at dawn, again at the third hour, again at the sixth hour, then the ninth hour and finally at the eleventh hour. Dawn signifies the world from Adam to Noah, the third hour represents Noah to Abraham, the sixth hour is Abraham to Moses, the ninth hour is from Moses to the Lord's appearance, and the eleventh hour represents the time from Jesus to the end of the world."[13] St. Augustine writes similarly in his Commentary on *Psalm* 62: "In the blood of Abel, the just one, the whole city speaks that has Christ as its king, and so on until the blood of Zechariah the prophet. That

---

13. This homily, given in the Basilica of St. Lawrence Martyr on Septuagesima Sunday (7th Sunday before Easter), is found in *Patrologia Latina* 76:1154. The Vatican in 1969 abandoned the designation of Sundays before Easter.

same city goes on speaking in the blood of John the Baptist, the blood of the apostles and martyrs, and in all of Christ's faithful." There is no need to add more church testimony to the fact that the redemptive grace of Christ reached back to every moment in the past and to each person. Whether this or that ancient person responded to grace is not different from the choice today to respond to God's grace for anyone living after Jesus lived.

Therefore, a situation of pure Original Sin, lacking the offer of any redemptive healing of it, never existed for any human being in all of history. Not only would it go against the convictions of eminent theologians like Gregory the Great or Augustine, it would force a picture of God that is unbearable. It would mean that God created human beings to live in a world of unchecked Original Sin, whose outcome in life is damnation because they live their entire lives enslaved to sin.

But why have I chosen to call the milieu of pure Original Sin—the milieu Augustine describes in so dire a fashion—a *what if* situation? Because it never actually existed *as such*, which is different from saying it has no reality.[14] Consider again Augustine's Question 11. To fully appreciate the good that a good God can bring out of evil, first appreciate the evil. Appreciate what a hopeless and wretched situation pure Original Sin would be if God out of goodness and in freedom *had not* "sent His Son into the world." Augustine wishes us to first recognize the great evil (Original Sin) that the greater blessing (God's love, Christ's redemptive grace) conquers. "For your sake God has become man...You would have suffered eternal death, had he not been born in time. Never would you have been freed from sinful flesh, had he not taken on the likeness of sinful flesh. You would have suffered everlasting unhappiness, had it not been for this mercy" (Sermon 185). This is why I have come to see the state or duration of pure Original Sin a "what if" situation.

But Original Sin is not simply a figment of imagination, an invention. The teaching of Trent demands otherwise. Admittedly, it is awkward to call an evil a *something*, because by definition an evil, whether physical like deafness or moral like lying, is the lack of a something, the lack of the power of hearing or the lack of the disposition to veracity. The good is clearly a something, and an evil amounts to a non-something in a defective reality; it lacks the good that ought to be there. This is fine philosophical talk, but in the everyday manner in which people talk, evils sound like realities. "I have cancer." "I have poverty." "I have an addiction." It's not a denial that cancer cells are in reality squamous or basal cells; it's that there is some absence of control of cell mitosis. A healthy body regulates; an illness is the absence of

14. I recognize that there are biblical passages that, if given a literal interpretation, mention a period of humanity's wickedness before Christ acted. "Someone might die for a really good person. But what proves that God loves us is that Christ died for us while we were still sinners" (*Rom* 5:8). I find such passages so formulated in order to assert another matter. In *Rom* 5:8, for example, it is God's surprising love.

a regulating principle.

Original Sin, considered as such, is a vast and complex evil that, as an evil, is lacking the good that ought to be present to human behavior. People like St. Anselm of Canterbury (1033–1109), and St. Thomas Aquinas after him, described it as the lack of a cohesive principle of personality, in which our emotions and passions are not subject to our reasoning and will power, and reason and the will, in turn, are turned from God as their ultimate happiness. St. Anselm called the cohesion "original justice," and Original Sin means the lack of it. However one describes what is lacking in the evil called Original Sin, the good that is restored to humanity is a graced existence, and the blessing is attributed to Jesus' life, death and resurrection. The good, restored and even augmented, is so awesome that an early church tradition called Adam's transgression "O happy fault" (*O felix culpa*).

Original Sin is a "what if" situation, as I've claimed. The actual existential reality from the very first humans down to me, and beyond me to the end of human earthly existence, is a healed-over human being. I want to propose that all of us have a healed-over flawed human nature, even if it sounds contradictory to join *healed* and *flawed*.

Because Christ's redemption is healing something, bringing to it the good it lacked, then underneath the healing, if one can use a *below/above* image, is a healed reality. It is human nature, mine, yours, everyone's. Human nature saddled with pure Original Sin never existed. A nature in some manner flawed, as explained below, but ever existing under a canopy of grace, that's ours. This is the sense I give to Trent's teaching that Original Sin is passed on to each one, although it is not the passing on of a personal sin, as Trent teaches. For me, inherited sin is a non-binding feature of the teaching.

What each human birth means is the emergence from the womb of a human nature that is not automatically directed to damnation, for that would be a moment of pure Original Sin; rather, it is human nature that bears the experience of something *flawed*. I struggle to describe it, and any analogy seems to falter, but here is the closest I can come. As a young man I injured my knee in sports. Had I not gotten the right kind of treatment, I might have had a limp for the rest of my life. But that didn't happen. I came to walk and to play sports in the same fashion as before without noticing anything except rarely. On certain days, when the barometer dropped very low, I felt stiffness. Underneath the "good" of my regained knee mobility was the healed-over remnant of a long-ago injury. Let me attempt to clarify further this conundrum.

EXPLAINING ORIGINAL SIN IN A NEW MANNER

Using suggestive language from Trent's Canon V describing Baptism as removing inherited Original Sin, it teaches that *concupiscentia vel fomes* remain in baptized people "for life's trials." I translate it as "potentially sinful propensities" remaining in them, the Latin word *fomes* having the sense of tinder that would burn easily. Potential propensities is a morally neutral assertion. They are not sins nor are they nothing whatsoever. As soon as you think in this manner, you are involved in the realm of free will. If a propensity leads to a sin, that is a misuse of freedom. If a propensity leads to a virtuous act, it is free will rightly exercised. A propensity can go either way, but can it tilt to one direction? This is the key question. Does human freedom have a tilt?

I have used the word *flaw*, as in "we're born with a flawed human nature," but *flawed* does not mean sinful human nature. I intended it as getting close to the sense of a nature's *tilt*. I draw an analogy. A robin is born. It has the avian nature of that species. Later, seemingly in automatic fashion, it builds a nest the way robins always have. It hunts as robins do. It avoids certain predators as robins do. From birth and throughout its life, its nature unfolds in predictable fashion. The individual robin does not have a flawed robin's nature. It has a nature built on instinctual patterns.

Human nature is so different because it unfolds with reasoning and free will operating, and the results are not predictable. (I do not deny certain instincts present, especially in infancy, e.g., sucking at the breast.) But a conundrum, in describing a flawed human nature, presents itself. If the first human beings, and everyone thereafter, bear a healed-over human nature, bear a human nature that would be a slave to sinning except for Jesus' redemption, doesn't the word *flawed* push back onto God the creation of human natures needing repair?

My way out of this enigma lies in the very grandeur of what God creates. In the words of *Ps* 8 describing human creation, "What is a person that you should be ever mindful, a mortal who claims your care? Yet you have made this person little less than a god and bestowed a crown of honor and glory." The glory and honor certainly refer to the gift of reasoning but even more, I think, to the gift of human freedom. To be made in God's image is to bear the gift of free will. Free will involves self-determination. Parents raising children know this truth first hand. At the "terrible twos age," children assert their wills, will cry if resisted. At the "fearsome fours," children will do exactly the opposite of what they're told.

My concern is the operation of free will in adults, at that time in life when we bear moral responsibility for how we exercise self-determination. It can be done in a selfish manner or in a selfless and altruistic manner. Proposing my answer to the enigma, God created the first human beings and every other human being with self-determination. It was meant to be a human asset used selflessly. It was meant to be loving, as God's nature is loving. What are the chances of its selfish use? I think quite high or at least high enough. I think human self-determination tilts to "I am my own boss. Self-preservation is paramount." It is more "I want" rather than "What can I do for you?" This is the tilt of human freedom's nature. Altruism needs to be learned. The experience of parenting comes to mind. If little children are never disciplined and instead have their demands constantly catered to, they will grow into egotistical adults.

Gifted artists have used their imaginations to depict human society in the throes of scarcity of goods and impending physical threats. They picture people who are combative, self-serving, and domineering.[15] I find such books and films very plausible. I think free will, self-determination, can go either direction (selfishness or selflessness), but it tilts to prioritizing the self, not the other. To sum up, then, the grandeur of being created to have self-determination is to bear a flawed human nature where *flaw* does not mean sinful but it connotes *tilt*. On the other hand, a human nature in which healing has taken root, that is to say, a nature empowered by the grace of redemption, is lured to tilt in the opposite direction. Grace inclines human nature to be loving and altruistic.

How do I compare the first human beings living hundreds of thousands of years ago to the Garden story about Adam and Eve and the literal approach to it that the bishops at Trent took? Unlike the Adam and Eve story, there was no prelapsarian period of natural bliss for ancient humans before some sort of "fall." In fact, there was never the situation of the first two human beings, or however many there were at first, who were given a test that they failed. Still, all of the religious teachings of the two creation stories apply to those first human beings. They are created in the image of God. They bear God's spirit (*ruah*) making them in body and in soul human. They are created with self-determination. I have called it having a flawed human nature, not sinful as such but nevertheless tilted to behavior that likely engenders sinning. And they surely sinned. The first primitive peoples killed each other, contesting for food or for territory. But they lived under a canopy of grace. How God moved their consciences to avoid such behavior, or to seek forgiveness having done it, I do not know nor do I know if God was successful in luring to repentance, but I do believe that they were not, as human beings, abandoned by the One who created them in the divine image. And why do I say this? God has promised humanity so much!

What notion of God did ancient humans have? They likely thought in terms of forces in the sky or in nature, and their notions were surely primitive. But they, and every later human being, are meant for salvation. I am connected to them, not because I inherit a human nature that they at the very beginning sullied, but because I am born with a human nature that tilts, too, as theirs did. So my ventured answer to why we are born with a flawed human nature is to say "we are all Adam, we are all Eve" in their pre-Fall

---

15. I have in mind the 1983 television film, *The Day After*, depicting how all social constraints fail following a nuclear attack on the United States, and William Golding's 1954 novel, *Lord of the Flies*, about a group of young boys stranded on an uninhabited island whose life together descended into savagery.

natures as it were, when they misused free will,[16] whereas we tend to think we are like Adam and Eve in some post-Garden worse-off condition. I ventured also that flawed human nature is human nature as such. Because it is everyone's nature, in this sense it can be described as being "transmitted," or "passed down." This agrees with Aquinas's insight about lacking full cohesion of the personality, and it meets Trent's requirement.

There is a description of sin in the J story that is prescient. I do not refer to the usual description in J about sin as disobedience to Yahweh's commandment, "There are many trees to eat from in the Garden but don't dare eat from that particular tree." I refer to the temptation associated with that tree, called the tree of the knowledge of good and evil in the story, and pointed to by the serpent: "If you eat of that tree, you will become like God, which God does not want." When treating this story earlier, I described the sin as seeking moral autonomy and the privilege to determine yourself what is morally right and wrong, God's prerogative be damned. This religious teaching of the nature of sin is an exact depiction of human self-determination described just above that tilts to self-centered behavior; it tilts, in fact, to asserting self over against God in the words of the temptation.

Sometimes, sharing one's faith in a mystery bumps up against an aspect of the mystery that eludes clarification. For example, how is it that Jesus' virginal conception leads to a human nature like our own that nevertheless lacked the genetic makeup that male semen normally contributes? My belief in virginal conception cannot answer it but it does not compel me to deny the doctrine because the "overshadowing" creative Spirit of God (Lk 1:35) can bring about what seems biologically impossible. The Garden story presents another aspect that, for me, eludes clarification. A consequence of the sin of Adam and Eve is that they are expelled from the Garden, meaning they no longer have access to eat from "the tree of life" in the Garden, meaning that they are now mortal. This consequence fulfills the story's aim to teach that human sin causes mortality and to reject the Babylonian myth that associates human deaths with divine jealousy against humans.

Saint Paul accepted the Garden story in a literal manner just as everyone else did for so many centuries. To repeat Rom 5:12 again but in its truer Greek sense, "Therefore, just as through one person [Adam] sin entered the world, and through sin death entered, and therefore death came to everyone inasmuch as all sinned." But why does sin cause dying? This stumps me. One explanation is to say dying means spiritual death. That makes sense because sin causes separation from God, which amounts to spiritual and everlasting death. But physical death is the symbol of spiritual death, as one reads in Wis 2:23-24: "God created human beings to be immortal for he made them as an image of his own nature. Death came into the world only through the

16. I veer from the CCC on this point.

devil's envy." So the question is simply pushed back: Why is physical death the symbol of spiritual death? Physical death is real. It is not just a symbol. It happens. So how is earthly mortality caused by sinfulness? As I said, I'm stumped, but not enough to deny its truth.

CHAPTER THREE

So What is God Like?

*"[God] dwells in unapproachable light
whom no human being has seen or can see."* 1 Tim 6:16

Following what I've shared on how the Bible works, and how the two creations stories in *Genesis* are easily misunderstood, it seems obvious to talk about God. God is, after all, the main focus of the Bible and the reason why there are creations stories at all. So what is God like? The short answer to the question is that we don't directly know. But this is no reason to end chapter three right here. People pray to God and they are not using make-believe thoughts. People talk about God and write about God, and their words are not mere guesses. St. Thomas Aquinas provides a way beyond the impasse. I do not propose to elaborate his strategy. I mention only a few of his pointers because he has been a mentor for me in what we can know about God and what we can't.

SOME SUGGESTIONS FROM ST. THOMAS AQUINAS

His foremost pointer is to maintain a healthy agnosticism to the question, "What is God like?" "I thought agnosticism meant that you can't know anything about God," you might wonder. Yes and no. If we are talking about the human attempt to grasp God, to have a concept of God much as the scientist, working on a nuclear reactor, can comprehend how nuclear fission works and have concepts about its nature, then we must remain agnostics in wanting to grasp God in similar depth. As Aquinas says, the human intellect is made to grasp realities of this world and is powerful enough to get to their essences, such as the nuclear scientist does. But the essence of God totally outstrips the most acute powers of our minds. God remains shielded in the "cloud of unknowing," to use the phrase of an anonymous medieval mystic.

But there is a difference between intuiting something and directly comprehending it, and this is his second pointer. Our minds can grow by drawing inferences, by experiencing an effect and inferring its cause, as when we see droppings in the morning and infer a mouse has visited the kitchen. We don't arrive at grasping the nature of mouse-ness other than that mice defecate, I suppose. If the "no" in the "yes and no" above referred to a healthy agnosticism, the "yes" refers to experiencing certain effects in our world from which it can be inferred that God is their cause. This is to know God in an indirect and very limited manner. I imagine indirect knowing to be like looking forward and inferring something behind your back, as when on a dark night walking west, you see your shadow moving in front of you and conclude that it is coming from the full moon to the east behind you.

A third pointer involves the words we use about God, about "God talk" as it is called. Our words about anything, and even words about God, come from our experiences of the world about us. If any word is to apply to God, it must be stretched from its normal setting, and any associated imperfections are shaved away. This process with the elasticity of words is familiar to teachers of English and lovers of poetry. Therefore, to say that God is *loving* is to apply to God a word we only know from our human experience with other people. A healthy reminder from this pointer is that words about God limp and can be true enough but vastly imperfect.

It would be something else if our human minds could grasp the divine essence so that arguments whether God exists or not would be passé. His truth or existence would be self-evident. It would be like asking a mathematician, who can grasp the nature of a right triangle, why the Pythagorean Theorem must be true. At the very beginning of his famous *Summa of Theology* (ST, I, q.2, a.1) Aquinas makes a seminal assertion about the Yes and No regarding knowing God, and I offer his words as a final pointer. "Our minds cannot grasp the divine essence, and therefore nothing about God is immediately self-evident to us; instead, our knowledge about God needs to derive from our reasoning about things that are more known to us, and here I am referring to our knowledge of the effects of God's reality, that is, to created realities." Drawing inferences about God from our concepts of created realities is no easy task, but it can be done. When in chapter eight I treat evolution, however, I'll consider the argument for God's existence from "Intelligent Design" in the universe. I think its proponents get it wrong.

Aquinas proposed five famous proofs for God's existence. They're not proofs in the normal sense of that word. They are five invitations—he called them five ways (*quinque viae*)—to reach a philosophical inference about God drawn from our experience of creation. Any one of the five is difficult to follow, and I am never sure "I've got it." Of what I am sure is that they are not the pathway for most Catholic laity to gain a knowledge of God. So what is that pathway?

KNOWING GOD IN A MORE READY MANNER

We know God by God's actions in history. This is still indirect knowledge about God because what we are knowing in direct fashion is the history of human life that bears God's imprint. We need to look through the imprint to what lies behind it and out of direct view. What are some expressions of this history? Foremost is God's revelation of Self in and through the life of Jesus, and this is also to include the death and resurrection of Jesus. There is also God's revelation of Self in the history of Israel, what Christianity has come to call *salvation history* and what Israel's psalms call God's *wonderful deeds of old*, the *mirabilia Dei* as the psalms in Gregorian chant have it. Furthermore, it is God's revelation of Self in the story of the church and especially in the nobility of its martyrs. In addition, it includes what has happened in the lives of people who in retrospect assert without qualm, "God has been good to me, good to us."

I don't wish to be Pollyannaish, oblivious to the evils that befell Israel, befell the church—I refer to its warts, its wrinkles, its scandals—and befell many individuals who have cried out, "Where are you in my need, God?" Yes, the presence of evil, as if evil were a thing, dampens and sometimes suffocates acknowledging God from the effects of His imprint in history. The experience of evil produces atheists, it must be admitted. So do one thousand unanswered prayers. If, too quickly, someone were to brandish Aquinas's arguments for God's existence against God-deniers, I would remind the enthusiast that immediately preceding Aquinas's arguments was his mention of the great stumbling block to grasping them, the experience of evil in the world.

So what is God like? Two signposts mentioned earlier remain my indicators. We have no direct knowledge of God "whom no human being has seen or can see" (*1 Tim* 6:16). But Jesus we can know by looking right at him, looking through the lenses of scripture, church writings, and our own experience as baptized persons bearing his imprint. We ourselves can become the Philip to whom Jesus spoke: "Whoever has seen me has seen the Father" (*Jn* 14:9).

The other signpost is our language about God and the fact that it derives from the language of earth-bound experience. God can be called Lord, Judge, Shepherd, and so forth; all such words derive from our experience of worldly counterparts, for example, human shepherds. Applying such words aptly to God involves what I think of as a stripping-away process of the imperfections that first accompanied these words into our imagination. But this stripping away, called technically "using analogous words for God," needs mention later because it is part of Catholic faith, part of my faith.

Jesus' life and his vocabulary are the direct reflection—this is something my mind can handle—of how I can know God without removing the incomprehensible mystery. My faith lets Jesus' behavior model how God is to be known. His own word for God, which has become paramount for me, is the Aramaic *Abba*, which is translated *Father* in the Bible. To capture the needed intimacy in Jesus' use of *Abba*, some have suggested *daddy* as a more accurate translation, the way in which adult American Southerners in a non-childish manner still call their biological fathers.

Did not all of us grow up with this word, *Father*, repeating it so many times over, when we blessed ourselves and when we prayed with "We ask this through Jesus Christ, who lives and reigns with the Father and the Holy Spirit?" "It should always have been prominent," a reader might retort. "What do you mean that addressing God as Father, but in Jesus' intimate sense of Abba, *became* prominent to you?" Indeed, I repeated *Father* in verbal prayers more times than I could count. But I shared at the outset that my prayer inclination grew more toward contemplation than to the habitual verbal prayers. As I immersed myself deeper into stories about Jesus and sensed the sheer specialness of his word *Abba* for God, I began attempting to live with its echo in my consciousness.

There's a misconception that Jesus originated the name *father* for God. He did not. There are several Tanak texts where Yahweh is called father, e.g., "You, Yahweh, are our father" (*Is* 63:16); "Father of orphans, defender of widows, such is God in his holy abode" (*Ps* 68:5).[1] But Jesus did originate an intimate and affectionate name for God, *abba*, which has no precedent in Judaism. The normal word for father is *ab* in Aramaic. To express affection for one's father, a child would say abba instead, as would an adult son or daughter later on. But for Jesus to call God *abba* must have sounded flippant or irreverent to other Jews. Yet he preferred the word, and he urged his disciples to experience the same affection and intimacy for God by using this startling word.

I desired for myself some share of Jesus' intimacy with God because I think Jesus invites all of us to do so. Therefore I began to repeat in silence, as a meditative mantra, the word *abba*, usually in the quiet of the morning upon waking. Not very fast, not as if the more times it is said, the better it works. Just reverently, just like knocking gently on a heavenly door to let the mystery of God in. At first I felt I was initiating the mantra, just as I might have initiated a familiar verbal prayer, the *Hail Mary, full of grace* for example. Later, I felt drawn into its repetition as if the One addressed, the Father, was pulling it out, not unlike St. Paul's observation, "From our spirit of adoption we cry 'Abba.' The Spirit himself joins with our spirit to bear witness we are children of God" (*Rom* 8:15-16). The repetition of abba produces its own inner stillness, similar to the "Jesus Prayer" mantra of the Greek Orthodox tradition, "Jesus Christ, Son of God, have mercy on me," which is claimed to lead to a holy silence for Greek monks. I've come to think that it is chiefly in stillness that we hear what God is like, confident that God wishes to inform us.

1. The Hebrew word for father in these texts is *ab* (אב), and it addresses God in a rather formal manner. In the Greek New Testament, the word *patēr* (Father) for God, used by Jesus and others, appears over 150 times. In three texts, the Aramaic *abba* is simply transliterated into Greek letters, αββα (*Mk* 14:36, *Rom* 8:15, and *Gal* 4:6). The Aramaic is clearly Jesus' word for the God of Israel.

What do I hear? I hear God dwelling within me, in my soul. (Of course I am using *hear* metaphorically, not literally. No voices are involved. You experience the lure, the attracting power of a person, Abba. Anyone who has fallen in love knows this pull.) Here's where the Father is located. Someone might say, "I thought your soul was within you, and that God was up in heaven." That was how I imagined things years ago, and furthermore, that my duty was to advance toward God, as if climbing to heaven. But I had the direction all wrong. I've come to see that the Father, Abba, has come to me. In John's gospel, where the divinity of Jesus is apparent—"The Father and I are one" (*Jn* 10:30)—the Father arrives with the Son to take abode within us. "Whoever loves me will keep my word, and my Father will love [you] and we will come to [you] and make our dwelling with [you]." I take to heart Jesus' words that "the kingdom (reign) of God is within you." I take to heart that I am a son of God by adoption, and that Abba did the adopting, not that I merited or won it.

When I was younger, I saw the Catholic Christian life as exerting efforts, as in follow this law, do that devotional practice. I am not against devotional practices, even now; it's just that the primary focus is that Abba has reached out to embrace me, not that I have done things to earn reaching Him. And if it seems that our love of the Lord and keeping his word is an exertion that thereby causes God to love us and to come dwell, we mistake the movement. We love God because God first loved us. A love coming from the invisible world induces our acts of love in this visible world. Still, it is all one and the same world, not us below and God up above.

NEWMAN'S INVISIBLE WORLD AND VISIBLE WORLD

This is the time to say a few things about up and down. We inherit from the Bible the imagery that God is up in heaven, and we labor down on earth, awaiting the end of our lives when we will be raised up to be with God in heaven. St. Maximus, a popular homilist who lived in fifth-century Turin (northern Italy), used this imagery to great effect: "Christ is risen! His Holy Spirit has unlocked the doors of heaven, which stands wide open to receive those who rise up from the earth. Because of Christ's resurrection the thief ascends to paradise, the bodies of the blessed enter the holy city, and the dead are restored to the company of the living. There is an upward movement in the whole of creation....Our Savior's passion raised people from the depths, lifts them from earth, and sets them in the heights." His language plays to our imaginations. Many Catholics pray the *Our Father* today by holding hands raised and eyes cast upward. Take *Ps* 113: "Who is like the Lord our God, who has risen on high to his throne, yet stoops down from the heights to look down upon heaven and earth?" The psalm reflects the P creation story in *Genesis* where God has located the waters below the earth, the sky about earth, the firmament higher still holding waters about it, and above all these works of God's hand sits God enthroned.

Yes, God as *up* comes easily to our imagination. And below the earth is darkness, the netherworld, the abode of the dead, even the abode of devils. It is often imagined a fiery place, as Matthew's Jesus expresses it: "Fool, you will be liable to fiery Gehenna" (*Mt* 5:22). And again, "The Devil who had led people astray was thrown into the pool of fire and sulfur, where the beast and the false prophet were. There they will be tormented day and night forever and ever" (*Rev* 20:10).[2] Imagining *down* to be something unknown, or even a hellish place, is probably derived from our experience with corpses. Save for the few cultures that cremate atop a funeral pyre, dead bodies are buried in the earth. The great Italian poet Dante (AD 1265–1321) put classical status on someone's being down below and out of sight, on being in the unending torment of hell, in his *Inferno* section of the *Divine Comedy* poem. Whatever the sources for our imaginations, we live with upwards being good and where God is, and downwards being bad and where devils and bad people are.

The language of an invisible world and a visible world overcomes the ways that up and down language can mislead. Heaven is not a place but a manner of existing. It is more accurate to say how God is rather than where God is. I realize that Mormons locate God the Father somewhere out in the cosmos, behind the cosmic body Kolob as some texts say, because Mormons conceive God the Father to have corporeality (and to have a wife) and to look physically as they themselves look. A corporeal divinity makes no sense to me, or perhaps I should say more gently that it is not the God to whom I assent. God is not composed of matter. Nor is heaven a location in the cosmos or is hell a physical place. Hell is a manner of existing alienated from God, alienated from any experience of personal fulfillment.

On the other hand, the visible world I inhabit consists in quantifiable and measurable realities. I have weight (*mass* more properly in physics) and this can be measured; light and radio waves and gamma waves have wave length and frequency, all of which can be measured. I move from place to place. And wave phenomena studied by physics propagate, not unlike ripples on a lake struck by a stone. It takes the visible electromagnetic radiation we call *light* eight minutes to come from the sun to earth. This is my world of sense experience. It is the world of science. It is the world of common sense experience for the most part. But there is an invisible world I experience, a world where God is present within me and all about me. It is distinct from the visible sensible world but not located elsewhere from it. It is as if the visible world and the invisible world are overlapping or penetrating each other.

2. Hell as fire is called apocalyptic imagery, of which imagery the *Book of Revelation* is stock full. It is not meant to be taken literally although some devout persons say it should because Jesus used it. Gehenna, the "Valley of Hinnon" in Hebrew, was a place southwest of Jerusalem where child sacrifice was practiced and where trash was burned later on. The punishment of sinners in a fiery hell is found in Jewish apocalyptic books, e.g., *Enoch* 90, 26.

I experience a visible world of stuff. I experience an invisible world wherein God dwells. It is a different kind of experience, to be sure, as different as loving a person is from knowing how tall and how heavy the person is. Also present to me from the invisible world are the workings of grace and the action of the Risen Jesus in sacraments. These realities are invisible to my optic nerve but not to the eyes of faith, not to spiritual sight. God and grace belong to my experience every bit as much as material stuff does. Thus I find it better to use Newman's words of a visible world and an invisible world. Up and down language ought to be left behind as misleading. Such words can remain if they're an aid to our imagination but not as descriptions of spiritual realities.

God's personal existence within us is given frequent expression in biblical imagery. We are a *home* in which the Father dwells. Theology would say that God's coming within us creates His dwelling, which I would propose is the proper understanding of *sanctifying grace*. St. Ambrose (AD 339–397), the bishop who converted and baptized St. Augustine, elaborates how we are God's home: "Let your door stand open to receive Him, unlock your soul to Him, offer Him a welcome in your mind, and then you will see the riches of simplicity, the treasures of peace, the joy of grace." *Temple* is another biblical image. God comes to dwell in us as in a temple. "Do you not know that you are the temple of God and that the Spirit of God dwells in you" (1 Cor 3:16). Small wonder that temple imagery came so readily to St. Paul, Jew that he was, since it echoes the divine presence of Yahweh in Solomon's Temple, where God is described as overshadowing the Ark of the Covenant.

The identification of sanctifying grace with God's personal presence within us may become clearer by recalling earlier catechism teachings on grace. "A sacrament bestows sanctifying grace" and "Ask God for the actual grace to avoid temptations." Even though the sanctifying grace vs. actual grace distinction is hardly ever preached these days, actual grace was understood as a divine empowerment to do this or that activity. Sanctifying grace was harder to describe other than to say that if mortal sin was present, it was not. The mistake was to think of sanctifying grace as a *thing*, as a something that could come and go, and to think of actual grace as a sort of empowering fuel. My parish church for over a year has had a poster in the lobby suggesting activities to receive the "outpouring of grace." I realize no one would say grace is anything like a liquid but the language makes it sound like a divine liquid. Rightly understood, sanctifying grace is the divine presence within us. The Father's presence—that of Jesus and the Holy Spirit as well because God arrives as the triune God—molds the temple He inhabits. Viewed from the angle of us as a temple dwelling, we are sanctified by the arrival of God. Viewed from what does the sanctifying, it is the indwelling Trinity or it can be ascribed specifically to the Holy Spirit. This is what the catechism phrase, *sanctifying grace*, means. To "receive" sanctifying grace, or to "have" sanctifying grace, simply means to "be entered into" by God, to "possess" God. Without coercing my freedom, God leads me from within to do good and avoid evil. There is no harm in calling this divine shepherding action the workings of actual grace.

ON BELIEF AND LACK OF BELIEF

Let me at this point work in what I've come to think about belief and unbelief, about being an atheist or being a theist. I start with a conclusion about which I have become more and more convinced. Being an atheist is a choice. Being a theist is a choice. There are many books today presenting arguments for atheism or for theism but one must be cautious about the word *argument*. When an argument is logically convincing, the conclusion is forced upon one's mind. Choice has no role in accepting the conclusion. Reasoning impels it. Geometry provides many clear examples, and here is one. Call the length of the sides of a right triangle A and B, and call C its diagonal length. It is fairly easy to prove the formula that $C^2 = A^2 + B^2$.

I used to read books by atheists, thinking my theism needed to be protected by seeing where the atheistic argument went wrong. But I saw that their arguments did not lead to a logical certitude ruling out the existence of God. What I did see in these books was the making of a case that no God existed, but the conclusion needed to be chosen, by an act of one's will, as plausible. The arguments never reached the certitude that the above geometric argument reaches. One such argument, and a tough argument it indeed is, goes this way: "If God exists, then God is supreme Goodness and underpins a good universe. But evils exist. The experience of evils, which cannot be denied, is incommensurate with believing in God." But note carefully: This is not a conclusive proof against God's existence. It certainly presents a difficulty with belief in God. But the atheism it might invite involves a choice, not a logical compulsion.

Other arguments for atheism come from scientists who insist on empirical evidence for the existence of whatever. Empirical thinking is a mode of inquiry that has proven its worth in beneficial scientific discoveries, especially in the world of diseases. If you begin in demanding that one must show, by measurement or experiment, the existence of X and the non-existence of Y, then you impose on the question under debate your quantitative way of reasoning. It works for the visible world where matter is measurable but not for the invisible world. And even in the visible world, when the subject under consideration tends toward the invisible, the "measurement only" requirement falters. For example, if you are a happily married scientist, your way of empirical knowing can never certify why your choice of a spouse was logically or empirically determined. I don't think spouse selections are blind choices. I think they are warranted, but the way of knowing in these situations is of a different nature from a scientific investigation and its way of knowing.

There are a whole host of other ways people are or end up atheists. I think some believers become atheists through an experience already mentioned, when I used the metaphor of *one thousand unanswered prayers*. "I have prayed unceasingly that my little son would not die of cancer, but he did. Where were you, God, in my time of need?" I can understand why people give up on God. Are these people really atheists? Not in the sense of proclaimed atheists such as Richard Dawkins, Christopher Hitchens and others who write books wishing to undermine religious belief as antithetical to being "really human." I think people who have given up on God because of the overwhelming pain and disappointment they have experienced need another name for themselves than the name we use for programmatic atheists. Whatever name might fit them, these people have come to be where they are, through choice. But I've come to think that it is not a choice for which God holds them accountable, by which I mean they are not being excluded from heaven.

On the other hand, what about making the case for the existence of God? The famous philosopher and theologian, St. Anselm of Canterbury, argued that the existence of God is immediately evident to the intellect once you accept the concept of God as "that greater than which nothing can be conceived." Later philosophers such as Descartes (AD 1596–1650) accepted the same validity of arguing from the mental notion of God to God's existence outside the mind. But other philosophers rejected this leap from the mental (the notion of God) to the extramental, one of them being St. Thomas Aquinas, writing 150 years after Anselm. He said that if your mind could have a concept of divinity as such, Anselm's argument works. But the human mind cannot grasp divinity in a direct manner. The human mind is made for grasping empirical realities. Call them created realities, as Aquinas did. From a metaphysical analysis of them, you can make an argument for God's existence as creation's ground and cause. But this is an indirect approach, an argument by way of drawing inferences.

Let that daunting word *metaphysical* suggest how unsuitable for most people is the method of Aquinas on behalf of God's existence. Cardinal Newman, no incompetent when it came to theistic matters, was never persuaded by such arguments. For him, the argument from the testimony of conscience to the existence of an exterior "Moral Governor," to whom our behavior and conduct are accountable, was persuasive. Newman thought it a more congenial argument for other people he knew. The Moral Governor is the voice of God within you prompting the doing of good and the avoiding of evil. When the voice is obeyed, peace ensues, and when it is disobeyed, guilt ensues. Of the argument from conscience, and of other arguments offered for theism, none of them will ever convince with the clarity that the proof of the Pythagorean Theorem possesses concerning a right triangle. The theistic arguments are not wrong; they are simply of a nature that invites a choice following the mental process of mulling them over. (If a seasoned philosopher is convinced of the logical cogency of a metaphysical argument, this is a different matter. This is where church teachings mislead in maintaining that the existence of God can be proven by reason.)

For these reasons I maintain that belief in God is a choice a person makes, just as atheism is a choice. Of these choices, I add two observations. Choices ought not to be blind. I grant that some people are theistic somewhat blindly, and some have accepted atheism for themselves equally untested. But for those who are conscientiously one or the other, their choices have warrants. The warrants are like plausible arguments. Let me give you the testimony of a scientist with whom I used to work out (played handball at Emory University) years ago. He was a professor in the medical school. His research was in embryology. He used to tell me of the thousands upon thousands of things that need to happen, and timed correctly, for a human embryo to arrive at healthy birth. He studied these processes to discover how medical science can help pregnancies when trouble appeared during the gestation period. Most pregnancies, of course, unfold in a healthy manner. He was profoundly struck by the immense complexity of gestation that seemed to unfold on its own, driven by the nature of things, such that he could not conceive of a human world not governed by God. His belief in God was a choice, not blindly made however, but with a warrant that was personally and powerfully persuasive to him.

My second observation is directed against thinking that I reduce warrants to sheer relativity. Granting that the choices for theism or atheism advance warrants in most cases, I would contend that the warrants for theism are stronger and more varied than those for atheism. The evidence that they are more varied reflects the pervasive belief in God in many cultures and over many centuries. One would have to be very cynical to claim that all those people, over all that time, arrived at belief blindly. I use the word god in a wide sense. I refer to the monotheistic god of Jews (Yahweh or Adonai), of Christians (Abba), of Muslims (Allah), and of Sikhs (Waheguru), to the polytheism of Hindus (Vishnu, Shiva, etc.) and to the personal being or Buddha of Mahayana Buddhism.

It would not be a valid counterargument to say, "Well, look at all the atheism in China." How was all that atheism arrived at? Imposition rather than freely-made choice is my answer for the mandated social order Mao Zedong bequeathed. Because the warrants for or against belief in God are very personal, and differ practically with the person and her experiences, to contend that theistic warrants for belief in God are stronger must simply remain my personal persuasion. But most important and not to be forgotten is that either believing in God or not believing are choices people make.

NAMES FOR GOD

Words for God should be considered in a chapter asking what God is like. Naming is the normal way we examine most things. Some names for God possess a referent. God is called Father, or Abba in Jesus' Aramaic language. We have a notion what human fathers do, and God is something like that. Jesus used this analogy. "What father would give his son a stone when the son needed bread? If you know how to give your children what's good, how much more will your Father in heaven give good things to those in need?" Other names work in this same direction. God is my Savior. God is my Shepherd. The name itself possesses an indication of God's nature by having us recall how a human being has saved us or how a herdsman works with sheep. On the other hand, there are names for God that have no referent. The name g-o-d is very interesting and important to me because it lacks all human or worldly references. *Bóg* (rhymes with Luke in pronunciation), the Polish word for God and used so often by Pope John Paul II, is the same. It names God without trying to specify God by a human referent. The word reminds us that God outstrips all our conceptualization and imagination. The simple word *God* reminds me of Aquinas's teaching that no human intellect or imagination can capture God's essence.

But that's a problem. If our human minds cannot grasp and capture conceptually the infinite nature of God, what's the use of words about God? Are they not like shooting arrows into darkness without taking aim? What is called the *analogical* use of words gets me out of this cul de sac. I learned it from Thomas Aquinas, and it enables me to describe my faith in God in a simple direct way without ever suggesting that I have now come to grasp God's essence. Certain words are *metaphorical*, such as calling God a rock. "Yahweh is my rock, my fortress" (Ps 18:3). The word is proportional, meaning that God supports me in the way that rocks stabilize a railroad track. *Analogy* is more than proportion, and this example gets closer. Food is healthy. Health does not really describe food. It describes a person's balanced organism. But because food contributes to metabolic balance, we can term it healthy. But these two words, *rock* and *health*, do not properly describe God and never can. Our notions of them remain locked into and restricted to material realities, rocks and healthy organisms. But what if we can think of something from our material environment, the application of which is not restricted to material things but can be stretched through intuition beyond the material that was the original source of the word. I noted earlier that poetry is a word-stretching endeavor. "She walks in beauty like the night" (Lord Byron).

Words like *person, wise, merciful, loving* seem elastic enough to be stretched toward the unlimited, toward the immaterial. My concepts of these words come from my grasp of human persons, wise persons, loving persons. But I can mentally shed from such concepts the imperfections in which they are realized in people. I never have a concept of God's wisdom because God is beyond intellectual grasp. But the language of being wise, taken from my experience of wise people, can be applied to God analogically through an intuition of how the word can be stretched beyond its usual usage. We do not have analogical concepts of anything but we can use words analogically and apply some of them properly to God. God is wise in a pre-eminent manner. Personhood describes the reality of God when personhood is stripped of all the limitations I experience in understanding, grasping, having concepts of persons I have known.

Let me describe how a warrant for believing in God and a word to apply to God analogically come together for me, personally. In those meditative moments to which I am inclined, I draw into myself and reflect on my very existence. Who am I and why do I exist at all? I begin to experience a reality that seems other than I am, one I did not fabricate. I experience myself sustained, propped up in existence. And the more I think of myself in this manner, I intuit—that is, not directly viewing and conceptualizing—its source, its ground. It is other than I am. I am not my own explanation for existing. The vague and confused awareness coming from this introspection I have about being real, about existing, becomes an intuition of the source of my existence and the source of all things existing. This self-reflection leads to a word, which can be applied analogically to God. He is *pure existence*.

The phrase, while true to my experience, strikes me as too philosophical and offsetting for readers. So let me begin again, this time saying that I experience myself as being created and as being sustained in creation. It is not two different experiences; it is two sides of the one meditative experience. I am not my own explanation why I am. I intuit God as my creator. Had I begun with describing myself as *created* and intuiting God *Creator*, someone might object that you begin with creation by assuming the conclusion, Creator. So I began with the story of reflecting on my own propped-up existence.

These discussions might have been easier to present of what is God like if I had come to faith from atheism. But I did not. I believed in God life long, in the way one is nurtured by family and church into theism and at some point at more mature age owning it as my own choice. Conversions from atheism to belief, however, have a drama and language all their own. Years ago I was much taken by the French play, *The Satin Slipper*. Because of the sensitive handling of the relationship in it between Rodrigue and Doña Prouhèze, the personal life of the playwright attracted me. Paul Claudel grew up Catholic but quit it and abandoned belief in God as he became more involved in diplomatic work and playwriting. But his personal life grew more depressed over the years. One dark rainy 1886 Christmas evening, he entered Notre Dame in Paris when the *Magnificat* of Vespers was being sung. "Such was the miserable tyke" (*Tel était le malheureux enfant*) were his words for the depression he carried into the Cathedral. But his words from *My Conversion* continue: "I stood near the second pillar at the entrance to the chancel, to the right, on the side of the sacristy" next to a fourteenth-century statue of the Virgin and Child. "Then occurred the event which dominates my entire life. In an instant, my heart was touched and I believed. I believed with such a strength of adherence, with such an uplifting of my entire being, with such powerful conviction, with such a certainty leaving no room for any kind of doubt, that since then all the books, all the arguments, all the incidents and accidents of a busy life have been unable to shake my faith, nor indeed to affect it in any way." Was it the Gregorian chant? Was it a fourteenth-century Madonna looking down on him? I think he would say, "I was overcome by the God I had forsaken who was welcoming me back home."

Edith Stein's conversion was similar but not with Claudel's suddenness. She was raised a Jew, was an atheist by her teen years, went to university to study philosophy with Edmund Husserl, and at some point began reading the Spanish Carmelite mystic, Teresa of Avila (AD 1515–1582). Soon thereafter, she embraced belief in God, got baptized into the Catholic Church, taught for some years in a Dominican Sisters school in Speyer, and became a Carmelite cloistered nun herself in 1933 with the name Teresa Benedicta of the Cross. When the Nazis began hunting Jews and Jewish converts to Christianity, she was sent to a Carmelite monastery in the Netherlands for her protection, but she was not able to avoid later arrest. She was dispatched to Auschwitz where she was exterminated in 1942. I think Edith, the atheist intellectual, was overcome by the human genuineness of Teresa's prayer life. It simply possessed her and highlighted an emptiness in herself. Without trying to fathom what else went on within the hearts (souls) of Claudel and Stein, I would simply quote St. Augustine and maintain it was God who converted them. Here are Augustine's words, one of the most profoundly succinct statements I've ever read about conversions. "God is the one who builds, admonishes, instills fear, opens the mind, and *bends perceptions* to the act of belief."[3] Whatever perceptions Claudel and Stein were experiencing, God bent them toward himself.

What about calling God a *person*? This is as important a name as anything else in saying what God is like. The name seems so simple and so unnecessary of validation. If prayer is talk, and I like to think of prayer as honest talk, Catholics need no convincing that they are praying to a person who is God. It is person to person. It's God and me. But what about naming God as Three Persons, as the Anglican poet and priest John Donne (AD 1572–1631) does in the famous words, "Batter my heart, three-person'd God, for you as yet but knock, breathe, shine, and seek to mend"? Catholics grow up with the catechism answers. Jesus has two natures, the human and the divine, united in one divine person. Jesus is not two persons. On the other

---

3. Italics mine. Augustine's commentary on *Ps* 126: Ipse [Deus] aedificat, ipse monet, ipse terret, ipse intellectum aperit, ipse ad fidem *applicat sensum vestrum. Corpus Chrisianorum Latinorum* 40:1858.

hand, God is one divine nature existing as three persons. The Trinity does not mean three gods. These two catechism answers are easy to mouth but practically impossible to grasp. What could I hope to share about my belief in God, the Blessed Trinity, in a simple manner?

GOD AS BLESSED TRINITY

To write about the Trinity is to risk trying to decipher incomprehensible mystery, akin to the futility of Sisyphus pushing a bolder uphill, only to see it slip and roll back down time after time. No topic is more baffling. Nothing is more contentious among the three large monotheistic religions—Judaism, Christianity, and Islam. For Christians, nothing touches the essence of God more than the name *Trinity*.

First, some caveats. We Christians are monotheists. We believe in the oneness of God, as do Jews and Muslims. But they think we aren't really monotheists. They remain convinced that calling God three persons amounts to tritheism, the belief in three different Gods. Like Dante's words in his poem over the gate of *Inferno* (Italian for *hell*), "abandon all hope, you who enter," I would say the same to anyone trying to convince a Jew or a Muslim that three divine persons are compatible with the oneness of God.

This leads to a second caveat posed in question form. "Is belief in God as Trinity only based on Christian scriptures, then?" The direct and simple answer is yes. Two things need to be noted. God as Trinity is not found nor implied in the Tanak, although some Christian Evangelicals think it is, as when the opening chapter of *Genesis* reads, "Let us make human beings in our image, after our likeness." There the Hebrew word for God is *Elohim*. It is a word in plural form that intensifies how God is God, and hence the grammar requires the use of relative pronouns like *us* or *our*, as explained in chapter two. The New Testament does reveal distinct personhood in God, but it does so with certain ambiguity. Cardinal Newman's sage remark earlier about Unitarians and Trinitarians applies. Invite both to sit and read the New Testament. The former will get up still Unitarian. Same for the Trinitarians.[4]

Our Catholic tradition has used a distinction to sharpen the issues: the immanent Trinity and the economic Trinity. The former refers to the internal divine life, the inner essence of God. The latter refers to the actions of God on humankind in history. But of the divine essence, the *immanent Trinity*, no intellect can grasp it, and therefore speculations on how the three persons of God interact among themselves are problematic. I used to be attracted by St. Augustine's psychological descriptions of the inner workings of love in

4. In his letter of 10 September 1875 to an unknown correspondent. His point is that the Bible conveys revelation but it does not teach doctrines. Churches and catechisms do, e.g., "Wesleyan schools turn out Wesleyan pupils, Congregationalists Congregational youths....If the Bible teaches doctrine clearly, why do some readers rise from it Trinitarians, other Unitarians, and others Calvinists?" *Letters and Diaries of J. H. Newman* 27:353, hereafter *LD*.

the Trinity, but he was reaching into what cannot be known in itself and only known by analogies, which were no better than inferences.

The phrase *economic Trinity* was coined to express a more external view of the Trinity, *economy* meaning simply God's involvement with the world. Since God is Trinitarian by nature, all actions by God in the world are actions of the entire Trinity. But does this mean that we can detect that God is Trinitarian by analyzing the world of nature, much as a scientist might? No. The three-person'd God, to use John Donne's poetic phrase, leaves on creation no Trinitarian prints. On what, then, is conviction based that God is Trinitarian? The New Testament!

If it were not for the Incarnation, the becoming human of the Son of God—"and the word became flesh" (*Jn* 1:14)—there would be no awareness of multiple personhood in God. The *Gospel of John* provides the clearest assertion of the divinity of Jesus. According to New Testament scholar Raymond E. Brown, Thomas the Apostle's confession of "my Lord and my God" in the Upper Room (*Jn* 20:28) is an undeniable assertion in the biblical record of Jesus' divinity. What Jesus had always been from the moment of his conception becomes known eventually to his disciples by the impress of his life on them, through his Resurrection appearances especially. To this biblical fact one must couple the fact that Jesus prayed to Abba as his heavenly Father. He was praying to God. Jesus was not praying to himself because that makes no sense.

I am certain that Jesus did not think in the categories of Trinity that we do now, as if his human consciousness thought of himself as God the Son and that he was praying to another Person of the Trinity. Put simply, he prayed to God, the Maker of heaven and earth, the God of Abraham, Isaac, and Jacob, the God who led Israel through the desert. He prayed to Yahweh, with the intimacy *abba* suggests. Did he think of himself as God, and here I am referring to the *human consciousness* of Jesus? I think not. In his human awareness he was a monotheistic Jew. But in his introspection into his life and vocation, which drives anyone's self-consciousness, which drives the "who am I" question, it is my belief that he perceived a connectedness with God so unique that he began doing things that an observant Jew would call a sacrilege. For example, he forgave sins that worked appreciation and change in the sinner and worked malice in his detractors.

Bear in mind what I wrote in chapter one on how the Bible works, especially the New Testament, and why it was important to begin the book with this topic. There are insights from Stage Two (the period of resurrection appearances) and Stage Three (the period of gospel formation) into the nature of Jesus that are retroactively inserted into Stage One (the Palestinian ministry of Jesus) by the gospel writers. If I maintain that I do not think Jesus went about thinking he was God and calling himself God, as if his human consciousness had a Trinitarian mentality, then the text "the Father and I

are one" (*Jn* 10:30) is not a rebuttal. By the time of the Stage Three gospels in
the last third of the first century, Jesus is being confessed as divine, and this
appears expressly so in the *Gospel of John*. It is another thing, and for me a
wrong thing, to say that the divinity of Jesus was expressly known by his first
followers during Jesus's lifetime in Palestine because Jesus expressed himself
clearly on it.

During Jesus's ministry in Palestine, I think that he became increasingly
aware of a unique intimacy he enjoyed with Abba, causing what I would
call the unfolding of "a functional divinity." He *did* things hitherto restricted
to God in Jewish thought. His behavior bespoke an intimacy with God that
later on will be termed an identity, and this is why he acted as he did. He
will come to be confessed as having the same nature as Abba, as Son of the
Father, in the words of the Nicene Creed.[5] But the Creed is clear: By Incarnation, he entered human life as divine; he doesn't become divine later even
if his disciples came only to recognize it later.

To sum up thus far my belief in the Trinity in as simple a manner as I can
forge: God the Father is the One to whom Jesus prayed. I perceive the Father
as the background mystery from which all originates, the primal Source as
it were. The Father is the foundation of existence from which everything
proceeds. God the Son is the personal identity of the human nature of Jesus.
As the Son, Jesus is the image, the reflection, of the Father's nature. In my
prayer, sometimes I pray to Abba, sometimes to the Risen Jesus, and mostly
simply to God as God.

God the Holy Spirit presents a difficulty for me in which I do not stand
alone. The separate personal identity of God the Holy Spirit remained
unclear at first.[6] Adopting a principle mentioned earlier about ecumenical
councils, namely, that their infallible teaching role comes into play when an
important truth is unclear or denied outright by some Christians, it was not
until the First Council of Constantinople (AD 381) that the divinity of the Holy
Spirit as a distinct person within the Trinity was taught definitively. This is
not to imply that earlier Christians were ignorant of the Holy Spirit's distinct identity—Saints Basil (330–379), his brother Gregory of Nyssa (331–395),
and their friend Gregory Nazianzus (329–389) preached passionately about the
Holy Spirit prior to the Council—nor is it being implied that it is not revealed
in the New Testament. It is only to note that it was an ambiguous truth in
earliest Christian reflection.

Regarding my belief in the Holy Spirit, the key scripture for me is *Jn*
7:37-39. Jesus is in Jerusalem during the Jewish festival of Sukkoth, an au-

---

5. The phrase *Son of God* in the Tanak does not mean divinity, only being righteous and
being special to God, as in *Wis* 2:18, *2 Sm* 7:14, or *Ps* 2:7.

6. The *Catechism of the Catholic Church* (1994), referencing *Jn* 14:17, 26; 16:13 presents the
Holy Spirit revealed as "another divine person" in the Last Supper promise of Jesus to send
"another Paraclete" (Advocate). See § 243.

tumn pilgrimage feast associated with grape harvesting and water. Jesus calls out, "Let anyone who thirsts come to me and drink. Whoever believes in me, as scripture says, 'Rivers of living water will flow from within him.'" The gospel writer then adds the clarification, "He said this in reference to the Spirit that those who came to believe in him were to receive. There was, of course, no Spirit yet, because Jesus had not yet been glorified."

Jesus becomes glorified when he passes through death into immediate resurrection; otherwise, the Incarnation would have come to a pause, which is unthinkable. His human nature, assumed at the Incarnation, becomes a life-giving entity, a Spirit-bestowing reality, in his being exalted to glorification. The resurrection of Jesus enables the bestowal of the Holy Spirit into the world, into the so-called *economy* of salvation, which is not only then in Palestine but also in the future and also retroactively into ages past. (Later I treat my belief in retroactivity of God's actions in and through the historical Jesus.)

Jn 7 enables me to grasp the working of the Trinity in a kind of unity, which of course has to be if it is to be the Trinitarian expression of the one single godhead. Jesus, ever the Divine Son, spends a human life and exercises his human freedom doing the will of Abba, his Father in heaven. He remains steadfast to his calling of preaching the reign (kingdom) of God even to the point of being killed for it. To Abba he prays from the Cross, "Into your hands I commit my life and its purposes," the very prayer all of us ought to say on our deathbeds. Abba responds by raising the human nature of Jesus into resurrection, and from the realm of glorification—sitting at God's right hand in biblical language—Jesus sends forth the Holy Spirit into other human hearts. The *Passover event* of Jesus, death into resurrection, unleashes the ultimate divine gift for people, surpassing simply being created in God's image (as in *Genesis*). It achieves a kind of deification of people by bestowing the Holy Spirit into them as into a temple, as an indwelling. Let us call the gift of indwelling a *Pentecost event*, described at first in the Upper Room "on the first day of the week" in *Jn* 20, that is, on the day after Sabbath (Shabbat); it is also described happening on the fiftieth day after Passover in *Acts*, and lastly it happens in any Catholic baptismal ceremony by using water (death and rising) and chrism oil (symbolizing the gift of the Holy Spirit).

I think I've come close to St. Basil's notion of the Holy Spirit as "the manifestation [in ourselves] of the divinity" of the resurrected Jesus but I lack his profoundness. Hear Basil himself:

> A spiritual person is one who no longer lives by the flesh [lives in a sinful fashion] but is led by the Spirit of God and is called a son of God, remade in the likeness of God's [own] Son. As the power of sight is active in a healthy eye, so the Holy Spirit is active in a purified soul….As the Father is seen in the Son, so the Son is seen in the Spirit….As we

speak of worship in the Son because the Son is the image of God the Father, so we speak of worship in the Spirit because the Spirit is the manifestation of the divinity of the Lord. Through the light of the Spirit, we behold the Son, the splendor of the Father's glory, and through the Son, the very *stamp* of the Father, we are led to him [Abba] who is the source of both his stamp, who is the Son, and of its *seal*, who is the Holy Spirit.

The image of light pervades Eastern theology, like Basil's above. God dwells in boundless light. Baptism is enlightenment. Faith is a light within us. The Holy Spirit enables a believer to see Jesus as the reflection (stamp) of the Father's glory or light. The Holy Spirit is the seal of our gifted enlightenment. *Seal* is a wonderful descriptor for the notion of being bonded with God and not easily shunted aside. We grow up thinking that when we do really bad things, God decides to go away from us. But think of God as entering into us and not wishing to be budged away. It is a feature of God to come to us bonded.[7]

A BRIEF SUMMATION

To sum up what I think God is like, as a way to conclude this chapter, I approach the most baffling portion of our faith, God as Trinity. I confess God the Father by thinking of God, of Abba, as the background mystery to all that exists, as the sustaining reality from which all originates, but who, as Abba, is as intimate and personal to me, even infinitely more so, as any human father or mother strives to be. I do not think of Abba as masculine, just personal, without gender. My wife calls Abba "my almighty friend," and this captures it, too. I think of God the Son as the humanization of God, as God experiencing the world in the manner Jesus did, fully, without caveats save one, namely, "like us in all things except sin" (Heb 4:15). This means Jesus was tempted. No temptation was off the table. No human joy was disallowed, either. He laughed with friends over stories, he shared meals with friends. He felt a mother's embrace. Perhaps one human joy was disallowed, and this by reason of his call to celibacy. He did not have the joy of holding a son or daughter in his arms. Weighing this possibility of what he was never meant to enjoy became also a temptation, of course, in his life. Not all temptations are toward sins. The Jewish men with whom he surrounded himself were married with children. If he was tempted to swerve from his messiahship, as the Satan temptations in *Matthew* and *Luke* recount, then he would have been

7. Basil's text is in his book, *Peri Tou Agiou Pneumatos* (On the Holy Spirit), *PG* 32:186, at the very end of chap. 26. His word for seal, sphargis, has the same import as the Latin sacramentum, the seal or oath of a soldier, marking him for membership in a Roman Legion. Medieval theology taught the idea of the sacramental characters or seals of Baptism, Confirmation, and Ordination, as being marked lifelong, hence unrepeatable sacraments.

tempted to swerve from his celibate calling because in traditional Judaism covenant people are meant to marry and have children. All of this became the experience of God by reason of "the Word becoming flesh." This is what Son of God of the Trinity means to me. The Holy Spirit means the divine reality that Jesus Christ in his risen and glorified humanity bestows on all called to salvation. The Holy Spirit is the invisible world impacting the visible world, to use the words of Cardinal Newman.

The bestowal of the Holy Spirit into me means my becoming almost divine. Some of the Church Fathers dare to leave out the world *almost*, but they do not mean pantheism, as if suggesting we humans become divine and become the same substance as God. Listen again to St. Basil the Great: "Through the Spirit we become citizens of heaven, we are admitted to the company of angels, we enter into eternal happiness, we abide in God. Through the Spirit we acquire a likeness to God; indeed, we attain what is beyond our most sublime aspirations—we become God." Basil's friend, St. Gregory Nazianzen, writes similarly: "What is this new mystery surrounding me....I am to be buried with Christ and to rise again with him, to become a coheir with him, a son of God, and indeed God himself." A fine and orthodox theologian like the medieval German mystic, Meister Eckhart (AD 1260–1328), had to so stretch German and Latin words to describe his mystical experience of sheer connectedness with the Trinity with the result that some critics have thought him a pantheist and therefore a heretic. They simply mistake the exuberance of mystical language.

In my faith about God entering into me, I have become convinced more and more that the true orthodox understanding of an abiding God, of sanctifying grace as the indwelling of the Trinity, is not pantheism but it is close to it. I must correct my wording. *Entering into* doesn't quite capture it because it seems to keep apart who enters and what is entered into. *Being absorbed by* is better language. It captures what God's indwelling achieves. God's reality absorbs me. My identity, which is never abandoned, shares in, participates in, is joined with, the nature of God. But what repetition of verbs can ever express being divinely absorbed?[8]

Our real fault is not by drawing too close to asserting pantheism—that God and I are the same in all ways—but in distancing ourselves from God's presence in wishing to feel humble or unworthy or disrespecting God's total transcendence, as I think much in Protestantism does. It was people like the Evangelist we call John, and St. Basil, and St. Gregory Nazianzus, and a little of Eckhart thrown in, with perhaps my contemplative bent coming in play, that has brought me to this conviction that Trinitarian indwelling is almost pantheism. If at the end of time we read that God will be all in all, why can't

8. My professor colleague and frequent proofreader on my behalf, Dr. Breslin, asked if being absorbed would have any application to receiving Holy Communion. See chapter seven.

God begin achieving it now?

I observed that the Risen Jesus bestows the Holy Spirit according to that significant passage in *John* 7. Jesus, in his dying moments, handed over his human life to the Father: "Into your hands I commend my spirit." And the Father raised Jesus from death into glory. It means, then, that the Holy Spirit flows from the relationship between Father and Son, between Abba and Jesus. The reflections of St. Thomas Aquinas on the Trinity utilized the biblical notions of processions, the Spirit coming from the Father/Son relationship, and the Son who proceeds from the Father, such as the many "The Father has sent me" texts in *John*.

Do I understand how God is one divine nature in three persons? Not at all. Will I, one day? Yes. I quote from an early pope who has in recent years become one of my favorite writers. "What mind can conceive, what words can express the great happiness of seeing God? Yet human nature will achieve this when it has been transformed so that it sees the Godhead 'no longer in a mirror or obscurely but face to face,' the Godhead that no man or woman has been able to see. In the inexpressible joy of this eternal vision, human nature will possess 'what eye has not seen or ear heard, what the human heart has never conceived'" (from a sermon of Pope Leo the Great on the beatitudes in *Matthew*).

It is all right to use words that you do not fully understand. This is clear in a marriage vow. "I take you for better or worse, etc." At the moment of making the vow, who would dare to say, "I grasp all it means?" It is even truer in Christian prayer. We pray to the one God but we use Trinitarian language that eludes full grasp. "We ask this, Father, through Jesus Christ your Son, who lives and reigns with you and the Holy Spirit." Or again, "Let us begin our prayer, 'In the name of the Father and of the Son and of the Holy Spirit.'" It is my belief that God is OK with the prayer when we pray in the darkness of understanding, so to speak. This, again, is what I think God is like. God accepts our words because He accepts us.

CHAPTER FOUR

On Prayer

"Prayer is the one thing that can conquer God." Tertullian (AD 160–225)[1]

Having just finished a chapter on what God is like, I turn now to the topic of praying. Wouldn't a chapter about Jesus make logical sense coming next, you might wonder? But I think the topic of prayer, touching as it does on crucial emphases that have just come before, makes more sense. God is personal. In fact, God is three persons, Father, Son, and Holy Spirit. You and I are persons. An important part of us, as important as anything else, is the need to communicate with other persons, to talk to them, to listen to them. And this would go with God who is more deeply personal than we can imagine. Prayer is personal dialogue with God.

Another element in the last chapter that connects intimately with praying is atheism. This looks misleading at first sight. If you are an atheist, you don't pray. That's very true. But I am thinking of persons who have become atheists though at one time in their lives believed in God. They are not atheists in the programmatic sense like Richard Dawkins and others who argue the case that God is a delusion and who seem to crusade in their publications against the foolishness of belief in the divine. No, the persons I envision have somehow slipped into nonbelief and make no clamor about themselves or what they previously accepted. I think of them as functional atheists, meaning that they look like atheists from the outside but the actual word is too mean-spirited to describe them. They are among that growing cadre of Americans, larger in number than any single Christian church, who are called *nones*,[2] meaning those who would check off *none* when filling out a survey asking for

1. "Sola est oratio quae Deum vincit." *Corpus Christianorum Latinorum*, I, "De Oratione" XXIX, 274.
2. Cardinal Newman, that great master of prose and poetry, coined a word for the nones of his day in the 1860s, fashioned after legitimate words like Trinitarian and Latitudinarian: nothingarian. "I should have the greatest repugnance [to use arguments to unsettle the solid religious views of Anglicans in Oxford]....Altogether another thing in a place like Birmingham, where nearly everyone is a nothingarian, an infidel, a sceptic." *LD* 19:352.

one's religious affiliation. I am convinced that some of the nones, not all of them, gave up on a prayer life, and the reality of God slipped as much into irrelevance as they slipped out of churches and synagogues. To believe in God and maintain a prayer life is crucial.

PRELIMINARIES

There are two preliminaries that need stating before I describe what praying has come to mean to my faith in it. The first one begins with a denial. I am not a two-dimensional or two-levelled person composed of a body and soul as if my body is just an outer garment to my soul, as if my soul or human spirit merely inhabits my body from the inside, as if my soul is really more fittingly aligned with my brain than it is with my hands or any other bodily part. I am an undivided unity.

Although having a physical body, for this is what medical personnel examine and test, I think of myself as a spiritualized body, or conversely, as an enfleshed spirit. The application to praying will be made shortly but for the moment this much can be said: It isn't that my soul prays and my body is along for the ride. My soul and my body can be mentally distinguished but they are not separate realities. Thus when I am praying and I become distracted, I cannot blame distractions on my imagination or memories and leaving my soul the victim, as if my spirit wanted to keep on praying but got sideswiped by my body. I was praying and I got distracted. The same holds in a positive vein. I was praying and I began to cry. It isn't that my body could not contain without emoting what my spirit was about. It is simply that I prayed with tears. So did St. Augustine just before his conversion in Milan. So did St. Dominic during Mass. So did Jesus.

Bodily postures are not unconnected with prayerfulness. Kneeling, sitting, walking, standing with arms extended, all these features are expressions of prayer and not accidental attachments. St. Dominic (AD 1170–1221), the Spanish-born founder of itinerant preachers who continue to this day and bear his name, is reported to have used nine prayer postures, such as a maintained bow, being prostrate on the floor, standing with arms extended in the form of a cross, standing with arms raised aloft, and five others. In my experience, sitting comfortably is a very suitable posture for praying or meditating. Kneeling in a church pew, quietly recollected, is a powerful image of Catholics at prayer. We needn't have yoga practitioners remind us of the value of postures as they search for mindfulness and as we Christians seek prayerfulness.

The second preliminary concerns different types of praying. Vocal prayers and meditative prayers were met already in the Foreword. The vocal prayers could have been done all alone or with others, as mentioned. But I did not mention yet another type: not simply praying to Jesus but also praying with him, as if swept up into his own praying. This for me is the most intense and fruitful way of praying, and if examined properly it is what our Catholic faith affirms as the way above all others. It deserves its special treatment in a short while.

DOES PRAYING WORK?

I think that the great challenge to praying, or let's just call it maintaining a prayer life, is to wonder if it works. Is it worthwhile doing? Am I just talking to myself when I think that I am directing the vocalized promptings of my heart to a listening God? And what about unanswered prayers that concern precious things, such as for a spouse with cancer who nevertheless dies, leaving behind young children? These are real questions that cannot be merely brushed aside as temptations to abandon prayer. For this reason, and in fact to provide my reasoned insight, I want to begin with a consideration of the question, is praying worthwhile? I have come across only one answer that makes sense to me. If there are other answers, which make sense to you, my readers, then be thankful you have them, because without an answer to the *is-it-worthwhile* question, people give up on praying. And when prayer slips away, everything else of the invisible world undergoes slow evaporation from our real apprehension of it, to use two phrases from Cardinal Newman mentioned when discussing *Style of Writing*. The spiritual becomes unreal. The *invisible* world becomes merely *notional*.

St. Thomas Aquinas, and St. Augustine almost eight centuries before him, are the two greatest influences on Western Christianity (that is, on Latin-speaking Catholicism) who have shaped my thinking. Both have asked the question, why pray if God already knows what we need? Their mention provides me occasion to share how they differ from each other in their basic orientations, and why it is that Aquinas's explanation of the value of praying answers better a person's skepticism about doing it. To distinguish these great theologians, I offer two code words: *desiring* and *reasoning*. Augustine's fundamental orientation is from the human heart and the value of desiring. Aquinas's orientation is from the human mind and the value of thinking something through. This is seen in their respective answers to whether praying is worthwhile if God already knows our needs.

Augustine wrote a lengthy letter to a noblewoman of the Western Empire, Anicia Faltonia Proba, a widow living in North Africa when they corresponded. "Why God should ask us to pray," Augustine writes her, "when he knows what we need before we ask, may perplex us if we do not realize that our Lord and God does not want to know what we want, for he cannot fail to know it, but he wants us rather to exercise our desire through our praying so that we may be able to receive what He prepares to give us. His gift is very great indeed but our capacity is too small to take it in....The deeper our faith, the stronger our hope, the greater our desire, the larger will be our capacity to receive a gift very great indeed." Desiring changes us; it enlarges our receptivity. This is common sense to anyone who has fallen in love. Augustine addresses the value of praying by focusing on the human person, her desires, his longings. But to a person turned off from praying, it leaves untreated why praying makes any kind of a claim on God, to borrow the quotation from Tertullian at this chapter's beginning. As true as Augustine's answer is, something more is needed, at least for me.

Thomas Aquinas lived when Western universities were beginning in the late twelfth and thirteenth centuries, those of Paris, Oxford, Bologna and Padua. His style of writing, and therefore thinking, reflected university culture. A professor's life was centered predominantly upon arguing a case, either a disputed topic or an exposition of a biblical book. Academic debates formed its background. Accordingly, reasoned arguments lie at the center of Aquinas's orientation and differentiate it from Augustine's *desiring*. Is praying worthwhile? He makes the case that it is, and the heart of his case is that God, in that eternal gaze of Divine Providence that encompasses all human actions and hence our free decisions, has connected *answers* to our prayerful petitions on the condition that we have chosen to ask. The heart of the case, however, has other considerations that make it more compelling, and these await our attention just below. His line of reasoning has become more congenial to my need to know why praying works.

In a very fine teaching method that deserves more use today, Aquinas began a topic by providing objections against the position he was to take. He then gave the briefest reason to look at the matter in the other direction, that is, in his direction. Then he proceeded to argue the case. But being left with objections against his position, he needed to answer them from some principle contained in his argument, in the spirit of *1 Pt* 3:15, "providing others a reason for your hope." The entire endeavor was to support the reasonableness of the faith and of Christian behavior that the church professed. Here, then, are those above features, as he elaborates them in II-II, question 83, article two of his most famous writing, *The Summa of Theology*.[3]

Aquinas begins with three objections against praying. They are hardly pushovers; they have teeth. (1) Prayer seems necessary in order to make known to God our needs. But Jesus in *Mt* 6 tells us that our heavenly Father knows our needs before we ask. So why pray? (2) In prayer we seem to be asking for a change of mind in the God we beseech. But the mind of God is unchanging, as we read in *1 Kgs*, "the God of Israel will not be moved by

---

3. *Summa Theologiae* (hereafter *ST*). What he called an article, we term a question. What he called a question, we term a tract or major section of related materials. Major subdivisions, such as our II-II above, delineate the *Summa*'s structure (I, I-II, II-II, III). *ST* has 2669 articles spread among 512 questions. Aquinas's work on his overall scheme stopped abruptly before he could finish it. After his death in 1274, the scheme was supplemented with 99 other questions (446 articles), lifted from earlier writings by Thomas's companion and secretary, Reginald of Piperno.

repentance." So it is useless to pray to God. (3) It displays more generosity to give benefits to people who had not asked for them, than it is to bestow gifts on petitioners. Aquinas quotes the Roman philosopher Seneca in support of this idea. But our God is the most generous of beings. Therefore our God does not need to be asked for what we need in order for us to benefit to the full. Turning the three into street creed: God already knows; God's mind does not flip flop; a most generous God doesn't need asking.

On the other hand—the famous *Sed Contra* in Aquinas's Latin—Jesus tells us in *Lk* 18 to keep on praying and not lose heart. The *Sed Contra* is meant to make our mind pause after reading very poignant objections at the start.

Aquinas develops his case in what is called the *corpus*, or body, of the article. Ancient Greek philosophers, he begins, harbored three erroneous ideas about praying: (a) Human behavior is not subject to divine providence, and so it is useless to pray or even worship God; (b) All events in life, even our free decisions, happen by necessity either because the divine order is inflexible or because the stars decree what happens, and so it's useless to pray; (c) Human behavior does fall under God's ordered plan but this does not mean our behavior is compelled, because divine providence is variable and prayers can change God's intentions.

The right answer involves navigating between these three false approaches, and Aquinas will incorporate a philosophical principle clear to his medieval listeners but not so clear today, the distinction between a primary cause acting on a secondary cause. Let me insert myself for a moment before picking up Aquinas again. A musician (primary cause) plays a violin (secondary cause) and produces in sound an idea or feeling in the listener. Then he plays a cello. Someone can easily say "That's a cello producing the feeling, the other was a violin." Thus, the instrument is a cause of the unique sound, and the musician is a more significant cause of the sound itself. In this older language, the musician is the primary cause of an idea or feeling expressed in sound, and the instrument is a secondary cause of the emotional effect. The musician expresses herself in and through the instrument without destroying the nature of the instrument; on the contrary, she utilizes its nature. And so it will be in Aquinas's presentation, with God as the primary cause from the invisible world acting upon all realities of our visible world, including human free decisions, all these being secondary causes used by God to bring about what God intends. Keep in mind that the nature of the secondary causes, such free human choices, are not altered by God's actions in and through them, as if God coerces our freedom, any more than musicians misuse the nature of their instruments.

Back to Aquinas. As a causative action of the invisible world, God's providence, or God's shepherding of the world, disposes what happens in the visible world and also the manner in which things unfold, as well as the network of secondary causes in the unfolding.[4] Humanly-made free choices, such as choosing to pray or not pray, are among the secondary causes under God's sway. Therefore, situations coming from free human choices are foreseen by God and are not surprises to God that alter his shepherding of the world; rather, these human choices are implementing effects and situations in the manner foreseen and arranged by God, on analogy with the cello channeling the will of the musician.

As Aquinas navigates between false alternatives, his insight about secondary causes is not so easy to grasp because the language is unfamiliar. Let me take another stab at it. God's will for us, which includes his "answers" to our prayers, does not arise from a fixed, pre-determined, program; rather, God's will for us achieves itself in the unfolding of our freedoms, which, by the way, can also include the choice to sin. The achievement of God's plan, for each of us and for the whole world, is foreseen—not predetermined I must stress—in God's eternal gaze, in God's all-at-once knowledge of our daily lives and destinies. (Chapter six and Boethius reprise this important idea of eternity.) To sum up Aquinas's insight, I translate his concluding observation: "We don't pray in order to change God's mind. We do pray that we might secure that which God had arranged would have been obtained through our free choice to pray. In other words, people pray so that, as Pope Gregory says in his *Dialogues*, they might deserve to receive what God decreed to give them from all eternity, should they have prayed."

An immediate misunderstanding of this final observation would be that someone has missed out on so much one could have received because he or she did not pray all the time, or at the right time, or with the right words. Aquinas covers this misreading in answering objection three. Let me take his answers to the three objections in turn: (1) apropos God already knows what we need, we nevertheless pray not to inform an unknowing God what we need but to remind ourselves that in all matters we stand in need of God's support; (2) apropos wanting to change God's mind, praying does not alter God's providential plan but praying does obtain those benefits that in God's eternal plan were set only to have been obtained through prayer; (3) apropos a most generous God not needing to be beseeched, I quote his words in full: "God bestows on us so many things from his boundless generosity that were not even requested by us. But for our own benefit, God has decreed to bestow certain gifts upon our prayerful request. In this way, our trust in the power of prayer grows, and we grow in appreciation of God as the giver of all good

4. Some years ago I detailed a complex set of causes, many of them human choices, behind the closure of steel mills around Youngstown, Ohio, due to shareholder profit-taking and cheaper offshore Oriental steel products, one effect being the unexpected unemployment of Youngstown laborers raising families and paying off mortgages in the Mahoning Valley. See "Praying When Troubled: Retrieving Boethius and Aquinas," in *Theology and Lived Christianity*, ed. by David M. Hammond (Mystic CT: Twenty-Third Publications, 2000), 289-306.

gifts. Thus St. John Chrysostom teaches: 'Consider what happiness is given you, what honor is bestowed on you, when you talk with God in prayer, when you dialogue with Christ, when you ask what you will, whatever you desire.'"

If you were to ask a very prayerful person if prayer works, say an older person who has made praying part of her years-long life style, she would answer without hesitation, "of course." Does it mean she received each and every thing for which she prayed, and at that moment? Of course not. Does it mean that she has come to see, especially in retrospect, how God "answers her prayers?" Yes, even if what she precisely prayed for was not to be the answer. Does it mean that she has come to experience being supported by God, guided by the kindly Shepherd of souls, and this without any doubts, or to use Newman's early phrase, with a real apprehension of the divine Shepherd? Yes it does. Does she need to offer justifications for praying to counter someone of a skeptical mind? No. She would simply feel compassion for this other person who lacks what she experiences. This imagined dialogue with a prayerful older person—I am thinking of my memories of my maternal grandmother, Annie Collins, as I wrote it—expresses what I have come to believe about prayer.

But I go beyond her clear and simple faith by my need to have further reasons why praying is not useless. This is because I am the person I have become, who has a questioning mind and who seeks a reason for the faith I carry, and Aquinas often does it for me. To pray or forego praying is a free choice I make. God as a cause, as a bestower of blessings, works through my free choice to pray, the prayer itself being a secondary cause, to bring about the God-willed blessing. God causes the blessing. My prayer causes the blessing. They work together like the musician and the cello. This is my reasoned faith why praying is worthwhile.

But common sense must prevail. There is no numerical formula such that if I have prayed on ten straight days "without an answer," praying on the eleventh day would have achieved it as if by a secret formula God has set. I take Jesus' words about being persistent, to keep knocking on the door, with common sense, and so with a common sense approach I stick at it, just as I continue to pray these recent years for the healing of the autism afflicting my cousin's son, little Danny.

Nor is there a formula for success such that these precise words I use are not as good as other words I might have used. Common sense means choosing to pray when conscience prompts. But don't fall into second-guessing and don't become obsessive about it. The God to whom I pray is on my side. This must always be remembered. And God doesn't play tricks that make me second guess how or when to pray. Incantations go by timing formulas and verbal formulas, and these rules befit religious superstitions and exotic religions, not Christian praying.

TYPES OF PRAYER

You might have noticed that prayers of petition, asking prayers, were the assumed type being discussed above. This was a reasonable way for me to begin. Most people, at least in their personal prayers, ask for help in this matter, relief in that matter. Prayers of petition lie behind that classical expression for soldiers on the battlefield, "there are no atheists in foxholes." But prayers of petition are just one way of conversing with God. Another way of praying is in the form of thanksgiving. St. John Chrysostom, mentioned just above, was getting at this style of prayer when he said "What happiness is given you…when you talk with God in prayer." There is a painting of a man, whose French artist I now forget, Jean-François Millet perhaps because the person is a humble peasant, an old man, hardworking and likely widowed. He sits alone at a table with a simple meal before him. His gnarled hands are folded together in the way people pray and his head looks to his lap. You just know he is offering God thanks for this skimpy mid-day meal before he eats and returns to the fields. The painting has stuck in my imagination for years. It has become for me, in Newman's language, a real apprehension of thanksgiving prayer at work.

Prayers of petition make sense because of the hard and painful lives we have, but they become wearisome if they are the only way we converse with God. Praying needs the spice—perhaps leaven is a better word—of thanksgiving talk with God. Simple blessings do invade our lives. Our health, even if not 100%, is still a blessing. Our children, our spouses, this or that special friend, count as blessings for whom to thank God. Even deceased parents, long after grieving their deaths have passed, are memories worthy of a thanksgiving prayer in retrospect. "I thank you, Lord, for them and that they begot me, and thank you, Lord, that *you* incorporated them in my being brought about."

That old Catholic catechism already mentioned, the *Baltimore Catechism*, which was the staple of religious instruction years ago, still retains currency in many matters. It taught that praying fell into four types: adoration or praising God, contrition or asking forgiveness for sins, petition or seeing a need, and thanksgiving or expressing gratitude. For me petition and contrition amount to the same thing, asking God for a felt need, whether it's for forgiveness or for a benefit. Prayers of thanksgiving I've just mentioned. Prayers praising God remain for mention. I have been assuming that petitioning God and giving thanks are done as private prayers for most people but thanking or petitioning God in the company of others happens frequently, such as in church. Prayers of praise in my private moments don't come readily to me, and I suspect they don't to most. Praising God in a communal prayer has a natural fit.

Just yesterday Kathleen and I attended Sunday Mass with one of our sons. After the first reading there was a lovely antiphon sung by the congregation, "Praise the Lord, my soul," which was repeated after verses of *Ps* 148, itself labeled by scholars a psalm of praise. I don't doubt that I could have prayed the antiphon all by myself, in the quiet of my home or in the bucolic surroundings of a nearby park. Still, everyone in church singing the antiphon seemed to make so much a better and more natural fit for a prayer of praise.

Might parents feel ill at ease with their children in conducting communal prayers at home, whether of praise or thanksgiving or petition? I suspect many do and therefore hesitate to do it. An easy and non-embarrassing way to do communal family prayer is simply to pray before meals. Even that little bit shows the children that their parents pray and that they are not ashamed to show the children, and more than that, to include the children, when the parents pray at the meal table. When the children were very young and were being "put to bed," nighttime prayers achieved the same thing. The challenge, and it is not easy, is to remain a prayerful family in later years.

BRINGING "MY SOUL" TO PRAYER

Having used the phrase, *my soul*, in the praise antiphon above, now is a fitting time to describe what the word *soul* means to my faith. When I was young, and in the days of the *Baltimore Catechism*, I had no idea what it really meant but it seemed to be something invisible inside me. "Pray that God will save your soul," I was told. "Remember in November the poor souls in Purgatory," I was urged. When I got older and into philosophy, I met up with Plato and read about the soul being the really valuable part of you that was imprisoned in the body. That seemed to fit with those earlier days of the catechism. This Platonic tinge got replaced with what I have come to know as the rich and proper heritage of the Catholic tradition. The soul is simply another manner of referring to the real me in my fullness and unity. I am not composed of two parts, a *soul* really noble and godlike and the other feature being the less noble body housing the soul as if imprisoning it. It is all just I myself. It's me.

Thomas Merton (AD 1915–1968), like St. Augustine, led a life of dissipation—both fathered a child outside marriage—before converting to Catholicism, and, like Augustine, was a gifted writer. Merton became a Trappist monk—Cistercian is the proper name—in 1941 and spent the rest of his life in the Abbey of Our Lady of Gethsemani, Kentucky, writing dozens of books on spirituality. One semi-autobiographical book, *My Argument with the Gestapo*, written before his conversion and only published the year after his death, expressed his pre-conversion search for his true self. His words capture the above meaning of soul. "If you want to identify me, ask me not where I live, or what I like to eat, or how I comb my hair, but ask me what I think is keeping me from living fully for the thing I want to live for."

Here is another illustration, close to home for me, of the meaning of the soul. I have a relative who became engaged. The days approaching the wedding unfolded. The date with the church was arranged. The church-required pre-marriage preparations happened. The photographer, the musicians, and the venues were contracted. Even the wedding invitations were mailed. And then, in the very shadow of the ceremony, she felt she could not go through with it. It had nothing to do with falling out of love. It simply had to do with sensing herself in a false position, that such a commitment would not have involved "the real me" as I would translate her reluctance.

I think almost any one of us gets into situations where we ask ourselves, "Is this the real me or not?" There is no dichotomy here of body and soul in posing such a question to ourselves. It's just me in all of my inexpressible uniqueness. The word *soul* is an expression for the real me. If we use the phrase *my personhood*, it never seems to be something inside my body. It doesn't seem to suffer from the dichotomy with which a Platonic philosophy has saddled the word *soul*. My personhood is the same as soul, and they both mean me. Recall those two creation stories from *Genesis*, God made me in his image—the P story—and God breathed his spirit into the molded clay to create a living human reality, me—the J story. There are important implications for this proper understanding of soul when the topics of death and resurrection are treated later. For now and for prayers of praise, the implication is simple. "Praise the Lord, my soul," means I praise the Lord. It means I did it as an embodied person. My singing voice, my vocal cords, praised the Lord. And I joined with many others in the melody.

EXPRESSIONS OF COMMUNAL PRAYING

I mentioned in the Foreword that monastic life taught me the value and attraction of communal prayer. My younger prior life in Philadelphia had prayers in common, where I joined with others. At a wake service, we mourners prayed the rosary together. People sang hymns in church. But I don't think most Catholics saw the Mass itself as a communal prayer. I didn't. But of course it was, and it involved the entire Church of the whole world, not just our gathered parish. This communal richness of the Mass deserves its own set of reflections shortly.

Communal praying offers a feeling of empowerment that private praying does not. I am thinking what happens when the sacraments are celebrated, especially after Vatican II made improvements in their rituals. Think of the members of the household joining with the visiting priest or deacon to conduct the Sacrament of Anointing for a very sick relative. All join in the prayer, all extending their hands in petition, much like someone being "prayed over" in Protestant evangelical settings. Think of a Catholic Baptism and everyone making the sign of the cross on the infant's forehead, and everyone involved in the ritual prayers save for the actual pouring of the water and chrism anointing.

Church hymns particularly are meant to engender the same sense of enhanced praying. Singing hymns is something that Protestants do better than Catholics. During the years I joined my fellow professors and our seminary students in bi-weekly chapel in Emory University's Divinity School, I experienced what good hymn singing was like and wished my own Atlanta Catholic archdiocese could have duplicated its force and fervor. But beyond the feeling of enhancement that comes with communal prayer, there is a theological insight on its behalf. St. Ambrose, the bishop of Milan who baptized Augustine, wrote about it. "If you pray for all and with all, all will be praying for you, for you are included in everyone. In this way there is a great recompense. Through the prayers of each one, the intercession of the whole assembly is gained for each individual. There is here no pride, but an increase of humility and a richer harvest from prayer."

MEDITATION

There is another form of prayer, called meditation, which at certain times reaches into wordless and time-suspended contemplation. I leave descriptions of the latter for those more adept in the spiritual life than I, and one such was Fr. Thomas Aquinas Keating, O.C.S.O., of the Cistercian monastery in Snowmass, Colorado, who died just weeks before I wrote this sentence. Keating gives it a simple title, *centering prayer*, and thinks it is quite possible for laity to experience it; it is not restricted to the reclusive life of monks. He describes it as becoming quiet, not forcing words through your brain. It is a letting go in the presence of God who is recognized as loving you beyond measure.

Meditation is somewhat similar and a prelude to contemplation. I experience meditation as a retreat into quiet recollection, into a realm of solitude. It is withdrawing into yourself, or as an older language said, into your soul. It cannot happen with noise, although some people use very soft music or even burning incense as helps. I prefer just silence, and my preferred time is early morning before newspapers or TV news or home conversations claim attention. Here is St. Ambrose again: "Our Savior says, *Go into your room and pray*. By the word *room* you must understand, not a room enclosed by walls, but the room that is within you, the room where you hide your thoughts, where you keep your affections. This room of prayer is always with you, wherever you are, and it is always a secret room, where only God can see you," to which I would add, where God speaks to you.

To unlock this door within myself, I have begun in recent years invoking God's name, *Abba*, in slow, quiet words from my heart. I take seriously, as all Catholics do, the need to imitate Our Lord. He called God *Abba* in his native Aramaic. The word's meaning was explained earlier, but sufficient to recall that it is a very endearing and trusting name for the All Holy God, Maker of Heaven and Earth, the Yahweh who spoke on Mount Sinai. Abba as a name for God expresses closeness and overcomes the coolness of divine transcendence. It reminds me that God is not present up there, out there, far away, but rather in me, knit to my soul. Abba dwells in me.

To achieve what I think Fr. Keating meant by centering prayer, I use the name Abba to become drawn toward God and I think this is how Jesus used it. Actually, I think it truer to say that God wishes to draw closer to me than that it's up to me to approach God. It is as if I am opening myself up, letting myself be more aware. After this repetition of God's Aramaic name, I then say the Our Father prayer slowly, as befits quiet meditation. What yoga devotees claim that rhythmic breathing accomplishes—restfulness, mind-centeredness, focus—invoking Abba achieves these features for me, moreso, because it involves God and me, not just me.

It is important to bring something to meditation lest the presence of God evaporate under the ardor of distractions, such as the things I intend doing the rest of the day. Here is a recent example of something I brought into this quiet time, the text in *Lk* 17:5-6: "The Apostles said to the Lord, 'Increase our faith.' The Lord replied, 'If you have faith the size of a mustard seed, you would say to this mulberry tree, Be uprooted and planted in the sea, and it would obey you.'" What a conundrum, this text! It doesn't have the ready grasp of the Lord's "Love your neighbor as yourself." So, without running to biblical commentaries or wondering how it went in the original Greek, I meditated on it by letting it rest on my mind and turning it over from time to time, like that John Denver song title, *Gentle on my Mind*. But mostly I allowed silence so that God would speak to me in solitude. For some days I let it rest gentle on my (meditative) mind. Finally a kind of intuition arose that I interpreted as God's voice to me. "Let your faith in Me not discount what I can accomplish on your behalf or on behalf of others for whom you pray." This was then my resolve coming from meditative prayer: Increase my faith, Lord, that I not discount how you can be God. The same thought is in *Ps* 147: "Great is our Lord, vast in power, with wisdom beyond measure," i.e., beyond being figured out.

We can bring to the invisible world of the meditative dialogue with God matters from the visible world, the real world in which I live, such as a trying tragedy, an experienced blessing, apprehensions of whatever sort. These things count and so do things like a reading from the Bible or the verse of a hymn. I myself in times past have been drawn to the beautiful melody of "Eternal Father, Strong to Save," sometimes just called the Navy Hymn, sung by a ship's company as they tended sailors killed in battle when the dead bodies were slid overboard. This melody brings to my dialogue with Abba the lives of soldiers and sailors cut short, families back home who will never see their spouses or fathers. I am thankful that my own Naval Officer father returned from battle alive for us and that my three younger sisters had the chance to be born.

SUPPORTS FOR PRAYING

There's an older phrase, *doing spiritual reading*, which I think for a prayer life is as true as ever and as necessary. While I grant some truth to the bromide, "You are what you eat," I think there is much truth for the spiritual life in the phrase, "You are what you read." For most people, and at the same time something easy to accomplish, it means reading the Bible with some frequency. If you adopt a meditative noiseless time, as I do, read a few verses from it, preferably words of Jesus in the gospels, before seeking to quiet down and get centered. Let a particular story become what gently sits on your mind. Don't try to bring brainpower to it or discursive thought or analysis. Do a gentle puzzling of the story, request God to speak to you but on God's timeframe. If nothing much happens, that's OK. Return to the story tomorrow. In meditation I remind myself that God is a person. I was created as a person. To be a person is to want to share and create connection. So I am always convinced that God by his very nature wants to share with me, to talk to me, but in the wisdom of his ways and his timeframe.

Just like the different kinds of novels people choose to read, there is a personal fit for choosing this or that type of spiritual reading. I mentioned Thomas Merton above. I've liked his books probably because my memory of spending overnights in the Cistercian monastery near Atlanta was so fulfilling to the personality I have. The books of Henri Nouwen, a Dutch priest psychologist who spent many years living in Canada and the US, offered rich imagery for me. At an earlier time I was captivated by the spiritual writings of Romano Guardini (1885–1968), a German priest and professor who was an influence on the young Joseph Ratzinger (Benedict XVI) and on Jorge Bergoglio (Pope Francis); I still read his *The Lord*, short meditations on the life of Jesus. And the sermons of John Henry Newman are as enriching spiritual reading for me as they were almost two centuries ago for Anglicans who described his preaching as "owning my soul." But above all these sources for feeding my religious imagination stand, of course, the scriptures themselves, followed close behind by the writings of the Fathers of the Church. But I repeat, spiritual reading is a personal fit. I see small books in the narthex of our parish church coming out of a very evangelical brand of Catholicism, in which I perceive a very conservative Catholicism to be present. I am not attracted to them but other people are. As long as spiritual readings feed your spirit and focus your meditative prayer, that is all that is important.

I return to why I picked out *Lk* 17:5-6, for it enables me to mention something about the New Testament that wasn't mentioned in chapter one. There I was concerned to describe "how the Bible works," especially the three stages of gospel formation in order to protect Catholic faith from a misleading biblical fundamentalism. *Matthew, Mark,* and *Luke* are the three *Synoptic* Gospels, the word suggesting a similarity they possess that the *Gospel of John* lacks.

Leaving the unique orientation of John to the side, *Mark* has few teachings of Jesus. *Matthew* and *Luke* have many. Matthew, who sketches his portrait of Jesus as the Giver of the New Law surpassing Moses the Lawgiver, clusters the actions and teachings of Jesus into five booklets in his gospel, an echo of the five books of the Torah connected with Moses. Luke, who writes for a more Gentile readership than Matthew did, bunches his major compilation of Jesus' teaching into Jesus' long trek to Jerusalem (*Lk* 9:51 to 19:27) where he goes to meet his death. I had mentioned already in chapter one how 9:51 sets the whole tone. "When the days for his being taken up were fulfilled [= when the time approached for him to die], he resolutely determined to journey to Jerusalem."

I've shared already my technique with Gwynedd's undergraduates, which bears repeating to illustrate the poignancy of Luke's arrangement. If a person's grandmother was dying in a distant city and sent for her grand-daughter in order to share some important facts about the family's history, the young woman would rush to her side and listen with an intensity unlike that given any other conversation. Why? These were the words of someone dear who is about to die. This is where Luke positions Jesus and his disciples. As they walk with him toward his death, Jesus wishes to teach them very important matters. They listen to someone soon to die. They, and we the readers, are meant to take in Jesus' words most intently. This is why I like to return to these chapters and ponder. I then told students, "If you wish to do something for Lent, don't just give up candy. Read a little each day from the *Gospel of Luke*, 9:51 to 19:27. It is an inspired approach to Good Friday."

JOINING OURSELVES TO WHAT JESUS PRAYS

I mentioned at the outset of this chapter that there is a style of Christian prayer that does not involve praying to Jesus but praying with him, and that this is perhaps the most powerful form of praying. It is time to explain it. It is the Mass, the Eucharistic Sacrifice, the Divine Liturgy as the Greek and Russian Orthodox call it, the Breaking of the Bread as the first Christians called it. Many people think of the Mass as something that the priest does, as something that I attend, as something where I go to receive Communion. These phrases were especially true before the Second Vatican Council. Since the Council, the accent has been on the laity's participation in the Mass. (This emphasis on participating has been successful. I rarely see parishioners praying the rosary while the Mass goes on, as people years ago did.) There is now an invitation to focus on what one is hearing, because the priest now prays in an understandable language, and aloud. Notice carefully, however, how the prayer of the Mass is actually unfolding. The Great Amen before the Our Father prayer is as clear a place as any other to perceive the point I wish to make. "Through him [the Risen Jesus] and with him and in him, O God, almighty Father, in the unity of the Holy Spirit, all glory and honor is yours, for ever and ever." And the people say "Amen." Remembering that the Hebrew word *Amen* means "so be it" or "this I believe," or "here I stand firmly," the people are asserting the same thing that the priest had been reading aloud, as if he was praying the words vicariously on their behalf. The *Amen* affirmation means, "These are our words." Although the Mass rubrics from the Vatican do not permit it, I have never met any theological or liturgical reason why the entire people could not pray "Through him and with him...."

And what do those few words mean? The Risen Christ is offering himself and returning honor and glory to God the Father. It is Jesus' prayer to the Father. And the words "in the unity of the Holy Spirit" bring the rest of us, laity and priest, into unity with Jesus' prayer, because the Spirit given us in Baptism united us with the Risen Christ and identified us with his redemptive life, and in this particular case, with his prayer life. (This is why the Holy Water font at the rear of the church acts as a sacramental, a reminder when you touch it and bless yourself, or just view it in passing, that the person entering the place of the Mass is baptized and is about to participate in the prayer of the baptized.)

Notice the language of the rest of the consecration prayer. It is replete with "we" and "us." Eucharistic Prayer I: "To you, most merciful Father, we make humble prayer...." "Bless these gifts which we offer you...." "We offer you this sacrifice of praise...." "Be pleased, O God, we pray to bless and approve this offering...so that it may become for us the Body and Blood...." It is not the prayer of the priest as if from him alone. It is the prayer of the congregation vocalized by the priest. Even when the consecratory prayer turns from "we" to a singular meaning, it becomes Jesus' words. "This is my Body....This is my Blood." All through, it is the prayer of Jesus offering the sacrifice of his life to God his Father, for the Father's glory and honor. In being the prayer of Jesus, the Mass is the most eventful and powerful Christian prayer there could be. We are drawn into participation with Jesus' prayer in offering honor and glory to God the Father, our Father. And we are drawn into joining Jesus' very words in the next event that follows the *Amen*, the *Our Father* prayer.[5]

Some conclusions about the Mass: We are not praying to Jesus but we are drawn into Jesus' own prayer and we pray with him to God the Father. It is our prayer in that we are joining ourselves to Jesus' prayer. Nor ought we to say, it is Father X's prayer or Father Y's Mass, as older Catholic language did. It is our Mass, the Mass of the baptized people. I do not deny that the role of an ordained person is necessary when Mass is celebrated. The idea of any

---

5. With the prayer of the Mass being the most powerful prayer possible, because it is Jesus' own prayer to which we hitch ourselves as being our own prayer, it makes no sense to me to have a celebrant lead the congregation in additional prayers when Mass has concluded, as if it bolstered what went before, for example, saying a prayer to Michael the Archangel that I have experienced of late.

persons on their own "doing the Mass," because the words and gestures can be easily imitated, makes no sense to me for reasons to be considered later in a consideration of Eucharist and the role of Ordination in chapter seven.

Furthermore, the word *our* in the Eucharistic prayers (the four canons) needs to be expanded beyond this or that parish congregation. A particular Mass, at a particular time and in a particular parish, is the prayer of the entire Mystical Body, that is to say, the prayer of the entire church. It includes the church in glory because we pray in union with this or that saint. It includes the local church of a diocese because it is prayed in union with its bishop and mentions his name. It includes the global church because it is prayed in union with the pope, whose function as shepherd extends worldwide.

Any discussion of Christian prayer cannot fail to consider that most excellent prayer that Jesus himself used and taught, the *Our Father*, sometimes called the *Pater Noster* from the fame over centuries of its Latin form. Jesus prayed it in Aramaic. Would that the church preserved a gospel in Aramaic that reported how Jesus might have spoken.[6] We have Matthew's Greek version (6:9-13), which in translation almost everyone knows from memory, and Luke's shorter Greek version (11:2-4), hardly known by heart at all. An insight from St. Cyprian (AD cir 200–258), a North African bishop and martyr, has shaped my belief that praying the Our Father is praying along with Jesus himself: "Let us pray as God our master has taught us. To ask the Father in words his Son has given us, to let the Father hear the prayer of Christ ringing in his ears, is to make our prayer one of friendship, a family prayer. Let the Father recognize the words of his Son. Let the Son, who lives in our hearts, be also on our lips."

Modern Catholic biblical scholarship has led me to understand the Our Father as an *eschatological* prayer. This seemingly fancy word refers simply to the end-times (*eschatos* means *last* in Greek), to the consummation of the world, when history will have come to an end and God will be all in all (1 Cor 15:28). St. Paul, just quoted, believed in an imminent eschatology, thinking that before he died, the world would end and Jesus would have returned in glory to gather him and others then still alive. He was incorrect on that point, but he joined with other Christians, as fitting in his time as for Christians today, in praying the *Marana tha* for the return of Jesus, whenever it would happen. "Do come, Lord" best translates this Aramaic phrase. There are very few Aramaic phrases maintained in the Greek New Testament; *Abba*, the *Eloi Eloi* cry of Jesus from the Cross, and this eschatological plea with which Paul concludes *First Corinthians* mark the sum of them. The earliest style of Christian praying was eschatological in this sense, praying for the

---

6. We saw in chapter one that the four gospels originated in Greek between the late 60s and middle 90s. In piecemeal items from Papias (AD 60–130) preserved by later writers, he claimed Matthew wrote teachings of Jesus in Aramaic. Actual writings of Papias have never been found, and scholars doubt seriously an Aramaic gospel existed.

soon return of Jesus.

Such is the Lord's Prayer itself. Three petitions are addressed to our *heavenly* Father. (The title *Father*, standing alone, was too abrupt and insensitive for those earliest Jewish Christians, to whom *Matthew*'s gospel was directed. The prayer in *Luke* begins with simply *Father*, quite suitable for Luke's Gentile readership.) These three petitions (your name be sanctified, your kingdom come, your will be done) had the earliest meaning of "You, God, bring about these realities, so that the end-time will arrive."

I make a brief aside on *your name be sanctified*, that is, may God make the world come to revere and hold holy His personhood. The all-holy God cannot become more sanctified but can become more revered by people. A frequent synonym for revere is to have the fear of the Lord, as shown in *Ps* 34: "Fear the Lord, you his holy ones, nothing is lacking to those who fear him....Come and hear me; I will teach you fear of the Lord." It has nothing to do with being fearful of God, which is hardly in keeping with the nature of God as loving and compassionate. The fear of the Lord, in the sense of revering God, is the "beginning of wisdom" (*Prv* 9:10). Hallowed be your name, may you be revered, is what our petition means. There are some occasions in the Bible where "to fear God" means to be fearful in our modern sense of trepidation, as in Jesus' words, "Don't be afraid of those who can kill only the body; rather, fear Him who can destroy both body and soul in Gehenna" (*Mt* 10:28).

Matthew's remaining four petitions are strategies for reverential or righteous living awaiting the eschaton. Father, forgive us as we forgive our offenders, protect us from the great trial (temptations) of the end-time, and deliver us from the Evil One at the end. Jewish literature described severe trials at the end of the world and the trickery of the Adversary, Satan.

Left unmentioned has been the petition, "give us today our daily bread." Its meaning is unclear and this is because the Greek adjective *epiousion* modifying the word *bread* has an unknown meaning. The word occurs only once in the entire history of the Greek language, here in *Mt* 6:11 of the Lord's Prayer and its echo in *Lk* 11:3. With no other contexts with which to compare it, scholars are stumped how to translate the kind of bread meant.

One approach is to break the word apart. *Epi* means on or upon or over. *Ousion* means nature or substance. The result is *supersubstantial* bread, as some early Latin translations of *Mt* 6 read, whatever that phrase itself might mean. An early writer figured that if you need it for your substance, then you need it on a daily basis. Another text had "tomorrow's bread," based on the manna-in-the-desert experience (*Ex* 16). Every day the Israelites were to go out of the camp and collect the manna on the desert floor, except of course on Sabbath when they were bound to remain in camp all day. So on Friday they collected Friday's bread and enough for tomorrow's (Sabbath) bread. In keeping with the eschatological dimension of the entire prayer, the petition likely refers to the bread of the Messianic banquet in heaven, tomorrow's bread, meaning end-time bread.

When I pray the Lord's Prayer, my faith goes to the end-time feature of the petitions. But I also know that when the return of Jesus was delayed indefinitely, the petitions became contemporized by later writers like St. Cyprian and St. Augustine. Their proposals: May your kingdom come within me; may I do your will today; may I not be led into temptations from my surroundings; may I feed on your heavenly bread, the Eucharist. The word *bread* can be expanded into whatever nourishment I need from my Father in heaven. Such are the many ways that reciting the Lord's Prayer, whether in private or in church, reverberate in my imagination. But guiding all of it is the image of being lured into the prayer that Jesus himself prays to the Father. It is our prayer, his and mine, and if prayed in church in communal fashion, his and ours.

SOME CONCLUDING OBSERVATIONS ON PRAYER

There are a few other matters to share about praying. They are like corollaries to what was said above. About distractions, first. You cannot talk realistically about praying without mentioning distractions. They happen all the time. They especially happen at Mass. It's almost impossible to maintain focus on the words of the Eucharistic Prayer without getting distracted if the microphone system is bad or if the celebrant doesn't articulate well enough into the microphone to benefit the back of the church. Or you find yourself simply thinking about how to get the Sunday dinner on. Distractions also happen in private prayer and especially in meditative prayer. Our minds and imaginations flit all over.

It used to be commonly taught that the devil is the cause of distractions because the devil doesn't want you to pray. I prefer to think that distractions in prayer are somewhat natural and reflect the human situations we carry to prayer. Take this case: I became distracted because I was thinking about my youngster's cough that has persisted for two days. And why wouldn't I get distracted? Rather than fight against it, just switch meditative gears and engage God in prayer about your child's health. If the nature of the distraction seems inopportune, then recognize it as such and refocus on that about which you were praying. As quickly as you darted away, dart back. My fundamental insight about distractions: They're natural and ought not to cause any sense of guilt or impatience.

Spiritual aridity. First, what is it? It is the experience of praying, or trying to pray, in which one feels that nothing spiritual is working and the very taste for praying is lost or at least seems sour. Perhaps God is felt to be absent or distant or uninterested. It is hard to keep at prayer when the experience of spiritual dryness is pervasive and long lasting. Spiritual aridity is never, or almost never, the material of sermons these days, and so for the laity it is uncharted vocabulary. When the letters of Mother Teresa were published after her death, letters she never wanted made known, it was a surprise to very many of her admirers to learn that she had experienced spiritual aridity for many years without break. It seems to have begun when she began caring for the poor and dying in Calcutta. The Carmelite mystic, St. John of the Cross (AD 1542–1591), gave it a name centuries earlier: the dark night of the soul. Whether this darkness of the spirit is part of a wiser strategy of God to advance a person in the spiritual life, I don't know. John of the Cross described it as a stepping stone to deeper union with God. But this I do know: That if getting spiritual consolations are the aim of your prayers, such as seeking to feel joy and bliss, then aridity awaits. Why? Your prayer is seeking something for yourself; it is not seeking God.

Seeking consolations as prayer's object is as self-defeating as conversing with a friend and expecting always to depart in a bouncy and fully uplifted spirit. I cannot say more about aridity. I've not really had it, or at least not much of it. I enter praying with the faith conviction that God is seeking to talk to me, around which conviction I don't erect parameters of expectations as to how, when, or about what. In silence I await God. God is more of me than I am of myself and addresses me from within. God wishes to talk to me even more than I wish to pray to God. This is another way that I see how I am made in God's image. I bear him within, ever communicating. Our God is a God who talks.

That fact that praying produces feelings of delight or of peacefulness is a quite different matter than someone praying to get them, as if all along this had been the sole aim. These feelings are—let me call them—side-effects to praying. One experiences a peacefulness, a rightfulness in one's conscience, a sense of no longer feeling alone because the one who said "all you who labor and are burdened come to me" has been met. The long tradition of Catholic writings on the prayer life of saints and mystics describes their experience of *sweetness*. The word is perhaps too saccharine for me to describe my experience. I find the word *peacefulness* works best. Praying makes me peaceful.

I want to share a beautiful description on prayer from St. John Chrysostom (AD 347–407), and I trust its length needs no apology. Caring for his widowed mother delayed John's becoming a monk and hermit, later a bishop. His eloquence—the nickname Chrysostom means golden mouthed—drew him into pastoral care, and against his will he accepted being Patriarch of Constantinople in AD 398. His courage in attacking the materialistic excesses of the Emperor's household—"God desires golden virtues, not golden vessels"—led to his banishment into snowy exile in the Anatolian mountains where he seems to have died from pneumonia. The woman Proba, mentioned earlier as Augustine's correspondent, wrote other bishops at the time to intervene because of his mistreatment. Chrysostom's text on prayer recalls an older student Dr. Breslin and I had in the Honors Program who cherished it when it was shared with the class. Hopefully readers will feel about it as Marianne did.

Prayer and converse with God is a supreme good. It is a partnership and union with God. As the eyes of the body are enlightened when they see light, so also is our spirit, when it is intent on God, illumined by his infinite light. I do not mean the prayer of outward observance but prayer from the heart, not confined to fixed times or periods but continuous throughout the day and night.

Our spirit should be quick to reach out toward God, and not only when it is engaged in meditation. At other times also, when it is carrying out its duties, such as caring for the needy, performing works of charity, giving generously in the service of others, our spirit should long for God and call him to mind, so that these works may be seasoned with the salt of God's love, so that they make a palatable offering to the Lord of the universe. Throughout the whole of our lives we may enjoy the benefit that comes from prayer if we devote a great deal of time to it.

Prayer is the light of the spirit, true knowledge of God, mediating between God and humankind. The human spirit, raised up to heaven by prayer, clings to God with the utmost tenderness. Like a child crying tearfully for its mother, it craves the milk that God provides. It seeks the satisfaction of its own desires, and it receives gifts outweighing the whole world of nature.

Prayer stands before God as an honored ambassador. It gives joy to the spirit and peace to the heart. I speak of prayer, not words. It is the longing for God, a love too deep for words, a gift not given by a human being but by God's grace. The apostle Paul say, "We do not know how we are to pray, but the Spirit Himself pleads for us with inexpressible longings."

When the Lord gives this kind of prayer to someone, God is giving this person riches that cannot be taken away, a food from heaven that satisfies the spirit. One who tastes this food is set on fire with an eternal longing for the Lord. This person's spirit burns as in a fire of utmost intensity.

Practice prayer from the beginning. Paint your house with the colors of modesty and humility. Make it radiant with the light of justice. Decorate it with the finest gold leaf of good deeds. Adorn it with the walls and stones of faith and generosity. Crown it with the pinnacle of prayer. In this way you will make your house a perfect dwelling place for the Lord. You will be able to receive Him as in a splendid palace, and through His grace you will be able to possess God, His image enthroned in the temple of your spirit.

Let me add to these corollaries on prayer two short expressions that I have shared with other people and which reflect what my faith in praying has come to mean to me. *Pray in the direction of your hopes.* This is my answer to the question, "What should I pray for?" "My spouse has a failing liver," or "My closest friend has lost her job." "Should I pray for these things?" "Of course" is my immediate answer because you should pray in the direction of your hopes. But let common sense prevail about this true principle. Should one pray for winning a horse race?" I put into a different category hoping to win very large sums of money at the Derby from hopes like those above.

What about praying for rain, or for lack of it? I grant that there are hopes in each direction on the matter of the weather and likely the same for other topics. A wedding party hopes that the following weekend will be sunny. A nearby farmer struggling with an anemic-looking harvest needs rain and lots of it. Both have conflicting hopes for the weekend's weather. I think that the weather is not a rightful object of prayers. On the contrary, I am convinced that the prolonged droughts in sub-Saharan Africa are prayer worthy, where famine rages and deaths multiply. Praying for quality of human life always makes sense, and for a country like Chad it means praying for rain. I pray for the famine-stricken people of Chad. And I pray in thanksgiving for people like Bill and Melinda Gates who sink money into sinking water wells there. It makes common sense.

My other short expression is my handy definition of prayer. Prayer is *honest talk* with God. People might wonder, "What words should I select? What should I say?" Just make it honest talk. Here is a good example of it. You go to sacramental confession. You don't have to go if there is no mortal sin. (Confession is only obligated if there were. This is a topic to be treated in chapter seven.) But we all come morally short in something or other, and so you are making what is technically called a devotional sacramental confession. Confession, like all sacraments, is a prayer. And so you say, "For doing this thing I am really sorry." You don't have to mention a litany of minor sins, just one transgression suffices. And *I am sorry* means I did it. No one else is to blame. It was all and fully my fault and I'm holding nothing back. Praying "I'm sorry" is honest talk. It is perhaps the most honest talk of which we are capable. For me it has always had a rock bottom quality of veracity.

The phrase "I love you with all my heart" addressed to God is certainly honest, too, but if you wonder "How do I know if I am loving God in the full manner God deserves?" or maybe you think you have secondary motives in saying "I love God," then you can make it fully honest talk by praying to God, "I *desire* to love you with all my heart." You may not have control over

"I love God as much as God deserves." But you do have control over wanting to do it. It is easier to say "I desire to love God." It's certainly honest talk.

In that book where Thomas Aquinas argued why praying is worthwhile, he had an array of other prayer-related questions. They are all germane and quite wonderful, and I might have gone through them but I am not giving a class on Aquinas any more than one on St. John Chrysostom. I'm just sharing some features of what my faith in praying has come to mean. So the question arises, what's possible to pray for, what's a legitimate need. I refer to prayers of petition, of course. Keeping in mind what I came to realize was the import of Jesus' example of the mulberry tree in ocean water, namely, having a faith that does not limit God being God, I don't enter upon praying by first asking what is possible to God.

But are there impossible requests? Take the instance of praying for a miracle. A soldier returns from a war zone with a leg amputated above the knee. Should one pray for an overnight miracle such that the soldier awakens with a full grown and as-good-as-new leg fully identical with his former leg? No, because it is not a miracle God would work. A child is born and begins to play and speaks up until almost three, then suddenly all speaking stops. He is diagnosed with severe autism and is now in his young teens with unchanged diagnosis. Autism, viewed at the behavioral level, is a serious developmental disorder that impairs the ability to communicate and interact. Should one pray for a miracle to heal the autism? Yes, and I do it daily for a relative, because it is a miracle God could work.

What is the difference in these two situations? The difference is the biblical teaching about miracles. A miracle requires faith in the requester in order to happen (Mk 6:5). Every miracle Jesus did had skeptics who denied that it came from God. "Oh, no, he did it by the power of Beelzebub" (Mt 12:24). Or, it didn't really happen. "Ask his parents if this man was blind from birth" (Jn 9:19). A miracle that necessarily invites an act of faith in God's agency is also grist for a skeptic and unbeliever's millstone because the miracle can be written off as luck or happenstance. So the first step in moving toward the difference in the two situations is bringing the eyes of faith to bear on the outcome and its possibility.

Second, a genuine act of faith is not something compelled but freely chosen; if forced, it's not faith. With these principles in mind, praying for an autism healing make sense. The disease is an abnormality in brain functioning even though not much is known conclusively. God could heal the abnormality. Medical science would say, "I cannot explain how it happened." The sceptic denies that God caused the unexpected to happen, just shrugs that something happened or "we'll discover why later on." The believer says I have prayed to God for a miraculous healing. It happened and I, like one of the ten lepers in the Gospel, return to Jesus to acknowledge his power and say thank you. As to the soldier's missing leg, for it to show up suddenly attached to the torso and even without a scar line would invite incredulity, or invite a kind of faith that was compelled to acknowledge God's power. But a compelled faith is a contradiction in terms. The God of miracles, who works where the eyes of faith can penetrate, does not do things that are more suitable to a magician's sleight of hand. A genuine miracle, along with its very possibility of happening, should it lie in God's providence, is suitable and even propelled—recalling *Mk* 6:5—by a living faith in the power of the invisible world breaking into my visible world.

Not all praying for a miracle comes to fruition. Some things for which I pray remain unanswered, if *answer* is taken to mean precisely what I desired to happen. In these matters, we all need to refer to Old Testament Job who refused to try to unravel God's wiser ways. The sceptic, of course, calls this a cop-out. But I don't live my faith life looking over my shoulder for sceptics and worrying about mollifying them. I pray for healing, do not get agitated if has not come, and remain confident that God blesses the situation in manners I cannot fathom, at least not yet.

The reason for maintaining reverence for God's eternal plan in this situation and in all situations is at the heart of the case Aquinas made for the worthwhileness of prayer. God has arranged by plan a world he shepherds, crisscrossed by causes and effects He orchestrates, some of which causes are my free-willed actions to pray, and that this world unfolds in a manner God foresees. This does not mean that God countenances misuses of freedom, called sins. This does not mean that God causes autism or causes war zones where nations battle. It does mean that a greater providence and wisdom can bring good out of evil as well as good flowing from good. I think the truth of this is best experienced in the solitude of meditation where the voice of God can be heard.

CONCERNING PSALM PRAYING IN PARTICULAR

In my reflections on praying, the next-to-last matter to share is not so much a corollary as it is a recognition of the unique value of praying the psalms. We have in the Scriptures an entire book devoted to prayers. It is the *Book of Psalms* in the Tanak. There are 150 psalms in it, some very short like the two verses of *Ps* 117 and some very long like *Ps* 119 that seems to go on forever and having countless synonyms for the word *law*, meaning the Mosaic Law of Mt. Sinai. Psalm is another word for hymn or song because psalms are meant to be sung. In weekend Catholic Masses this happens following the first reading from the Tanak and involves one particular psalm with an antiphon. In monasteries around the Catholic world, those of men and others of women, psalmody in abbey churches happens seven times a day such that in the course of a week, almost all 150 psalms are chanted in monastic choirs.

I've known the range of psalms since my monastic years, but it has only been in recent years that I've come to value them especially as a way of praying. One particular source of support stands out. From time to time something is happening in my life that is unsettling. When I am really worrying about it, it causes me to wake up early, long before my wife might. Just trying to think my way through the anxiety doesn't remove it, just the opposite. So I go downstairs and grab our psalm book and pick a random selection. Most times it seems like a providential pick. When it isn't, as when the psalm is describing Yahweh as an avenging warrior on behalf of the oppressed Israelites, then I make another random selection or two. Praying the psalm has a marvelous calming effect on my worries. Whatever is causing the anxiety is not somehow evaporated out of existence. The issue remains but I now experience God holding me in the palm of his hands. I am less unsettled, less feeling alone with the issue. I know that there are New Testament passages having the same effect, such as the *birds of the air* or *flowers of the field* text in *Mt* 6 ending with the words of Jesus, "So don't worry about tomorrow; tomorrow will take care of itself." Psalm praying has been doing this service for me, too.

The English translation has a lot to do with the effect of the psalms on me. The *New Jerusalem Bible*, which is so wonderful in its footnotes on the Hebrew language nuances of the Tanak, or the Greek nuances in the Septuagint version, has a less prayerful cadence for me in its psalm translation. The *New American Bible* is better. This is the translation used by the American bishops for the Mass readings. Best for me, however, is The Grail translation.[7] It flows prayerfully and poetically, and liturgical musicians inform us that it is the best translation adapted for music. I like that it translates God's frequent name in the psalms, Yahweh, as Lord. I accept that the Hebrew text has Yahweh as God's most frequently used name, but the word in its Hebrew casting rattles the spirit of my praying. *Lord* is a comfortable and inviting name for God. Tommy, a boyhood friend, born on the same day and in the same Lankenau Hospital as I, married a wonderful Philadelphia woman. He died too early. I was honored that his wife asked me to give the eulogy. I then purchased a Grail book of psalms, which I gave her after the Mass, suggesting that when she gets up during those lonely mornings and makes a cup of coffee, she might read a psalm or two before her day gets going. I hoped for her what the Grail psalms accomplish for me.

I offer a caution when selecting psalms for praying. The *Book of Psalms* reflects the different stages of Israelite experience. Some psalms reflect their struggles conquering the Promised Land such as "Do not grant the wicked their desire....Let coals of fire rain upon them, and may they be flung into the mire once and for all" (Ps 140).[8] Other psalms come from the Exile Period

7. London: Collins, 1963.

8. Recall that most Psalm numbers in Jewish Bibles, Protestant Bibles, and newer Catholic Bibles run one higher integer than in older Catholic Bibles. Grail translations follow the older numbering. See footnote 7 of chapter 2.

such as "By the rivers of Babylon we sat and wept at the memory of Zion [Jerusalem]. On the trees we hung up our harps. When our captors asked us for a Zion song, how could we sing in a foreign land?" (Ps 137). Consequently, psalms carry historical echoes that may not be apparent or conducive to your needs at that moment.

I am somewhat hesitant to advise one to simply pick up the *Book of Psalms* and to start praying them, especially if the person lacks enough sophisticated knowledge of how the Bible works. (This was the focus of chapter one.) *Psalm* 18 provides an example of my hesitancy. It unfolds clearly and positively enough. "As for God, his ways are perfect. The word of the Lord is like purest gold. He is indeed the shield of all who take refuge in Him" (v. 30). But soon the theme takes an uneasy direction. "You [Lord] girded me with strength for battle. You made my enemies fall beneath me....I crushed them fine as dust before the wind; trod them down like dirt in the streets" (v. 42). To this anathema can be added the awful wish concluding *Psalm* 137: "A blessing on anyone who seizes your babies and shatters their heads against a rock." It is no comfort to explain that *Ps* 137 describes the ill treatment exiled Jews received in Babylon and therefore infanticide was their hoped revenge. All such themes are far removed from the Lord's words, "love your enemies, do good to those who hate you." I think, then, that a more sophisticated understanding of a psalm's historical context and of the earlier Israelite attitude of being an embattled people help to remove such rants from psalm praying and to avoid concluding that they are, or earlier were, part of divine revelation meant to be embraced by readers today.

Most of the psalms have a generalized religious experience, as suitable to the people who composed them thousands of years ago as they are today. "I trusted, even when I said, I am deeply afflicted" (Ps 116). This is a religious cry of the heart that applies to anyone who believes in God. There are psalms to trust in the power of prayer: "A humbled, contrite heart you will not spurn" (Ps 51), and "If there had been evil in my heart, the Lord would not have listened" (Ps 66). There are psalms of thanksgiving: "My soul, give thanks to the Lord, all my being, bless his holy name. My soul, give thanks to the Lord, and never forget all his blessings" (Ps 103). And there are many deeply consoling psalms, such as the famous "The Lord is my Shepherd, there is nothing I shall want" (Ps 23), whose French music from Genineau mesmerizes me.

CONCERNING MARY AND THE ROSARY

I would be remiss in sharing Catholic faith insights and describing praying, as done above, without mentioning Mary and praying the rosary in particular. Catholics pray to saints, which is more properly phrased as Catholics pray to saints to intercede on their behalf with God. (The meaning of intercession awaits chapter eight.) This proper phraseology preserves the truth that God, and God alone, is the object of praying, the one and only prayer partner in the act of worship. And it is God who answers prayers, which was the whole point of Aquinas's *Is Praying Worthwhile*. Still, devotional language uses phrases like "I pray to the Blessed Mother," "I pray to St. Jude." And further, "Mary answered my prayer," or "St. Anthony answered my prayer and I found my lost money." For now, let's consider these expressions as inexact for what Catholic faith requires, but devotionally understandable. This kind of pious speaking can be tolerated without danger, and it is the way many Catholics speak.

Mary enjoys a very large role in Catholic veneration. Perhaps even stronger than in Roman Catholicism is Mary's importance for Orthodox Christians, so easily sensed in the icons displayed in Orthodox parishes and basilicas and the multiple feast days in her honor. In both branches of Christianity, both "lungs" of the one body as Pope John Paul II called the churches, Mary is especially venerated.

In Roman Catholicism, devotion to Mary is so pervasive that, to outsiders like Protestants, it seems that Catholics put her on a par with Jesus. This is not true, of course, but it must be acknowledged that pockets of extreme Marian sentiment have existed. During the third session of Vatican II (Fall of 1964), when the document on the church, *Lumen Gentium*, was being hammered into final form, a vocal and assertive minority of bishops and some cardinals wanted Mary proclaimed as co-Redemptrix and Mediatrix of graces in chapter eight because they could not secure a separate council document about her alone. The majority resisted them, insisting it's Catholic faith that Christ alone is Mediator and Redeemer.

This extreme Catholic fringe must not obscure the preeminent role of Mary in Catholic devotions, as she is in Orthodox devotions. Of all the ways to pray to Mary (i.e., for her intercession), the rosary is paramount.[9] I wish to note two features of the rosary that support the focus on prayer of this chapter. (1) Most world religions have repetitive prayers or sounds, and the rosary is its expression in Catholicism. With the rosary, the Our Father's and Hail Mary's are said so fast that it is the hum of the rhythmic cadence that is important. It is impossible to be thinking of the meaning of each phrase in them when prayed at that speed. (2) But there is place for reflection, and it is the announced biblical story or mystery for each decade of the rosary (the ten Hail Mary's preceded by the Our Father). For example, the Annunciation to Mary by Gabriel is the first mystery of the Joyful Mysteries sequence. I provide in Appendix E how one might meditate on the Annunciation when praying the rosary's first decade or set of ten. Without thinking about the

---

9. The Orthodox do not use the rosary to express devotion to Mary. In every celebration of the Divine Liturgy, no matter whose feast day is being celebrated, they sing the *Theotokos Hymn* to honor Mary. "It is truly fitting to bless you, Theotokos [bearer of God, hence Mother of God], ever blessed and most pure. More honorable than the Cherubim, more glorious than the Seraphim...."

words and praying with a kind of rote, we are invited to reflect on the biblical stories associated with the other decades. Some historians claim that the rosary was devised to help medieval laity, most of them unable to read, circle through biblical stories in their minds.

So powerful is the material structure of rosary beads, and everyone has probably seen a pope walking in the Vatican Gardens "fingering the beads," that rosary beads are placed into the fingers of an embalmed corpse when Catholics gather around an open coffin to view the deceased at a wake service. And then, what comes next at the wake? Pray the rosary, of course.

SOME CONCLUDING POSTSCRIPTS

I do not intend to break new ground on the topic of praying but only to repeat a few principles met above.

Principle One. Keep in mind who your prayer partner is: God. And who is God, really? My wife has come to think of God as her Almighty Friend, the *almighty* capturing the divine transcendence of God being all-powerful, all-knowing, and eternal, the *friend* capturing the intimacy of God who dwells within. I think of God as the shepherd of my soul, the provident and benevolent reality leading my life. Therefore God to whom you pray is not disinterested or aloof or unlistening. God is not waiting for you to hit the "correct prayer button" to gain his response. In using this phrase, I refer to a temptation that wonders if certain words must be used or certain places must be utilized for prayers to work. Your prayer partner is an ever-loving God whose loving is never turned off. It helps praying to know with whom you are conversing.

Principle Two. Keep in mind the need for being recollected. Call it being quiet enough. Conversation is a two-way matter: speaking and listening. God is never unlistening. But are we listening enough? The speaking aspect of our praying seems clear: Saying the *Our Father*, reading psalms, expressing short invocations such as *Do come, Lord* as the earliest Christians did. But listening, that's not so easy a matter. In the older Catholic spiritual writings, it was called "putting yourself in the presence of God." "Get focused" is its modern maxim. I've shared how repeating *Abba,* Jesus' Aramaic name for the Father, eases me into the quiet presence of God. Other helps to becoming recollected are reading a short passage from the Bible or praying a psalm. Or to become recollected in order to offer thanks or praise to God, think of a concrete experience of a blessing you have received. This is a kind of listening, offered in advance, to what you pray of praise or thanksgiving to God.

Principle Three. I mentioned that prayers of contrition and prayers of petition—two of the four types from the *Baltimore Catechism*—are essentially similar. They both fall under *asking.* I ask for forgiveness. I ask for the return of health of my son. Suitability is no problem for contrition prayers. It involves my awareness of my sins. To say "I am sorry" is one of the great examples of prayer as "honest talk." Suitability is trickier for prayers of petition. Do I pray for this weekend's weather? Do I pray for a winning lottery ticket? My principle is to pray in the direction of your hopes and let your conscience, or common sense, discern suitability. Praying in the direction of your hopes keeps concrete that for which you pray: my son's health, finding a job, a depression I cannot shake, passing an examination, and so forth. They capture Newman's definition of *real apprehension*. Notional apprehensions brought to prayers of petition are generic, often vague, and more rarely met: that evil in the world cease, that peace prosper, that all people be saved and come to the knowledge of the truth (*1 Tim* 2:4). I do not discount these types of prayers of petition, of course. They are met weekly in the collective Prayer of the Faithful at Mass. For one's personal petitions, I recommend real apprehensions of topics, but not without that most beautiful of generic topics, "thy will be done."

Principle Four. Pray liturgically, and let me refer to the instance met most frequently, the Mass. I've mentioned already how the Mass is an example of our prayer being swept up into and joining the prayer of Jesus to his Father. I would merely repeat its bidding. In a spirit of recollection, align yourself with the words of the Mass and especially those words in the Eucharistic Prayer, the canon of the Mass. Do not just be overhearing what the priest prays. Be saying to yourself, these are my words of prayer, and I own them. The final sung *Amen* is an ownership expression.

Principle Five. Don't give in to what I have called the tipping point for many who have ceased believing in God, "the one thousand prayers that went unanswered." I believe that their disappointment in God, before God was jettisoned, was their expectation, perhaps need, that God's answer to their prayers had to be what they calculated it needed to be. This is the false understanding of "praying in the direction of one's hopes." A truer understanding involves trusting in a benevolent God who listens and who wills, from a depth of wisdom outstripping ours, the blessings meant for our hopes. St. Thomas's answer to one of those earlier objections captures it nicely, and I repeat him. "God bestows on us so many things from his boundless generosity that were not even requested by us. But for our own good, God has decreed to bestow certain gifts upon our prayerful request. In this way, our trust in the power of prayer grows, and we grow in appreciation of God as the giver of all good gifts."

To sum up everything, prayer is personal dialogue with a divine friend.

CHAPTER FIVE

The Life, Death, and Resurrection of Jesus

"You are the Christ, the Son of the living God."
Peter answering Jesus in *Mt*

Thinking about a phrase to introduce this chapter, I settled on a passage from *Mt* 16:16, in which Jesus posed this question to Peter and the earliest followers: "Who do people say the Son of Man is?" and received Peter's confident reply: "You are the Christ, the son of the living God."

I've chosen Peter's answer to Jesus to begin this chapter about my faith in Jesus for a simple reason. If you ask most Catholics today what it means to be Catholic, the answers are likely to run along themes like "love one another" and "help your fellow human beings in their needs." Or some might say that "Catholics have the Mass and have the pope." Some might say, a bit inexactly but making a distinctively Catholic point, "I believe in the pope."

These responses are understandable enough, but they do not move to the essential core behind the question. The most fundamental answer is that Catholics confess Jesus as the Christ (i.e., Messiah) and as the Son of God. Other Christians do, too, and good that they do. Implications of confessing this identity of Jesus lead, however, to differences among Christians on such matters as the role of authority concerning ethical issues, or the structures of the church, or whether a church is needed at all if everything relies on individual convictions, as the evangelists of non-denominational TV programs propound. Jews do not confess belief in Moses, although he is esteemed as the great lawgiver who provided the Torah. Muslims do not confess belief in Muhammed although he is acknowledged as receiving from the Angel Jibril (Gabriel) direct divine revelations in Arabic that became the text of the Qur'an. But Christians confess belief in Jesus. It is their essential self-identity, and all four gospels stress and confirm this belief.

In selecting an organizing scheme for this chapter, I took my cue from St. Anselm of Canterbury who wrote in his *Proslogion*: "I was made to see you, and I have not yet done that for which I was made." These words reminded me of the Season of Advent in our church, a time of waiting and hoping to see the face of God. "Your face, Lord, I seek. Do not hide your face from me" (Ps 27:8-9). In fact, Anselm's image of *seeing* opened up the full range of features that we call the Liturgical Year: the seasons of Advent, Christmas, Lent, the Passion Period, Eastertide (which includes Resurrection, Ascension, Pentecost), and a generic liturgical season that overlaps others, called Ordinary Time. The latter considers the teachings and actions of Jesus during his adult earthly life, and it concludes with end-of-worldly-history scriptural readings when Christ begins reigning as King in the green pastures of eternity, to use that marvelous image from Pope Gregory the Great. With the Sunday feast of Christ the King, the Liturgical Year comes full cycle, and the Advent Season in Catholic churches begins anew.

I will follow this liturgical format and use its seasons. It traces my effort to share my faith in Christ alongside how the church itself presents Jesus to the laity. With the regularity of a cyclic year, the church's biblical readings and its preaching begin with Advent motifs and themes, followed by Christmas teachings and then the other seasons, ending with the teachings of our Lord met over the months of summer and autumn. There are so many teachings to be pondered during Ordinary Time that three yearly cycles of biblical readings are required: cycle A for *Matthew*, cycle B for *Mark*, and cycle C for *Luke*. My faith sharing calls for selectivity, of course, because so many features of the Lord's life can be associated with Ordinary Time in the liturgical-year motif I am following.

ADVENT FEATURES OF MY BELIEFS

Advent is a Latinized word (*adventus*), meaning *coming toward* and hence its related connotation, waiting for the arrival (of someone, of something). For the Christians of the first centuries, Jesus' birth in Bethlehem represented the "First Coming." After his death and resurrection, Christians awaited Jesus' "Second Coming" at the end of the world to judge the living and the dead, thus bringing the history of the world to an end. Jesus' Second Coming in glory also goes by the Greek word *Parousia* (being present or arriving), often used untranslated in English discourse for his arrival at the end of time.[1] In the words of St. Cyril of Jerusalem (about AD 350), "We do not preach only one coming of Christ, but a second as well, much more glorious than the first. The first was marked by patience; the second will bring the crown of a divine kingdom."

Centuries later, a third sense of Advent came to be emphasized: Jesus' coming into the lives of Christians themselves. St. Bernard (1090–1153), abbot

---

1. This word occurs about two dozen times in the Greek New Testament. Does Jesus' return initiate a thousand-year period, or conclude a thousand-year period before the world ends? Hence the nineteenth-century Protestant sects teaching Pre-Millennialism or Post-Millennialism, some of them calculating the very day of Jesus' arrival.

of Clairvaux and practically the founder of the Cistercian Order, gave it clearest expression in one of his Advent sermons:

> We know that there are three comings of the Lord. The third lies between the other two. It is invisible while the other two are visible. In the first coming he was seen on earth and lived among us. In the final coming "all flesh will see the salvation of our God, and they will look upon him whom they have pierced" [Jn 19:37]. The intermediate coming is a hidden one; the elect will see the Lord within their own selves....Because this coming lies between the other two, it is like a road on which we travel from the first coming to the last coming [at the end of the world].

I must confess that I do not yearn with eagerness for Jesus' Parousia, which amounts to yearning for the end of the world. The first Christians did, including St. Paul who thought Jesus' arrival was imminent. Nor does my Catholic faith have any kinship with sectarian millennialists, who combed the Bible (especially the *Book of Daniel* and chap. 20 of *Revelation*) for revealed secrets of when and how the world ends. My Advent-inspired beliefs in Jesus focus on the First Coming and on Bernard's middle sense. It is especially Bernard's middle sense that addresses this question: How do I experience God?

What was the *when* of the advent (coming) of God, or of Jesus, to me? At my conception, first of all. God created me in his own image. I bore God's likeness. Another coming of God was my Baptism (10/06/1940) when I was baptized into Christ, clothed with Christ. I bore Christ's image. I might as well have been called *Christopher*, a name meaning "bearer or carrier of Christ." My First Communion (05/02/1948) is another arrival, in which the coming is phrased as "receiving Jesus." I didn't have a real apprehension of the Eucharistic Jesus, and my mind was too young to grasp it notionally. Perhaps by the time of my First Communion one might argue with me, "You must have known what was happening." Maybe a little bit. I certainly didn't want to chew the consecrated host with my teeth as if, without knowing it, I shared in that medieval Eucharistic heresy of a physically present Jesus in the Host. For many years I swallowed the consecrated Host without chewing.

Since I do not believe that God, or the Risen Jesus, is involved in leaving and returning later to me, all that is left is that God's presence, which arrived as early as my conception, invited a growth later on in notional apprehension of it, that is, people taught me about it. Eventually, growth in a real apprehension of an advent-natured God dwelling within me awaited the arrival of a mature Christian faith. These phrases I use, *notional* and *real* apprehensions, awaited also a later time in my thinking, after I had read Newman.

I need to share how I experience God's presence, God's long-ago arrival, in a manner befitting real apprehension. The key to it is the realization of God's goodness. Such a simple word. Such a profound strategy.

I first met writers describing the goodness of God when I began reading the Greek-speaking Fathers of the (Eastern) Church. Their style didn't attract me initially because I was reading them after I had studied Aristotle and Aquinas for some time. Although a profound philosopher, Aristotle was an atheist. His highest reality was the "unmoved mover" that explained why everything happens, a *that*, not a *who*. Aquinas took the best of Aristotle's philosophy, "baptized" it in the memorable words of G. K. Chesterton, and described the highest reality as an "uncaused cause" and "underived existence." Definitely a *who*. Aquinas was writing about God, a person. This was the best way to talk about God, I originally thought. But I overcame this leaning the more I read people like St. Basil and his brother, Gregory of Nyssa, and St. Athanasius who influenced the Council of Nicea, and the two Cyrils (one of Jerusalem, the other of Alexandria). They wrote with such a vivid realization of the Divine Goodness within their lives and permeating all creation. Nothing merely notional and conceptual is met here; they wrote of divine goodness being as real to them as their hands in front of their faces.

This brought me to an insight about myself. I do experience myself as having a derived existence and needing God. I am not my own answer. But this experience of God enabling my existence bounces between the notional and the real, with more tilt to the notional. And it is certainly the most difficult experience to explain to another person, unless the person is philosophical. But to experience God's goodness straight away, that's an altogether different matter. I experience it in my day-to-day life, and in simplest language let's call its instances *blessings*. I experience abundant blessings that I perceive derive from God. Among the greatest was holding my firstborn Brian in the Tallahassee delivery room, and later Kevin at Georgetown University Hospital. If some cynic or skeptic had said to me, "You don't know for sure God is behind all this," I might have said something like "Get behind me, Satan," as Jesus said to Peter on Peter's resistance to Jesus' understanding of being the Messiah.

There is no doubt that experiencing a blessing and seeing it as derived from God's goodness requires eyes of faith, as all the Lord's blindness healings in the gospels require. And there is no doubt in my mind, too, that perceiving Divine Goodness from one's concrete and vivid experiences in life is a trickier assertion to make than trying to experience one's derived existence. Many people have had painful experiences in life, too many of them in fact. Urging the goodness of God on them, even if it's my experience, seems hurtful for them all over again.

I cannot answer those tough life situations that invite my empathy and compassion except to remain respectfully silent at times when in the presence of people who are hurting. But there are many people, and perhaps I should particularize it, many Catholics I know, who experience the goodness of God in their lives. Recently at her funeral I heard the testimony of a 96-year-old woman, written for her daughter before she died, widowed some 9 years after a marriage of 64 years, and mother of five, who wrote of God's goodness:

God has been good to me. As of today, I have five children, thirteen grandchildren, and ten great grandchildren. And all of them have made me proud and happy. I have been blessed with great friends (though many of them have gone to their reward in heaven). All my siblings have died, so I am the last of the clan. And just think when I go to join them, what a happy reunion it will be! Best of all, I will see the love of my life, my beloved husband and best friend, whom I still miss after nine years. What a lot of catching up we will do! I count my blessings, have had a great life, and now it is time to say goodbye. Pray for me.[2]

Because the experience of God's goodness is so vivid and arresting for Anne Brown, left unsaid in her testimony are any of the hard times, the times that elicited apprehensions and tears, which surely were met in a life of almost one hundred years. The advance of years gives a stronger authenticity to the voice of someone bearing witness to God's goodness no matter what life brought with it. "As silver is tried in the fire," goes the biblical text, so is the real apprehension of God's goodness all the more genuine in the voice of "an elder keeping watch by the city gates," as another biblical verse describes older holy people.

Years ago, a friend shared with me the turning upside down of familiar words found in the *Baltimore Catechism*. The flip, described as a sea change in how she viewed God, captures very well just how expansive is God's goodness. "Why did God make us?" was the question, and its old answer was: "God made us to know him and love him and serve him in this world and to be happy with him forever in heaven." Upside down the answer runs: "God made us so that He could know us and love us and serve us in this world and be happy with us in the next." This vision of God is not far-fetched. Expressed differently, the same thought is found in the words of William of St.-Thierry (1085–1148), medieval mystic and monk: "And this is the clear reason [why You, our God, love us]: You first loved us so that we might love you, not because You need our love, but because we could not be what You created us to be, except by loving You."

Why have I come around to the Eastern Greek Church Fathers? Their focus on the Divine Goodness, rather than on something like Underived Being, lends itself to real apprehension and hence to my real assent to God's reality. To my apprehension of God I can bring my personal life experiences of blessings. These experiences are concrete and vivid. The apprehension of

2. Testimony of Anne H. Brown, read by her daughter and my Gwynedd Mercy University colleague, Tricia Brown O'Hara, at Mrs. Brown's funeral on 24 January 2019.

them is real, in Newman's sense.

CHRISTMAS FEATURES OF MY BELIEFS

To retain the focus on faith as a real assent, based on a real apprehension of God's invisible world, let me begin with some pastoral words from one of St. Augustine's sermons to his flock in North Africa. "We cannot yet behold him as the Only Son, abiding eternally with his Father, so let us recall his coming forth. We are not yet ready for the banquet of our Father, so let us contemplate the *manger* of Jesus Christ our Lord."[3]

In late December weeks when some Christmas decorations are out, I have meditated in early morning hours while pondering our family manger, a wonderful crèche given us by my mother when we first married so that Christmas decorations, as she said, "started out right." The crèche has Magi, shepherds, animals, angels, Joseph, Mary, and the baby Jesus. I'm reminded of the story in *Matthew* where Magi come, led by a star, but a vengeful Herod awaits. I think of the different story in *Luke*, which has heavenly angels singing and poor shepherds arriving, and Jesus being birthed outdoors—stable or cave matters not—but birthed not unlike most poor people around the world today. My imagination focuses on the real, not the notional, pondering that manger.

Here is Jesus, the Word of God, but he cannot even speak. (The Latin behind our word *infant* actually means "unable to speak.") He is eventually to be perceived and confessed as fully divine and fully human. The idea of being divine outstrips being imagined. Being human does not need much help being imagined. He enters the world needing the antibodies from her nursing, just as he needed the immunities of Mary's blood, in utero. He grows from her nursing as well as their skin-to-skin contact that only more recently has become appreciated regarding protection from bacteria. He needs to be held close to her to experience intimacy. Later he has to learn to talk—it will be in Aramaic with her Galilean accent—and he has to learn from Mary and Joseph the Jewish prayers. Some of them, like the *Shema* (Dt 6:4), will be in Hebrew and recited daily. His story is our story, as infants and children, only the slants on the stories being different. Such are for me the real apprehensions of him that issue from the visible world of that crèche.

There is another apprehension of the "babe in the manger" that so partakes of the invisible world that it is surely at first only notional—being taught us, that is—and takes some effort over years to reach a real apprehension of its truth. Its scriptural foundation is from the opening hymn in the *Gospel of John*. I refer to Jesus' divinity. "In the beginning was the Word, and the Word was with God, and what God was, the Word was...And the Word became

3. "Nondum idonei sumus convivio Patris nostri, agnoscamus *praesepe* Domini nostri Jesu Christi. *PL* 38:1017. My italics in Augustine's Latin and my English translation are meant to highlight the physical reality of the manger.

flesh."[4] The Word, of course, means Jesus, and the Word became flesh—*sarx* (flesh) is the Greek word suggesting vulnerable existence—when conceived by Mary. The manger leads to the belief in Jesus as a human baby and as God-with-us, Immanuel. The manger weds the divine and the human. The manger contains the Incarnation.

Catholics are traditionalists, not in the sense used today of progressives vs. traditionalists, or liberals vs. conservatives, but in the older sense of *tradition*, that is, something being "handed over." Handed over to us today, and to generations before us, has been the content of faith itself, the language about the mystery of God. It was milled out during that early age we call "the Era of Church Fathers." The voices were many of the people I quote today to express my own faith. Wrong ideas about the nature of God or the person of Jesus were the grist with which they contended. Sometimes their thoughts were in their sermons—most were bishops—or their treatises; at other times, they banded together in a council or synod to make collective binding teachings, whenever erroneous viewpoints—called heresies—appeared too destructive for the church at large. The reality of church tradition brings to our confessions of faith today their efforts, their struggles, their legacy.

In an earlier chapter I mentioned that it was important in professing Catholic faith, which in this book I am proposing to be doing in the manner that has become my settled faith, to understand some history of the church and its ancient teachings. Church history is like the skeleton in which Christian beliefs navigate, mature, and become nuanced. And so in an earlier chapter I wrote about ecumenical councils, and who convoked them, and who came to them, and how the role of infallible teaching entered. I want now to report on the first four of those councils, in the briefest fashion, as they bear on what the manger projects: the visible world—it's a baby—and the invisible world—he's God enfleshed.

The hammered out language is short and well known. There is only one divine nature in God, who exists as three Persons. Jesus is one of those persons who exists with a fully human nature and a fully divine nature. There it is, simple to say but not simple to grasp. I want to list the troubling ideas that occasioned this formulaic language, three persons in God, two natures and one divine person in Jesus.

The first heresies arrived early, by the first century's end. They claimed that Jesus was a divine figure who came down from heaven to teach special knowledge (*gnosis* in Greek) meant for chosen clientele. He was so extraworldly that Jesus only seemed (*dokeō*) to be human. No ecumenical council

4. "...and the Word was with *the* God (*ton theon*) and the Word was God (*theos*). The Greek text makes a verbal difference between "the God" (i.e., God the Father) and "God" without the definite article. Equality, yet difference. It's like arguing, "You are human. I am human. Therefore, you are me," whereas the conclusion should be "what you are, I am." Thus, my preferred translation above.

yet dared to exist to combat this Gnosticism and Docetism because Christianity was still suspect to Roman authorities. But Christian writers did answer:
The biblical author of *1 John*, "The Word whom we have seen with our eyes
and touched with our hands," and St. Ignatius of Antioch's (about AD 100)
Letter to the Smyrnaeans, 1.1, "Jesus was truly born of a virgin…and truly nailed
in the flesh under Pontius Pilate," and the book that St. Irenaeus (about AD
180) wrote against Gnosticism itself.

A later vaster heresy was that Jesus was the highest of God's creatures
but was not equal to God; he was not divine. Such was the teaching of Arius
(AD 250–336), a priest of Alexandria, who stumbled over texts like "God begot
me, the first of his creation" (*Prv* 8:22) and "The Father is greater than I" (*Jn*
14:28). I think of Arius as the original biblical fundamentalist. His teaching
(Arianism) spread over the entire Roman Empire, and it occasioned the First
Ecumenical Council, Nicea (AD 325), called by Emperor Constantine to address the doctrinal mess. St. Athanasius (AD 296–373) led the bishops to use a
non-biblical word to capture what the Bible truly entailed about Jesus: *homo-
ousion*, Greek meaning having the same nature or being. (Recently, the Vatican mandated that the word in the Nicene Creed be translated *consubstantial*,
replacing *one in being*, in use since Vatican II, yet the latter struck me as clearer
for the laity.)

The First Council of Constantinople (AD 381) addressed a matter not yet
fully clear, namely, that the Holy Spirit refers to a distinct person in the Godhead, hence is fully divine. The doctrine of Trinity became enjoined by the
Council as official Christian faith, and a further adapting of the Creed of
Nicea, in the Greek language of the gathered bishops, was promulgated.
This is the creed Catholics, Orthodox Christians, and many Protestants pray
on Sundays.[5]

The next jolt to the commonly accepted belief in a Trinitarian God concerned not that issue itself but understanding how Jesus is God, and it brings
us back to the image of the manger and Mary next to it. She certainly is
mother of Jesus as a man. Does this make her mother of God or *theotokos*
(Greek for *bearer of God*)? Praying certain words either unites you or gets you
into trouble, and this is an example of the latter. Nestorius (386–451) became
the patriarch of Constantinople in the year 428 and led a faction objecting
to the usage of *theotokos* for Mary in prayers. Mary mothered the human
person but hardly can be said to mother the divine person. St. Cyril (376–444),
patriarch of Alexandria since 412, led a vigorous counterattack. At stake was
whether Jesus had a dual personality (Nestorius) or was a single person, at

---

5. A precision. The Creed of 381 describes the Holy Spirit as "proceeding from the Father" only. Proceeding from the Father *and the Son* (*filioque*) crept into Western texts, especially
around the year 800, when Charlemagne was standardizing the Latin liturgy in his kingdom.
About 1000 the *filioque* was adopted finally by the popes. To this day the inserted phrase, *and
the son*, is considered novel by the Orthodox churches and repudiated.

once God and man (Cyril). Emperor Theodosius II convoked the Council of Ephesus in 431. Cyril and his partisans arrived first and began the proceedings without waiting for supporters of Nestorius to arrive or even waiting for the legates of Pope Celestine. Nestorius's view was condemned, He was deposed from the patriarchy and excommunicated. How Cyril's strong-handed methods were later resolved can be skipped, but the doctrine of Ephesus—Jesus is human and divine but is not split up—enters the legacy of church tradition, as does calling Mary *theotokos*. "...holy Mary, *Mother of God*, pray for us sinners...." Nestorians never died out after Ephesus. They fled the Empire to Persia and continue today as the Chaldean Catholic Church and the Eastern Assyrian Church.

Sensing Cyril's personality, it's understandable to suspect that he overstated the correct doctrine. To describe Jesus Christ, he used, perhaps inadvertently, the phrase *mia physis*, one nature. This helped to bolster a faction, called the Monophysites (i.e., the one-nature people), led by Abbot Eutyches in Constantinople, enjoying imperial court connections and was as opposed to Nestorius as Cyril. These Monophysites claimed that Jesus had only one nature, a divine nature, and they pressed for imperial sanctions against opponents.

In 451, the Emperor Marcian convoked the Council of Chalcedon in a present-day suburb of Istanbul to quell the infighting. Pope St. Leo the Great (c. 400–461), though absent from the proceedings, played a significant role in resolving the complexities. His two legates to the Council were invited to speak first. They read a letter Leo had written two years earlier to Patriarch Flavian that expressed succinctly and clearly how the Latins understood Jesus: Jesus is one Divine Person in whom the human nature and the divine nature are sustained, the natures being permanently united though unconfused (each maintaining separate properties) and unmixed (that is, not blended together). The Council adopted his words into the Greek resolutions they promulgated. "Peter has spoken through Leo," the bishops shouted in appreciation.

Because the first four Ecumenical Councils articulate my faith in Jesus, as they do the faith of the Catholic Church and the Orthodox churches, I felt it important to share how and why these binding early church teachings came about. From this tangled history came the seemingly simple confession of faith: Jesus is one person, existing fully human and fully divine. To leave these councils unmentioned is tantamount to trying to describe the nature of Catholicism today without ever mentioning the role of the Second Vatican Council.

What did the Incarnation bring about? It brought about God assuming a human nature that was united to his divine nature in the single personhood of the second person of the Trinity. This is very true but as verbalizing Christian faith, quite incomprehensible. It expresses what is called the *Hypo-*

static Union and is implicitly answering the question, what did the Incarnation bring about in Jesus? In Pope Leo's words, God united as one person (*hypostasis* in Greek) "both natures in an alliance so wonderful that the glory of the greater would not annihilate the lesser, nor the taking up of the lower diminish the greatness of the higher. What belongs to each nature is preserved intact."

But what did Jesus' Incarnation bring about in us? This is the question I am seeking to answer. And the short answer is that it has made us different, supremely different. This will take some careful explaining, and the idea of solidarity is at the heart of it.

A common notion of Original Sin, a notion I find misleading as explained in chapter two, is that every human after Adam inherits Adam's same guilt for Adam's disobedience. His personal penalty, becoming mortal, is our fate by inheritance; we are meant to die. "If by the sin of one person, death comes to everyone..." (*Rom* 5:17). The idea follows on a presumed solidarity. Adam and we are connected. St. Paul uses this presumed solidarity to teach another solidarity, its opposite and counterbalance, our real solidarity with Jesus. What is accomplished in Jesus becomes our reality, too. Paul's real focus was our solidarity in Jesus' death and resurrection. But solidarity with Jesus began happening at the moment of his Incarnation, and this is what I have come to see as true. As the human nature assumed by God is then borne by a divine person, Jesus' human nature becomes the story of all human nature. He, who is human, is divine. We, humans in solidarity with his humanity, are divine in a derived sense.

This has become an important feature of my faith. Allow me to move more slowly and present myself as someone who underwent a change of thinking. At a younger age and even after beginning to study theology, I thought the Incarnation happened in order to provide the possibility for Jesus, later on as an adult, to undergo suffering and death, thus redeeming humanity from the contagion of Original Sin. To this viewpoint were connected the many texts about Jesus dying for our sins, shedding blood for our salvation, in other words, the many texts that make the Cross, rather than the Easter Lily or even the manger, the symbol of Christianity. I didn't attribute redemptive value to the Incarnation as such. The reality of Bethlehem was at the service of the reality of Calvary. But I was wrong in seeing the Incarnation in this limited sense, as merely providing the possibility of a physical body that would bleed and die. And if understood in this narrow manner, it opened up an awful prospect: God sent his Son to die and wanted it to happen. My faith needed some kind of balance that would allow seeing love, love from God and Jesus' love directed to God, as the driving force behind redemption. I needed to see redemption as a blessing and driven by the energy of love between Jesus and Abba.

If the Incarnation was not to be merely a setup for later suffering, then how was it meant "for us and our salvation" just by itself? The Fathers of the Church were up to answering it. Consider St. Athanasius, the great defender of the Incarnation at the Council of Nicea: "By taking our nature, the Word was to destroy it completely and then invest it with his own nature....The salvation of the whole human person, that is, of body and soul, has really been achieved in the Word himself....Our body has acquired something great through its communion and union with the Word." Athanasius has moved redemption into the manger crèche, the milieu of God's love for us and for Jesus. "God so loved the world that he gave his only Son" (*Jn* 3:16), where *gave* means the gift of the Incarnation according to the *NAB* footnote on it.[6]

O admirabile commercium is a Latin phrase that has become famous in church liturgy, particularly in monastic chant. It occurs in Vespers of the Octave of Christmas, now renamed the Feast of the Mother of God on New Year's Day. The famous Italian Renaissance musician, Giovanni de Palestrina, put it to music. The antiphon in full runs: "*O wonderful exchange* that the Creator of the human race, in taking a living body from the Virgin...has gifted us with his Divinity." The *exchange* idea is the same as saying *God became human so that humans could become gods*.

St. Irenaeus, the second-century theologian who wrote that book against Gnosticism, remarks in the Preface to Section V, "The Word became what we are so that we become what he is." St. Athanasius wrote that "the Son of God became man so that we might become God." To add two Latin writers as witnesses to this compelling insight: St. Augustine in a Nativity sermon writes, "Beloved, our Lord today became our Savior by being born of a mother....God became man so that man might become God." St. Thomas Aquinas, a theologian not given to overreach and who composed the liturgical feast of Corpus Christi, observed that "never now nor in the past has any nation been so honored as to have gods approaching it as we have our God being with us. The Only-Begotten Son of God, wishing that we become partakers of his divinity, assumed our nature in order that by becoming human he might make humans gods."[7]

We met earlier the astonishing teaching in *Gen* 1:27 that "God created humans in his image; male and female he created them." A phrase from Pope St. Leo brings the teaching full circle: "Wake up, men and women (*Espergiscere homo*), recognize the dignity of your nature. Recall that you were made in the image of God, and even if it became corrupted in Adam, in Christ nevertheless it has been restored." Using the notion of an implied solidarity, Leo

6. The New American Bible translation appeared in 1986. The Old Testament was revised in 2010. Since then, the translation has been called the New American Bible Revised Edition (NABRE).

7. Aquinas's last sentence runs "Unigenitus siquidem Dei filius, suae divinitatis volens nos esse participes, nostram naturam assumpsit ut homines deos faceret factus homo." *Opusculum* 57 for Corpus Christi feast.

is teaching that the Son of God, taking unto himself a human nature, has recrafted the reality of anyone who is born human. The word *restore* means, for Leo, to overlay with the reality of the Incarnate Jesus.

St. Peter Chrysologus (AD 380–424), bishop of Ravenna a few years before Leo became bishop of Rome, put it succinctly: "The creature that God had formed out of earthly clay he now makes heavenly; what he had endowed with a human soul, he now vivifies to become a heavenly spirit." The Incarnation is redemptive by this process of divinization, of solidarity between God's nature and our natures. Being created in the image of God is truly astounding but it is not as awesome as being divinized. It fulfills the formula that began chapter two: *Having, Losing, and Regaining More.* Redemption doesn't merely restore the sullied image of God. It enhances humanness.

In an earlier chapter about what God is like, I offered my insights on the indwelling of the Holy Spirit, quoting from St. Basil and St. Gregory Nazianzen, who have helped inform my faith in how God is present in me and recreates me in a divine manner. "Almost pantheism, but not exactly," I then wrote in a manner to protect my orthodoxy and theirs. The thoughts of these two Greek Eastern Fathers are applicable here and need not be repeated. Instead, I follow a summary from a respected Russian religious philosopher, Nikolai Berdyaev (1874–1948), in his autobiography, *Dream and Reality.*

> The central idea of the Eastern Fathers was that of *theosis*, the divinization of all creatures, the transformation of the world, the idea of the cosmos and not the idea of personal salvation….Only later Christian consciousness began to value the idea of hell more than the idea of transfiguration and divinization of the world….The Kingdom of God is the transfiguration of the world, the universal resurrection, a new heaven and a new earth.

The Christmas Season concludes with the Feast of the Epiphany. Epiphany does not add to what I have shared of my faith in the Incarnation, but it has two aspects worth noting, one historical and the other about biblical insight. We do not know when in the calendar year Jesus was born.[8] The Epiphany—the word means manifestation—feast began being celebrated on January 6 in the East sometime in the early third century. God's glory was manifested in the birth of Jesus, in his baptism by John, and in the Cana

---

8. His year of birth is more certain, *cir.* 5 BC. How is this possible? Early Christianity followed the Julian calendar, devised by Julius Caesar, whose starting or zero point was the legendary founding of the city of Rome centuries earlier. About 500 years after the birth of Jesus, a monk living in Rome, Dionysius Exiguus (Denis the Humble), decided to depaganize the calendar since the whole world he knew was Christian. Using records at hand, he calculated how many years back to a new start, the birth of Jesus. He did a masterful job but undershot it by about five years. Jesus was born while King Herod lived. From reliable records but unknown to Denis, Herod died 4 BC. Our calendar today follows Denis's tabulation. Jesus was actually born five years before whatever year today is.

wedding miracle. The Latin church of the West, on the other hand, faced a lingering pagan festival of the "Unconquered Son" around the winter solstice when the sun began to rise earlier and set later. To dislodge it and get it out of people's imagination, the birth of Jesus was positioned on December 25 sometime in the fourth century. Jesus was, after all, the real light coming into the world. The Western feast of Epiphany focuses on the visit of the Magi (the festival of *Dia de los Reyes* in Spanish nations today) and includes the baptism of Jesus on the following Sunday, and in cycle C only, the Cana Wedding Miracle reading on the subsequent Sunday.

The Magi (*magoi* in Greek meaning sages) appearing in Matthew's gospel provide the biblical insight. No number of them is given in the Bible. The number three likely came about because these travelers from the East came with three gifts, one carried by each, one must suppose. They are the first Gentiles to believe in Jesus. They are sages, wise men, able to read the stars as befits secular wisdom in those days. But Jesus is the true Wisdom who has come into the world. The secular wisdom of the world bows before the true Wisdom and offers gifts. This then is the motif in the rest of the *Gospel of Matthew*. Jesus brings a wisdom superior to the world's wisdom (the Magi) and to that of Moses himself on Sinai. Jesus gives a New Law from a new mountaintop, the Sermon on the Mount.

LENTEN FEATURES OF MY BELIEF

In describing above how the Incarnation itself begets redemption by means of our divinization, because God assumed a human nature in which we enjoy solidarity, I don't intend to downplay the role of the Cross in achieving redemption. There is simply too much scriptural affirmation of it. In order to show how the Cross is, as the Incarnation is, a work of love between Jesus and his Father in heaven, I need to share two features of the life of Jesus that I have come to realize as being the real causes in how redemption is achieved in the Lord's suffering and death. If redemption is not driven by the reality of love between Jesus and Abba, both in Jesus becoming incarnate and in undergoing crucifixion, then the essential nature of God as love is overturned. Explanations such as "Jesus died to appease God's wrath" slip in. The two features of the life of Jesus to which I am referring are his faith in God and his unswerving obedience to God's will. Both features undergo challenge by temptations Jesus faced.

The season of Lent recalls at the start, fittingly, the role of temptations. Lenten readings begin here. I think that temptations are often misunderstood in the life of Jesus and in our own lives, too. So I wish to share where my faith stands regarding temptations.

TEMPTATIONS

Jesus was led into the desert for forty days and was tempted. *Mark* only says this much, but *Matthew* and *Luke* describe three temptations. The descriptions are stylized. I don't think them to be actual events as if Satan haggled Jesus or led him around. But the temptations, as depicted, are insights into Jesus' actual life. They symbolize temptations to give up his Messianic calling. This indeed must have been something Jesus faced frequently, especially when kingdom-of-God preaching wasn't unfolding easily for him. The temptations of Jesus also echo how the Israelites, in their forty-year desert trek, succumbed to the same kind of issues. Jesus throws the temptations aside with biblical injunctions. The Israelites in the desert fell prey to them. In this stylized manner in the Gospel accounts, Jesus is portrayed as the true Israelite fulfilling the prophecy, "Out of Egypt I have called my Son" (*Mt* 2:15; *Hos* 11:1). I will return to the idea of Jesus as the faithful Israelite when I share how I believe that Jesus redeems us in undergoing death.

With the mention of temptations, I believe the words of scripture that Jesus was tempted "in every way that we are but without sinning" (*Heb* 4:15). This means that nothing was off the table, if I may express it so. Take his sexuality. It was a Jewish virtue, even an expectation, for a man to marry and have children. Jesus' perception of his calling by Abba to proclaim the kingdom involved his choice of celibacy, an unusual decision shared only by Jeremiah and a few others in Israel's history. Was he tempted, in his human pondering, to wonder if the normal married Jewish life might be his calling, as marriage was for most other prophets, including Moses? I certainly think it would have crossed his mind.

Not every temptation is to something sinful, and to ponder the possibility of marriage is an example. Temptations to something evil are easier to brush aside. For example, should I inflate my charitable donations to the Salvation Army when I itemize deductions on my Federal 1040 because the Feds would never know? There should be an easy "no" to this temptation to cheat. But consider the case of a whistle-blower employee who perceives dishonesty. Should he or she speak up and likely lose the job that's so necessary for the family's sustenance? Being called by God to one good thing and away from another good thing is tougher going. Besides the fact that I think no temptations are excluded in principle from Jesus, the reason I picked Jesus' sexuality as an example is because I think most Catholics would feel repelled by a sexuality temptation or by a temptation to cower regarding Jesus, and yet they acquiesce easily with Jesus being tempted by the devil to fall down and worship him because "it's in the Bible."

That "no temptation was off the table" for Jesus is most important for us when we consider its context in *Heb* where we read of a compassionate High Priest who can identify with all our temptations and struggles. No temptation or struggle is off the table for us, of course. "Let us have no hesitation to approach the throne of grace…when we need help" (4:16). Jesus, with a human nature like ours that met temptations and struggles like ours, has entered heaven as the empathetic High Priest who intercedes for us, which amounts to empowering us and seeing us through our trials in life.

The reader may wonder, "Why don't I read in the gospels about Jesus' daily temptations and struggles as you suggest he had them?" The question takes us back to how the Bible works, treated in the opening chapter. The aim of the apostolic preachers who walked with Jesus and later had resurrection appearances was to present to potential converts Jesus as Messiah, as Savior, and as possessing other such redemptive identities. It was not their aim to present how Jesus was tempted every day away from messianic purposes. Here's an easier example to make the same point. Jesus calls the first disciples. They are fishing. Without hesitation, they drop what they are doing and follow him, with the implication that they kept following him every day thereafter. But if this is taken literally, then Jesus is party to spousal and family abandonment. That cannot be. So what is the truth lurking in the accounts we have? To prioritize God's call! That's what the story is meant to preach to later generations of readers; it is not about leaving family responsibilities behind. Do we prioritize what Jesus means? How the brothers Andrew and Peter, and the brothers James and John, pulled off "following him" and yet remained as providers for their wives and children is a matter the gospel text does not relate. We do know that in the post-resurrection period of preaching, the apostles were accompanied by their wives (1 Cor 9:5).

To be sure, some struggles Jesus faced do surface in the gospels. Jesus retreated frequently to solitary prayer (Mk 1:35, Mt 14:23) and at times it lasted all night long. "In those days he departed to the mountain to pray, and he spent the night in prayer to God" (Lk 6:12). Part of struggling is seeking discernment from God about what to do. This describes Jesus and why he prayed all night long. The text above is followed in the morning by Jesus' choice of the Twelve from among a larger number of disciples. A clear text about struggling is the Garden scene—Luke alone reports the anguish—where Jesus prays, "Father, if you are willing, take this cup away from me." When read in church, the next words follow immediately, but I think much time happened before Jesus said, "still, not my will but yours be done" (Lk 22:42).[9] Praying for discernment means seeking to see things as God wants you to see matters, even when the matter is painful and takes time to accept.

You might wonder, "If Jesus is divine, could he not know all things straight off?" Even the astute Thomas Aquinas, to whom I am indebted for many insights, had difficulty perceiving limitations in Jesus' knowledge. He attributed vast perfections to Jesus' human nature because that nature, and hence its thinking powers, had been assumed into union with the Word of

---

9. A skeptic might carp that these words are bunk because no one was close enough to hear them. Yes, some words are put on Jesus' lips in the later preaching, not out of thin air but justified from the long relationship the disciples had with him and hearing how he prayed. They would have sensed Jesus' apprehension before his capture.

God. Aquinas thought that Jesus enjoyed the Beatific Vision from the beginning of his human life. I do not believe that the human mind of Jesus during his Galilean ministry possessed such vast and unequaled knowledge. Neither do Catholic theologians nor biblical scholars today think so. I am raising Aquinas's view of Jesus' human knowledge because I suspect many Catholics view Jesus' human awareness of situations in practically the same way.

Here is a test case question. When Jesus selected Judas Iscariot as one of the Twelve, did Jesus know then that Judas would betray him to his enemies later on? Some think yes, as Aquinas did. I think Jesus did not know, and that the betrayal was all the more painful because it came from someone Jesus originally counted on. My view of Jesus' 'imperfect human knowledge' does not detract from the meaning and dignity of the Incarnation. Of the human nature assumed by the Word of God as it came to exist from Mary through the creative power of the Holy Spirit, I believe that Jesus was *fully* human, not that he was *perfectly* human. He did not possess every conceivable human perfection. I am not alone thinking so. That Jesus was fully human are the measured and sober words of the Ecumenical Council of Chalcedon.

Let us move through the Season of Lent to approach its pinnacle, the Cross.

OUR LORD'S PASSION

The very becoming human of the Son of God is redemptive in itself. According to the Greek Church Fathers, quoted above, the very fact of the Incarnation causes our divinization. "God became human so that we would become gods" was the shorthand formula used to express our redemption, that is, our humanness being profoundly graced because the Word became human, became *flesh* in the language of John's gospel.

But a difficulty immediately inserts itself. If the Incarnation, in and of itself, is redemptive, where does this leave Jesus's suffering and death as being redemptive with all the scriptural texts asserting it? How can you have redemption being caused by being born, the Incarnation, and being caused by the Cross, undergoing death? How can there be two seemingly opposite events causing the one single mystery of redemption? I propose that there are not two contradictory events, and so I will make a "modest proposal."

My faith sharing must get theological at this point. I might have taken a more devotional approach, sharing how Jesus' sufferings and death are deeply wrenching, even causes for tears, much as certain stirring sermons achieve. But I wish to share my faith on what redemption means. How is redemption pulled off? This surely sounds like a flippant question to describe a mystery, a blessing from God that's held to be so sacred and revered. But the directness of the question gets to the heart of the matter. The reality of Original Sin, if *properly understood* as in chapter two, is the backdrop to any explanation of redemption because the answer to "redeemed from what?" cannot be "nothing whatever." I begin with some explanations that had or still have some prominence in the Christian tradition even if they assume an understanding of Original Sin as an inherited guilt from Adam.

The Ransom Approach: Because of Original Sin, Satan gained certain rights over the descendants of Adam and Eve. Humans became slaves to sin, hence to Satan, hence became children of Satan. God's own Son, Jesus, came under the power of Satan by being delivered up to death as if he were deserving of death like everyone else. But the blood of Jesus "buys away" Satan's rights.

Even granting that ransom language occurs in scripture ("The Son of Man came not to be served but to serve and to offer his life as a ransom for many" *Mk* 10:45), how can any explanation of redemption incorporate the devil as a key player whom God or Jesus pays off? I bring up this approach, as outlandish as it is, to simply caution against grabbing onto biblical phrases like *ransom* and *slaves to sin* uncritically.

The Penal Substitution Approach: An effect of Original Sin as traditionally understood is being a sinner, unable to act otherwise. Sin causes God's wrath toward us, witness the many wrath-of-God texts in scripture. Christ takes on himself the sins of the world. Christ then becomes the object of God's wrath. God the Father permits his Son to die in place of ourselves who should have been the ones to endure God's wrath. Jesus' death mollifies God and removes God's wrath from us.

The problems with this approach should be evident. It makes the relationship between Jesus and Abba, his heavenly Father, one of wrath. And the appeasement of God's wrath is the starting point for "how it is pulled off." Where is a loving God in all of this? I have appreciated much Protestant preaching I've heard in my life but certainly not the redemptive preaching of this sort. It continues in some pulpits. Its foundations lie in the writings of John Calvin (AD 1509–1564).

> If Christ had died only a bodily death, it would have been ineffectual. No—it was expedient at the same time for him to undergo the severity of God's vengeance, to appease his wrath and to satisfy his just judgment....By these words [Calvin is referring to "he was wounded for our transgressions" of Is 53] he means that Christ was put in place of evildoers as surety and pledge—submitting himself even as the accused—to bear and suffer all the punishments that they ought to have suffered.[10]

A Making-Satisfaction Approach. It derives from eleventh-century St. Anselm of Canterbury. His language reflects the feudal concepts of class stratification and debt obligations of his epoch. Its logical power has held a certain place of honor in the Catholic tradition. It runs as follows: Any offense against a

---

10. John Calvin, *Institutes of the Christian Religion*, II, chap. 16, § 10.

person disrupts the rightful social order, and amends must be made. The more dignified the offended person, the greater the offense. Because God is of infinite dignity, sin is an infinite offense. The offenders (human beings), because they're the sinners, must make amends (satisfaction) but mere human beings cannot make sufficient amends. Only the sufferings of One who is both fully human and fully divine can offer satisfaction that comes both from within humanity and also carries infinite sufficient value.

Pluses and Minuses? Long before psychiatrist Karl Menninger's famous book, *Whatever Became of Sin* (Hawthorn, 1973), reminded the public of an avoided truth, Anselm's argument underlined the serious nature of sin and the boundless dignity of God. It also took seriously the nature of the Incarnation, as taught by the Council of Chalcedon. The argument's juridical temper, which on the other hand is reflective of its feudal milieu, chose debt-repayment over love in understanding redemption.

A Modest Proposal based on God's love. Some things I wish to avoid in expressing how I and you, my readers, are redeemed should now be clear enough. The devil has no role in the affair of redemption. My treatment of Original Sin in chapter two was meant to lay groundwork for Christian doctrines, and Satan received no mention in it. There is no role for *wrath*, either in God directed at us or between God and Jesus. Nor does buying God's favor play any role, even if the word wrath is downsized to something like God's *displeasure* with sinners. If redemption is God's initiative, God's blessing, then any explanation of redemption needs to start there. It needs to start with God and be driven by God's intrinsic nature, which is love.

Anselm's explanation starts with a definition of *sin*, and this is understandable and in fact necessary if the dynamic of redemption, the how-is-it-pulled-off aspect, is humanity's need to make amends. There is a role in Catholic thinking for amend making on the other side of getting God's forgiveness, such as the Sacrament of Reconciliation requires. But if the role of God's love is to be at the heart of how redemption happens, then making amends, such as Jesus to the Father on our behalf, does not express it. So what understanding of redemption expresses love?

When discussing the Bethlehem manger, I made the observation that the Incarnation, in and of itself, changed the nature of all humanness.[11] Actually, the Incarnation augmented how we are human. Everyone is born imagining God (Gn 1:17), which is already a type of God-connectedness. But being in communion with God, which means "being common" with God (*theos*), is an effect of the Incarnation and our resulting divinization, our *theosis*. Still, it would be false to think that Jesus' suffering and death were not essential to what redemption means and how "it was pulled off." However, if the In-

---

11. The phrase *potentially changed* is being assumed, of course. To grasp it clearly, mentally replace the word *grace* for divinization. Everyone is offered grace. Not everyone might accept it, and some later might abandon it.

carnation is seen as an event founded on God's love, and if the suffering and death of Jesus is seen as based on the love between the Father and the Son, then the one single mystery of redemption becomes based on the nature of God as love. And this is the modest proposal I wish to make.

Three principles lead me to think about redemption as I now do: (1) God did not will for Jesus to die as if to mean that it was God's direct wish for it to happen. (2) Jesus did not wish to die himself. If that were so, then our religion is based on a suicidal propensity, which seems unfitting. (3) The effects of Jesus' redemption need to benefit retroactively all human beings, from their beginning in the world to its end. If it's not retroactive, then for millennia before Christ, human beings came about who would be created in God's image and end up damned upon their earthly demise because they were saddled throughout life with a flawed human nature that tilted ever more strongly to sinning until sinning became an inevitable habit. (Recall discussion of Original Sin in chapter two.) How could this outcome befit the nature of God Creator as love, or in the words of Greek Church Fathers, as sheer Goodness?

My modest proposal of how the suffering and death of Jesus ought to be seen is based on the two features of faith and obedience that characterized Jesus' entire Palestinian life. The notion of *covenant* in Israelite faith led me to appreciate these features in Jesus.

The covenant is God's initiative. God does the calling, the choosing, and the promising. "You, Israel, are my own people. I will be your God *if* you worship me alone and *if* you obey my laws. I, Yahweh, will protect you from your enemies and I promise you a land of your own to live out the covenant." It's like a deal. Israel's two obligations are a lived-out monotheism and daily obedience to God's commandments. The first is captured by the Hebrew prayer said daily, the *Shema Israel*: "Hear, O Israel, the Lord is God, the Lord alone." The commandments are those revealed at Sinai and those obligations later understood to be obliging, such as how to provide food for strangers and aliens and how to worship in the Temple. One should think of these commandments, these *mitzvahs* of the Torah, as directions to live by God's wisdom and not merely as legal dictates.[12] To use abbreviated Hebrew words for their behavior, Israelites were held to acknowledging Yahweh alone (doing *shema*) and obeying Yahweh's directives (observing *torah*).

God's obligations to the covenant are a promised land—recall that the Israelites at Sinai has been landless for four centuries—and protection from enemies. The later stories in the Old Testament depict how Israel faltered in the deal, repeating failings against *shema* and *torah* to such an extent that

12. Having more influence today on regulating Jewish observance than passages from the Torah, especially with the Orthodox and even with Conservative Jews, are the regulations of the Mishnah, the second-century rabbinic commentaries on the Torah, and the fifth-century commentaries on the Mishnah itself, the Talmud.

hopes among them arose for a God-sent deliverer, a *messiah* (a word meaning an anointed one), to rectify covenant life because Israel could not. Admittedly, my account is overly simplified but the general lines as supplying backdrop for Jesus' behavior are sufficiently accurate.

The temptation stories in *Matthew* and *Luke* present Jesus as the true Israelite, obeying God's will and refusing worship to anyone but God alone. Jesus achieves the obligations of *shema* and *torah* throughout his entire life because the temptations "throughout forty days" did not end then. They symbolize lifelong temptations to his calling.

Jesus did not come to throw out the old covenant arrangement and start a new religion. He came, as he said, to minister to the House of Israel and recall it to its ancient covenant commitments. The phrase "old covenant" as we have come to use it today for the Tanak does not mean passé but rather *originating*. The phrase "new covenant" does not mean brand new but rather *renewed*. Jesus was about renewing the covenant. When you examine closely the details of Jesus preaching the kingdom of God and presenting God's nature as a father to everyone he addressed, does Jesus advocate anything brand new to what Israel already knew but wasn't achieving? I think not. "Love God with all your energy, and love your neighbor as you love yourself." (Implications of Jesus' preaching become sharper in later church developments: preaching to Gentiles, the reality of resurrection, understanding God as Trinity. These are rightly called new.)

The Gospel portrait we have of Jesus' life is of a faithful Israelite who maintained the vision of God, of Abba, as uppermost in his thoughts and affections (*shema*), and who sought always to do the will of his heavenly Father (torah). Discovering Abba's will required discernment for him, as it does for us, and this is why Jesus led a prayerful life and a reflective live. Jesus' life of faith and obedience reaches its greatest and most poignant expression in his suffering and death. How is this so and why is it so?

It's a quandary why someone preaching good news ran into such a buzz saw of animosity, but he did. He didn't back off. I suspect some of strife he aroused had to do with his preaching of *repentance*, a word that really means to change your thinking, your religious mentality if necessary. This can be unsettling for people already convinced that the God of Israel sided with them and how they viewed Mosaic religion. Whatever be the rancor in the minds of his opponents, it began to involve getting rid of him. "They planned for his death" is an idea met in the gospels.

Did he want to die by his own intention? He did not but he accepted death because it became tangled with preaching the kingdom of God? Yes, he accepted death in that sense of remaining obedient to why he felt called. An understandable analogy comes from the case of a parent who would willingly thrust herself in front of a fast approaching car, knowing she could die, because her youngster had wandered into the car's path. She does not want to die. She wants to push her youngster aside. She does not turn from the possibility of dying. She is simply being obedient to a higher calling of loving her youngster. This is how I see Jesus being "obedient unto death, even death on a cross" (Phil 2:8). It is driven by Jesus' love for the Father, whose will Jesus obeys, and love for those for whose benefit the Father has sent him. This is the Crucifixion facet of redemption *happening as love*.

Abba did not send him to die any more than I would intentionally send one of my sons into mortal danger, even though *Rom* 8:32, if taken literally, seems to say the contrary. We are at this point thrust into the mystery of evil. It is as if evil ensnares God's intention to divinize us, which the Incarnation in itself implies. It is as if God's Incarnational plan gets pulled into a death strategy in order to untie death's hold on life. A text that I have found very powerful in this conundrum comes from Pope Leo. "For unless the new man, by being made in the likeness of sinful humanity, had himself assumed the nature of our first parents, unless he had stooped to be one in substance with his mother while sharing the Father's substance and, being free from sin, united our nature to his, the whole human race would still be held captive under the dominion of the devil. *His Victory would have profited us nothing if the battle had been fought outside our human condition* (italics mine).[13]

Considered earlier in this chapter was the mystery of the Incarnation, God becoming human. And why? "God so loved the world that he sent his only-begotten Son..." To this frequently quoted *Jn* 3:16 can be added *Jn* 17:23: "That the world might know that you sent me, and that you loved them even as you loved me." The foundation is made clear. The Incarnation *happens as love*.

Therefore, both the Christmas crèche and Good Friday's Cross express the role of God's love as their foundations and causes. This, then, becomes my modest proposal for how the redemption is pulled off. God's love for us and the love between Jesus and his Father are doing the pulling.

With both Incarnation and Good Friday being differing expressions of redemption being achieved through divine love, let me share what Holy Saturday represents. It is a "what if" day for me. Holy Saturday symbolizes the absence of God. I am not a fan of the phrase, the death of God, because it seems to imply that God has ceased. But I am a fan of a liturgical setting that helps me imagine a world as if God were not. It is harder to come by now because Catholic churches on the Saturday after Good Friday are busy with volunteers getting everything ready for the Easter Vigil that night, and this preparation of the sanctuary starts bright and early. But I recall Holy Saturdays from my youth, and from days I visited the Cistercian monastery

---

13. Because his last sentence is so linchpin, I give Leo's own words: "Nec uti possemus triumphantis Victoria, si extra nostram esset concerta naturam." It is in Letter 31 (*PL* 54:792), sent to the Empress Pulcheria (AD 399–453). It was she who assisted her husband, Emperor Marcian, to convoke the Council of Chalcedon in 451, discussed earlier.

in Georgia, how vacant everything was on Holy Saturday morning. How utterly bare and barren was the parish church, the abbey church. No Mass, no statues, no anything, just an empty tabernacle with doors wide open. There is coldness when there are no representations of the invisible world. It is my Lenten wish that everyone should pause and feel the coldness of those moments when we imagine what if there were no God, no Incarnation. Call it the shudder that Holy Saturday produces.

EASTER FEATURES OF MY BELIEF

There is a visual difference between crosses in Roman Catholicism and crosses in the Orthodox churches, Greek, Russian and others. The crucified Jesus hangs on ours, and so the cross is rightly called a crucifix. On Orthodox crosses there is no dead body. It has just the shape of a cross. Sometimes jewels are placed on it. It is as if proclaiming the biblical words, "He is not here [among the dead], he is risen."

Our western minds tend to take things chronologically, sequentially, and so I wrote about Good Friday. My description was essentially incomplete. A most important feature of the Cross was left unmentioned: the Resurrection. But our western mentality tends to consider Jesus' resurrection as the next thing to happen, as if it happened three days after his death. I don't follow this tendency but rather return to a teaching found among some Fathers of the Church that Jesus dies into his resurrected state. There is no delay. Because our own passage from death to resurrected life mirrors what happened to Jesus, as St. Paul frequently teaches, notice the immediacy in these words from St. Cyprian: "What an honor, what happiness to depart joyfully from this world, to go forth in glory from the anguish and pain, in one moment to close the eyes that looked on the world of men and in the next to open them at once to look on God and Christ! The speed of this joyous departure! You are suddenly withdrawn from the earth to find yourself in the kingdom of heaven."[14] I believe that this was Jesus' story and it happens to us, too.

JESUS' RESURRECTION

In the Foreword I mentioned Baroque Catholicism, that unique period of behaving and thinking that held sway after the Council of Trent up to the dawn of Vatican II. The resurrection of Jesus was not fully appreciated in these centuries. Catechisms and seminary texts taught that Jesus' resurrection had two aspects: It proved Jesus' divinity, and it was God's reward to him for having laid down his life to save us. Except for teaching that Jesus was dead for a period of time before he was raised[15] and that at the end of

14. Some Church Fathers perceived a delay between Jesus' death and his resurrection. The early Christians were immersed three times when baptized. Cyril of Jerusalem says each immersion corresponds to each night Jesus was in the tomb.

15. The language of the Bible is that Jesus was *raised*. His human life came to an end and

the world people worthy of heaven would be resurrected, the meaning of his resurrection seemed to stop there.

Deeper meaning to the resurrection is seen with St. Paul. "We believe in the one [God] who raised Jesus our Lord from the dead, who was handed over for our sins and was raised for our justification" (Rom 4:25-26). This deeper meaning is found in Leo the Great: "By dying he submitted to the laws of the underworld; by rising he destroyed them. He did away with the everlasting character of death." St. Thomas Aquinas also connects Jesus' resurrection to our own: "Thus, the resurrection of Christ is the effective cause of our own resurrection through the power of [his united] divinity, to which belongs the role of raising the dead to life."

From time to time a book appears that has an explosive impact on theology. Such was the biblical study in 1950 on the resurrection by French Redemptorist scholar, François-Xavier Durrwell, *La Résurrection de Jésus, mystère de salut* (ET *The Resurrection: A Biblical Study*, Sheed & Ward, 1960). It prodded theologians before and after Vatican II to reclaim the more connected view of Jesus' death and his resurrection. This integrated view has come to shape what I think resurrection means, Jesus' and ours.

Jesus' death and his resurrection are the outside and inside of the same reality, its convex and concave sides one might say. Jesus dies into resurrection. The phrase *Paschal Mystery* has gained currency among Catholics, and it means the same thing: death directly into resurrection. Do we not pray at funeral liturgies for dead friends that God would have already received them into heaven? Jesus experienced the same immediate doorway from death into exalted life, to arriving at God the Father's right hand.

If a passage of time were needed before his resurrection happened, then the union of the Son of God with a living human nature would have come to a pause with his dead corpse. But a pause is impossible for our faith. It borders heresy. The human nature of Jesus, taken from the flesh of Mary in order to be exactly ours, a human nature with limitations and mortality, dies. Its vulnerability comes to an end at the moment of his death. This much is true. "What an exchange to wonder at," says Augustine, "we gave him the ability to die and he gave us the ability to live." But Jesus' human nature lived out in Palestine is vivified, becomes transformed, becomes resurrected and exalted, as he passes through death. The Hypostatic Union of his divine personhood with a human nature never becomes severed. Only the manner of being human changes, from having a non-resurrected body to having a resurrected body. The Incarnation does not come to a pause; it endures from a life this side of death to a life beyond death.

This view requires rethinking certain assumptions, which Durrwell's

---

the Father raised him up. It belongs only to divinity to resurrect. If one focuses on the divinity of Jesus, that Jesus *resurrected* himself becomes possible to say. I will use the biblical language that Jesus was raised. Abba raised up Jesus.

book prompted people to do. For the simplified faith views I want to share, I need now to say something about "he was raised on the third day" and that his corpse was buried in a tomb that was found empty when disciples visited it "on the first day of the week," i.e., Sunday. The idea of a time delay in Jesus' resurrection seems to get in the way of my proposal.

The first thing to note is that nowhere in the New Testament is the actual resurrecting process described. His moment of death, sure. His appearing as the Risen Christ to this or that person, sure. Newman's visible/invisible world distinction is wonderfully illustrated. Realities of the visible world—his capture, his trial, his crucifixion—happen in our space-time dimensions. A reality of the invisible world, such as the transformation of being raised from the dead by Abba, eludes our space-time reckonings.

The second thing to note is that the phrase, "on the third day," possesses biblical meaningfulness, not chronological meaningfulness. It is a biblical expression to convey God's providence, not to convey clock time. To quote Vincentian biblical scholar Bruce Vawter, "the third day was traditionally the day of deliverance, of reversal, of victory snatched from the jaws of death and defeat." The biblical instances are numerous. "Let us return to Yahweh....On the third day he will raise us up" (Hos 6:1). God (Elohim) directed Abraham to sacrifice his own son, Isaac. Abraham obeyed and on the third day, he built an altar, tied up Isaac, and took out his knife. Then the "angel of the Lord" (a circumlocution for God himself) said to stop (Gn 22:4). On the third day, Esther began her task to save Israelites from sure destruction (Est 5:1). On the third day Jonah's prayer was heard and he was freed from the belly of a great fish (Jon 1:17, 2:10). Because the third day is the moment of divine reversal when all seems lost, it describes most fittingly the resurrection of Jesus. The hopes of Jesus' followers were crushed. The male disciples fled, not so some women. Why? We can only surmise. They feared for themselves. They were disillusioned. Perhaps they concluded it was all a mistake and fled home to resume their earlier lives. Whatever the reasons, the resurrection appearances to them were truly God's expression of Jesus' victory over death when all had seemed lost. The appearances certainly changed the disciples' fear and flight into courage and loyalty. It's the biblical "third day of vindication" applied to experiencing Jesus as risen.

I risk getting technical about features of Jesus' resurrection as described in the Bible because the tendency is to read them in the same manner one might read how a sick person got well. To recall Newman, we forget that the invisible world does not allow the easy description that the visible world does. St. Paul has the same caution: "We look not to what is seen but to what is unseen" (2 Cor 5:18). What are some of these features?

Regarding Jesus' resurrection, the New Testament has two kinds of stories, and both have complexities. The first kind are "empty tomb" stories, and here the complexities involve who came to the tomb, who rolled back the entrance stone, who was already there (one or two angels), and what was said to the visitors.[16] My faith in Jesus' resurrection from the dead is not based on people finding the tomb empty. A biblical scholar once quipped that if resurrection faith is based on an empty tomb, it is as empty as the tomb is. Even the account in *Mt* gives a contrary explanation for emptiness. "They stole the dead body," said the Jewish leadership. A revelation from God is the only true explanation why the tomb is empty. But it doesn't stop there with an angelic message. The Risen Jesus instills the truth of his resurrection by means of his appearances to followers.

The second kind of story, then, involves these resurrection appearances. When did they occur, and where, and to whom? Here we meet greater complexities. Given that I believe Jesus' resurrection happened immediately upon death, when did he first appear from the realm of glory to someone in this space-time world, being mindful that "on the third day" is not clock time? Although it is not in scripture or church tradition, I believe he appeared initially to his mother, maybe after sundown on Friday, maybe on Saturday. I don't know when but I cannot accept the fact the he appeared later to others—Peter, Mary Magdalen, etc.—without bringing relief to a grieving mother first. The Jesus and Mary relationship is too strong and central in the Roman Catholic and Eastern Orthodox churches to not consider seriously this possibility. I believe he appears to his mother quite early on, perhaps in her home when Sabbath laws imposed seclusion.

When did he appear first to the Eleven? (The biblical title, the Twelve, accounted for Judas Iscariot, who's now missing.) It was in Galilee according to *Mt* 28 and the original shorter ending to *Mk* 16. It was in Jerusalem according to *Lk* 24 and *Jn* 20. What kind of risen body did Jesus have? Some texts make it quite physical, a body like ours. Other texts make it very different, as if befitting the invisible world of spiritual realities. He is not recognized at first, he appears and disappears, he comes through locked doors, and so forth. All these complexities I would treat and attempt to clarify in a theology classroom but not here. I want only to share what I have come to believe.

An appearance of Jesus is the breaking into our world of the invisible world of God. Jesus' human nature has been transformed and glorified. It has become an "end-time" reality, to use that technical term *eschaton* mentioned earlier, and therefore an indication of what everyone in heaven will be like. The disciples encounter Jesus as real, not as a ghost or as a hallucination. This is why I think overly physical descriptions of Jesus were employed, especially by Luke, to counteract such mistakes. But the disciples are not seeing a physical person of such and such height and weight. If this were so, then Jesus' resurrection simply amounts to resuscitation of a corpse.

16. As always with angels in the Bible, read their lips. *Angel* in Greek means messenger, hence their words are messages from heaven, i.e., revelations. Their words in *Lk* 24:5 say it all: "Why do you seek the living among the dead. He has been raised."

Let's imagine that video cameras existed then, and someone else, like an outsider, was filming a resurrection appearance, for example, to the Eleven in the Upper Room where Jesus appeared and said *shalom*. Nothing would have been recorded. But Jesus is nevertheless recognized *by them* as the one they knew. An old theology colleague used a phrase I've found helpful over the years: The disciples had *believing seeing*. The risen Jesus caused it.

Believing seeing is simply restating Aquinas's formula of encountering the invisible world with the "eyes of faith." There is a phrase in the Galilean appearance story in *Mt* 28:17 that is telltale. When the disciples saw him on the mountain top, "they worshiped but they doubted." *Doubted* does not signal disbelief but rather the type of hesitancy someone experiences in confessing "I assent" but fully aware that it is not like assenting to seeing a tree outside your window. The disciples are assenting to experiencing the Jesus they knew as now alive, albeit transformed. "I have seen the Lord" becomes the common expression used, and they begin to apply the title *Lord* for the Risen One.

Lest the word *seeing* gets in the way, the word to see, *ōphthē* in biblical Greek, does not only mean seeing with one's optic nerve; it also includes seeing the invisible God, as Abraham is able to do (Gen 12:7).[17] Because I think we bring into death the autobiographies that our lives in earthly freedom created, the disciples perceived the appearing Jesus bearing "the mark of the nails." These texts are also telltale for my faith. The Jesus they recognize with the eyes of faith is the Crucified One because he brought into his death what he suffered and why he suffered. His wounds are now victorious because his earthly human nature has become glorified. The wounds, which at first were mere gore, have been victorious and salvific wounds. Recall my caution: They are not seeing wounds with the optic nerve the way I now see wounds.

Of course, they received much more in a resurrection appearance. A resurrection appearance is revelatory. I mentioned this feature in chapter one when explaining how the gospels originated. The disciples came to perceive the deeper import of everything Jesus taught and did when they walked with him. They perceived how God's providence unfolded in his life and how it was foreshadowed in the texts of the prophets. This is the deeper significance of the Emmaus appearance when Jesus[18] opens the minds of the two disciples, one named Cleopas, to how the Jewish scriptures point to him (Lk 24:13). Jesus went unrecognized at first. "Their eyes were prevented from recognizing him," another indication that recognition is not optic-nerve seeing but believing seeing. He becomes recognized in the "blessing and breaking of the bread," and then he vanishes.

The phrase *believing seeing* seems to put all the initiative on what the dis-

---

17. He *appeared* is the passive voice of ōphthē in Greek grammar.

18. The only time in all the gospels when he is addressed simply and only as Jesus is when the "good thief" in *Lk* 23:42 says, "Jesus, remember me when you come into your kingdom."

ciples contribute, as if it were like "I am seeing the tree." We have to return to the simple catechism teaching that God causes faith. God opens our eyes. Or in the words of St. Augustine used earlier, God bends our perceptions into the act of belief. In any appearance story, the initiative comes from the invisible world into disciples of our world. Without ever assuming a physical appearance, the Risen Jesus creates an encounter of believing seeing. Could this or that disciple have refused the approach of a wanting-to-appear Jesus? I suppose in theory it is possible but in actuality I leave it to the mystery of how God has elected many people in salvation history, beginning with Abraham, to respond to a call without being coerced. Could Mary have refused the invitation from Gabriel? In theory she could have—with people hanging in the balance for her free yes, as St. Bernard of Clairvaux in Appendix E imagines—but she did not refuse the divine overture.

The only sacred author in the New Testament who actually had a resurrection appearance was St. Paul *(Gal 1:12, see also Acts 9:4)*. Recall what was mentioned about how the Bible works: The four evangelists were anonymous, and they wrote in the last third of the first century. Matthew the tax collector and John, son of Zebedee, were indeed disciples who received resurrection appearances, but they did not write the gospels that only in mid-second century began bearing their names. So we are left with Paul as the only recipient who wrote about resurrected bodies. His descriptions were very sober and restrained and respectful of how different a resurrected body is. In *1 Cor* 15:35-44, using the analogy of a seed sown in the ground and undergoing transformation, he describes how our earthly bodies are transformed into resurrected bodies, patterned on Jesus' resurrected body. "It is sown perishable, it is raised imperishable. It is sown in dishonor, it is raised in glory. It is sown in weakness, it is raised in power. It is sown a natural body *(sōma psychikon)*, it is raised a spiritual body *(sōma pneumatikon)*." Everyone knows what a natural or physical body is. We have them. But what is a spiritualized body? I leave to the next chapter what I think having a spiritualized body in heaven could mean.

JESUS' ASCENSION

After Easter in the Liturgical Year comes Ascension Thursday, 40 days later. To share what I believe about Jesus' ascension into heaven involves unraveling another biblical time expression, and it is symbolic, too. A number of events in salvation history have happened after 40 years or 40 days. The earth was covered with water for 40 days, killing off everything except what Noah took into the ark. After the Golden Calf idolatry, Moses went back up Mount Sinai for 40 days and nights while new stone tablets of Commandments were written. The Israelites wandered in the desert for 40 years. After Jezebel threatened to kill Elijah, he walked for 40 days to Mt. Sinai where God promised protection, and Elijah returned to preach. Jesus spent 40 days in the desert after his baptism. And, of course, there is the well-known Ascension text: "For 40 days Jesus continued to appear to them and tell them about the kingdom of God....Then he was lifted up and a cloud took him from their sight" (Acts 1:3,9).

This array of forty-numbered instances suggests their deeper meaningfulness, and it is not chronological. It refers to a period of whatever length that introduces the next stage of salvation history. After Noah came a renewed world. After the second time on Mt. Sinai, the Israelites were ready to commit to covenant living. After arrival in the Promised Land, living out a covenant life begins. Elijah returned to Israel and so did Israelite prophecy. Jesus emerges from the desert and begins his preaching ministry. After Jesus ascends, church ministry begins.

Two conclusions follow. When did Jesus ascend into heaven? Immediately. Upon dying, Jesus enters the realm of glory as the Risen Lord. He has ascended to Abba's right hand. (Biblically, to be at someone's right hand is to be given a share in the person's power and prerogatives.) Each separate resurrection appearance, and there were several, involves a descent from heaven and an ascension when it is finished. This is the special up and down language I mentioned earlier that should not be taken literally. Heaven is not up. Heaven does not answer to a *where* question but to a *how* question.

Second, why tie a departure of Jesus to 40 days? At some date the resurrection appearances of Jesus ended, sometime in the middle part of the first century. We know he appeared to Paul on the Damascus Road, and Paul's conversion is at least three years after the Crucifixion. I grew up with the teaching—and it is true enough if properly understood—that revelation ended with the death of the last apostle, and I was probably taught that *apostle* meant one of the Twelve (the original Eleven plus Matthias who replaced Judas). Leave to the side the identity of who qualifies as an apostle. Paul was certainly one, and he wasn't one of the Twelve. Mary Magdalene was one. Paul said that Jesus appeared to "more than five hundred brethren [men and women] at the same time" (1 Cor 15:6). When? Where? Who knows? What alone is important is that they received an appearance with all that it entails. Since an appearance is revelatory, revelation stops when the appearances stop. Call that ending of the last appearance and Jesus' departure *the* Ascension with a capital A. It is pegged at 40 days for the reasons indicated: Jesus revealed deeper levels of the Kingdom of God, and the ministry of the church is the next (and current) phase of salvation history.

Understanding *ascension* in this manner avoids the awkward and unnecessary question, where did Jesus go after he appeared in the Upper Room, or at Emmaus, or wherever? He didn't go anywhere as if he stayed on earth concealed. He appeared to disciples from the realm of glory, without ever really leaving it. An appearance simply ended, which only means that their experience of the Risen Jesus in that special revelatory moment came to an end.

PENTECOST AS ACTION OF RISEN JESUS

Ten days after Ascension Thursday comes the feast of Pentecost, described in *Acts* 2. It is connected with a dramatic bestowal of the Holy Spirit and is often called "the birthday of the church." I want to avoid how I would teach in a classroom its many symbols, such as the tongues of fire and speaking foreign languages. My faith focuses on the truth that the Risen Jesus bestows the Holy Spirit. To be a life-giving Spirit, to use Paul's words, is another definition of being the Risen Jesus. Read in parallel the Upper Room story in *Jn* 20. The Risen Jesus appears to the disciples. Even though the text mentions the absence of the male apostle, Thomas, I cannot conceive that the collective term *disciples* excluded women because Mary of Magdala, just recently, had brought news to the disciples that Jesus was raised. Jesus appeared to the disciples and said, "Peace. As the Father has sent me, so I send you." And he breathed on them and said, "Receive the Holy Spirit." This is as much a Pentecost-like event as the traditional event described in *Acts*. In fact, I believe every appearance of the Risen Jesus is Pentecostal and Spirit sharing. It's just its nature.

Having placed in their proper contexts *raised on the third day* and *appeared throughout forty days*, I wish to propose a reconstruction of what transpired from the Last Supper meal to the end of the resurrection appearances.

First of all, the Jews have a seven-day week, each day going from sundown to the next sundown. They have different names for the days of the week, and *Sabbath* is from Friday sundown till Saturday sundown. Hence, the "first day of the week is from after sundown all through daylight Sunday.

On Thursday Jesus wished to celebrate a Passover meal with his followers. We've come to call the meal his Last Supper because he was dead the next day. The narratives in the three Synoptics present it as a Passover meal for Jesus and his twelve male apostles only, although I think others were present, including women. (Thursday's Last Supper in *John* is the day before Passover occurs, with the result that Jesus is shedding blood on Friday while Passover lambs for that evening's meal are being killed in the Temple.) The Synoptic viewpoint is understandable and is used by the church as the motif of Holy Thursday, because the meal is viewed as a renewal of the covenant. "This cup is the new covenant in my blood, which will be shed for you" (*Lk* 22:20). The twelve apostles are meant to recall and represent the twelve male patriarchs of the originating covenant. To describe others at the meal muddies the symbolism. But I think it implausible that Jesus told the Twelve earlier that day to ready Passover for themselves and told the other (faithful) disciples, men and women, to prepare their own Passover. Leonardo da Vinci's painting on the Dominican refectory wall in Milan, *The Last Supper*, showing Jesus and the Twelve, has implanted the Synoptic scene into our imaginations as being the way it was. It is not a defined Catholic doctrine who was present and who wasn't. Some could say the presence of "men only" is defined by inference because the Last Supper words of Jesus became at a later time the basis for priestly ordination and for repeating ritually at Mass Jesus' sacrifice, a role till now restricted to males.[19]

Later that night, while Jesus was at prayer in a garden, he was captured. He had two inquisitions, one before Jewish leadership and one before the Roman Procurator, Pilate. In the meantime, his disciples fled and Peter outright denied knowing him. How frightened they were! When you are very afraid, you go back home. The people from Galilee fled home. Those from the Jerusalem environs stayed closer but out of sight. Jesus was crucified during the daylight hours of Friday. Some female disciples, including Jesus' mother, "watched from a distance" (Mk 15:40). Sabbath neared because sundown was approaching. The Romans did not want to spark Jewish outrage by leaving dying Jews on crosses when Sabbath arrived. So deaths—the texts describe two others but many could have been given death sentences at that time—were hastened by breaking legs. Death on a cross is by asphyxiation, and to catch a breath, the condemned person pushes up with his legs. But if legs are broken, this is impossible and death comes quickly. Jesus was already dead when the Romans came to break legs. Jesus was removed from the cross and placed quickly in a tomb. Sabbath's arrival presented no time to do the ritual washing and anointing of a corpse, a task for the female members of one's family. Jesus had no siblings. (His "brothers and sisters" in *Acts* 6:3 refer to relatives, perhaps cousins.) So the task fell to female companions.

The women could not do it on Saturday because of Sabbath. After sundown of Sabbath it was too dark to do it. So the texts make sense that women went to the tomb on the "first day of the week," Sunday, to anoint the body. And the body was not there.

Even though some texts present first-time appearances to the male apostles in Jerusalem, and other texts place them clearly in Galilee. I believe the Galilean apostles fled Jerusalem right away and Jesus appeared later to them in Galilee. The appearances begin happening in different places, to different people. The next Jewish festival that would bring everyone together back in Jerusalem was the early summer pilgrimage feast of Shavuoth, called Pentecost by Greek-speaking Jews, fifty days after Passover. (Jews observe three pilgrimage festivals that involve travel to the Temple, the first in middle spring called Pesach or Passover, followed by this one, and then a third festival in early autumn called Sukkoth, or Booths.) The disciples likely reconvened in Jerusalem for Pentecost to seek more sense among themselves about what had

19. I agree with the findings of the pope's own biblical resource, the Pontifical Biblical Commission, that the New Testament, by itself, does not solve who can be ordained. "Can Women be Priests?" Report of the PBC, April 1976. English translation in *Origins: CNS Documentary Service* (July 1976). Other documents are restrictive. The Code of Canon Law, § 1024, and the *Catechism of the Catholic Church*, § 1577, confine ordination to baptized males.

been happening to them. It was there that another resurrection appearance (Acts 2) happened to them, described dramatically not in terms of Jesus but of the bestowed Holy Spirit he causes.[20] More appearances awaited disciples in upcoming years, such as to St. Paul on the Damascus Road, but resurrection appearances did come to an end at a date that cannot be determined. We are simply left with the later church formula, "revelation ended with the death of the last apostle." But we can no more determine who he or she was than we can determine who were the five hundred to whom Jesus appeared, "some of whom are still alive" (1 Cor 15: 6) when Paul wrote the letter around AD 55 or 56.

The abiding presence of the Risen Jesus with the disciples and the later church is another matter. The presence of Jesus during an appearance to the disciples is a unique way of being present to them, for reasons indicated. It begins and ends. He is to be present in other ways, as taught during the appearance on the mountain in Galilee when he commissions the apostles to preach to "all nations" and promising that he will remain present to them always, until the world ends.

---

20. Luke calls his book *Acts of the Apostles*. This is a misnomer. Except for Peter and Paul and brief mention of Philip, it is not about the activities of each of the Twelve. (By this moment Matthias has been chosen to replace Judas and to reconstitute Twelveness). The book should be called "How the Church left Jerusalem and spread all over the known Roman World." The Spirit came over them at Pentecost and they began speaking all the known languages of the Empire, a symbolic expression of where Spirit-empowerment will lead the Church. The book began in Jerusalem and ends when Paul gets to Rome, the symbolic center of the known world. It began with preaching to Jews and ends when Paul, in frustration, says to Roman Jews rejecting him, "the Gentiles will listen."

CHAPTER SIX

Other Features of Resurrection Belief

"Eternity is the complete, all-at-once, perfect having of unending life."
Anicius Boethius

If *the* Ascension of Jesus is to mean coming to the end of his several resurrection appearances, whenever in the middle of the first century it was, it does not mean his risen presence among the disciples ceased. His invisible presence continues in a visible earthly reality called church.[1] Before turning to church-related matters in chapter seven, there are some features of my Catholic faith additionally connected with the invisible world that Jesus' resurrection occasions. I hold these features to be genuinely Catholic but they will not always be in conformity with their treatment in the *Catechism of the Catholic Church* (CCC). I offer this comment by way of *full disclosure*, as writers feel called to do and as I promised earlier I would.

I must explain why I begin this chapter with words from a sixth-century philosopher, Boethius (AD 480–524), who for most people today is an obscure figure at best. Not so for educated Christians of the Middle Ages. After the Latin Vulgate Bible, his book, *The Consolation of Philosophy*, was the most read piece of literature for them. In this book he provides a definition of eternity. Thomas Aquinas knew it and used it, as did other philosophers and theologians over the centuries. In the medieval seminar mentioned in the Foreword, we used his book annually, and his definition of eternity began to exercise ever greater impact on my thinking about my faith. His definition became my gateway to thinking why *eternal life* underlies so much about understand-

---

1. Our English word *church* is derived indirectly. The New Testament used the word *ekklēsia* for it, which literally means "the called together people," the convocation. This Greek word replicates exactly the Hebrew word for the forerunners of the church, the *qahal Yahweh*, the *called together people* of God, i.e., the people set apart or chosen. Romance languages keep the connection with ekklēsia: *ecclesia* (Latin), *église* (French), *chiesa* (Italian), and *iglesia* (Spanish). Germanic languages seem to derive from the Greek *kyriakon*, "belonging to the Lord (*Kyrios*):" *church* (English), *Kirche* (German), and *kerk* (Dutch). Being a called together people seems to get lost on English ears.

ing the invisible world and hence the title I've chosen for this book.

THE NATURE OF ETERNITY

"Eternity, therefore, is the complete, all-at-once, perfect having of unending life."[2] I provide Boethius's Latin below because everything hangs on how to properly translate *simul*. Sometimes the word means *simultaneously*, as in "it was raining in Philadelphia while simultaneously in Chicago it was snowing." At other times the word means *all at once*, as it does in his book. There is no passage of time. It is immediate and now, with no before or after moments. The usual fault with envisioning God in heaven, or the blessed in heaven, is to think of heavenly life as perpetuity, as if heaven were a ticking clock that never stops ticking, as if it were simply duration without beginning or end. But eternity is not perpetuity.

Let me say a few words in defense of *perpetuity* before repeating again that it's not eternity. Our imagination is something human and earthbound and conditioned by what's temporal. We can imagine perpetuity or unendingness without much difficulty. Mark Twain poked fun at the Protestant sermons about heaven he heard as a boy in Missouri, writing that Christians who went to heaven played harps and sang *Hosannah* forever, moment after moment after moment. It would never cease, but how boring and tedious it would become.[3] He flipped the preacher's perpetuity sermon upside-down. Our own Catholic prayer tradition uses concluding phrases like "who lives and reigns forever and ever" or "Glory to the Father, and to the Son and to the Holy Spirit...world without end, Amen." These phrases suggest perpetuity, and who can fault them because they speak to the manner we imagine God living forevermore. But to assert, as a matter of faith, that God continues in perpetuity is to assert that God has a past and that God awaits a future. This no Catholic should want to assert.

Initially, I applied this newly appreciated sense of eternity to thinking about when I would die. There is no middle ground between eternity and the passage of time on earth. To be earthbound is to be temporal. Things begin and end. Things have duration. There comes a precise moment when I die. However, to be with God in heaven is to be as God is and *how* God is, not *where* God is. I would be existing in eternity because I am absorbed into God's life. So my death is the passage from existing in time to existing in

2. *Aeternitas igitur est interminabilis vitae tota simul et perfecta possessio*, Consolatio Philosophiae, bk 5, passus 6. *Tota simul*, if taken together, conveys the same idea: the instantaneously total.

3. In Twain's caustic view of religious piety, he describes the Archangel Satan going down to earth to examine the insane humans that the "Master Intellect" [God] created, then sending letters back to fellow Archangels Gabriel and Michael about the insane things he was seeing and hearing. See *Letters from the Earth*, "Letter Two," reproduced in *The Norton Anthology of American Literature*, Vol C, (Norton: New York, 2012), 340-41.

eternity. There is nothing in-between.[4] I don't die and then have to wait for eternity to happen. Precisions need to follow: Do you believe in Purgatory? Yes, and it needs explanation. Do you believe in dying and waiting somehow for a general resurrection of the dead at the end of the world? No, and this needs explanation. Does sharing God's life only start with being in heaven? No, and one implication, also needing explanation, is that I have Eternal Life now; I'm not just immersed in time. Do you think Christ was in the tomb for three days before entering into resurrection? No, even though St. Cyril of Jerusalem (315–386), from whom I have learned much about sacraments, thinks differently. He wrote: Baptizing with three immersions represents Christ's three days in the tomb.

Our Lord died at some precise moment on that Friday, leaving a corpse impaled on a cross, a corpse that was then removed to a tomb. But he wasn't to be consigned among the dead because, without a passage of time intervening, God the Father resurrected him into a state of glory even though his corpse remained visible. Jesus' death was the moment of transition into exaltation, into taking his place at God's right hand. The biblical texts have it "that he was raised on the third day in accordance with the scriptures" (1 Cor 15:4). There is no doubt that early church writers took three days literally, as Cyril above, meaning that Jesus died before Sabbath began and he was resurrected on the day after Sabbath, Sunday for us. But as pointed out in the last chapter, *on the third day* proliferates in the scriptures. It does not possess calendar meaning.

This does not mean that we do away with the liturgy of Easter Sunday celebrating Jesus' resurrection any more than we do away with Ascension Thursday, forty days after Easter, celebrating Jesus' final departure into heaven. The liturgy has incorporated temporal shapes to aid our imaginations in prayerfulness and for careful consideration of the many aspects of a mystery. Save for celebrating a martyr's death when we have documentation for the date it happened, a liturgical feast day, normally, has no more historical specification than saying that Gabriel's annunciation to Mary happened in the springtime because the feast day is March 25, exactly nine months before Christmas day.

JESUS WENT INTO SHEOL (HELL)

I promised to point out where I depart from what the *Catechism of the Catholic Church* presents, and now is one such point. The *CCC* teaches "the separation

---

4. Not everyone agrees. "The aeon (aevum) differs from time (tempus) and eternity (aeternitas), lying somewhere between the two" (*ST* I, 10, 5). St. Thomas is joined by contemporary Parisian professors St. Bonaventure and Alexander of Hales in speculating about aeviternity to measure how angels and saints exist, short of God's eternity but far above temporal duration. Aevum is a medieval curiosity for me and plays no role in what I believe about heaven. About angels, see later.

of his soul from his body, between the time he expired on the cross and the time he was raised from the dead" on the third day (§ 624). Christ really died "but because of the union his body retained with the divine person he is, his was not a mortal corpse like others for 'divine power preserved Christ's body from corruption'" (§ 627). I've come to see Jesus' Paschal Victory differently because there is no in-between reality of existence between earthly life ending—what Newman called the visible world—and eternal life beginning, the invisible world of God's eternity.

During his earthly life, Jesus' human nature was united to the person of the Son, and in resurrection his glorified or transformed human nature remains united to the person of the Son. If the transition from Jesus' death to resurrected life needed an in-between period, say three days when his human soul seemed to be suspended without a body, then the mystery of the Incarnation would have come to a pause. That prospect seems implausible to me, and it seemed impossible to St. Hilary of Poitiers (AD 315–367), the preeminent Latin theologian before St. Augustine: "When the Word became man, he actually clothed himself in our flesh, uniting it to himself forever." The Son of God is never without an assumed human nature, whether it is unglorified while in Palestine or receiving glorification upon dying.

What the *CCC* sees happening in this middle period when the human soul remained united to the person of the Son, and the entombed corpse remained a dead reality, is that Christ (human soul united to the Son) "descended into Hell" to liberate those meant for heaven but held captive because redemption hadn't happened until that moment. The real significance of this last phase of Jesus' "messianic mission" is "the spread of Christ's redemptive work to all men [and women] of all times and all places, for all who are saved have been made sharers in the redemption" (§ 634). I agree fully with this last sentence, and I wish to share the manner in which my faith in redemption has become simpler in understanding it.

Jesus' "descent into Hell" would not be a topic for consideration were it not for an enigmatic text in *1 Pt* 3:18: Christ, put to death in the flesh, brought to life in the spirit, and in the spirit "went to preach to the spirits in prison who had once been disobedient…in the days of Noah." It would have been relegated to a list of other isolated and hard-to-decipher texts were it not for its use in the *Apostles Creed*, which runs "he was crucified, died and was buried; he descended into hell; on the third day he rose again from the dead." This creed first appeared in the early eighth century in the West, and by legend it was thought to be a joint composition of the Twelve Apostles. The Eastern Greek-speaking church did not know of the Apostles Creed and of Jesus' descent into hell (Sheol).[5] Our western Catholic church retains it

5. We are left with the meaning of the enigmatic "Jesus preached to the disobedient spirits in the times of Noah." The mention of Noah suggests that these are the bad angels, also known as sons of God, who had intercourse with the daughters of men, producing the leg-

and prays it at Mass when the Creed of Nicea-Constantinople is not selected; furthermore, Catholicism teaches the Apostles Creed in its catechisms for young children.

Every church teaching takes pains to assert that the Risen Christ did not go to the hell of the damned. Damnation means an existence alienated from God, and for God to go there is a contradiction in terms. Hell meaning *Sheol* is another matter, and let me explain this strange word. The earliest Israelites had no sense of life after death. One simply died and returned to dust (recall *adamah* from the Garden story in *Genesis*). In later reflection, people died and went to Sheol, sort of an underworld, and reflecting an undeveloped and shadowy Jewish belief in future life. Later still, belief in life-after-death emerges in clarity. In Jesus' day, the Pharisees believed in resurrection, the Sadducees did not.

But what about everyone who died in the many millennia before Jesus lived? As the *CCC* teaches, the human soul of Jesus before his resurrection went to them in Sheol to bring the blessings of redemption. I've been contending that Jesus dies into resurrection, and his glorified human nature brings "the mark of the nails," or however one expresses the biography of a salvific life, into the Eternal Life of God. Without the Incarnation ever having come to a pause, Jesus enters eternity, with his human identity shaped by how he lived. His redemption is eternalized. Could the effects of Jesus' redemption extend to human beings who lived and died before him without mention of visiting Sheol? My belief is *yes* and retroactively!

Jesus' death and resurrection have brought the blessings of his redemption into the eternal plan of God because he entered eternity to sit "at the Father's right hand." This is why its effects are retroactive as well as forward looking since God's eternity embraces past, present, and future earthly times. People of the past died with the prospect of entering, without delay, the blessedness of heaven or entering the condition of damnation instead. To the latter possibility I return later in this chapter.

An imaginative illustration of redemption becoming *eternalized* is suggested by a shining light. If you imagine the Risen Savior as being an intense source of light who shines on the whole sweep of time on earth, all at once, such that the past, the present, and the future fall under the same beam, then God's eternity is embracing past, present and future events. If light and its beam are made to stand for God's knowledge, then God knows everything without having to recall it or await its happening. If the light and its beam stand for the blessings of redemption, then the blessings of Jesus' victory reach every human being, especially retroactively, which is what the *CCC* essentially teaches in § 634 above and why I agree with it.

---

endary prehistoric giants whom the Israelites called the *Nephilim* (*Gn* 6:1-4). So the *1 Pt* text is a mythical way of teaching that Jesus' victory over death crushes the Satanic forces. *Jn* 16 teaches the same idea: Jesus' resurrection begets the condemnation of the Prince of this world.

What was said about Original Sin in chapter two needs recalling. It is not an inherited guilt from ancient parents. The phrase stands for the human nature shared by everyone whose feature of free self-determination, as God's gift to it, tilts to misusing self-determination, as earlier explained. What is the eventual prognosis for humanity without some provided remedy or antidote? As if it were a virus replicating itself in a pandemic, misused human freedoms, left to themselves, would mushroom into a human society dominated by the power and pervasive clutch of sin. And such are his words about slavery to sin in St. Paul's depiction of human society without Christ. But this dire picture of the reign and triumph of sin is a "what if" situation. What if the Incarnation never happened to bring healing to freedom's tilt, to block its proneness to misuse from becoming rampant? Recall St. Augustine's principle: to appreciate a grace or blessing, envision its absence.

Because of a milieu or canopy of grace covering all human history, Original Sin, that is, the tilt of human freedom to misuse, has always existed as a *healed over* situation. The retroactive and prospective effects of Jesus' redemption provide this canopy of grace over the first humans, over us, and over future generations to work out, in freedom, our "divine vocations" (see Vatican II below). A canopy of grace does not preclude egregious misuses of freedom from happening: the Nazi extermination camps, the Cambodian *Killing Fields* of the Khmer Rouge, the West African slave trade, are just a few horrors from more recent times.

Boethius's definition of eternity has informed my faith, and I have used it to describe how the blessings of redemption are retroactive to the very beginning of the human race and reach forward to the end of history, without recourse to accepting, in literal fashion, that Jesus descended into Sheol.

There are other ways to teach the stretch of redemption to the whole human race. The rich Israelite notion of *firstfruits* is one of them. The very first and best portion of a harvest belonged to Yahweh, and therefore to his Temple priests, since he had given Israel the land itself. The firstfruits of the harvest were offered the Temple in thanksgiving and begot the consecration of the entire harvest. "But now," St. Paul teaches by analogy, "Christ has been raised from the dead, the firstfruits of those who have fallen asleep" (1 *Cor* 15:20). Christ's resurrection is not just a solitary achievement for himself; it achieves the consecration (resurrection) of all who have died.

The notion of Christ as head of the church and the notion of ourselves as the body of the church is another way to describe how redemption overflows in all temporal directions. Thomas Aquinas used the imagery of head and body, wherein the body, that is, the church, receives from Christ the head the graces that are his in fullness and which his salvific life earned for us. Aquinas's head and body image translates the image in *Jn* 15, "I am the vine" and you are the branches that draw life from the vine. "The body, which is the Church," writes Aquinas, "is made up of people who have existed from the beginning of the world up to the very end of the world."[6] Aquinas joins the early Fathers of the Church in accepting their notion of *Ecclesia ab Abel*, the church existing from Adam and Eve and their son Abel until the world ends.

Catholic faith makes it incumbent to maintain that the possibility of salvation is denied no single human being who has ever lived and who had, in being conceived, carried the nobility of having been made in "the image of God." Note these words from one of Vatican II's more solemn documents, *The Church in the Modern World*: "[Hope for resurrection] is true not only for Christians but also of all persons of good will in whose heart grace works in an unseen way. For, since Christ died for everyone, and since the final vocation of everyone is in fact the same, and divine, we ought to believe that the Holy Spirit, in a manner known only to God, offers to every person the possibility of being associated with this pascal mystery" (*Gaudium et Spes* § 22).

WHAT HAPPENS WHEN I (AND YOU) DIE?

Two other questions are connected with this question. What about Purgatory? What about the resurrection of bodies only happening at the end of the world? The same fundamental belief met above will apply to these questions: There is no time delay between dying and being resurrected. Resurrection belief is stated in the Nicene Creed ("I look forward to the resurrection of the dead") and in the Apostles' Creed ("I believe in…the resurrection of the body"). When it happens is not mentioned in the Creeds.[7] The belief in Purgatory is not in the Creeds but it develops in writings of the Church Fathers, especially in the West. It plays a large role in Roman Catholic belief but it is less specific in Orthodox Christian belief. Both Catholics and Orthodox, however, maintain a strong tradition of praying for the welfare of the dead. The Protestant reformers rejected belief in Purgatory.

PURGATORY

What, then, about belief in Purgatory? Let me be clear about myself: I believe in the reality of Purgatory. It is a wonderful church doctrine if understood correctly. The traditional understanding about it comes from the Middle Ages and the distinction then made between the guilt a sin produces and the reparation or amends owed for the sin. God's forgiveness removes the guilt. But reparation remains, either to be undertaken as doing penance in this life or, if not completed sufficiently, doing penance after death. This led to seeing Purgatory as a penal period preparing a person for entry into heaven,

6. "Corpus Ecclesiae constituitur ex hominibus qui fuerunt a principio mundi usque ad finem ipsius." *ST III*, 8,3.

7. The Creed, first formulated at the Greek-speaking Ecumenical Councils of Nicea (AD 325) and expanded at Constantinople (AD 381) began with the word "We believe" (*Pisteuomen*). When the Creed began to be used in individual Baptisms, *we believe* became *I believe* and became hallowed as *I believe* (*Credo*) in Gregorian Chant. I remain perplexed why our Mass avoids using "We believe…" because everything else prays as *we* e.g., *Our Father*.

because the deceased person, while no longer bearing sin's guilt, still needs to make amends for offending God. A problem that is immediately sensed with the traditional understanding of Purgatory is that it envisions God as a strict legalist: God demands of someone meant for heaven every last measure of making amends even though God has already forgiven one's sins.

Catholic language spoke of souls in purgatory, and praying for "the poor souls" in the month of November. Because Purgatory lasted for however long amend-making was needed, certain actions of devotion from Catholics still living (almsgiving, pilgrimages, saying prescribed prayers, and other practices) led to the practice of "gaining indulgences." Indulgences carried specified timed merits in order to shorten the time period in Purgatory for oneself and for "souls" still suffering there. (The vocabulary of *souls* assumed that the deceased were alive but without bodies.) I do not exaggerate this description but it is wrongly framed. It is wrong mainly because it inserts a time period between death and resurrection. Purgatory cannot be some duration of suffering, a sort of waiting room before entering heaven. And it is wrong to think of Purgatory as even a situation regulated by timed indulgences, such as a "ten-year indulgence" that one meets in some Catholic devotional literature.

My understanding of Purgatory begins with the church's conviction that only the "pure of heart" can see God (*Mt* 5:8). Only the godly can be in the presence of God, the all-holy. Most people, one would hope, died loving God and wanting to have loved better, but they were not perfect. They brought into death their imperfect biographies. Therefore, Purgatory means the transforming action of God in resurrecting a person and, at the same moment, a perfecting of the person, a cleansing if you will. It is an effect of God's love for the individual and enabling "purity of heart," therefore enabling entering into the holy presence of God.

But why the language of *purgatory* as a suffering reality? Our language for God's activity is always drawn from our own earthly experiences by way of analogy. What is my own experience of how I grow in holiness and purity of heart? It is through a purging of my sinful inclinations, a freely undertaken self-discipline that chastises what is ungodly in me. It seems to be a law of the spiritual life that growth in holiness involves penances, not all the time to be sure because developing virtues plays its own holiness-making role, but not skirting penances either. For this reason we stretch imaginative language to describe the transformative feature of our resurrections as a purgation, a purgatory.[8] To paraphrase words of Pope Benedict XVI that support my proposal, if there were no purgatory, then we would have to invent it, for who would dare say of themselves that they died being worthy to enter into the

---

8. A fuller description is contained in my "A Roman Catholic View of Death," *Death and Bereavement Around the World*, vol. 1, *Major Religious Traditions*, eds., John Morgan and Pittu Laungani, (Amityville: Baywood Publishing Co., Inc., 2002), 87-102.

all-holy presence of God.[9]

Prayers for the dead count. Our Funeral Masses count. Lighting a candle or visiting a grave counts. If stripped of a temporal algorithm, our indulgences on behalf of deceased persons count, for the matter of an indulgence from our perspective is our performance of a good work or a voiced prayer, or another holy action undertaken, offered to God from a contrite heart. We are all keepers for each other in the Mystical Body, even beyond the other's death. "It is a holy and wholesome thought to pray for the dead" is the familiar rendering of the older *Douay-Rheims* Catholic Bible for *2 Mc* 12:46; the NABRE runs: "Thus [Judas Maccabeus] made atonement for the dead that they might be absolved from their sin." Our prayers for the dead enter into the eternal hearing of God and are retroactive. We influence the fate of others even if Purgatory is actually God's blessed transformation and instantaneous achievement of someone entering heaven.

THE DAY OF JUDGMENT

So many strands of thought converge under this topic, and it is difficult to sort them without confusion. From the Jewish tradition, Christianity inherited the "Day of Yahweh," and it was understood in two different ways. At the end of the world God would appear as victor, either gathering all the nations [Gentiles] together to recognize and worship the God whom Israel served, and peace would reign (i.e., the lion would rest beside the lamb) or, on the other hand, that God would return in vengeance when he brought the world to an end because evil held such sway. Christianity translated the Day of Yahweh into the Parousia, the Second Coming of Jesus at the end of the world, "coming from the right hand of the Father to judge the living and the dead" (*sedet ad dexteram Patris unde venturus est judicare vivos et mortuos*). Such read the brief Latin creedal formulas known to Saints Hyppolytus, Ambrose, and Augustine. And the contemporary Greek formulas of faith read the same about God judging the living (*zōntas*) and the dead (*nekrous*).

The phrase about the Risen Jesus coming to judge the living and the dead had made its entry into both the earlier Nicene Creed and the later Apostles Creed. Its stature in these two important creeds made me cautious

---

9. Benedict's 2007 encyclical on Hope, *Spe Salvi*, presents Purgatory similarly. "Before his gaze all falsehood melts away. This encounter with him, as it burns us, transforms and frees us, allowing us to become truly ourselves....His gaze, the touch of his heart heals us through an undeniably painful transformation "as through fire" (*1 Cor* 3:25)....But it is **a blessed pain**, in which the holy power of his love sears through us like a flame, enabling us to become totally ourselves and thus totally of God.... The transforming "moment" of this encounter **eludes earthly time-reckoning**—it is the heart's time, it is the time of "passage" to communion with God in the Body of Christ" (§ 47). [If Purgatory is the individual's encounter with a transforming God], "how can a third person intervene? When we ask such a question, we should recall that **no man is an island**, entire of itself. Our lives are linked together. No one lives alone. No one sins alone. No one is saved alone....So my prayer for another is not something extraneous to that person, not even after death" (§ 48). Bold print mine.

to suggest that the Day of Judgment at the end of the world should be understood differently, but I have come to think so.

Let me list some texts bearing on end-time judgment that have made me hesitant. The sole New Testament text using these words that became part of the two creeds is *2 Tim* 4:1. "Before God and before Christ Jesus, who is to be judge of the living and the dead, I charge you [Timothy] in the name of his appearance [coming] and his kingdom, preach the word...." There are New Testament echoes elsewhere, of course, two of them using words from Jesus himself. "When the Son of Man comes in glory, escorted by all the angels, he will sit on his glorious throne, and all the nations [every human being] will be assembled before him. He will separate" the good (sheep) from the bad (goats), as a shepherd partitions his flock. The bad "will go off to eternal punishment, but the righteous to eternal life" (*Mt* 25: 31-46).[10] "Amen, amen, I say to you, the hour is coming and is now here when the dead will hear the voice of the Son of God....The [Father] gave him power to exercise judgment because he is the Son of Man....The hour is coming in which all who are in the tombs will hear his voice and come out, those who have done good deeds to the resurrection of life but those who have done wicked deeds to the resurrection of condemnation" (*Jn* 5:25-29).

Only two other texts bear on end-time events. Paul evangelized the Thessalonians around AD 50, and he surely preached his personal conviction that the end of the world, hence Jesus' return, was near. Events forced him to leave the city before explaining what would happen to someone who dies before Jesus returns. Hence we have the following in his letter to them: "About those who have fallen asleep, do not grieve for them as others do who have no hope. We believe that Jesus died and arose again, and that in the same way God will bring with him those who have fallen asleep in Jesus....We who are still alive for the Lord's coming (*parousia*) will not have any advantage over those who have fallen asleep" (*1 Thes* 4:13-16). Although it is not an end-of-the-world judgment text, Paul's letter does refer to the resurrection of the righteous, of those who have "fallen asleep in Jesus," at Jesus' Second Coming. The other text is clearly judgmental and frightfully so. It describes the Last Judgment scene in the *Book of Revelation*, a book that brims with apocalyptic imagery that must be carefully interpreted, pure literalism avoided.

> Next I saw a large white throne and the one [the Lamb of God] who was sitting on it. The earth and the sky fled from his presence and there was no place for them. I saw the dead, the great and the lowly, standing before the throne, and scrolls were opened. Then another scroll was opened, the book of life. The dead were judged according to their

---

10. The judging criteria are the famous "when I was hungry, did you feed me or not, clothe me or not?" Neither *2 Tim* nor *Mt* 25 used *parousia* for Jesus' return but both texts refer to the Second Coming at the end of history.

deeds, by what was written in the scroll. The sea gave up its dead; then Death and Hades[11] gave up their dead. All the dead were judged according to their deeds. Then Death and Hades were thrown into the pool of fire....Anyone whose name was not found in the book of life was thrown into the pool of fire (*Rev* 20:11-15).

Taken literally and on face value, these four texts would seem to support the words of the two creeds that the Risen Jesus will return at the end of the world to judge the living and the dead, with doers of good resurrecting into Eternal Life and with doers of evil to everlasting punishment, the *pool of fire* in apocalyptic language. But two matters give me pause about seeing our Catholic faith in this manner. The first is a matter of textual interpretation. Jesus and his first followers, hence the Paul who wrote to the Thessalonians, inherited the Old Testament descriptions of the Day of Yahweh, such as its description in *Malachi* 3, when Elijah, who seemed transported to heaven without dying (*2 Kgs* 2:11), returns at the end of the world, when evil-doers perish and the righteous are saved. These texts are end-of-the-world answers to the perennial question, "Why in this life does evil seem to flourish and goodness gets trampled?" The prophet Malachi even puts this pointed question on the lips of Yahweh's critics, "Where is the God of fair judgment now" (*Mal* 2:17)? I think it is natural to push to an end-of-the-world trial how the scales of justice get balanced with goodness rewarded and evil punished, especially if many people, good and bad, died without experiencing in their earthly lives this clear-cut reckoning.

The second matter giving me pause is the implied notion that the people who die before the world ends somehow continue to exist as pure disembodied souls. This would refer to "the saved" going back to "Adam and Eve" in biblical language, that is, back to the beginning of the human race. In the meantime, all of them would lack a body because it became a corpse that rotted in the earth or disintegrated in the sea or was cremated. In addition, the end of the world and a final judgment of the living and the dead have thousands upon thousands of years still to go—this is my guess—before the righteous get judged and receive resurrected bodies. This idea amounts to countless disembodied souls awaiting the final judgment day.

Besides the vast numbers involved of persons awaiting judgment (resurrection or damnation), how is all this possible? Where do human souls without bodies exist? Is there a location for them, which by definition cannot be earth or heaven, and is not Purgatory? I trip over these questions. What I envision seems more reasonable. Everyone dies into resurrection with no time delay. Human beings are unified realities. They are spiritualized bodies

11. The Greek word translated Hades is *thanatos*, meaning the underworld. It is met throughout Greek mythology.

or, conversely, embodied souls. People are not composites of body and soul as if two parts. I think a human being never becomes disembodied, even on the other side of death; otherwise, one ceases to be a human being. Left behind in death is a corruptible body, the corpse. Gained on the other side of death is the acquisition of an incorruptible body, a resurrected body. This glorified body is of God's making in the manner described above. It is my glorified body. It is I, as God gifted me to be.

When it would pertain to our Catholic faith, I promised to provide some examples of church history, and this very topic is one such occasion. The question of disembodied human souls existing before the general resurrection of bodies at the Final Judgment enjoyed a curious papal debate in the late Middle Ages with one pope condemning his predecessor. Both popes accepted the reality of disembodied human souls after a person's death. They differed on whether such human souls had to wait until the end of the world to enter heaven and enjoy the Beatific Vision. Pope John XXII [Jacques Duèse] was the second Avignon pope after the papacy relocated there in 1309. (It was he who approved the canonization of Thomas Aquinas in 1323.) John XXII taught that the righteous, upon dying, only begin to enjoy the vision of God after the resurrection of bodies on the last day when everyone gets judged.

His successor, Benedict XII, condemned this opinion and taught instead that human souls, either not needing purgatory after death, or having achieved a "pure in spirit" life before death, enter forthwith (*mox*) into heaven where they enjoy the Beatific Vision, not needing to await the general resurrection at the end of the world to receive resurrected bodies. Benedict's wording of his 1336 document—"By this Constitution, which is to remain in force forever, we with apostolic authority define the following"—has led a few theologians to think that this solemn wording introduces infallible papal teaching.[12] I do not consider it fulfills the needed conditions for expressing papal infallibility, and I also think Benedict XII was wrong about disembodied human souls existing in heaven awaiting resurrected bodies. But this papal clash, in which both popes accepted without quibble the possibility of disembodied human souls existing, as if in suspended animation, shows how ingrained this manner had become of conceiving how a person existed between one's death and the end of the world. Catholic language about "souls in purgatory" is of similar bearing.

END OF THE WORLD

The end of the world is another way of saying the end of human existence because the "earth and its fullness" (Ps 24) is God's provision for the human life God created. Without people, an ongoing world makes no sense. This is

---

12. *Denzinger-Schönmetzer Handbook of Church Teachings*, § 1002, edition of 1965 reflecting the new numbering.

the implication of the two creation stories in *Genesis*.

And what will be the human situation when the end of our planet draws near? Will it have become a human family in harmony, or a chaotic mess where groups and religions are at loggerheads? And does the world end by our sun becoming a Red Giant star as it depletes its hydrogen supply, toasting to cinders the inner planets of the solar system, which includes Earth? This is the accepted scientific prediction. These are questions beyond my reach. But one question isn't. What is the end of the world for the human race?

For those meant for salvation, each individual death brings immediate entry into resurrection. Therefore, all deaths, viewed collectively and unfolding over time, is the end of the world for the human race because it means that everyone meant for salvation has achieved it. This has been the central insight I have shared. In this belief there is no role for the corpses human death left behind. They decay. They are not needed for the resurrected bodies God fashions for us even though some early church writers thought otherwise.[13]

There is one exception to this point, and I can see no way around it. It involves Jesus' corpse and I believe that it is a unique case with Jesus. I've shared my belief that Jesus died into immediate resurrection and glorification. But resurrection preaching by Jesus' disciples was to follow his death and appearances to them, as we saw in chapter two. If opponents to this preaching—and there were many in those first decades—could point out his corpse, preaching Jesus' resurrection would never have taken hold. His corpse needed not to be present and observable. The Empty Tomb stories certainly attest to the absence of a corpse at least, although they do not attest to proof of his resurrection. But how Jesus' corpse came from being observable—remember it was removed from the Cross and carried to a tomb—to becoming no longer observable is a matter on which the Bible is silent and about which I can only conjecture.

I rely on my understanding how God's act of creating is forever happening and is not a once-for-all action of the past. God, as Creator, actively sustains in existence everything that ever existed, now exists, or will come to exist in the future. Everything is propped up in existence and would lapse into nothingness without the Creator's support. Corpses, too, are sustained in existence, and they undergo decay into materials themselves propped up.

Because in God's providence the success of resurrection preaching about Jesus required the absence of his corpse, I conjecture that his corpse simply lapsed into non-existence in the tomb. God Creator ceased to sustain it in existence. Below, in treating the topic of *hell*, I will apply this same idea of being sustained in existence, or lapsing into non-existence, to ponder if there

---

13. St. Augustine is an example. "The Lord, by dying, destroyed death....His body did not see corruption; our body will see corruption, and only then will it be clothed through him in incorruption at the end of the world."

is anyone damned for all eternity.

Some biblical texts, besides empty tomb stories, support my surmise that something of this nature happened to the no-longer-existing corpse of Jesus. In the Septuagint (LXX) version of Hebrew psalms, *Ps* 15:10 reads: "You will not abandon my soul to hell (*Hades* in Greek), nor will you allow your holy one to experience corruption." The New Testament sacred authors, including the writer we call Luke, used the LXX. Although writing years after the events he records, Luke reports six early sermons about Jesus' resurrection in *Acts*, the first five attributed to Peter and the sixth to Paul.

In the first one, Peter's so-called Pentecost sermon, Peter quotes David's prophecy, i.e., *Ps* 15, that God would not abandon his Messiah to Hades nor let his body undergo corruption, because God raised him up (Acts 2:31). In the sixth sermon, Paul is preaching in a synagogue in Antioch of Asia Minor that God raised Jesus from the dead, quoting the classical resurrection prophecy of *Ps* 2, "You are my son, this day I have begotten you," and *Ps* 15, "You will not allow your Holy One to see corruption" (Acts 13:37). There is unequivocal stress on the fact that the body of Jesus did not experience corruption, even though decay is the fate of anyone else who dies. I believe the incorruptibility to be true, and I believe it to be a unique case with the corpse of Jesus, which soon ceased to exist at all. To preach later on that God did not allow his Anointed One to undergo corruption is equivalent to proclaiming Jesus is resurrected into glory and his earthly corpse is no more.

My faith has simplified concerning our deaths and resurrections. A person dies and is transformed by God into resurrection. In St. Paul's language in *1 Cor* 15:44, we who once had a physical body (*sōma psychikon*) now have a spiritualized body (*sōma pneumatikon*). The physical body, the corpse, is prepared by the family for burial or for cremation. But the corpse is not the person. It is an assemblage of chemicals, even of organs that can be donated to another person needing them. The real person, now spiritualized, has entered into the Eternal Life of God, as if absorbed by God to share God's nature. The resurrected person and all other resurrected persons have come to experience "end-time" reality, the *eschaton* in the Bible's words, which is what the teaching about a universal judgment at the end of the world was meant to convey. But a literal understanding of the teaching is not needed.

Entering eternity has a particular implication, and it staggers my temporally-inclined imagination I must confess. Because existing in eternity means there are no before or after moments in it, entering eternity, entering heaven, means that no one gets to be in heaven before anyone else does. *Before* doesn't figure in an eternal milieu. However, a certain priority belongs to Jesus' entry into heaven because he is the cause of, the pattern of, the firstfruits of, our resurrections into eternity. *Col* 1:18 calls him "the firstborn from the dead." The resurrection of Jesus enables the resurrection of all others, even if they lived and died before he did. Jesus and all others die at different times in history, but they enter resurrected status at the same instant, from heaven's perspective.

How is this conundrum to be understood? Thomas Aquinas has a help-ful distinction: priority of nature *vs.* priority of time. The latter means that something occurs in time before something else. We meet this in our lives all the time, e.g., one person dies before another. Priority of nature means that something is the cause and enablement of others things in its category. It comes *before* the others in this causal sense. Jesus' resurrection enjoys priority of nature. Therefore it is true to say that the resurrection of Jesus enables the heaven of the saved to come about. Jesus enters heaven first, in terms of priority of nature. Jesus and everyone else enter heaven together because eternity has no before and after, even if someone lived long before Jesus and had died into immediate resurrection. This, of course, is language describing the invisible world of heaven. In the visible world, the world of my senses and memory and hopes, people die before others, and Jesus is eternally interced-ing for all of us. The invisible world permeates the visible world (Newman); eternity acts in history (Jesus the High Priest); the eternal Word lived in Pal-estine (*Jn* 1:14). These things take pondering.

My understanding of everyone arriving in eternity together is reinforced, I believe, by the idea of heaven's undiluted happiness. If I were to die and go to heaven, and my children and my grandchildren were not present with me in the company of the blessed, if they were still working out their possible salvation, how could I be fully happy not knowing the outcome? But if being in heaven really means being in the company of the blessed, all of them, then there is no "waiting for someone." *Waiting around* is another of those phrases out of sync with what eternity means.

A final comment about facing divine judgment upon dying. The notion developed slowly and by the Middle Ages achieved definitive shape that each individual faced God's judgment upon dying. It was called the Particular Judgment as opposed to the General Judgment of everyone at the end of the world. The Particular Judgment engendered a sense of apprehension or even fear of "what will happen to me?" "Will I be saved?" One's family was anxious that a dying member receive the "Last Rights" of the Church (an anointing, confessing of sin, and receiving the Eucharist if swallowing it were possible) lest he or she fail the Particular Judgment's scrutiny. I have tried to share, on the contrary, that we bear within ourselves Eternal Life during our earthly lives and into death. The way I have described dying into resurrec-tion, with Purgatory being a moment of healing grace, replaces the scrutiny of a particular judgment and a final general judgment. I do not see two separate judgments happening to me but only one reality, and this event, my resurrection and simultaneous healing, is a moment of grace. The Eternal Life within me, which I carried into death, achieves its full blossom.

HAVING RESURRECTED BODIES

There is an expression in popular Catholicism that one hears occasionally, and in times past heard frequently. "Upon death the soul leaves the body." It flies to Purgatory, or to somewhere to await the general resurrection at the end or, God forbid, it goes to hell. Never mind that no explanation was given how souls travel. The medieval imagination pictured spirits flying; notice the wings on angels in medieval paintings. I've been at pains throughout this book to use words that do not imply the soul and the body are two entities that separate off at death. I used the phrases *embodied spirit* or *spiritualized body*. Body and soul can be distinguished mentally but they are not separate in reality. I am the only reality. But does my careful terminology reach an impasse when I die? The embodiment of my soul, as I experienced it in earthly life, is left behind. It is now a corpse and not me. Someone might then say, "You really do accept that your soul departs your former body, goes off as it were. There's no other alternative."

But there is. It has been my proposal all along. When I die, I die into resurrection without any delay, with a resurrected body God has formed. It has long been a Catholic conviction that the human soul is immortal. It began to be but it does not die. I agree, of course, and I am only adding my conviction that being embodied does not cease either. In other words, I do not cease. Rather than saying that the human soul is immortal, I prefer to say that I am immortal. You are immortal. We all are.

Let me return to people who use the phrase, "the soul leaves the body" at death. Although I disagree with their words, I do think that their instinct about someone's soul is correct. Their instinct concerns someone's personal identity. This is what I think they are seeking to retain when describing death, and so do I. They see someone's personal identity as if it's a book listing good and bad deeds of their soul, and the deceased brings that personal moral scorecard into the punishment of Purgatory or before the judgment throne of God.

Leave aside their descriptions of the postmortem process about Purgatory and Judgment. I agree with them that my soul retains my personal identity through death into risen life. Before death, my body and soul, existing in an essential oneness with each other, was simply *me*. In my everyday life, I gave expression to who I was, and hoped to be, and feared being, and all the other factors of psychological life, which also involved, of course, biological life. That was who I was, as I unfolded my life in free choices about myself, others, the surrounding physical world, and about God, even were I someone who asserted, "There is no God."

This is my dynamic personal identity. If I was living many years with a spouse, and was transparent about myself, the spouse would come to know the real me, even underneath the unfolding events of my life over several years, even when I went from one job to a quite different job or to unemployment, or we went from having no children to having several, or living through the deaths of loved ones. Spouses grasp the personal identities of each other. There is an aphorism that says "All good things come to an end." For many things in life this may be true, but for the most important thing in life, my personal identity, it is not true. The personal identity I have forged for myself before dying is the personal identity I bring into resurrected life, scoured of imperfections if need be by the gifting process I've called Purgatory. In resurrection I come out a better me but it is still my continuing personal identity.

Explaining death is hard. We trip over the words. In saying that our personal identities endure through death, I am brought back to something mentioned in the Foreword. When Easter Week days are warm and non-rainy, my wife and I would sit on our outdoor deck, a glass of a suitable wine in hand, and share thoughts on resurrection and what heaven will be like.[14] Only later, after reading St. Augustine's life, did I realize we were doing exactly what Augustine and his mother, Monica, had done at Ostia, preparing to sail from Rome's seaport to Africa. "The two of us, all alone, were enjoying a very pleasant conversation overlooking the garden. We were asking one another in the presence of the Truth [God] what it would be like to share the eternal life enjoyed by the saints" (*Confessions*, IX, 10). Shortly after, Monica took ill and died in Ostia.

One of Kathleen's early questions to me was, "How will I recognize you in heaven?" Because we will not have the recognizable bodies we carried about on earth of being so tall, so heavy, etc., I answered, "You will recognize me from the personal identity you came to grasp about me over the years. Didn't you used to advise me—whatever the proposal was—'I don't think you should do this because it doesn't fit you'? And didn't I respond, 'I think you know me better than I know myself at times'?" A person in a resurrected condition retains the personal identity, the recognizable identity that was formed in earthly life. In heaven we will exist with the flower of our historical personalities, a fullness reflecting the grace of Christ and what God has predestined for each one.

If personal identity worked out over a lifetime supplies our fundamental identity, what about parents who lose infant children to death? At that time of grief, they consoled themselves, and friends consoled them, "You will join little Mark in heaven—this is a true story of one of my aunts—and you'll be together." How do I describe the personal identity of a baby who lived only a few days? *Ecclesia supplet* (the Church supplies)[15] is a principle to cover the validity of a sacrament when a factual error of jurisdiction happened. The sacrament is still validly received, the church supplying, as it were, any defect in the ritual. Regarding little Mark and many similar situations, I can't make

14. The earliest possible date for Easter is March 21 and the latest date is April 25. Easter occurs on the first Sunday after the first full moon after the spring equinox.
15. Canon 144 in the New Code of Canon Law.

the case for an achieved personal identity to solve it. So I just say, *Deus supplet*. Let God be God and unite knowingly in resurrected life those meant for each other. However one tries to describe heaven, a healthy and rightful "I can't say how" needs to remain.

It is surely easier to describe what a resurrected existence is not. It is not happening in a location, however idyllically imagined. Heaven is not a place. The word *how* rather than *where* befits heaven. It is not an existence unfolding in perpetuity. Resurrected life has the nature of timelessness. The physical characteristics of earthly life do not translate over. It is silly to ponder how tall we will be, or how heavy, or what earthly age we will reflect. (A Catholic ethicist in a recent book proposed the role of intercourse happening in heaven—*could be envisioned* was her proposal—that I find similarly silly and more so when a person has had two or more spouses.)

We need to fall back on scriptural revelation to say what resurrection involves in order to avoid silly proposals. The ability to *see* God *as God* is a recurrent theme, expressed imaginatively as beholding the face of God, as *Ps* 42:3 does: "My soul thirsts for God....When can I enter and see the face of God?" The Beatitude from the Sermon on the Mount, which I used in explaining the nature of Purgatory, uses the image of seeing God: "Blessed are the pure of heart for they shall see God" (*Mt* 5:8). Paul describes afterlife in like fashion: "At present we see indistinctly, as in a mirror, but then face to face" (*1 Cor* 5:12). In the Johannine tradition we have "Beloved, we are God's children now; what we shall be has not yet been revealed. We do know that when it is revealed, we shall be like him, for we shall see him as he is" (*1 Jn* 3:2). Thomas Aquinas used this Johannine text to teach that seeing God precisely as God requires God gifting the blessed with an illumination—he called it the *light of glory*—enabling the saints to see what by the nature of the human mind they could not grasp on earth, the very essence of God. This illumination, in effect, divinizes persons. "By means of this light [resurrected persons] are changed into godlikeness, that is, made similar to God."[16]

I am unsure when the phrase *Beatific Vision* entered into the Catholic lexicon but certainly the many teachings of Thomas Aquinas about seeing God in God's glory had much to do with its acceptance. As a phrase, Beatific Vision is simply another expression for heavenly life or bliss. As an illumination, it is God's direct and unmediated self-communication of himself, as Trinitarian persons, to the personalities of the blessed. The aspiration of human life to know God as God is—recalling the hopes of Augustine and Anselm—is met and satiated.

However, there is with Beatific Vision an emphasis on the intellectual (knowing) feature of a resurrected person. But this is only part of the picture of heaven, and not the paramount part. Knowing leads to loving. This is

---

16. "Secundum hoc lumen efficiuntur deiformes, idest Deo similes" (*ST* I, 12, 5).

as true in afterlife as it is in this life. Seeing God face to face, grasping the Trinitarian nature of God as God has willed to be seen—this is what God's self-communication means. And this is to see how loveable God is. Therefore God is loved unrestrictedly by the blessed. This intensity of loving God seems to be anticipated in this life, however slightly and by those few whom we call mystics. As I have studied—more accurately struggled to grasp—St. John of the Cross's (1542–1591) *unitive* way, he reports that mystics experience such an unrestricted love of God that the passage of time comes to a standstill. To anyone skeptical about such an experience, I would ask: Why cannot God grant to mystics a foretaste of what heaven will be like?

I've attempted to avoid quoting modern theologians, with the exception of Cardinal Newman, because I wanted to avoid that type of writing fit for theology journals. To express my faith as simply as I could, it was enough to quote the Bible, the Fathers of the early church, and occasionally some medieval writers. But I wish to acknowledge the influence of a modern theologian, Karl Rahner, S.J. (1904–1984), on two aspects of my thoughts how the blessed in heaven know and love God. On these matters he himself was actually influenced by Thomas Aquinas.

Regarding seeing God face to face and grasping the essence of God through an empowering illumination, as described above, the Beatific Vision "does not annul God's incomprehensibility."[17] God is never known in the unlimited sense God knows himself. The experience of God's incomprehensibility (*Unbegreiflichkeit*), when the saints are seeing the face of God, differs from the incomprehensible God we experience in this life. However, and as unimaginable as it seems, God's incomprehensibility leads to the bliss of love, a heightened love if you will, in the hearts of those in heaven. Rahner connects the Beatific Vision's experience of the incomprehensible God with augmenting the bliss of the love of God that the saints possess. Rahner is a very deep thinker but his point about an augmented love of God seems plausible.

His second contention is more plausible to me but it is equally speculative. To be in heaven is not only to know and love God but also to know and love others. What others? Certainly my family, relatives and friends, for what would heaven be like if it were not so. But how far is the net to be stretched? Let us assume, and I think it is a good assumption to make, that the number of the saved who lived from when human life began to when the world ends is a very large number indeed. Let us just say countless. To know and to love God and others is to have recognition and awareness of them. Does it make sense to claim that my recognition of fellow saints involves an astronomical number of them? The prospect borders on the bizarre, but I do not discount what God can achieve. How wide is this net of knowing and loving fellow

17. See K. Rahner, "Beatific Vision," *The Concise Sacramentum Mundi* (New York: Crossroads, 1989).

saints? Rahner observes that "all others are known and loved in the manner it *concerns us*," and he refers to III, 10, 2 of Aquinas's *Summa*. Let me render Aquinas somewhat freely. "Each created intellect [i.e., each resurrected human being] does not grasp in the Word [of God] all heavenly realities whatsoever but only proportionally as many realities as [this person] more perfectly beholds the Word. Nevertheless, no blessed knower in grasping the Word is without awareness of those others who *pertain to* that blessed person."[18]

Aquinas reads *spectant*, Rahner translates *concerns us*, and I have rendered it *pertain to*. I find Rahner's speculation plausible because it avoids the silliness of saying that in heaven, in loving the reality of God, who after all caused the assembly of the redeemed to be who they are, we will be aware of a person from thousands of years ago no more or no less than we are aware of parents or a spouse or children. This can't be so. Instead, our heavenly awareness of others has a limited reach without experiencing deprivation.

To this plausible idea I connect my idea of carrying into resurrection one's personal identity. It is my identity and by its personal nature it is limited in scope. Limited in number are the persons I have known, have befriended, have injured and sinned against, and have been objects of my prayers of petition. In heaven I want to be aware of St. Augustine and of this or that martyr whose story seared me. So many are likely to be the full number of the blessed—Catholicism prays weekly in its Masses for the salvation of the world beginning to end—that I am reminded that the first hunter/gatherers of my human family, whom I hope are in heaven, are as unknown and distant from me as if they came from another galaxy. But they did not. They were created in the image of God. They experienced the lure of redemptive grace. Humanity began with hunter/gatherers and it ends in heaven with knower/lovers.

Because loving God in heaven has been mentioned, the loving faculty of a resurrected human nature remains the human will. This means that loving is an expression of human freedom, as was our earthly experience of loving. But in heaven, the will always acts in freedom to love God. We cannot not love God and we in full freedom do it. Expressing it negatively, we cannot sin in heaven. Why are we sinless in heaven but not on earth? The act of knowing! Our earthly experience is that the will responds to what the intellect sizes up. If we could grasp the truth, then we in freedom would choose it because it is seen as good-for-us. And if it is good for us truly, and in the manner of *the truly* reflecting *the godly*, then we would never sin. But this is heaven's situa-

18. For readers knowing some Latin, the text runs: Uniquisque enim intellectus creatus in Verbo cognoscit, non quidem omnia simpliciter, sed tanto plura quanto perfectius videt Verbum. Nulli autem intellectui beato deest quin cognoscat in Verbo omnia quae ad ipsum *spectant* (italic mine). Aquinas has another principle lurking behind *perfectius* (more perfectly). The greater the illumination a resurrected person receives in Beatific Vision, the more perfectly God is seen. Such is someone who dies possessing more love (*qui plus habet de caritate*) *ST* I, 12, 6.

tion. We see God as God in truth is. Therefore in freedom we love God and cannot choose otherwise. This is not a diminishment of human freedom but its highest accomplishment. With a certain irony and not at all unexpected, heaven is the antithesis of what pure Original Sin on earth would have been if a reign of sin ever existed. In the latter, one cannot not sin yet one sins freely and under no compulsion. In heaven, one cannot not love, yet it is done freely, in fact, supremely freely.

In the most succinct manner I wish to conclude this section about what I believe life in heaven means. Through a special illumination, we are gifted to be able to see the very essence of God, to see God face to face in biblical language. We know God but we do not comprehend God because our human natures remain created, even though resurrected. Our knowing God is never equal to God's self-knowing. Experiencing God and God's incomprehensibility is not experienced as a limitation but rather as heightened bliss, for which Fr. Karl Rahner is to be thanked. And such is the nature of our loving. Because the object of our knowing and loving is God in the fullness of Trinity, which in the Son of God means Jesus Christ, we experience all other humans *of moment to us*—my other translation of Aquinas's *spectant*—because Christ brings into eternity his entire Mystical Body of the saved. This is happening in eternity, where *happening* does not mean an unfolding moment-after-moment event. It is rather a timeless *now* of ecstasy and awareness of others. This cannot be imagined because imagination is tied to temporality. We are left with "Eye has not seen, nor ear heard, nor has it entered into our hearts [read imaginations] what God has prepared for those who love him" (1 Cor 2:9).

ANGELS

Who else is in heaven? The traditional answer is that the saints join the angels who are already there. This wording seems to violate what I said about eternity lacking *before* and *after*, so I need to return to it. For now I just want to reflect on angels. Who are they? In terms of function, they are God's messengers or agents. The word *angelos* (αγγελος) means messenger in Greek, as does the Hebrew word for them, *mal'āk*. So a rule of thumb strategy for encountering angels in the Bible is to read their lips. What they speak to people is communicating to them God's revelation. Notice the words of the angel(s) in the empty tomb: "Jesus is not here; he has been raised." In terms of their makeup, they are creatures (as we are), they have natures with an intellect and will (as we do although ours function differently), and they are immaterial (as we are not). Christian writings influenced by Greek philosophy worked with a hierarchical universe. At the highest level is God, an uncreated spiritual being, next came created spiritual beings (angels), then came created spiritual/material creatures (humans) and lastly came purely material creation (everything else on earth).

Any teaching about angels meets with certain difficulties at the present time. The chief difficulty is whether angels exist at all. Many people assert unabashedly that angels do not exist. I do not know how anyone can confidently claim this because you cannot prove a negative contention. You cannot prove "angels do not exist" any more than you can prove the Cryptic Treehunter, a Brazilian rain forest bird, does not exist. All you can say is that I haven't seen the bird in a very long time. Lest my own position gets lost in what follows, let me say it outright. I don't know if angels exist, but I am not going to claim that they don't. Must you believe they exist? That's another question, to which I'm going to say no.

Why my caution when angels are met all through the late Old Testament and in the New Testament, and even on the lips of Jesus? The *CCC* teaches that the church has defined their existence as binding on one's faith (see §328), making reference to the words of the Fourth Lateran Ecumenical Council (AD 1215): "By his omnipotent power God created from no preexisting reality (*de nihilo condidit*) creatures both spiritual and corporeal, namely angels and things of earth, and then (*deinde*) humans who are of body and spirit" (Denzinger §800). These medieval bishops and abbots of AD 1215 clearly were repeating the picture in the P creation story, although angels are not itemized in the P story. Still, I need to proceed respectfully because an Ecumenical Council has been referenced.

Angels appear late in the Tanak texts, almost like an incursion. In the earliest biblical witness, the "angel of Yahweh" (*mal'āk YHWH*) is Yahweh himself. The story of Moses at the burning bush (Ex 3) shows the identity clearly. First, the angel speaks from the bush, then it is Yahweh speaking after all. When Jacob departed Laban in Mesopotamia, after obtaining Rachel as wife, "God's angels encountered him, and Jacob named the place, 'This is God's encampment'" (Gn 32).

There are mythical angel stories, as when "the sons of God" came down to earth and ravished the daughters of men, producing the legendary giants (*Nephilim*) of old (Gn 6). This story, besides being a preparatory event for the Noah's Ark story of a world becoming more evil, also reflects how angel stories from ancient Near Eastern cultures infiltrated Israelite thinking. In all of them, god (or gods, if pantheistic) was envisioned in a heavenly court surrounded by angels to do the divine bidding. In Isaiah's vision (Is 6) and Yahweh's conversation with Job (Jb 38), angels form the heavenly court and sing Yahweh's praises. In the late-appearing *Book of Daniel*, angels are guardians of nations, and when Israel was oppressed by Persia, Israel's guardian angel Michael had to do battle with Persia's angel (Dn 10). The apocryphal *Book of Enoch* has a highly developed angelology. So I would conclude that existence of angels in the Tanak seems to be an incursion from existing external cultures rather than a revealed defining event, as the Sinai Covenant or the monarchy under Saul, then under David, are revealed events.

With the New Testament, the existence of angels is taken for granted. Our Lord himself sanctions the popular belief. Some will claim that if Jesus talked about angels, that solves it. But recall the official Catholic teaching about the three stages of gospel formation in chapter one. I need to repeat what I then wrote. "Church teaching asserts that Jesus was a fully embodied inhabitant of first-century Palestine. His thinking involved current thought forms, just as ours does today. His language used the idioms and vocabulary limitations of the Aramaic that he and everyone else spoke. His outlook was of the specific time, location, and circumstances in which he lived. If the culture then thought that the sun moved and the earth did not, so did Jesus. If the general Jewish sense at that time was that King David composed every psalm in the Tanak, then Jesus would have thought the same as apparently he does (*Mt 22:43*)." I am merely trying to answer someone who says, "That solves it because Jesus said it." It may, but it is equally plausible that Our Lord was not proposing a divine revelation about angels that requires the assent of faith but was only reflecting a cultural viewpoint he and his listeners shared.[19]

The rest of the New Testament, the writings of Fathers of the Church, and church teachings such as the Fourth Lateran Council, write with the assumption that angels exist. That's pretty powerful harmony. It is never clear to me, however, that angels are the direct object of what's being taught, even in those clear words of Lateran IV where the opponents were, in fact, the dualistic-thinking Catharists of the south of France. Angels may be part of the wider context, an assumed background as it were, to what is being taught and required for belief. All through this book I have been presenting the teachings of the Fathers of the Church as sources of true insights and shapers of my personal faith in so many matters. I never found angels to be their direct focus. They believed in them in the same way that they believed Adam and Eve to be the first humans and lived in a Garden only a few thousand years before these bishops were living. As I showed in the chapter on Original Sin, the bishops of the Council of Trent believed in a literal understanding of the Garden of Eden story. I don't take the story literally and I trust most thoughtful Catholics today don't either. Still, the Garden story if understood properly, and Trent itself, taught religious truths that ought to be part of our faith.

I don't wish this to become more of a history on angels than it already is. I do want to take two cases where I could be challenged with "How do you explain that away?" The angel Gabriel appears to Mary with the announcement of the Incarnation, a message that is actually an invitation for Mary to say "Be it done unto me according to your word." Recall the principle of *read my lips*. The words of Gabriel are actually God's revelation to Mary. How could anyone deny that God approached Mary, communicating a revelation

---

19. When Jesus taught, "he followed the modes of reasoning and exposition that were in vogue at the time. He accommodated himself to the mentality of his listeners." § VI, 2 of the *Instruction on the Historical Truth of the Gospels* (1964), approved by Pope Paul VI.

of His will, without denying the Incarnation itself? I don't. Gabriel represents the fact that a divine revelation happened, but what more than that is being revealed? Was actual speaking involved? *Angel* means God's messenger but Gabriel, as a purely spiritual creature, lacks vocal cords. So nothing struck Mary's ear drums. And as a spiritual creature, an angel cannot be seen with human eyes. This is only saying what didn't happen. I don't know how God revealed his will to Mary in a direct private revelation but I affirm it happened. Christians have had direct private revelations from God—I tend to call them discernments of God's will—leading to a life-changing decision that "God has called me to do such and such." A skeptic listening to this explanation might say, "But Mary missed her period and her womb kept expanding, so her *discernment* is quite different than other callings from God." I simply part company with such skepticism because I accept what "the power of the Most High" can do when it "overshadowed" Mary (*Lk* 1:35) following her *yes* to a calling.

The second case is similar but I believe I have a better grasp of the discernment involved. In *Mt*, Mary is already pregnant in her betrothal period with Joseph, but he is not the cause and ponders dismissing (divorcing) her without publicity. Then an "angel of the Lord appeared to him in a dream," Hebrew idiom for "God spoke to him in a dream." A message through a dream was another vehicle in Judaism for a divine revelation. God's revelation to Joseph was that the pregnancy was conceived "through the power of the Holy Spirit" (*Mt* 1:20) and he ought not to divorce Mary. "When Joseph awoke, he did as the angel of the Lord commanded," the Josephite form of "Be it done unto me according to your word."

How did his discernment happen, especially given the precarious nature of dreams from our own experience? I think it was based on two testimonies. The first was Mary's own. "I cannot explain the pregnancy but it is not from intercourse with another man." Joseph struggled with how fine and virtuous a person he knew Mary to be, on the one hand, and with the fact that men cause pregnancies on the other. The clincher testimony, if I am allowed that word in this sacred context, were the words of Mary's parents, known to us today as Saints Anna and Joachim. Their names come from a mid-second century apocryphal gospel, the *Protoevangelium of James*, but I focus on them as the real persons they were, because Mary had parents. Perhaps Mary and her parents, and Joseph and his parents, lived in the same village, given that parental agreements led to betrothals. Joseph would have known Anna and Joachim to be devout and trustworthy Jews. Knowing their daughter and her virtue, they would testify on her behalf. I believe that their corroborating testimony that Mary's words are to be accepted as true led Joseph to accept them, too. I place Joseph's discernment in the corroborating testimonies. Is this my surmise? Yes. Does Joseph come to accept Mary without suspicion? Yes. Was this the will of God all along, hence a revelation? Yes. Did it require angels? You be the judge.

I do not perceive that there is a binding doctrine of the church that re-quires the existence of angels for the particular doctrine to be true. I have just considered one of them, the Incarnation, that is, the coming to be of Mary's conception of the Word of God. I am not about to treat all the other church doctrines. I have spent a long life studying Catholic doctrines, which led me to write how I began this paragraph. Speaking personally, an awareness of and devotional attention to angels do not form part of my beliefs today, cer-tainly not in Newman's sense of real apprehensions. And apparently not in diocesan preaching, either. I cannot recall pulpit sermons, whose direct ob-ject was the existence of angels. At an earlier moment, when I was a child, my belief in having a guardian angel might have been very real. But I've come to think that my belief in the words of *Ps* 23 amounts to the same truth as persons claiming that God has sent a guardian angel to lead them. "The Lord is my shepherd, there is nothing I shall want....Near restful waters he leads me, to revive my drooping spirit. He guides me along the right path. He is true to his name." That God (or Jesus) is the shepherd of my soul, this is a matter of real apprehension for me.

An important caveat bears repeating. No one can prove that angels do not exist. I'm simply not sure that they do exist, and for the many Catholics who believe in angels, which is probably most of them, I make no quibble or criticism of them. In fact, I confess to having the same uplifted spirit that they would have when, at the end of a Funeral Mass and the coffin is being wheeled out of the church, we and the choir are singing the medieval *In Paradisum*: "May the angels guide you and bring you to paradise and may the martyrs come forth to welcome you home. And may they lead you into the holy city, Jerusalem." My emotional side of being Catholic is pulled to think-ing it all may be true.

DEVIL(S)

In the Mae Sai region of mountainous northern Thailand, near the Myan-mar boarder, twelve young soccer players and their coach explored a cave on June 23, 2018, that suddenly became their tomb as rising monsoon rain water blocked their exit. They were forced to retreat two miles inside the cave to escape drowning. Their location and even their lives were unknown until two British cave divers found them on July 2. Other divers, with food and medicine, joined up with the boys. All rescue options were risky. The uncer-tain plight of the thirteen riveted the world's attention. By July 8, with oxygen levels in the cave dangerously low, the risky option to swim them out with div-ing gear was made. Outside the cave, the international presence of experts, and sundry diving gear, and many medical stations were everywhere to be seen but also in evidence were the fishing nets hung by Buddhist women. The fishing nets were strung to keep evil spirits from entering the cave. A world of evil spirits is as real to the Buddhist culture as are its pagodas dotting the land. The children and rescuers swam out safely except for one Thai rescuer who died. Many around the world, I included, thanked God for the courage and expertise of the divers. Others were thankful because evil spirits had been held powerless.

For the 1.8 billion Muslims in the world, angels exist and this is crucial because one of them, Jibril (an echo of the Hebrew Gabriel), appeared to Muhammad and revealed the full Qur'an to him. Bad angels, called devils, also exist. Allah made all angels from light, but the bad angels rebelled. Iblis, corresponding to Satan, was the angelic tempter of Adam and Eve. Allah permits him and the rest of the devils to engage in evil ways until the Day of Judgment. In addition, creatures called jinns exist, spirits made from fire who can do both good and bad deeds. As with Buddhism, the Islamic cosmos is populated with spirits, good and bad.

Evil creatures proliferated in older cultures, likely merely mythically as we today assume but their reality was not in question for ancient peoples. Gorgons were angels of death to anyone making eye contact with them. In Norse stories, Valkyries assigned who was to die on the battlefield. Harpies were half human, half hideous monsters who snatched people to the realm of the dead. And the Irish have their fairies, whether a Banshee wailing the prediction of death or a Pooka in the form of an animal doing bad deeds or the more popular and gentler Leprechauns, the wee-folk bearded men causing all sorts of mischief. The listing seems endless from all cultures, describing malevolent forces acting on humans.

The worlds of the Old Testament and the New Testament are not immune from evil spirits. In relation to the earlier question of who is in heaven, it can be asked if there were once angels in heaven who sinned and were expelled as devils. *Yes* is the scriptural reply. But does this testimony reflect the infiltration of mythic ideas from outside cultures that had drifted into becoming assumed and as taken-for-granted background material for biblical teaching on other topics? This is not easy to decide.

The shifting biblical vocabulary about evil spirits doesn't help solve matters. A common biblical phrase for demonic forces is *Principalities and Powers.* "Our struggle is not with flesh and blood [humans] but with the principalities, with the powers...with the evil spirits in the heavens" (*Eph* 6:12) but in *Col* 1:16 they, with the thrones and dominions, are part of all things created in and through Christ. In later Christian theology, when the ten rankings of angels were formulated, powers and principalities ranked 6th and 7th. Our word *Satan* comes from the Hebrew word S-T-N—the Hebrew alphabet has consonants only—and it simply means adversary. So in the *Book of Job*, Satan makes a wager with Yahweh that the "blameless and upright man Job" would cave in and curse Him if Satan was allowed to remove blessings from Job's life (e.g., children, property, reputation, health). Yahweh accepts the wager,

Satan despoils Job, but Job remains steadfast amid the sufferings of his life. In *Job*, Satan is submissive to God's control, practically an agent merely employed to test Job, but Satan's meaning elsewhere in the Bible is as a more terrifying opponent of God and truly malevolent.

The name Satan became synonymous with the devil. He was the prince of the angels who rebelled against the Creator and fell from heaven. "I watched Satan fall," Jesus cautioned his disciples (*Lk* 10:18). He was called Lucifer, in the Vulgate Latin translation for the *Morning Star* who fell from heaven into the abyss (*Is* 14:12). He is a murderer, a liar, indeed the father of lies (*Jn* 8: 44). He is the force against Jesus—"Satan entered into Judas" (*Lk* 22:3)—while the Passion and Crucifixion of Jesus is happening. A combat between the kingdom of God and the kingdom of Satan unfolds, not only in the temptations-in-the-desert scenes in *Mt* and *Lk*, but especially throughout the *Gospel of Mark*, the most exorcism-focused of the four gospels. Jesus casts out devils.

The *Book of Revelation* brims with Jewish apocalyptic imagery describing the eventual triumph of good over evil. It has also been a hazardous minefield for literally-inclined interpreters who, lacking a background in Jewish literature, pontificate on what the unworldly scenes mean. It is in *Rev* that the battle between Michael, the archangel protector of Israel (*Dn* 10:13), and Satan is described, likely an expansion of the *Is* 14 text above.

> Then war broke out in heaven. Michael and his angels battled against the dragon. The dragon and his angels fought back but they did not prevail. The huge dragon, the ancient serpent [who seduced Eve], who is called the Devil and Satan, who deceived the whole world, was thrown down to earth with his angels (*Rev* 12:7-9).

> An angel came down from heaven, holding the key to the abyss and a huge chain in his hand. He seized the dragon, the ancient serpent, who is the devil or Satan, and chained him up for a thousand years....When the thousand years are over, Satan will be released from his prison. He will go out to seduce the nations in all four corners of the earth, and muster for war the troops of Gog and Magog...They invaded the whole country and surrounded the beloved city where God's people were encamped. But fire came down from heaven and devoured them. The devil who led them astray was hurled into the pool of burning Sulphur, where the beast and the false prophet had also been thrown. There they will be tortured day and night, forever and ever (*Rev* 20:1-14 passim).

The biblical acceptance of the reality of evil spirits and especially of Satan became in effortless fashion the inherited view of Christianity. The possibility was never raised that devils were merely the mythological personi-fication of evil experienced in one's life or in the world itself. Besides entering into its preaching, the devil entered into the church's liturgical prayers. For example, posed at Baptisms long ago and still today is the question, "Do you renounce Satan and all his pomps?" Two thousand years of an acknowledge-ment of devils, within the bundle of beliefs and practices carried along in the handed-down tradition of Catholicism, is a fairly strong reason to accept the reality of Satan and devils.

Has the existence of the devil, however, ever been taught by the Church in a manner binding on a Catholic's faith? Many think so, including the *CCC* (see §391), and reference is always made to the dogmatic teaching of the Fourth Lateran Council in AD 1215. This source was referenced earlier regarding God's creation of all beings, spiritual (angels), humans, and the world of matter. It goes on to teach that "the devil and other demons were created by God and created in a good nature but they, through themselves, became evil" *(Denzinger* §800).

The usual manner to interpret what an Ecumenical Council is teaching infallibly is to focus on the error it is opposing or the truth it sees as endan-gered. In the case of Lateran IV, it is commonly acknowledged that the her-esy is Catharist dualism. Catharism is also known as Albigensianism because it flourished at that time in Albi, a city in southern France. It held that the world was a battleground between spirit, the agent of good, and matter, the agent of evil. People were believed to be spirits trapped in matter. It repre-sented a reappearance of third-century Manichaeism, the philosophy that captured the young St. Augustine, which taught that there was a spirit world of light in battle with a material world of darkness or evil.

With this background, the wording of Lateran IV makes complete sense. There is, contrary to dualism, one source and principle of all things, God. God, using no pre-existing stuff *(de nihilo)*, creates everything that exists: spiri-tual and material creatures, and humans who express both body and spirit. Finally, God created the devils, but they were not inherently evil as a dualist philosophy would hold. They were created good but became evil realities by their own choice. If the Bible accepted, almost as a matter of fact, that devils exist, and the church, almost as a matter of fact, followed in course, then the later teaching of Lateran IV was not defining the existence of devils (or an-gels) because their existences were accepted as a matter of fact and denied by no one. What needed correction was any sort of dualism in the convictions of medieval French "fallen-away Catholics" that affirmed a principle of evil on a scale equal with God, the principle of good. If angels and devils did not exist, the Council's teaching against dualism would still hold because what-ever exists began as something good from the creative hand of God. Nothing evil is God's equal opponent. I think Lateran IV was not teaching infallibly that devils exist. It was teaching that Catharist dualism is false.

Dualism explains the problem of evil very easily, which is what caught the young St. Augustine's attention. Evils are caused by the principle of evil, call it the devil, call it the Force of Darkness in Manichaeism, call it Ahriman in the ancient Persian religion of Zoroaster. It is Christianity that has the difficulty of explaining the existence of evil: If God is perfectly good and creates nothing evil in itself, why is there evil? Christian piety drifts into a soft dualism, I think, when someone says "the devil made me do it." It's an echo of Adam saying, "Eve made me do it," and Eve saying "The serpent made me do it."

This brings me to say something about temptations, especially in any Catholic context that accepts Satan as real and the words of *1 Pt* 5:8 as sobering: "Be vigilant. Your adversary the devil prowls about like a roaring lion, seeking someone to devour." It has been constant Catholic teaching, and my considered belief, that you will never be tempted beyond your strength to resist the temptation, even if you think that Satan is adding strength to its appeal. It is also good moral theology used by the church, especially drawing from Aquinas's virtue-oriented ethics. Using the example of lying, the more one fosters the virtue of veracity, the less one feels tempted to lie, and the more one chooses to lie, the easier it is to give in to the temptation to lie again.

The existence of devils—and angels for that matter—has become increasingly difficult for modern people to accept, especially for those who are scientifically inclined, as I am. I would offer this caution, however. When you reflect on your experience in the world, or within your own psyche, I would admit that there are no intimations of the existence of angels. But when you do the same introspection, the intimations of a world of evil spirits, or of the devil, become more plausible. In the words of the theologian already met, Karl Rahner, who is not given to naïveté, "the sinister seemingly superhuman power of evil in history" cannot be easily explained by personal sins, even by a conglomeration of them. The breathtaking evil of the Holocaust, of Stalin's Gulag, or the Cambodian killing fields invites suspecting the evil-causing role of the *principalities and powers*.

I suspect I need to address a quandary about Satan that some readers have sensed. If what I said about eternity and about enjoying the Beatific Vision are true, then how do I envision a Satan, or Lucifer, being created good in nature—as is everything issuing from God's creative hand—and then sinning? If sinning later on, it implies heavenly duration, which is not eternity. If created in enjoyment of the Beatific Vision, how can Lucifer cease loving God, which is what angelic sinning would require? Patristic and medieval theologians speculated on the "fall of Satan from heaven." The speculations began to point in a single direction. In the very instant of Satan's creation, he[20] had an angelic intellect able to perceive, in that same initial moment, the nature of God as creator. But in that same instant and from intellectual pride, Satan rejected the subordination of his nature to God's nature that creatureliness required. Had pride not ruled, then the grace that enables Beatific Vision would have been his lasting gift. Pride of wanting equality led to the "fall from heaven." This is speculation of a very high order from many older theologians, and I am happy to report it is not suitable for pulpit preaching and rarely tried.

My treatment of the devil needed the length it got because I wanted to show how complex the evidence was, for or against. I wanted also to show how every serious church document, like that of the Fourth Lateran Council, needed to be scrutinized in order to sift what is binding on the faith and what is mere background, assumed to be true but not the direct object of binding teaching. This was not unlike the chapter on Original Sin where the Council of Trent was shown to teach certain matters infallibly but other portions of the text were assumed as true but are not received today as true, such as two individuals living in a garden paradise not that long ago and having one type of human existence before their "fall" and another after it.

Where stands my faith in the matter of devils? What I know to be untrue are any claims that a devil, or an angel for that matter, appeared in some physical form that one's optic nerve beheld. Spiritual creatures lack quantity and measurable extension. They are not avatars. A good example of an avatar, admittedly mythological to my mind, is the Hindu god Vishnu, adopting physical form as Krishna in the famous poem, the *Bhagavad Gita*, where he appeared on earth as a chariot driver to teach the duties of the warrior caste to Prince Arjuna. He was as physical and touchable as the Hindu warrior he rode beside. Medieval artists painted devils as horrifying beings with horns and tails and usually having red skin. Leave that sort of stuff to the painters. Real devils and real angels, should they exist, wouldn't have bodies that can be seen or touched.

As with angels, I cannot assert that devils do not exist. But I also think that their existence is not infallibly taught. The cosmos is filled with powerful forces, but I think of these forces in terms of gravitational and electromagnetic waves, not in terms of principalities and powers. I am well aware, from reading all sorts of literature, ancient and modern, that personifications of the *invisible world* happen. Are all of them myths? I do not know. I do know that I conduct my Catholic life as one who believes in many realities of the invisible world: the Risen Lord, the workings of the Holy Spirit, the workings of grace, the communion of saints. I recognize how evil can be in my life and how I can be attracted to an external evil, but I do not use the word *devil*

20. Angels and devils are persons but without gender. I use *he, his* because the English use of pronouns stumbles.

to understand it. I listen to the words of the Lord, and since he has words of Eternal Life, I resist thinking Jesus was simply indebted to mythological language and never rose above it. I say this even though I am aware that Our Lord worked from the same cultural viewpoints, some mistaken, that the Jews of his time had. Finally, I am aware that the last petition of the *Our Father* is not simply "deliver us from evil" but more correctly in the reconstructed Aramaic that Jesus would have used, "deliver us from the Evil One." I say the prayer both ways. Do I waffle? I'll let Abba, to whom I am praying, sift it.

HELL

Readers of a mature age will recall the famous "last four things" from the *Baltimore Catechism*: death, judgment, heaven and hell. In the narrative above, I have shared my faith in the first three of them. What about hell? Does it exist, and is there anybody in it?

What is it, first of all? Forget the images of fire and perpetual scream-ing but I would never deter anyone from reading Dante's captivating poem, the *Inferno*, where he names people consigned there who are suffering things comparable to how they sinned in this life. Whatever of the mythological was taught and preached in Catholic churches in years past, I join with our more recent popes in understanding hell as alienation from God in which damned persons would have full realization of their human unfilled essence. They would know that their nature was made to be with God and therefore, in having chosen alienation and separation in a fundamental misuse of their human freedom, they have made themselves incomplete. This sounds very abstract. But when damnation is grasped in these proper features, it is far worse than any unending pain associated with flames, and without resur-rected bodies, how would flames punish them anyway? The damned would not even have the support of suffering with other damned persons. They would experience alienation from God and aloneness within themselves, as if in unending solitary confinement.

Before addressing who, if any, are in hell, I would like to correct the language often used to describe "someone going to hell." God is envisioned as judging everyone's life at the final judgment, sending the elect to heaven, the reprobate to hell, and the not-yet-perfect to Purgatory. In the words of Lateran IV, "Christ comes at the world's end to judge the living and the dead, basing someone's damnation or election on each one's deeds in life, the former meant for perpetual punishment with the devil, the latter for eternal glory with Christ" (*Denzinger* §801).

But does this mean that Jesus is a judge who dispatches people to hell? Such an image of a judge comes from our common experience how legal punishment works. Judges send people to jail or to execution. This doesn't fit God's nature, as goodness itself, to cast people into hell. It is better to think that damned persons create their own hell. They bring into death a personal story that achieved alienation from God. In death they go to hell without God having to put them there.

To accent the idea I wish to propose, I suggest a variation of Jesus' parable in *Mt* 25 about the sheep and the goats. "When the Son of Man comes in his glory," he separates the sheep (people meant for heaven) from the goats (people meant for "the eternal fire prepared for the devil and his angels"). I propose that a shepherd, all along, had been leading the sheep and the goats. The *good* listened to his voice, but the *bad* drifted away. At the end, the bad did not need to be sent away because they had already drifted away from the shepherd. They ended up lost.

Stark lines have been drawn. Heaven *vs* Hell. Is anyone in heaven? The answer is yes, which the teaching of the church affirms in its liturgical prayers and in its canonizations, most recently that of St. John Henry Newman on 13 October 2019. Is anyone in hell? I don't know and the church does not teach that this or that person is there, apart from devils. In the Mass the church prays for the salvation of the world, praying that is retroactive, forward-looking, and meant for the here and now. So we pray as if no one is in hell. However, using common sense, one would think that there have been some exceedingly evil people who died that way unrepentant. Repentance requires free will and that once someone is dead, the exercise of free will has ceased. Think of someone doing great evil and dying in a hail of police bullets while doing the heinous act. Still, who can judge and assign what it must forecast? There are situations when you must let "God be God." Let divine justice and divine mercy arrange themselves in ways that our human minds can't fathom. Let the exact moment of death remain unknown when God can no longer approach the heart of one who seemed an inveterate sinner. Or, could God have lured him or her to repentance?

Hinduism is unlike Christianity because Hinduism is the religion of ultimate success. Everyone gets to be *saved*, which is my western word for what Hinduism calls escaping the wheel of rebirths, escaping *samsara*. Samsara is the cycle of deaths and rebirths through reincarnation until each soul achieves, through *karma* or good living, ultimate release (*moksha*) from the cycle. Christianity has one earthly lifetime and one reincarnation, called resurrection. Everything rides on that one lifetime but it needs always to be recalled that everything does not depend on us alone. We were each created in God's likeness. God calls us to salvation. God helps us achieve it, through grace, through shepherding. But the fact remains that a person can fail being saved through the person's own fault.

One of my favorite Fathers of the Church is Origen (AD 185–254) whose brilliance as a biblical scholar influenced so many others after him. He was also a speculative theologian, and one of his speculations is germane to the matter of hell. Death does not finally decide someone's fate, he thought. Chances to choose God are still provided everyone, angels, humans and devils, until the end of time. But God's grace is victorious and everyone gets saved. The church has never called him St. Origen because of such speculations. Of him and his well-documented holiness of life, I would add that he suffered torture for his Christian faith for a long time during the bitter Decian Persecution of *cir.* 250. I think he qualifies for being called a *confessor.* Had he died in the persecutions, *martyr* would have been his title.

Although Origen's theory of post-death salvation processes does not make sense to me, I have speculated on his motive for thinking this way and concluded, rightly or wrongly, that it was driven by his conviction that a supremely good God could not allow hell to be a final and contrasting reality to heaven. I am tempted to a similar thought but not about the non-existence of hell. I am thinking about damned human persons, the reprobates. They, like the blessed, are made in God's image. Granted that they defiled that image appallingly, they came into existence, as you and I did, as beings continually sustained by our Creator, continually propped up from the possibility of nothingness. As horrible as it is to imagine the eternal damnation of the damned, and knowing the nature of God Creator as Goodness, I began to think or at least to wonder that they might not enter forever into a hell of their own making, but rather God would cease to maintain them in existence upon their death. I began to wonder if, on death, they simply cease to be. Why would God maintain them in existence just to punish them eternally? Would this give satisfaction to God, which is another way of asking whether someone's eternal damnation fulfills the requirement of divine justice? It doesn't seem to square with the nature of God as Goodness, as Love.

This chapter has offered my beliefs in realities of the invisible world: Jesus' resurrection, our own resurrections, the nature of heaven, the nature of purgatory, angels, devils and faith matters of this sort. The notion of eternity has been a linchpin. The next chapter and the concluding chapter after it turn more emphatically to matters of this visible world, again to use Newman's terminology.

CHAPTER SEVEN

Eternal Life in the Church on Earth

"Those who love me will keep my word, and my Father will love them, and we will come to them and dwell within them." Jn 14:23

I know of a man, younger than I but not by much, a father and then a grandfather, who with his wife scraped by on a blue-collar salary in order to pay the tuitions for their children to attend parochial school. The Catholic religion was very important to him because it was important to his parents and to their parents before that. In a word, his Catholicism was ingrained. But today he no longer attends church or has any emotional attachment to the religion that defined him for so long. He didn't lose his Catholic faith as much as it was yanked from him. The clerical sexual abuse of children by priests and by a few bishops, plus the cover-up of pedophile priests by many bishops, broke his faith apart.

His experience has been multiplied among Roman Catholics many times over. One of the most astounding statistics of the last twenty years is that the number of Roman Catholics who have quit the Catholic Church is equal to ten percent of the American population. "Every tenth American you meet is an ex-RC," is the spicy way the newspapers reported it. It is certainly true that many factors are at play in the large number of departures: joining another church or a synagogue or Asian meditative movement, getting divorced and not wanting to be considered—a mistaken but widespread view—second-class Roman Catholics, being swamped and overtaken by secularist or relativistic convictions and becoming one of the *nones* (unaffiliated with any religion) described earlier. Nonetheless, it remains true that the clerical abuse scandal has been the reason for the departure of many Catholics.

There was a time not so long ago, certainly during that first period of my pre-Vatican II life in Philadelphia described in the Foreword, when almost all Catholics were proud of being Catholic and proud of their priests. The Catholic priesthood carried a mystique. Even Hollywood tapped into it with films about grand priests—Bing Crosby's Fr. Chuck O'Malley based on the

real Fr. Eugene O'Malley, Spencer Tracey's Fr. Ed Flanagan based on the actual founder of Boys Town in Nebraska. Those uplifting clerical times seem
so long ago and so hollow now in comparison. The pervasive pride is gone
and a kind of embarrassment has settled in. When the clerical abuse issue
first received national reporting with the *Boston Globe* investigations in 1992,
I concluded in a somewhat self-protective manner for maintaining esteem in
my church that this number of abusive priests was a very small percentage of
ordained clergy, and practically all Catholic clergy were not like that.

That was true then and still now. My own experience of priests—because
of my background it has been an extensive experience—is that they are generous and virtuous men, and they are as ashamed of and angered by abusive
priests and covering-up bishops as I am. Their priestly ministry is harder to
perform these days because they work under the shadow of suspicion cast by
derelict priests who quit ministry or have been forced out. They have more
work to do as they age, not less; they experience loneliness as multi-priest parishes grow scarce; they are hesitant to hug anyone, especially a child. Later, I
want to examine the notion of *clericalism* when considering the sacrament of
priestly ordination. I think that a clerical culture was the breeding ground for
abuse-prone priests to operate "under the radar" and explains why bishops
thought they were doing the right thing to "move around" to ever newer as-
signments these sexual predators in order to "keep things quiet" and to avoid
scandalizing the laity. The irony is that the episcopal strategy of reassigning
"problem cases" to keep the scandal undercover led to far greater public
scandal when mass media and grand jury reports exposed it.

Any of us who follow the statistics about contemporary church life have
seen the consequences for Catholicism: the diminished numbers attending
Mass, the drop in the number of Baptisms, the drop in marriage ceremonies
performed in church and witnessed by an ordained person, and not to be left
unnoticed, the drop in collection basket receipts.

I've not dropped out and have felt no temptation to do so. It is not because I take the scandals less seriously or less to heart than others who have
quit the Catholic Church. Two things have helped me remain committed
to Catholic identity even though I remain embarrassed for my church and
angry about its behavior.

One help has been my awareness of church history due to teaching theology for many years. I am aware of the vicissitudes that the Catholic Church
has experienced in its two millennia of history. These vicissitudes resemble
the ups and downs of someone's lifelong health: well-being followed by illness, regained health, illness again, then another recovery. For Catholicism
it has meant periods of decay and recovery. For example, the lay investiture
feature of medieval feudalism—bishops appointed by and under the thumb
of secular rulers—was followed by the reforms of Pope Gregory VII that reclaimed episcopal independence and spiritual priorities; the time when there

were two or even three bishops claiming to be the rightful pope was followed by the Council of Constance deposing all claimants and electing Martin V to unclutter the mess; the embarrassing lives of Italian Renaissance popes like Alexander VI, who fathered several children with different mistresses and was more intent on enriching his Spanish Borgia family than spreading the gospel, and like Pope Julius II who built the new St. Peter's Basilica by selling indulgences. But this decadent period was followed by the years that produced Saints Ignatius Loyola and Francis Xavier and the Jesuit renewal, and illustrious women like St. Angela Merici. Some say that the church's illness at the present moment is the nadir among all past failures. That may be true. I don't know. But I know that God heals what is broken because it belongs to God. In Jesus' words, the gates of hell shall not prevail.

This leads to my main reason why I have no temptation to drop out. The Roman Catholic Church in its institutional and social features shows forth all these ups and downs. It shows what people are made of, for good or bad. But the church is decidedly more than the sum of its human features. It is the presence of the Risen Jesus. In shorthand formula, it is the Mystical Body of Christ and its well-being comes from Jesus' renewing presence.[1]

When I was teaching ecclesiology to undergraduates, it was very difficult to share with them this interior view. Thinking structurally and institutionally came easier to their minds, prompting questions such as how do popes get chosen? How do they go about teaching? What does this or that teaching mean? And why, by the way, can't priests get married? Their curiosity was about marriage and sexual topics mostly: What is the church's teaching on LGBT issues? What is an annulment and what are the rules for getting one? Is dissent from church teaching, such as about artificial contraception, permitted? To lead them to view the church in terms of its soul, that is, to view how the Risen Christ is active in the church's visible features, proved too difficult for me. So I stopped teaching ecclesiology because I didn't want to reduce ecclesiology to current problems that were normally of a controversial nature.

I, on the other hand, tend to view the church in its spiritual features (Newman's *invisible world*) without in any way disregarding contemporary and controversial topics. Take attending Mass as an example. I am aware that the music may be good or bad, that the preaching may be engaging or boring, that the adornments of the altar may be tasteful or not. As important as the musician, the homilist, and expressions of beauty are, I am more keenly aware that the Mass is a prayer of the Risen Jesus to God the Father, and I am being incorporated into that movement of praising God. This is how I

---

1. This inner reality of the church, and the reason why it is itself called a kind of sacrament, is a revealed truth met in scripture. Karl Rahner, an influential theologian at Vatican II, wrote that the church itself is an *object of Christian faith*: Die Kirche ist selber *Gegenstand seines christlichen Glaubens. Schriften zur Theologie* XIV, 323.

measure the Mass, and this suggests the main reason why I do not measure the value of the church by the abuses of individuals who disfigure it. I do not say "I am not hurt by them," or "I just cover up my eyes," or "I won't fight for renewal." I just say, "I'm not leaving."

I've shared already how Eternal Life is what we live on the other side of death. But Eternal Life is also lived out on this side of death where our lives on earth and in the Catholic Church unfold. Chapters seven and eight of this book invite me to share my beliefs about the church here and now. It will primarily concern the Roman Catholic Church. There are other Christian realities called churches. Think of the Greek Orthodox Church whose Eucharist is as valid as ours. Think of the United Methodist Church whose students I prepared for ministry during my years teaching at Emory University. My focus, however, will be on Roman Catholicism.

Because the church is the presence of the Risen Jesus—I agree with Augustine who said "He did not leave heaven when he was born among us, nor did he withdraw from us when he ascended into heaven"—the church is therefore the earthly presence of Eternal Life. This is especially true regarding the church's sacraments, the subject of this chapter. The passage from *John* 14 at the beginning relates an awesome promise: Jesus, the Father, [and the Spirit] will dwell within an individual who keeps to heart Jesus' words and who seeks to love as he taught. God brings about Eternal Life wherever the divine presence is experienced: in ourselves through indwelling, and in the church's principal expressions of her mystery that we encounter.[2]

ENCOUNTERING THE DIVINE IN LITURGY

A text of the Second Vatican Council's document on the liturgy, describing how God is met, was quoted so widely that it became almost a cliché.

> To accomplish so great a work, Christ is always present in His Church, especially in her liturgical celebrations. He is present in the sacrifice of the Mass, not only in the person of His minister, "the same one now offering, through the ministry of priests, who formerly offered himself on the cross" [quoting Council of Trent], but especially under the Eucharistic species. By His power He is present in the sacraments, so that when a person baptizes it is really Christ Himself who baptizes. He is present in His word, since it is He Himself who speaks when the holy Scriptures are read in the church.

2. Encountering Eternal Life in the church's sacraments, because Jesus is the sacrament of God *par excellence*, is a phrase due to Flemish Dominican Edward Schillebeeckx with whom I was privileged to live years ago in Leuven and Nijmegen. Encounter, *ontmoeting* in Dutch, means more than just meeting up with. It suggests entering into and sharing life. He titled his 1963 influential book, *Christus Sacrament van de Godsontmoeting*. Christ is the sacrament of encountering God, and the church's sacraments enable encounter with Christ.

He is present, finally, when the Church prays and sings, for
He promised: "Where two or three are gathered together for
my sake, there am I in the midst of them" (Mt 18:20).[3]

Various ways for God to be present are enumerated: in the Mass as a sacrificial prayer, in the Real Presence of the Risen Jesus in the bread and wine
that the prayer of the Mass effects, in the other sacraments as their actual
celebrant, in the proclaimed scriptures at the Mass, and in the congregation
at prayer. I wish to elaborate especially upon the presence of the Risen Lord
in sacraments, in some cases indicating how my thinking has developed over
the years.

SACRAMENTS CONSIDERED GENERALLY

I grew up with the catechism definition of a sacrament being "an outward
sign, instituted by Christ, to give grace." This definition is true enough but
it can mislead. *Instituted by Christ* sent people plumbing the New Testament
for texts where Jesus of Palestine instituted this or that sacrament. Apart
from the case made for Eucharist at the Last Supper, one searches in vain
for some of the other sacraments in Jesus' life. In the life of the church after
Jesus' death, sacramental developments are another matter. Saint Paul's letters describe baptizing in the name of Jesus as a prominent activity of church
ministry. What saves the catechism definition is the word *Christ*. The work of
Jesus continues on after his Resurrection as the Risen Christ shepherding his
Church. And this means that subsequent developments in the later church
came to be seen as sacraments expressing the will of Christ, hence "instituted
by Christ."

It does not bother me that Confirmation, as a sacrament done separately
from Baptism, emerges much later in Christian consciousness. (The Orthodox churches celebrate Baptism, Confirmation, and receiving the Eucharist
altogether, even for infants; our Roman Catholic Church spreads them out
over time.) Nor does it bother my faith that marriage was not grasped as
one of the seven sacraments until well into the Middle Ages. Christians who
married in earlier centuries following the secular customs others did to get
married. But they who "married in the Lord" (1 Cor 7:39), that is, marrying another Christian, were as sacramentally strengthened as you and I are today.
It is simply that what was a sacramental reality in all those earlier marriages
was not appreciated as such, although it happened.

Outward sign was easy enough to picture, even when it wasn't physical
materials. In the Sacrament of Matrimony it was verbalizing lifelong vows.
Baptism's sign was pouring water over the person's head, or since Vatican
II allowed it, a threefold immersion under the water. The Anointing of the

---

3. *Sacrosanctum Concilium*, § 7. The document is often referenced simply as *SC*. The divine
presence is described in terms of Christ because it is about the Church, his Mystical Body.

Sick's sign was the blessed oil applied to the person's body. There are lots of physical signs in our lives, such as a handshake or a kiss, but to call these seven signs *sacramental* signs, which indeed they are, is a difficult matter to grasp. Try explaining to a youngster learning about Holy Communion that Jesus is really present under the appearances of bread and wine, and that the consecrated wine in the chalice is not similar to human blood, and that if you were to chew the Host, it is not grinding up Jesus. The short answer, of course, is that the eating and drinking of the Eucharist involves consuming a *sacramental* sign, not a physical sign. But how do you describe to a youngster preparing for First Holy Communion what the crucial adjective *sacramental* means? It's not easy.

To give grace is the third element in the classic definition that can readily mislead. The Latin word *res* means *thing*, and from it comes a phrase used by theologians: to *reify* something, that is, to conceive a spiritual reality in thing-like fashion. Here are traditional phrases that seem to reify what grace is: We *receive grace* in a sacrament as if it's an arriving something. Grace is said to flow from the heart of Jesus. "The church novena next week is an occasion for the *pouring out* of grace." Such phrases, which are traditional Catholic expressions, reify grace and make it akin to an invisible spiritual substance that inoculates the recipient.

Let me use this moment to share what I think grace is. In later medieval theology a distinction arose between sanctifying grace and actual grace, which is still met today. The former describes how God elevates a person's human nature to participate in his divine reality; it is also called habitual grace or living in "the state of grace." Mortal sin "removes sanctifying grace from the soul," the catechisms tell us, but the forgiveness met in the Sacrament of Reconciliation restores sanctifying grace. (This language seems to *reify* grace, especially as something that comes and goes.) Actual grace is the divine help to a person to accomplish this or that virtuous action; therefore, actual graces are God-given temporary assistances. However, the language of request tends not to be "God, come to my aid" but more likely "God, give me grace to help me." The language about grace seems to make grace into a thing.

I prefer to think of sanctifying grace as simply God's presence in a person. From the influence of the Greek Fathers on me, I see God's indwelling in me as in a temple, changing me, divinizing me; that's sanctifying grace. From his being the "shepherd of my soul," God empowers me to act fittingly as being the temple of his presence that I am. This is how I see actual graces without using the phrase. I focus on God, without making God seem to be a thing that comes and goes and without making his empowerments, his shepherding, thing-like infusions of actual graces.

I would propose the following definition for a sacrament that implies what a sacramental sign is without tripping over having to explain *sacramental*:

A sacrament is a liturgical ritual, that is, a church prayer, which in its external features symbolizes some sacred reality, and that in the act of symbolizing it, the ritual prayer brings about what is symbolized. Take Baptism. Although an ordained person is called the celebrant of the Baptism, and in certain circumstances a layperson can baptize, it is Christ who is the actual celebrant and who brings about in the invisible world what is symbolized or acted out in the visible world. Being washed or immersed brings about a graced or divinized life. The symbolizing action is accompanied by words, because it is a prayer.

In Roman Catholic liturgies the words could make it seem as if the priest or deacon is the cause of the spiritual effect and not Christ himself: "I baptize you [name] in the Name of the Father and of the Son and of the Holy Spirit." In Orthodox churches, the wording avoids any confusion of prioritizing the baptizing priest: "The servant of God [name] is baptized in the Name of the Father [first immersion] and of the Son [second immersion] and of the Holy Spirit [third immersion], Amen." For Roman Catholics and for the Orthodox, the symbol of pouring water for spiritual cleansing or the symbol of immersion into water for dying and rising brings about what is symbolized in their performance during the prayer. This is how a sacramental sign works. And it explains more easily the formula sacraments work *ex opera operato*, a formula used constantly in Catholic theology and sometimes met in catechisms to mean that the sacramental ritual achieves its effect in the actual doing of it.

In an earlier chapter I suggested that "we should pray out of our hopes" and then asked if we have any assurance that prayers, at least some prayers, bring about what we are hoping for. Sacraments are efficacious prayers because they work. They achieve what is being prayed for, as when parents bring a newborn to the parish church for Baptism so that their son or daughter might become God's adopted child, however the parents are imagining their hopes in their own words. The ritual prayers come from the parents, the godparents, and whoever else is present, along with the celebrant's unique role to wash the infant's head and pronounce "I baptize you...." The Risen Christ is Baptism's real celebrant, and he brings about what is prayed for. He causes divine adoption by doing the adopting. Sacraments are prayers that work.

All the sacraments bring about grace. Because I think of grace as God's indwelling life and as God shepherding me, the sacraments beget Eternal Life. This could be the initial arrival of Eternal Life in Baptism—below I will make some precisions—or the ways in which Eternal Life takes stronger grip on me, which is the work of the other sacraments. I was tempted to write that the other sacraments enable Eternal Life to grow in me—growth in grace being common Catholic catechism language—but for my simplified faith such language makes sense for me no longer. Eternal Life is God, and God cannot grow. But if I am a temple in which Eternal Life dwells, then I can always be a better temple and become more fully aware of my Godlikeness. Perhaps a better phrase captures it: With sacraments we are *absorbed* more deeply by the divine mystery possessing us.

BAPTISM AND CONFIRMATION

The Sacrament of Baptism is a good place to start because medieval theologians called it the *janua sacramentorum*, the doorway to the sacraments. A Catholic cannot receive any other sacrament without being baptized first. In what follows for Baptism and other sacraments, I do not intend to present my full faith view of each sacrament. As said in the Preface, I don't wish to formulate a catechism of my convictions. The *Catechism of the Catholic Church* provides this service, and I think it does a good job. I wish only to share how my thinking and my faith have become simpler and in certain areas have changed over time. This will involve proposing some insights that the *CCC* does not mention, and in some instances incorporates an explanation that veers from the *CCC*.

I used to think that Baptism was necessary for salvation, and there are enough scriptural and church texts that appear to say so. But this is not true, and the teaching from Vatican II supports me. In its document on the nature of the Roman Catholic Church, it lists various levels of linkage that other religions and individuals have to the Catholic Church and to God's offer of salvation. Closest to Roman Catholics, the document begins, are other baptized Christians (Orthodox, Anglicans, Protestants) who are linked to Christ's church in varying manners. Switching from *church* to *People of God* language, which also applies to the aforementioned Christians, Jews are linked foremost to God's people because the promises and covenant were given them. Other linkages follow:

> God's plan of salvation [for his People] also includes those who believe in God the Creator, first among whom are Muslims....Furthermore, God is close to those who seek the unknown God in shadows and images. [This is council language for Hinduism and any polytheistic religion, and also language for varieties of Buddhism that often are more philosophies than religions.] Furthermore, God does not deny his help for salvation to people who, through no blame of their own, do not even know a God exists, yet these people strive to live an honorable life, thanks to the invisible working of God's grace. [Here are found agnostics and atheists.][4]

I've quoted the Council's *Dogmatic Constitution on the Church* for two reasons: First, it gives the teaching that all sorts of people can be saved without ever

4. *Lumen Gentium*, §§ 14-16.

having been baptized. Second, it cautions readers to be wary should they have grown up hearing and accepting in a literal manner that "Outside the Church, no salvation." The official teaching of the Catholic Church stands contrary; it is very expansive official teaching regarding who can be saved.

Within the confines of Catholicism I ask this question: Imagine a Catholic couple having a newborn and having arranged a Baptism for two months after the birth. But, God forbid, the baby dies abruptly of SIDS. Can this unbaptized Catholic baby go to heaven? The answer is, "Of course the baby is saved. For how could God create this baby in His own image and likeness and predestine that it not be saved?" (There is no limbo possibility for the baby as a backstop because this was never official Catholic teaching, only a medieval hypothesis, as Pope Benedict XVI once wrote. Limbo needs to be discarded.) Anyone, then, who would maintain the absolute necessity of Baptism for salvation needs to explain what happens to this baby.

This raises a conundrum needing explanation. Because the baby is saved, which means it dies redeemed, does this not imply that any person approaching Baptism already experiences the grace of redemption before the actual liturgy of Baptism happens? The other side of the conundrum is that a sacrament, in symbolizing, accomplishes what is symbolized in the ritualized doing of it. Baptizing redeems and doesn't merely remind. Both contentions are true for Catholic faith. But how can they coexist?

The difficulty lies in our thinking that effects only happen after their causes happen. An arsonist lights a match to gasoline-soaked rags and the building burns down. If this is made the one and only norm of cause and effect, logicians called this restriction the fallacy of *post hoc, propter hoc*: Y happened after (*post*) X did, therefore X (*propter*) caused Y to happen. We need to expand our notion of *cause* to include some causes producing effects that came into existence beforehand, by anticipation as it were.

I propose that Baptism and its redemptive effects coexist in the same manner that Jesus' redemptive victory in first-century Palestine had retroactive effects on people living centuries before him, yet his Palestinian redemptive life was the necessary cause. I need to return to an idea from chapter two on the meaning of Original Sin. As there explained, Original Sin is a *what if* situation describing what would have been the human predicament if Jesus' redemptive victory had never happened. But it did happen, and God caused its effects to reach both forward and backward in time. Consequently, people long ago existed within a milieu of redemptive grace, as if a canopy of God's empowerment to salvation overshadowed them. In parallel fashion, the symbolizing ritual of Baptism portrays redemption, and St. Paul's description is crystal clear about it: By immersion into the water, we are baptized—Greek word *baptizo* means to immerse—into Jesus' dying and rising in resurrection (Rom 6:3-4). The water ritual of *pouring* portrays in its unique manner, therefore accomplishes, the full effect of Jesus' death and resurrection, namely, being washed clean and regenerated. But when?

The ritual of Baptism in the church, which is usually in the back of the church or to the side of the altar area but never at the altar reserved for Eucharist, symbolizes in truth the redemption of the baptized baby and causes it. But redemption can extend backward in time. The baby, or even an adult person about to be baptized, never existed without the canopy of overshadowing grace because Christ's redemptive act is retroactive. They are like a redeemed Abraham and others who lived long before Christ did. Therefore, in the baptismal ritual, we experience a reality being caused—the ritual is not play acting nor mere recollection of Calvary—but we do not restrict its workings to the *post hoc, propter hoc* fallacy that effects can only follow after the cause happens.

There are, on the other hand, situations in which *post hoc, propter hoc* formulas are true, besides the burning down of a building. One of them does apply to the baptismal ritual under another aspect. Baptism, along with Confirmation and Eucharist, are called sacraments of initiation. They cause the person to become a member of the church. Up to that point, neither the baby nor the catechumen awaiting Baptism is a member of the church in the full sense. When the baby is baptized, the baby becomes a member of the church, even though Confirmation and First Eucharist are years off. A baby in an Orthodox Church ritual receives the three sacraments of initiation together, and the parents bring the baby back for Eucharist on the next few Sundays. Reception of Eucharist is by means of a very small portion of the consecrated wine being placed on the baby's tongue. An adult Roman Catholic catechumen receives all three sacraments at the Easter Vigil and becomes thereafter a fully initiated member of the church.

There are many other features about Baptism that can be consulted in the *Catechism of the Catholic Church*. I have chosen a feature of my faith—the *post hoc, propter hoc* fallacy applied to ritual Baptism, that is not envisioned in the *CCC*. Whether it would be denied, or viewed as reasoning too convoluted to be acceptable, I do not know. But it addresses a conundrum I am attempting to solve: Baptisms work and a yet-to-be-baptized baby is not in danger of damnation.

There is not much for me to share about the Sacrament of Confirmation that isn't valuably proposed in the *CCC*. There has been debate in Roman Catholicism about why it became separated from infant Baptism. There's also been debate on its meaning. Long ago I sided with those liturgists who viewed it as equipping the baptized young adult, through the grace of the sacrament, for witnessing to one's Catholic faith.[5] And there has been constant debate on when to confer Confirmation in a youngster's life. In second

5. "Confirmation as Ecclesial Commissioning," *Louvain Studies*: Festschrift In Memoriam Dr. Piet Fransen 10 (1984), pp. 106-21.

grade? In eighth grade? During high school years, as Fulton J. Sheen (1895–1997), following his inspirational television career in the 1950s, chose when he became Bishop of Rochester, New York? What seems to be an unfortunate sign of the times regarding Confirmation and public school youngsters in religious education programs, the CCD of yesteryear, is that most students stop attending the religion classes after receiving Confirmation. It's a requirement placed on their parents that if Confirmation is wished, their youngsters must attend religious instruction classes beforehand. But carryover instruction in the Catholic faith for many young people halts after Confirmation is received.

THE EUCHARIST

There are many features of my faith that I wish to share about this "most august sacrament," as St. Thomas Aquinas calls it. I begin with the Mass. The phrase, *the Eucharist*, has meant for Catholics for a very long time the Real Presence of Jesus, under the appearances of bread and wine, which comes about at Mass. And for a very long time Catholic laity never got to gaze on the consecrated wine because after consecration the priest consumed all of it. (Since Vatican II, laity have had the possibility of receiving communion under the two appearances of bread and wine, or under both species in official church language). But well before Vatican II, at a prayer service called Benediction, the laity gazed in veneration upon a large consecrated host[6] in the *monstrance* [*monstrare* means *to show*], a richly decorated receptacle in which the host was visible.

The phrase *the Eucharist*, however, has a more fundamental meaning. It means the Mass itself, and it accentuates the prayer of the Mass as giving thanks, which is what the Greek word behind *Eucharist* means. Orthodox Christians call the Mass the *Divine Liturgy* to emphasize that this earthly prayer of thanksgiving imitates the prayer of praise of the angels and saints in heaven. Protestants tend to call the service involving bread and wine (or grape juice for those religions against alcohol) *the Lord's Supper* because it recalls Jesus' Last Supper with his followers. It was originally called the *Breaking of the Bread* in the early church, echoing the Last Supper words of Jesus, "he took bread, giving thanks, he blessed it, broke it...." Because there would be no Eucharist-as-Real-Presence without a celebration of the Mass consecrating it into existence, I begin with reflections on the Mass itself. As shortly to be seen, not all Christian religions believe in the Real Presence of Jesus coming to the bread and wine. Catholicism does.

A number of things about the Mass have already been shared in the chapter on prayer and do not bear repeating. It was an achievement of the

6. The word *host* is being used synonymously for the consecrated bread. Host, from the Latin *hostia*, connotes the idea of victimhood. Jesus is the sacrificed victim on Good Friday; hence, there's another phrase Catholics use, the Sacrifice of the Mass.

Second Vatican Council to reclaim the full sense of the Mass as a liturgy of the Word and a liturgy of the Eucharist, Word and Table joined together and enjoined for attendance beginning to end. Protestants had accented a liturgy of the Word: readings, hymn singing, preaching especially so, and often nothing more in the Sunday service. Older Catholicism accented a liturgy of the Eucharist in unmistakable ways: If you arrived in time for the Offertory, the Consecration, and Communion, you fulfilled your serious obligation to attend Mass. It mattered not so much that you missed the scripture readings and the sermon. (With a sense of financial savvy, perhaps, it was determined that the collection of money was taken up only after the Offertory began.)

The Prayer of Consecration in the Mass, called the Eucharistic Prayer for short, begins after the "Holy, Holy, Holy" segment and concludes just before praying the Lord's Prayer. There is a mentality that wonders when the precise moment occurs in the Eucharistic Prayer when Jesus becomes present in the bread and wine. I used to have that mentality. I don't any longer, and I want to give my reason why.[7]

Roman Catholicism has acted as if the words of Jesus at the Last Supper, when repeated in the Eucharistic Prayer, is the moment that the change happens. Bells ring. People standing in the back of churches kneel down. Just after these words, the celebrant says aloud, "the mystery of faith," and the congregation says or sings a response. It is a solemn moment indeed.

The Orthodox churches of the East, however, locate the transformative moment of the Eucharistic Prayer happening when the Holy Spirit is invoked to come upon the bread and wine and change them into the body and blood of Christ.[8] It is akin to the Holy Spirit overshadowing Mary and she conceives God's Son. In Roman Catholic Masses at this moment, the celebrant extends his hands over the elements and blesses them. If a deacon has been standing behind him, the deacon kneels and remains kneeling until after Jesus' Last Supper words. The Eucharist Prayer of the Orthodox also repeats Jesus' Last Supper words.[9]

When, then, is the moment of transformation, of transubstantiation if you will? Or is it misplaced to think of a single moment in the Eucharistic Prayer? Consider the following: The Roman Catholic Church teaches that Orthodox Churches have a valid Eucharistic liturgy and have correct

---

7. The Eucharistic Prayer is also called the *Canon of the Mass* or the *Anaphora*. The latter word is used only by liturgical scholars. The former term used to be used more widely by laity, but today less so. Vatican II introduced four different Eucharistic Prayers. Eucharistic Prayer I is the ancient Roman Canon and was left mostly unchanged from its 1600-years use in Latin.

8. The Orthodox call it the *epiclesis*, when the Spirit is invoked (*kalein*) to come upon (*epi*) the bread and wine.

9. There is a third key moment in a Eucharistic Prayer, called the *anamnesis*, a word literally meaning *remembering*. It refers to those words of the Eucharistic Prayer recalling to mind the Passion and Resurrection of Jesus, with the understanding, from Jewish tradition, that "to remember" means "to make present again."

beliefs about it. And the Orthodox think similarly about Roman Catholics. But if each group locates the paramount moment differently, then one concludes—and I have—that to wonder about the precise moment of change is misplaced. Every Eucharistic Prayer has these elements, and I prefer to think that the entire prayer is consecratory, beginning to end. I believe that precise-moment thinking is similar to maintaining that pouring the baptismal water is the precise moment when the baby gets redeemed.

Admittedly, there are precautions to be observed. If a celebrant were to have a sudden heart attack before he reached the Eucharistic Prayer, and there was no other nearby priest to finish the liturgy, the bread and wine would be simply returned to the sacristy for another time because consecration has not happened. If the accident happens within the Eucharistic Prayer, then the elements should be consumed as consecrated, as being the Lord's presence. I realize that some Roman Catholics might say, "Consume them only if the celebrant had reached and completed the words of Jesus at the Last Supper." That's too risky for me if the *epiclesis* has been reached.

How to think about the consecrated elements? Our Catholic tradition is clear, going back to all the Fathers of the Church. The elements, the seeming bread and wine together, or each *species* considered separately, are the risen Jesus Christ. Testimony from two of the earliest Fathers will suffice. St. Ignatius of Antioch (around AD 100), travelling from Syria as a prisoner meant for death in the Colosseum, wrote ahead to Christians in Rome: "I take no pleasure in corruptible food or the pleasures of this life. I want the bread of God, which is the flesh of Christ…and for drink I want his blood." And to Christians in Smyrna he wrote in route, "The Eucharist is the flesh of our Savior Jesus Christ." Not fifty years later St. Irenaeus is writing: "He declared that the [wine], which comes from his creation, was his blood….He affirmed that the bread, which comes from his creation, was his body. When the wine we mix [with water] and the bread we bake receive the word of God, the Eucharistic elements become the body and blood of Christ, by which our bodies live and grow." How the transformation happens, that is, the elements receiving the word of God, is a topic to be considered under the Sacrament of Ordination.

Not all Christians believe that the Eucharistic elements become Jesus and cease being actually bread and wine. The Orthodox do. I refer to Orthodox Christians in all their independent (autocephalous) churches, the Greeks, the Russians, the Serbs, etc. Lutherans do, in a sense. Lutherans believe that the elements become Jesus but that the realities of bread and wine remain. The word consubstantiation rather than transubstantiation applies. It is both Jesus and it remains bread. Anglicanism—the Episcopal Church in our country— varies. High-Church Anglicans, such as Newman was before he became Roman Catholic, believe in Real Presence. Others, reflecting a more Calvinist influence, do not believe the elements change when they attend Mass (or

Communion Service) in the Episcopal Church.

Calvin believed that Christ ascended into heaven and remains there; he cannot then become present here below in the bread and wine. The elements are symbolic of Jesus' Calvary experience, and by consuming them Calvinists, such as Presbyterians today, partake in the effects of Jesus' atonement. The Anabaptist tradition, called the "Left Wing of the Reformation," believed that praying over the bread and wine is remembering Calvary and is a sign of achieved fellowship that began when, as adults, they were re-baptized (*ana* + *baptizo*). After that first generation had left Catholicism, their children were baptized as adults (believers baptism). Many Christian communities fit here, Mennonites and Amish among them. (Amish communities in Pennsylvania celebrate a communion service only twice a year.)

The Catholic belief in Real Presence led to predictable phrases such as "eat his Body, drink his Blood." The Jesus of Palestine had an actual body with blood coursing through it. The body was tortured and the blood was spilled out. This is not the *body* and *blood* meant in those phrases, even when at Mass communicants are handed the consecrated wine with the phrase, "the Blood of Christ," to which they reply, "Amen" [I believe]. *Blood of Christ* can possibly mislead, and it certainly confuses youngsters. That the Eucharist recalls the tortured and bloodied first-century Calvary event and subsequent Resurrection is not being denied. But the consecration of the Mass does not change wine molecules into Jesus' red blood cells and white blood cells.

Regarding the transformed—transubstantiated in technical language— elements, I propose the simpler "Risen Jesus Christ" as the answer to the "what is it" question. What is it that looks like bread after the Prayer of Consecration? The Risen Jesus. What is it that looks like and tastes like wine? The Risen Jesus. What is it that a communicant receives after first receiving the Host and then the Chalice? The Risen Jesus, not two times but one reception of him in the sacramental gesture of eating and drinking. There is an old-time Catholic formula that supports the simplicity of "It is the Risen Jesus" who is present. "The body, blood, soul and divinity of Jesus" is present in the Eucharist, under each visible form of bread and wine. This older formula was simply declaring what I expressed in chapter five as my Easter faith. Jesus lives eternally as fully human and fully divine in his resurrected state. Without ever leaving the realm of glory, it is this risen reality that becomes truly present as these visible signs.

To support the Catholic belief in Real Presence, I referenced the Fathers of the Church for a simple reason. You cannot simply quote the New Testament to prove, beyond argument, belief in the Real Presence. Protestants read the same New Testament, and most do not believe in Real Presence. Ulrich Zwingli (1484–1531) is a case in point. He was a Swiss priest who left Catholicism over abuses he experienced, and he developed a view of the Eucharist as merely symbolic. "The sixth chapter of John, where Christ speaks of our eating his flesh, must be understood within its context, which has to do with believing in him….The verb *is* must be understood in the sense of *signifies*, as in so many other cases in which Christ says that he is a door, a shepherd, or a way." Therefore, the elements are not Christ. They are reminders of Christ, especially Christ the Victim.

But the Fathers, most of whom were Greek speaking, read the Greek New Testament in their mother tongue. They knew how the Lord's words were to be understood. When all the Church Fathers coalesce around the conviction that Jesus' declarations, *This is my Body, This is the cup of my Blood*[10] refer to a reality and are not merely symbolic, their convictions should be taken as true interpretations of Jesus' words and intentions.

Thomas Aquinas crafted an insightful exposition of the Eucharist in his academic writings and in his poetry, an example of the latter being the last two stanzas of his *Pange Lingua* poem that comprise the famous *Tantum Ergo* hymn sung by generations of Catholics at Benediction services, even if they didn't know much Latin. I think one of his best insights involved how the sign value of the Eucharistic elements worked. Through the power of the spoken words over the elements, the bread and wine become the body and blood of Christ, or as I propose in simpler fashion, they become the Risen Christ. But the sign value of the bread and wine is that they are to be eaten and drunk. "Unless you eat my flesh and drink my blood…."

The times when people attended Mass and did not communicate, did not feed themselves because they felt unworthy or felt uninvited, are long gone, thankfully. The sign value of the Eucharist as being a meal—Aquinas's prayer[11] calls it a *sacred banquet in which Christ is consumed*—is not to be confused with the false understanding some Christian churches have that Christ becomes present only when the elements are actually consumed and ceases being present in any leftover elements. In Catholic conviction, Christ's presence remains after the Eucharistic Prayer and Rite of Communion (feeding) at Mass, and unused elements are reserved in a special receptacle called a *tabernacle*, reserved for veneration, yes, but chiefly reserved for further feeding of the faithful, such as bringing the Eucharist to the at-home sick or to those approaching death who can still swallow (called *Viaticum*). Almost always it is the Eucharistic bread that is reserved because the consecrated wine is nor-

10. The New Testament word used is *potērion*, meaning cup. St. Jerome translated it into the Latin of his day as *calix*, meaning cup (*Lk* 22:20). The Latin transliterates into c(h)alice. Chalice is not a biblical word but it was imposed by the Vatican as the translation to be used in the Mass. It is unfortunate because all the rich references to cup in the Bible are lost: "Can you drink the cup I am to drink" (*Mt* 20:22). "Abba, take this cup from me" (*Mk* 14:36). "The cup of salvation I will raise and call on the Lord's name" (*Ps* 116:13 in newer Catholic Bibles).

11. *O sacrum convivium, in quo Christus sumitur.* This short and most beautiful prayer goes on to say that the meal recalls the memory of his Passion (*recolitur memoria Passionis ejus*), grace fills the communicant (*mens impletur gratia*), and the pledge of Eternal Life is bestowed (*et futurae gloriae nobis pignus datur*).

mally fully consumed at its Mass.

These considerations return us to St. Thomas and some inferences he draws from the sign value of the Eucharist as meant to be eaten and drunk. Some readers will find his practical conclusions startling. In examples Aquinas actually gives, what happens if the reserved Eucharistic bread decays or gets accidentally pulverized? What happens if the consecrated wine, the Blood of Christ, was reserved, then forgotten about, and spoils—Aquinas describes it in Latin as the wine losing its *sapor*. His answer is that the presence of Jesus ceases because the sign value of elements as meant to be drunk or eaten is gone.

Let me share his very words and crucial sentences following his original Latin, and then an implication I find very liberating:

> We observe with our senses that consecrated hosts go bad and decompose....It is obvious in our experience that bread-like features[12] are destroyed when the nature of bread itself is destroyed. After consecration, the bread-like and wine-like features can also cease to exist even after the natures of bread and wine had already been replaced [by Christ]....
>
> There are two ways these features can cease existing. Although the body and blood of Christ have succeeded to the substances of bread and wine in the Eucharist, if change happens to the bread and wine-like features but it would not have been enough to destroy actual bread and wine were they still present, the body and blood of Christ would not cease to be sacramentally present (*non desinit corpus et sanguis Christi esse sub hoc sacramento*). [Thomas gives examples of such small changes to the bread-like feature as dividing it in half, or the taste of wine becoming ever so slightly different.] But if the change to the bread and wine-like features would have destroyed the natures of bread and wine were they still

---

12. Aquinas uses a language from Aristotle no longer intelligible to most people. Here's a short primer. Substance refers to the nature or essence of something in that this nature stands under and supports the nature's perceptible features. E.g., the apple is red. He calls the perceptible features accidents, which have nothing to do with the word's modern meaning. The apple (the substance) has existence in itself; its redness has a directed toward existence (to some underlying reality). Redness exists only in another reality, the substance apple. In Eucharistic consecration, the reality of Jesus replaces the substances of bread and wine, but their accidents remain existing, suspended features without any underlying bread and wine. This deviation from the laws of nature, suspended accidents without substrates, is where Aquinas places the miracle of transubstantiation. God's power can achieve it. For modern-day clarity, I use bread-like features to replace the accidents of the substance bread. Aquinas also uses sacramental species to refer to the suspended accidents of bread, and of the wine, after consecration happens. Again, I use bread-like features.

> present, then Christ is no longer sacramentally present (*non remanent corpus et sanguis Christi sub hoc sacramento*) ST III, quest. 77, art. 4

For the bread-like or wine-like appearances of the Eucharist changing so drastically that the presence of the Risen Christ ceases, Thomas gives examples of qualitative changes to them (bread decays, wine spoils), and examples of quantitative changes (the host becomes pulverized, droplets from the chalice fall).

This is a liberating insight based on the sign value of eating and drinking. Where eating and drinking are no longer possible, such as when the host rots or is a barely visible crumb, or when the consecrated wine has spilled, the Risen Christ is no longer present. Why is it liberating? Accidents (in the word's modern sense) happen. Things get spilled. I know that all priests are very careful to avoid knocking over the chalice after consecration; in fact, they're apprehensive about it. But it can happen. With all of the wine-like features of the Risen Christ permeating the altar cloth in a spill, is it any longer the Eucharistic Jesus? The test question: Is anything there to be drunk? No. So it is not the Risen Jesus. (The parish of my youth had a special sink in the sacristy going directly into the earth to wash such altar cloths.)

There is a part of the Mass called the Fraction, coming after the Eucharistic Prayer, when the priest breaks in half the large just-consecrated host. From high-speed photography of the event, we know that many microscopic portions of the host fly off. And Catholics of a pre-Vatican II age can remember the celebrant after Communion scraping multiple times the white cloth (called the corporal) with his golden plate (called the paten) to gather up God-knows-what. Was there anything on the corporal maintaining the sign value of something to be eaten? No.

Here's a somewhat different question: How worthy do you have to be to receive the Eucharist? Given how sacred, how august in Aquinas's words, is the Risen Christ under bread-like and wine-like features, some Catholics in the past—I do not include ancient Church times—concluded that they were unworthy to partake of "the sacred banquet." No one would go to Communion. Why they thought that the priest was worthy to consume the Eucharist came from an unjustified exaltation of his personhood. The laity's hesitation was overcome slowly but a residual qualm remained. People would not communicate on Sunday unless they went to confession on Saturday. I am not referring here on the need to confess mortal sins but simply to confess any lesser faults.

It must be remembered that the Eucharist is food for sinners, not for the perfect, and no one is perfect. Should someone feel unworthy to communicate, the prayer in the Mass before Communion should be taken literally: "Lord, I am not worthy that **You come to me**; just speak and I shall be healed."[13] We communicate because we are not perfect and we wish to become more like Christ.

I'm struck frequently by the devout and recollected manner most Catholics display when they go to Communion. They walk forward with different anxieties, different experiences of pain, different blessings received, and different hopes. I have no idea who they are but I think my surmises fit them closely. I look on all of them with a quiet admiration.

What's happening to me when I receive the Eucharist? I am not receiving additional Jesus. I possess already the indwelling presence of God. In Baptism I was clothed in Christ and received Eternal Life. Lifelong I have been a *Christopher* in symbolic name, one who bears Christ (*Christus ferens*). Eucharistic reception does not make more of Christ coming into me because divinity cannot be expanded. The word *reception* of the consecrated host can possibly mislead. *Reception* denotes *ingesting* but with a crucial difference. Ingesting natural food makes more of its nutrients inside me, such as the potassium absorbed from bananas I eat. Ingesting the food and drink that is the Risen Christ moves in the opposite direction. I do not do the absorbing; Jesus does. I am more fully pulled into, absorbed by, what's divine. Therefore, divinity does not expand, I do. I become more godlike. If we are comfortable with the traditional phrase, "Communion makes me holier," and I think most Catholics are, can we not say, "Communion makes me more like God?" The writings of the Eastern Fathers and Augustine and Aquinas in the Latin West would support it.

Like comes to like when we receive the Eucharist. The nourishing Christ (Eucharist) comes to the indwelling Christ (Baptism). "If you, therefore, are Christ's body and members, it is your mystery that is placed on the Lord's Table. It is your own mystery you are receiving. You are saying Amen to what you already are."[14] Is this so confusing? I understand the reality of *love as being present to*. We love other people who are to various degrees loveable, to various degrees open to our being present within them. We want our loving them to make them more loveable. In this way I experience being loved when I consume the Eucharist.

I share a final experience more directly understandable. We all understand having been given promises. Receiving Communion entails a hope, yes, and even more, it entails a promise. In the mid-second century, St. Irenaeus

13. I give the direct way it is prayed in Dutch/Flemish Catholic parishes. Heer, ik ben niet waardig dat **Gij tot mij komt**, maar spreek en ik zal gezond worden. In recent years the Vatican imposed the translation "I am not worthy that you come under my roof...." This is not how Americans talk. It is found in the New Testament (*Mt* 8:8), but there the Gentile centurion was asking Jesus to speak a healing from a distance for his home-bound servant because "I'm too unworthy for you to enter my home."

14. Si ergo vos estis corpus Christi et membra, mysterium vestrum in mensa Dominica positum est. Mysterium vestrum accipitis. Ad id quod estis, "Amen" respondetis, et respondendo subscribitis. Sermon 272 of St. Augustine.

of Lyons wrote: "Just as bread from the earth, when it received the invocation of God, is no longer common bread but the Eucharist…so also our bodies, in receiving the Eucharist, are no longer corruptible because they have the hope of resurrection." Thomas Aquinas, in mid-thirteenth century, made this insight immeasurably stronger. He expressed resurrection hope in the words of a divine *pledge* (*pignus* in Latin. See footnote n. 11 above.) We have been given God's pledge for resurrected life when we feed on the Eucharist.

RECONCILIATION

The Sacrament of Reconciliation, familiarly called the Sacrament of Penance or simply "Going to Confession," has become a rare practice for Catholics. Some clergy decry the falloff as weakened Catholic commitment, and they hanker for the "old days" of long confessional lines of laity awaiting forgiveness of sins as signs of a vital Catholicism. Other observers, I included, see the lessened use of the Sacrament in less dire tones, see it in fact as a kind of adjustment to some wrong ideas that had been propagated, such as the above mentioned "You ought not go to Communion without going to Confession first."

I wish to share my beliefs about the Sacrament of Penance but first a few related topics. There are two fundamental distinctions in moral theology to be kept in mind: between something being right or wrong, and between an action evaluated as good or bad. These two distinctions are often, and wrongly, equated. An action that is right or wrong, meaning that it is virtuous or sinful, falls to God's judgment alone regarding sinfulness. God alone judges that someone's behavior is a sin, is wrong, the single exception being the individual person who can come to the judgment, in conscience, that "I have sinned." No one else can or ought to make a judgment that this or that behavior is committing a sin, not a pope, not a pulpit preacher, not a busybody. Virtuous behavior, however, can be judged by others, and this is what happens when church authorities judge a deceased person to be called *Venerable* in the process leading to the person's Beatification or Canonization. A virtuous life can be judged, not only by God but by others.

The distinction between good and bad actions is altogether different. Certain types of experts, moral theologians and ethicists and I would also include popes, make this distinction. Certain actions considered in the abstract can be evaluated as good or bad. Take stealing. What is its nature? If it is judged in general to be bad, when might exceptions play a mitigating role, or an excusing role? What is a charitable contribution? What makes it good in itself? When might it be masking a bad action, such as buying influence with it? This good vs bad distinction abstracts from the individual person doing the action. You can almost hear the mind of the moral theologian working the issue.

A problem arises from equating the two distinctions. Take artificial contraception. Some have argued, as popes and some moral theologians have, that a Catholic married couple commit a sin if practicing contraception other than the rhythm method of periodic abstinence. They have a right to say it is morally *bad* behavior and appears being beyond what a personal conscience ought to justify, but to label it a *sin* encroaches on God's territory. It could be a sin, especially if it is an ongoing strategy to avoid having any children for admittedly selfish reasons. Still, the judgment of sinfulness belongs to God. The classic violation caused by conflating the two distinctions was all the pulpit preaching, years ago, about committing mortal sins if Catholics miss Sunday Mass. Be wary if you hear someone pontificating, "This is a sin."

Common American expression confuses these distinctions. It is common to say that racism is morally wrong, perjury is morally wrong. Above, *wrong* was used to mean a sin, something reserved to God's judgment. *Bad* was used to express an ethical or moral judgment people can make. But calling something morally wrong carries a rhetorical power to it. The words practically thunder. So I will refrain from quibbling about it. Calling it merely bad sounds wilted even though it more accurately expresses what's unethical. Regarding whether this person's racism or perjury is a sin invites those perceptive words of Pope Francis: "Who am I to judge?" Such sidestepping doesn't absolve racism or perjury or avoid assessing such behavior in itself. It simply refuses to play God in labelling someone a sinner who acts this way.

What about sins? The distinction between mortal and venial sins is quite ancient. The *CCC* § 1854 references only *1 Jn* 5:16-17 describing deadly and "not deadly" sins. My concern is not venial sins—what Augustine called *light* or *daily* transgressions and Aquinas called *disorders* that remain compatible with having charity—but mortal sins, literally deadly sins, sins that if not forgiven would lead to damnation. This prospect of dying with "mortal sin on your soul" has gripped many Catholic consciences with fear. Some precisions are necessary. What exactly is mortal sin?

After using Aquinas's explanation of actions incompatible with charity[15] to describe mortal sins, and Aquinas thought that mortal sins could be multiplied, the *CCC* comes to the clearer definition of it as the loss of sanctifying grace in the sinner (§ 1861). If truly a mortal sin, I would agree but this amounts to the loss of God's presence, God's indwelling, in the person. If a person were to die this way, bereft of God, then of course damnation would follow, by definition. God is either present within you or absent when you die. I think that the possibility of the latter situation is very rare for a Christian wishing to be good person most of the time but who has faults, even serious ones. Lest I be thought too soft or uncritical, why do I think that committing

---

15. In Aquinas's theology, charity is a virtue (God's empowerment of our will and hence an elevation of our natural inclinations) to love God in Himself. It is sanctifying grace. As mentioned earlier, I prefer to think of this empowerment as the presence of God within me luring me to Himself as my definitive happiness.

mortal sins, during this life or carrying them into our deaths, to be rarer than much Catholic preaching has made them out to be? (I make no conjecture about a hardened sinner with a fixed malice of will, who lives and dies that way.)

First, there is scripture. "Can a mother forget her infant, be without tenderness for the child of her womb? Even should she forget, I will never forget you" (Is 49:15). I grant that the prophet's original reference was to Jews in exile in Babylon; however, Yahweh's promise on Isaiah's lips is heard in Christian worship as applying to all individuals. Many other texts teach the same commitment of God to people whom God created in his own image. I have a difficult time thinking of sanctifying grace coming and going, as if God is coming and going, based on our sins of whatever seriousness. It's rare I depart from Aquinas but on this topic I do.

My second reason has to do with the three conditions laid down for committing a mortal sin (CCC § 1857). They are the work of moral theology, and I find them an important legacy. They liberate from the likelihood, and the apprehension that goes with it, that mortal sins happen frequently. The first condition is that the behavior, the "matter" in the language of moralists, must be grievous. There is a big difference in seriousness between flirting and adultery, between a loud argument and physically maiming the other. The chief beneficiaries of this first condition are scrupulous people, people inclined to judge their faults as far more serious than they really are. I am also of the opinion that in years past, writers on moral matters lined up too many behaviors under the *grievous matter* category.

The second condition is that you must give sufficient reflection to what you are about to do, or to omit doing, for a mortal sin to happen. But think what this means. The person must be reflecting that if I do such and such, I am severing my life with God. This proposed activity and God's presence within me are incompatible. And this the person must be thinking in order to fulfill condition two. I do not think that this condition is easily met.

The third condition is not easily met, either. It runs: To commit a mortal sin, you must give the action (or omitting what you ought to do) the full consent of your will. You cannot drift into it impaired in any way, especially by fear or pressure or whatever else is pushing your will power. You must be clear-headed about your decision, especially in light of condition two. To meet condition three, your choice is basically expressing "I know the spiritually lethal consequences of my choice, and I accept them."

I prefer to divide sins into mortal and venial, and subdivide venial into Augustine's light sins done practically every day, and more serious offenses, without trying to define *serious* or indicate where the dividing line is between *serious* and *grievous*. This would invite the casuistry of yesteryear's moralists splicing up the moral life.

But I do wish to share from personal experience when I think a sin of whatever nature happens. Based on the faith view that God dwells within us, as in a temple, I experience sinning as a *disconnect* with God. The more I studied John Henry Newman on the nature and role of conscience, the more I drifted toward this personal experience of being disconnected with, or being at variance with, the presence of God within me. The more I savor the Eternal Life that is mine by divine bestowal, here in this life and as a pledge in resurrected life, the more I sense a sin as drifting from what God wills me to be. Admittedly, this is a subjective appraisal of sin, hardly applicable to people with a deadened conscience. But I am writing to share my beliefs with conscientious readers who are interested in, or at least curious about, their Catholicism.

With these shared thoughts on the topic of sin, I return to the Sacrament of Reconciliation. The first thing to note is that the history of this sacrament is very complex. It did not exist in the early Church in the manner it does now. The early church had a reconciliation ritual for three lethal actions, the death of faith through apostasy, the death of a marriage through adultery, and the death of another person through murder. Reconciliation with God and with the institutional church involved a period of public penance, sometimes lengthy, followed by a public reconciliation with the bishop, often at the Easter Vigil, followed by receiving Communion. But what about reconciliation for all other types of sins in those early centuries?

It happened in a manner that did not involve the Sacrament. Here is the teaching of St. John Chrysostom, from AD 400, about how sins are forgiven: (1) Accuse yourself for "if we admit our sins to God, He will forgive us," quoting *1 Jn* 1:9; (2) Forgive those who sin against you and God will forgive your sins; (3) Have a prayer life that "is fervent, careful and comes from the heart;" (4) almsgiving (*eleēmosunē*); (5) Living "a modest humble life...takes away sin. Thus have I shown you five paths of repentance (*pente metanoias dromous*), condemning your own sins, forgiving your neighbor's sins, prayer, almsgiving, and humility." St. Augustine, writing about the same time in the Latin-speaking church, teaches practically the same thing. Praying the Our Father removes our everyday sins (*peccata quotitdiana*). Almsgiving removes our sins but "do not suppose that those abominable sins (*infanda crimina*) that disallow life in heaven, if repeatedly done, can be atoned by almsgiving. Life must be changed for the better (*melius vita mutanda*)." For Augustine, almsgiving can atone even for mortal sins as long as there is resolve to change behavior.[16]

The Sacrament of Penance as we know it, involving confessing sins privately to a priest, had arisen by the early Middle Ages, but church legislation about it was often misused. A great instance of later misuse is the following legislation: The obligation to confess sins holds only if someone has commit-

---

16. Augustine, questions 70 and 71, in his *Enchiridion ad Laurentium* (*PL* 40:265). Chrysostom, from Sermon II on diabolical temptations in *PG* 49:264.

ted mortal sins. This obligation comes from the Fourth Lateran Council (AD 1215), an Ecumenical Council mentioned earlier when I discussed the existence of angels and devils. Councils normally teach dogmatic decrees and then a number of canons, which for the most part are disciplinary church laws. Lateran IV had seventy canons, the first two of which are actually decrees about matters of faith, and the remaining sixty-eight are clearly concerned with church discipline.[17] Canon 21 is germane: "All the faithful of both sexes, after reaching the age of discretion, should faithfully confess to their proper priest (pastor) all their own sins (*omnia sua solus peccata*) at least once a year and to the best of their ability perform the penance imposed, and reverently receive the Eucharist at Easter."

The word for sins (*peccata*) meant mortal sins, and the word still meant mortal sins three hundred and thirty years later at the Council of Trent, when it was further stipulated to list the types and frequency of each mortal sin. The conclusion is simple: If you don't have mortal sins, you do not need to use the Sacrament. This proviso got lost. To add to the confusion, listing the types and frequency came to be applied, in the popular mind, for confessing venial sins. To use an example from my childhood, "I hit my little sister five times since my last confession a week ago." There is little wonder why enough Catholic adults today rarely use the Confessional booth or room when this type of penitential recipe on how to go to Confession was taught them as children.

Having said that you do not have to go to Confession if there are no mortal sins—and I think a conscientious Catholic likely doesn't commit mortal sins—the conclusion should not be drawn that the Sacrament of Reconciliation is useless. On the contrary, it serves a very beneficial purpose in the spiritual life. Its use, absent having mortal sins, is called a *devotional* sacramental confession. There is a great value to vocalizing to Christ, who is the one being encountered in the Sacrament, your sense of sinfulness. The focus is venial sins, some more serious than others. How many sins to vocalize? The penitent chooses. It can be just one fault if you like. Recall that *type* and *frequency* were wrongly applied after Trent to confessing venial sins when Trent meant them for mortal sins. Whatever fault is chosen, just make it *honest talk*, to echo what I shared in the chapter on prayer.

How often to make use of a devotional confession? Again, the penitent chooses. Some laity, for devotional purposes, go weekly or monthly, others every year or so. A Catholic adult should have no hesitation to say to the priest confessor, "it's been so many years since my last confession that I cannot remember." All that matters is that this is the moment in your life that the

17. Some examples of its canons: Schoolmasters should be appointed in churches to teach the poor § 11. Churches should not be without a pastor for more than three months § 23. Tithes should be paid before taxes are paid § 54. Jews and Saracens (Muslims) must wear distinctive clothing in public § 68.

wish to vocalize your sin(s) is prompting the use of sacramental Confession. I like to think that God's lure is behind the prompting because the Holy Spirit is everyone's spiritual director.

Being audible travels in two directions in a devotional confession. Vocalizing a sin or two, something for which you feel deep contrition, leads to that therapeutic and cleansing expression that concludes the penitent's words, "for this and for all the sins in my life I am really sorry." Being really sorry is your "Act of Contrition" and your resolve to amend. The audible expression in the other direction comes from the loving compassion of God, "your sins are forgiven." God absolves, not the priest, even when the words of the Latin Rite from the mouth of the priest run, "I absolve you from your sins...."

Using any one of John Chrysostom's five ways of repentance brings about forgiveness of venial sins of whatever degree of seriousness. All of them remain interior to your conscience, and therefore silent. Devotional confessions enable sounds to be made and heard, your profession of sin and God's declaration of forgiveness. The spiritual life needs such vocalization from time to time, with whatever frequency your conscience dictates. We don't want to end up in our spiritual lives like those adults in their wounded lives who say of their deceased fathers (or mothers), "I never heard him (or her) say out loud that I was loved."[18]

ORDINATION

The Sacrament of Ordination follows logically from those of Eucharist and Reconciliation. Only the ordained, but not deacons, can celebrate Mass and express God's absolution. I use *celebrate* in the sense that sacraments are symbolic actions that bring about what is symbolized in their ritual performance. Ritual symbolizing requires human agents (e.g., a priest for Mass, a man and woman for marriage) and material things (e.g., oil, water) and prayed words. There is a truer sense that the Risen Christ is the primary agent or celebrant in sacraments, the one who causes their outcome.

Like the history of Reconciliation, that of Ordination is equally complex. When it began as a sacramental ceremony is not clear. Saint Paul traveled quickly through Asia Minor on his second and third so-called missionary journeys in the mid-50s of the first century, leaving behind newly founded churches and presumably pastoral leaders. These earliest churches celebrated the Eucharist but who led liturgies and how did they become enabled to do so remains unclear.

By the end of the century, the need for church organization had

18. I have gone into this matter at some length because I shared it in a retreat I gave adults at McKenzie Bridge, Oregon, women between the ages of 30 and 75. So many came to me afterward expressing appreciation for a positive view of the Sacrament of Reconciliation. They had lived for years with an oppressive view of it.

emerged.[19] Communities had leaders, sometimes called bishops, sometimes presbyters (elders). A structure of a presiding bishop, assisted by presbyters, and helped by deacons (literally people who *serve*) emerged and then continued as the paradigm. Yet it is to be noted that a residential structure of community leadership would emerge, where the bishop led the Eucharist. However, there is a document dated around AD 100 providing two Eucharistic prayers and teaching that travelling prophets be permitted to offer Eucharist "however they wish." But if they stay around too long, presumably requiring food and lodging, or ask for money, treat them as false prophets and have them move on.[20] So the picture of who presides at Eucharist is quite unclear at first. I have no wish to unravel the complex history of ordinations. Good Catholic encyclopedias serve the purpose.

My thinking has changed on an aspect of Ordination as it applies to celebrating Mass and it involves the notion of sacred powers. To introduce the topic, I need to recall two legacies from the Fathers of the Church. The first comes from St. Ignatius of Antioch, that wonderful example of a martyr's bravery who wrote seven letters to fellow Christians at the end of the first century while being led in chains to martyrdom in Rome. To him and to others we owe the organizational structure of a bishop presiding over a local church. Regarding valid Eucharist:

> Let no one do anything that has to do with the church without the bishop. Only that Eucharist which is under the authority of the bishop (or whomever he himself designates) is to be considered valid. (*Letter to the Church of Smyrna*, § 8)

St. Ambrose of Milan articulates the second legacy and other writers have repeated its substance. In retelling the contest-by-fire story between Elijah and the 400 pagan priests of Baal to cremate a bull, where they could not get their gods to send down fire, Elijah even drenches the bull and then prays to Yahweh to send fire to consume the bull, which Yahweh does. Ambrose applies the story, not to Elijah winning the contest, but to the power of sacred words.

> So far we have been considering instances of what grace can do through a prophet's blessing. If the blessing of a human being had power even to change nature, what do we say of God's action in the consecration itself, in which

19. The need can be seen in the two letters to Timothy and the one to Titus. They are attributed to St. Paul but actually come from the hands of Pauline disciples writing late in the first century according to the best Catholic biblical scholarship. These and other late NT writings reflect what is called *early Catholicism*, a portrait of the church reflecting the later Catholic Church.

20. The document is the *Didache*, its longer title being *Teaching of the Twelve Apostles*. See section ten. It is the earliest document to call the Lord's Supper the Eucharist. St. Clement of Alexandria and Origen considered it sacred scripture.

the very words of the Lord and Savior are effective? If the words of Elijah had power even to bring down fire from heaven, will not the words of Christ have power to change the natures of the elements [bread and wine]? You have learned that in the creation of the whole world *He spoke and they came to be; He commanded and they were created.* If Christ could by speaking create out of nothing what did not yet exist, can we say that His words are unable to change existing things into something they previously were not? ("On the Mysteries" in *Sources Chrétiennes*, 25:186)

Augustine adopted Ambrose's teaching to describe sacraments. Every sacrament has *materia* (physical stuff) and *verba* (God's scriptural words). When they come together, the sacrament happens. St. Thomas Aquinas adopts this idea, calling it the *matter* and *form* of a sacrament, and this formula became the Catholic legacy to the present time of what constitutes a sacrament. He is very clear that the power lies in the sacred words themselves, not in the person pronouncing them.

Before the sacramental words, it is just normal bread on the altar. When the consecration happens, the bread becomes the body of Christ. How is this possible? By whose words and whose voice is the consecration happening? The Lord Jesus! All the other things that are spoken refer to words of praise, prayers of petition for the people in general, for rulers, etc. But the sacrament is brought about (*conficitur*), not by the priest's own words but by giving voice to the words of Christ. (From the Feast of Corpus Christi composed by Aquinas *cir.* AD 1264)

I follow the centuries-long tradition of Catholicism that the celebration of the Mass requires the presence of an ordained priest or bishop, and where this is lacking, there is no Eucharist. The Ignatian legacy is that the Eucharist is under the pastoral oversight of the bishop,[21] either celebrated by him or by priests he designates. Such oversight amounts to the same reality as the later church language of requiring *validly* ordained priests to celebrate Mass. But it removes it from the realm of church canon law about validity, where authoritative documentation settles matters, to the Christ-centered reality of the church, the local church supervised by a bishop according to St. Ignatius.

How, then, to apply to Masses today the Ambrosian legacy that the power of consecrating lies in divine words and the Ignatian legacy of the bishop-supervised church? Vatican II reclaimed for Catholic consciousness the teaching that the local church, the diocese, is a full expression of the world-wide Mystical Body of Christ. The local church is not a department

---

21. The Greek word for bishop, *epi* + *skopos*, literally means to *look over*, to supervise, to practice oversight.

or subsection of the universal church but rather an instance of it. Therefore, for a Eucharist done in a parish, the liturgy expresses the words of the Risen Christ (Ambrose) as well as needing to be led by a priest designated by the bishop (Ignatius). The power of consecration lies in the Lord's voice, not in those of the priest as if he possesses a sacred power in and of itself.[22]

You cannot have a sacrament, any sacrament, without human participants involved in the symbolizing action, and therefore someone is needed to vocalize what Aquinas called the *form* of the sacrament. "I baptize you in the name of…," which can even be vocalized by a lay person in certain circumstances. "I absolve you…," is vocalized by the bishop or priest confessor. "I NN, take you, NN, for my lawful [spouse]…," can only be vocalized by the couple marrying themselves. The couple is the celebrant of the Sacrament of Marriage, not the attending cleric who functions as a church witness and as the representative of civil society if the marriage is to be civilly recognized.

In all cases, Christ is the one who brings about the effect of the words (*form*) directed over the *matter*; in these three sacraments the matter is water pouring or immersion into it, the contrition and resolve to not sin, and the freely-willed choices of two baptized people to forge an enduring life together. And likewise with the Mass. The matter is bread and wine, and it is the words of Christ that transform them into himself.

What, then, is the role of the ordained priest in the parish Mass? He connects this small congregation to the diocese because he is assigned there by its bishop (the Ignatian principle), and by praying in communion with his bishop and with the pope—"Remember N our bishop and N our pope"—his ordination connects these parish believers with the rest of the diocese and with the wider church. This is why I do not think Eucharist happens without the presence of an ordained person.[23]

I began this chapter recounting the story of someone who quit the church because of the clergy sexual abuse scandals. I mentioned there that I thought it was a type of clerical culture that begot the breeding ground of the scandals. This requires explanations. I begin with a positive explanation of the Sacrament of Ordination: Ordained people serve the other baptized people, which we see clearly in the persona and behavior of Pope Francis. Expressed in the thematic of this chapter, and of this book itself, ordained people serve the Eternal Life of the faithful. Enabling Eucharist to happen is the paramount expression of it. Ordained persons do not thereby occupy a

---

22. My opinion deviates from the *CCC* § 1538: Ordination "confers a gift of the Holy Spirit that permits the exercise of a 'sacred power,'" quoting § 10 of *Lumen Gentium* of Vatican II. Closer to my approach is *CCC* §1567: "Priests can exercise their ministry only in dependence on the bishop and in communion with him."

23. Therefore, there is a real difference between the ministerial priesthood and the priesthood of the faithful, the latter enabling the baptized to offer the "sacrifice of praise." Luther denied reality to the former. I do not.

pedestal above the baptized as if they possess the sacred power to consecrate the bread and wine that the rest lack. It is not a matter of power but service. Priests serve the faithful in the manner of St. John Vianney (aka Curé of Ars, 1786–1859), their patron and standard.

Next, a negative explanation of Ordination: Some of the ordained think that ordination confers on them sacred powers, the power to consecrate and the power to absolve sins, which they feel privileges them. Any priest whose seminary training inculcated the thinking of receiving sacred powers—recall that Vatican II in *Lumen Gentium* §10 teaches the conferral of sacred power at Ordination—but who has always exercised his ministry to the laity in terms of service, availability, and compassion, is not an example of a clerical culture that accents superiority. A ministry of a service culture, yes, of a clerical culture, no.

Why do some priests succumb to a clerical culture? To use "the matter and form" language of sacraments, the *matter* of Ordinations, to which the ordaining bishop's words (the *form*) are enjoined, is the ordaining bishop placing his hands on the heads of candidates, reminiscent of the many examples of hand imposition in the New Testament, such as when the leaders of the Antioch Church laid hands on Paul and Barnabas to go forth and evangelize. But these priests, I think, focus on an auxiliary ritual in the Ordination ceremony, the anointing of their palms with sacred oil. This is a secondary symbol in today's Ordination ceremony, not sharing in the primacy of imposition of hands, but it readily suggests sacred empowerment, reminiscent of the anointing of the Israelite High Priest in *Leviticus*.

So powerful is this symbol in the imagination that the custom arose to save the cloth that dried off the oil and keep it for the burial of the priest's mother, placing it around her hands in the coffin along with the traditional rosary beads. (I do not criticize this custom. It itself it is very beautiful, for the priest, for the mother thinking about her death to come, and for the entire family.) The primacy of symbolic oil has also taken root, wrongly to me, in the minds of some laity who insist on receiving Holy Communion on their tongues because "my hands were not anointed to touch the Host like the priest's hands were." I do not discount other devotional reasons for receiving Communion on the tongue, but this one I do.

Thinking that ordination confers sacred powers leads to language like "my Mass," and unnecessary focus on "my Ordination." (That someone can have a festive celebration for being ordained fifty years, or however long, is a different matter, in fact, a laudable matter.) I've become convinced, however, that the perception of possessing sacred powers leads to a clerical culture, called clericalism, which is now hurting the Catholic priesthood.

Much these days is written about it. I mention only its more salient features. It is an *attitude* of some priests and bishops, some cardinals in Rome too, of expecting deference from others, of seeing themselves privileged because of their sacred status, of living a life style befitting the upper class, hardly the middle and poorer classes and hardly in the spirit of Pope Francis shunning traditional papal trappings. It expresses itself in meetings where the priest has, and is expected to have, the last word. It is quick to remind lay persons that their opinions, while invited, are only consultative. It reflects the hierarchical thinking of the Middle Ages up until Modern Europe that accepted three social realms: the First Estate (clergy), the Second Estate (nobility) and the Third Estate (commoners).

Regarding clergy pedophilia, this culture contributed to the strategy to cover up the abuses from public knowledge, especially from Catholics in the pews, lest the priesthood lose its aura, lest priests (or bishops) get arrested, lest scandals undermine the deference of the laity. As I mentioned at the start of this chapter, and it bears repeating, the majority of priests and bishops today are very good people and are as embarrassed and angered by the pedophilia abuses as others are. But they, unfortunately, get tattooed with the fallout from the recriminations directed at abusers and their enablers.

Much has been published of the sexual abuse of young people. The crimes are not only by Catholic clergy. Abusers have included Protestant clergy, school teachers, and Boy Scout leaders. There is one aspect regarding Catholic offenders that I've not seen mentioned much, and I end with it. The abusive clergy entered the seminary system already beset with dysfunctional psycho-social-sexual development. They didn't become the culprits they became only after ordination. Imposed celibacy was not the cause either. The fault was the seminary oversight system. Why weren't they weeded out? They brought into the seminary a dysfunctional personality; this seems to be the testimony of the experts. Why wasn't this sensed by seminary officers? Seminarians are meant to keep discerning, "Is this my vocation?" Seminary officers have a role in discerning the suitability—they have four to six years to do so—and it isn't just whether the seminarian is pious enough, or orthodox enough in his theology, or is congenial enough. Oversight may be happening now, or at least happening better now, but where was it in the 1960s, the 1970s, and the 1980s when most of the clerical abusers "got through the system?"

MATRIMONY

Sharing my faith about the Sacrament of Matrimony is both important in itself in keeping with this book's aim and it is personal. God's Providence led my wife and me to meet, to choose to wed, and to be blessed with two sons, both of whom are now wed themselves. It was and remains a family life with sufficient financial supports. I began chapter one with two fundamental faith convictions: that God exists beyond doubt and that God providentially leads my life, lest these two assents would have gotten lost behind a welter of other things I wanted to share. I experience marriage as a providential gift. This is not the experience of many Catholic couples getting married. Almost half of such marriages end these days in divorce. In other marriages, couples have had so many children—I think of Catholics in Africa and Latin America—that their family lives border on poverty. And there are those—instances in my own family tree come to mind—whose first marriage in the church ended in divorce, and a civilly-contracted second marriage occurred that precluded receiving the Eucharist.

In sharing faith convictions and some pertinent observations, I do not aim for a theology of marriage in its many aspects. Lots of good books do that. Instead, I wish to offer clarifications where I think confusions exist about sacramental marriages and where I've come to see other matters differently from church teachings on them. Although these teachings were not being proposed infallibly, that is, requiring belief, the church nevertheless expects adherence to them. One deviates from them with caution and with respect, which I hope my reasons do.

Some clarifications about sacramental marriages: They are marriages between a baptized woman and a baptized man, provided both are free to get married, which normally means the absence of a previous marriage for each one. If the two are Catholics, or a Catholic marrying a Protestant, then there are requirements for conducting the ceremony to order to be a valid sacrament. If the two are Protestant Christians, how the ceremony happens (e.g., before a minister, before a Justice of the Peace) does not jeopardize its sacramentality. When the ceremony happens, the sacramental union between the couple is presumed to be lifelong, binding until the death of one spouse, even if Protestant thinking differs about this feature of marriage.

Suppose a civil divorce occurs. Civilly, this means that the marriage is dissolved, and each partner is free, in the eyes of society, to marry again without committing bigamy. But the sacramental bonding endures because it is presumably lifelong. I will return to the presumed sacramental bond below, called *putative* or *presumptive* in church language.

If the divorced Catholic partner remarries in a civil ceremony because a church marriage is not allowed, the Catholic person is not excommunicated but is not permitted to receive the Eucharist. This is one reason why such Catholics stop going to church because they have to remain in their pew when practically everyone else goes to Communion. It's too hard not to feel second class. If the Catholic partner did not remarry civilly, he or she is welcome to receive the Eucharist. For these Catholics, it was hard enough to undergo divorce, and nothing should make them feel like second-class Catholics because they are not.

What about that word *putative*? It is the presumption that the conditions necessary for entering into a sacramental marriage were present at the beginning and continued to exist. What are some opposite conditions? Not wanting to have children. Not accepting that these are lifelong marriage vows.

Not making the vows freely, because feeling coerced or being psychologically immature. These factors become crucial if the divorced Catholic pursues an annulment and, if they can be substantiated, become the reasons for successfully getting it.

What's involved in the approval or denial of an annulment request (petition)? It is a juridical process in what is called the *external forum* of church bureaucracy, involving the testimony of witnesses, documentation, and an ecclesiastical tribunal having a judge. (*Internal forum*, the counterpoint to external forum, involves Pope Francis's proposal below.) If the divorced Catholic obtains an annulment, then he or she is free to contract a sacramental marriage in the church. An annulment is a declaration of nullity from the tribunal that the first marriage lacked one or more reasons that stopped it from ever being a sacramental marriage. Therefore nothing of a lifelong obligation remains.

The first marriage was always and simultaneously a civil marriage—one reason why the attending priest needs to be civilly recognized by the city, county or state to conduct marriages, and the marriage must be civilly registered—and therefore the children of an annulled marriage are not illegitimate. They were born in a civilly-recognized marriage. Legitimacy and illegitimacy of children are civil realities and not affected by annulments. This is often misunderstood.

I hope this short primer removes a lot of misconceptions. Are divorced Catholics excommunicated? No, not even if they get civilly remarried. Does an annulment process cost money? It used to, to cover bureaucratic expenses, but Pope Francis has urged dioceses to make them cost free. Do annulments take a long time? They used to, and in some foreign countries they still do, but the American church has benefited from streamlined procedures Pope Francis introduced.

What makes an annulment petition very awkward? Take a Catholic, approaching marriage for the first time, falling in love with a divorced Protestant who had been married to another baptized Protestant. For the Catholic to get married in the Catholic Church, an annulment of the intended spouse's Protestant marriage is required since it was presumptively sacramental. It is the Protestant who needs to present before a Roman Catholic tribunal his or her first marriage for appraisal. Understandably the Protestant party could resent this obligation, both because the person is not Catholic to begin with and especially because all annulment processes require engaging or at least notifying the former divorced partner. There are other factors that can make annulment petitions awkward or problematic, but this one is, for me, the thorniest. Whatever the alleged factors, the petitioner needs to be civilly divorced before seeking an annulment.

Certain cases have their own thorny character when the *grounds*—what the church process calls the offered reasons—truly exist for obtaining an annulment but that the grounds cannot be substantiated before a tribunal, that is, in the external forum. Without proofs, the marriage tribunal is hand-cuffed. Consider this imagined case: A church marriage between two young Catholics happens that will eventually end in divorce. Both persons pledge lifelong vows before the priest but one of them, let's say the man, maintains a silent reservation about permanency. After some years, he loses interest in the marriage, leaves her, and a divorce follows in time. She seeks an annul-ment eventually, based on his lack of vowed permanency from the outset, which is something he confided in her after marital problems arose. If this could be substantiated, it is grounds for annulment. But it cannot be proven. It is only her word; he has rebuffed all contacts from the church to ascertain his thoughts about the original marriage. She meets a Catholic man, never married before, with whom she falls in love. They marry civilly because her first marriage stands in the way of a Catholic ceremony. They live together in happiness many years, raising children to share their Catholicism, attend-ing Mass, but not taking Communion. They may feel second class, and they long for a church-recognized marriage. Unprovable grounds differ in distinct cases; nevertheless, the situation, the impasse, is not untypical for many un-recognized second marriages of Catholics.

Pope Francis addressed this pastoral dilemma as well as other family challenges in "On Love in the Family" (2016), known by the more familiar Latin title, *Amoris Laetitia*, a papal *exhortation* that is just below an encyclical in authority. He had convened two gatherings of bishops for their analysis and pastoral advice, the 2014 and 2015 Synods on the Family, and *Amoris* was the result of the consultations. His proposals regarding divorced civilly-remar-ried Catholics—termed *irregular* situations in canon law language—drew the most press attention and, from conservative voices, the most criticism.[24]

The criticism is that couples in irregular marriages cannot receive Eu-charist because they are in unrecognized marriages and therefore are con-stantly committing adultery. If no annulment, then no Eucharist, these critics maintain. The pastoral inclination of most of the Synodal bishops, and of Francis himself, is that couples caught in the dilemma of impossible-to-get annulments often feel that their present marriages are true marriages, and the earlier ones were not. "Those who made every effort to save their first marriages and were unjustly abandoned...are sometimes subjectively certain in conscience that their previous and irreparably broken marriage had never been valid" (§ 298 of *Amoris*).

Where insisting on meeting an existing rule (read: either live as brother

---

24. Except for chapter eight of *Amoris*, where controversial topics are treated, the rest of the *Exhortation* has wonderful teaching on family life today. I think paragraphs 120-141 ought to be required reading for Pre-Cana Conferences, those pre-marriage preparations conducted for engaged couples. Anticipating critics of *Amoris* a year later, my own response appeared in an op-ed essay in the *Philadelphia Inquirer* (10/22/15). See Appendix C.

and sister or obtain an annulment) is like "stones to throw at people's lives" (§ 305), what is possible for irregular marriages is undertaking "a responsible personal and pastoral discernment of particular cases...[recognizing] that the consequences or effects of a rule need not necessarily always be the same" (§ 300). Controversial footnote 336 notes that this principle applies to sacramental discipline [read: receiving the Eucharist] because discernment can recognize that no grave sin exists in many irregular marriages. How does an "irregular" couple arrive at this discernment?

> A sincere reflection can strengthen trust in the mercy of God which is not denied anyone. What we are speaking of is a process of discernment which "guides the faithful to an awareness of their situation before God. Conversation with the priest, in the internal forum, contributes to the formation of a correct judgment on what hinders the possibility of a fuller participation in the life of the Church and on what steps can foster it and make it grow....For this discernment to happen, the following conditions must necessarily be present: humility, discretion and a love for the Church and her teaching, in a sincere search for God's will and a desire to make a more perfect response to it" (quoting bishops' report from the 2015 Synod).

The internal forum refers to decisions made in conscience that never reach the public record as do the external forum decisions of a marriage tribunal (see current Code of Canon Law § 130). The former can happen within the sacramental context of Confession or outside of it, but in both instances it involves conversations with a pastor who is present as a guide to conscience formation, not as decision maker, or rectifier of decisions. It happens likely outside of sacramental confession because it involves the priest helping two people to discern God's voice in their consciences. It becomes their own decision for which they are willing to stand before God in judgment. The decision might be to begin receiving Communion, or the decision to continue to refrain, or the decision to try the annulment process once again. How is God speaking to them in their hearts? This is what the couple works to discern.

The biggest kerfuffle in my lifetime regarding the Sacrament of Marriage happened on July 29, 1968. Pope Paul VI's encyclical *Humanae Vitae*, the so-called Birth Control Encyclical, eagerly awaited for fifteen months, was released to the public. It reiterated the church teaching condemning the use of artificial contraceptives, including the recently discovered anovulant "pill," to regulate pregnancies. What alone was permitted couples to avoid pregnancies was the so-called *rhythm method*, that is, restricting intercourse to the few days in a women's menstrual cycle—for many spouses pinpointing them proves nearly impossible—when conception was unlikely. If couples used artificial means for intercourse, it was branded as "intrinsically wrong", and Paul VI referenced Pope Pius XI's 1930 *Casti Connubii* (Chaste Wedlock) that labeled artificial contraception an action "against nature," incurring the "guilt of a grave sin."[25]

Consternation filled the Catholic world in the summer of 1968, although conservative Catholics rejoiced that the traditional marital teaching did not change. Most married couples were using artificial contraception, and now the specter of sinning mortally was raised anew. Theologians, many clergy, and most laity were anticipating an expansion of permissible means, beyond the rhythm method, to regulate pregnancies. Why this anticipation?

During the initial session of Vatican II (Fall 1962), some Council bishops wished to reconsider the prohibitions from previous popes against artificial contraception. Pope John XXIII assigned the topic to a small commission, which Pope Paul VI continued and expanded with bishops, theologians, and laity after John's death on June 3, 1963. It was called the Commission on Population, the Family, and Procreation. The commission, reaching nearly 70 members over three years, produced a document favored by the episcopal participants (four cardinals and five archbishops), opposed by one cardinal and two bishops, with an overall membership vote of 64 in favor of changes to 5 opposed to any changes. The document, henceforth called the Majority Report and meant only for the eyes of Paul VI, favored expanding legitimate birth control means, leaving decisions to the married couples themselves. The Report got leaked to two Catholic newspapers in April, 1967. During the fifteen months before *Humanae Vitae* was released, hopes for a change in the church's teaching on contraception grew very high.

I wish to share one event in the life of the Commission I find crucial and one teaching from the Commission I find true. Patty and Patrick Crowley, the Chicago-based leaders of the world-wide Christian Family Movement (CFM), were lay appointees to the Commission. It became quickly apparent to them that the Commission needed to hear the voices of committed married couples from the global Catholic world about the difficulties they faced in trying to live by current church rules. With help from survey experts of Notre Dame University, they collected a massive amount of testimonies describing how hard an affectionate married life was if rhythm was the only way to space or stop having children. These written testimonies played a crucial role on the Commission's final decisions to advocate changes. And it occasioned a pointed exchange. One of the conservative theologians, who remained to the very end opposed to any change in church teaching, Jesuit Marcelino Zalba, asked: "What about the millions we have sent to hell if these present norms were not valid?" Patty Crowley responded: "Father Zal-

---

25. The Latin phrases are crucial: *intrinsece inhonestum* in *Humanae Vitae*, § 14; *contra naturam* and *gravis noxae labe commaculari* in *Casti Connubii*, §§ 54, 56. In 1930 Vatican language, grave sin meant mortal sin. The *CCC*, § 2370, references *Humanae Vitae* § 14 and labels artificial contraception "intrinsically evil."

ba, do you really believe God has carried out all your orders?" The import of the Crowley contribution to the Commission bears on what is called the laity's instinct about what their faith means, called technically their *sensus fidei fidelium* or simply *sensus fidelium*.

Sensus fidelium is an important feature of the faith of Catholics and merits a short explanation. Two things it is not: It is not public opinion brought to bear on what church authorities teach. And it is not unique to the laity. It is a property of being baptized, and thus bishops and laity share in it. Essentially, it is a supernatural instinct caused by the Holy Spirit bestowed in Baptism to testify what this or that feature of faith has come to mean in living it out. Lived experience is crucial, even if someone objects, "Ought not people simply believe what pope and bishops teach, so look to the teaching church and forget personal experience?"

Cardinal Newman was the great champion of *sensus fidelium* in the nineteenth century after he studied how many bishops in the mid-fourth century were still teaching Arianism after the Council of Nicea condemned it, but it was the laity for the most part—bishops like Basil and Gregory of Nyssa and a few others joined them—who maintained the anti-Arian teaching of the Council. He then wrote an essay in 1859, *On Consulting the Faithful in Matters of Doctrine*, after being provoked why the English bishops, intend on imposing education restrictions, did not consult Catholic laity concerning the education of their own children.

Prior to Pope Pius IX's defining the dogma of the Immaculate Conception in 1854, he wrote the world's bishops in 1849 to ascertain what their laity and clergy believed about Mary and her Immaculate Conception. (Newman's *Essay* noted this consultation.) Pope Pius XII did likewise. He wrote the world's bishops in 1946 prior to defining the dogma of Mary's Assumption in 1950. Both popes consulted the faithful (clergy and laity) on the content of their faith.[26] Vatican II canonized the topic when it wrote in its chapter on the laity in *Lumen Gentium*, "[Christ continues to protect his Revelation] not only through the teaching hierarchy…but also through the laity. For this purpose He made the laity witnesses and gave them understanding of the faith (*sensus fidei*) and grace of speech" (§ 35).

The Majority Report claimed to be in continuity with the church's tradition that has always affirmed the *goodness* of procreating and the *rightfulness* of marital intercourse. It affirmed four principles: (a) A hedonistic motive for using contraceptives is always immoral; (b) Decent contraceptive means, ordered to fecundity in the *totality* of a couple's married life, is not contrary to church teaching; (c) The laity's *sensus fidelium* is to be listened to, namely, that heroic abstinence is not the answer; (d) There has been a development

26. *Ubi Primum* of Pius IX, 2 February 1849; *Deiparae Virginis Mariae* of Pius XII, 1 May 1946.

in church teaching regarding marriage, moving from asserting the primacy of begetting children to the equal importance of spousal love and affection. The Majority Report also noted that the rhythm method itself was banned until Pius XII permitted it in 1951.[27]

It is the principle of totality that I find to be true. It also seems necessary in many married lives for regulating conceptions when the rhythm method seems unworkable because unpredictable. The encyclicals of Pius XI and Pius XII taught that each separate act of marital intercourse must be open to the possibility of procreating, and any action artificially precluding it is immoral. The principle of totality asserts that the long married life of a couple is oriented to procreating, to fecundity, but that each single act of intercourse need not be.

Vatican II's *Gaudium et Spes* (§ 50) had asserted in 1965 the principle of responsible parenthood regarding the decision of couples concerning when and how many pregnancies are intended, and it also asserted that "where the intimacy of married life is broken off, it is not rare for its faithfulness [read: adultery or divorce] to be imperiled and its quality [read: an unwelcomed pregnancy] of fruitfulness ruined" (§ 51). When measured by the church's unitive (spousal intimacy) and procreative requirements for marital intercourse—language introduced and used by *Humanae Vitae*—applying the principle of totality to the whole of a couple's married life seems to meet the two requirements. One needs to measure over the whole life of a marriage openness to children and affection between the spouses.

The principle of totality applied to morality is not something new. Bodily amputations were judged immoral until Pius XII, in an address to the Congress of Urology in 1953, reasoned that preserving a diseased organ threatening the whole organism was itself wrong. Totality also applied to transplants from a living donor. They were judged to be immoral mutilations of the donor's body until Pius XII in 1956 extended the principle of totality to reckon it as an act of Christian charity to other human beings, not unlike Christ's sacrificial act for others.

Humanae Vitae had many fine things to teach about Christian marriage and love. It asserted strongly the role of responsible parenthood, contrary to the notion that Catholics are expected to procreate as much as possible. Readers, perhaps understandably, jumped immediately to paragraph 14 on "Unlawful Birth Control Methods." Besides maintaining the traditional

---

27. The Majority Report can be found readily online. Before the advent of internet searching, it was difficult to discover. The key early source I used was *Love & Sexuality*, ed. Odile Liebard, (McGrath: Wilmington NC, 1978). After the four principles, it listed four cautions: All contraceptive sex must be expressive of true love; Effectiveness of the means is to be in proportion to the necessity to avoid conception; Every method of prevention has negative features; Extrinsic factors, such as availability and costs, can influence the choice of contraceptive means.

church teaching on procreation without any new developments to it (§ 14), the encyclical also discounted the principle of totality, saying it is "intrinsically wrong" (*intrinsece inhonestum*) to group with the fertile acts of a whole marriage those single acts in themselves deprived of fertility.

When Vatican spokesperson Msgr. Ferdinando Lambruschini gave the document to the press on 29 July 1968, he noted two things about it. The pope did not repeat the idea of grave sin that Pope Pius XI used for artificial contraception in 1930. Second, the document is not an infallible teaching. Understandably, he did not say it could be wrong, but this possibility cannot be excluded. Professor and later Federal Appeals Judge of the Ninth Circuit (San Francisco), John T. Noonan, a Commission member from the very first, was more explicit. "The new document is not an infallible statement. It is a fallible document written by a fallible man in the fallible exercise of his office."

If having credible moral teaching authority means that people listen openly and in most cases deferentially to what church authorities (pope and/or bishops) teach, then *Humanae Vitae* was a disaster. Most Catholic married couples, already using artificial contraceptives, including "the pill," continued using them. Theologians published the criteria for dissenting, in good conscience, from papal non-infallible teachings. This provoked anger from bishops and it caused many theologians to lose teaching positions. (See Appendix D for various levels of the church's teaching office, called *magisterium*.) *Humanae Vitae* began the unraveling of Catholic confidence in church teaching about sexual ethics; moreover, the influence of the moral voice of the Catholic bishops on other church or societal matters diminished. Finally and unfortunately, Catholic laity in large numbers quit the church. So chaotic were the encyclical's effects that Pope Paul never published another encyclical.

The Pew Research Center in 2016 reported that 89% of American Catholics believe that artificial contraception is either morally acceptable or not a moral issue at all. One must assume, contrary to traditionalist skeptics discounting them as simply disloyal malcontents, that many of the respondents in the Pew survey were Catholics committed to their faith and devotional practices. Deeply faithful Catholics, whose integrity was beyond question, were indeed the CFM couples, especially from third world countries, who responded to Patty Crowley in the 1960s. It must be asked, what is the *sensus fidelium* in this matter of personal conjugal life in the Sacrament of Matrimony? Whose lived experience of the faith counts more? Celibate ecclesiastics or Catholic married couples? What is the Holy Spirit teaching the church through the laity's ongoing testimony of non-compliance with *Humanae Vitae*?

I think church teaching gets caught in a paradoxical situation in being opposed both to the use of contraceptives in general and being opposed to abortions. Sexual intercourse makes babies, not all the time but many times. If people having intercourse ought not to be conceiving fetuses, although they do—I am thinking mainly of the unmarried in our sexually permissive hook-up culture—and if church teaching about abstinence for the unmarried and the married does not work to a large extent, Catholic moral exhortation ought to be more flexible on the contraception issue if it wishes to oppose abortions. The church needs to have its argument against abortions not to be cluttered by a teaching that seems to favor, unintentionally, pregnancies happening. Abortion involves two human beings, the woman and the fetus, and the conflicting rights of each fuel today's Roe *v* Wade debate. Using contraceptives to avoid a pregnancy comes nowhere near the moral exigencies of a human fetus. The right to not get pregnant ought to be recognized if the right of the unborn fetus to live ought to be prioritized.

Having abortions is one matter not being supported: not by the laity, not by the Majority Report, not by *Humanae Vitae*, and not by unbroken Catholic tradition. I used to make the case against abortion in a somewhat philosophical way. Human life cannot be said to begin at some moment during gestation or only at successful birthing. What is the difference between a one-week old infant and a fetus at eight months kicking and moving around *in utero*? If none, then what is the difference between a fetus at five months and a fetus at one month? In all cases, and this includes infants in their first years after birth, they are human because they have begun developing toward a fuller expression of humanness: listening and comprehending voices, talking in monosyllables, feeding themselves, returning hugs, learning words and concepts, painting and orchestrating imaginative play games with siblings/parents/grandparents, exercising free will, praying to God, eventually deciding to leave home and strike out for themselves in life. When does unfolding humanness ever stop, or ever begin for the first time? Unfolding humanness, from conception on, was always happening. So ran my philosophical approach.

But my thinking against abortion runs along a stronger line now. Recall the Bethlehem manger in chapter five when I described the Christmas features of my belief, which was actually an extended meditation on the Incarnation. The Incarnation is God's assumption of a human nature at its first instance of existence within his mother. The Incarnation did not await the second month *in utero*, or the ninth, or the first moments outside the womb to begin. It came about as she became pregnant by the overshadowing of the Holy Spirit. The Incarnation began at the first moment of being conceived. Thus, any human life begins to be human at the very beginning. So runs my theological approach, and I believe it to be more persuasive.

My position against abortions also includes a more subtle use of principles of moral theology to justify terminating a pregnancy in rare cases. I have long accepted the conditions of the Hyde Amendment. This 1976 amendment, named for Congressman Henry Hyde who successfully introduced it into law, banned the use of federal funds to pay for an abortion except to save the life of the mother should the pregnancy continue, or if pregnancy arose from incest or rape. When a woman becomes impregnated through incest—usually a very young family member—or rape, the woman is a victim of a horrible evil. I do not see how it is God's will that she must be obligated to carry the pregnancy to term. It seems a second instance of being victimized.

Without making the case in detail, I note that terminating pregnancies in these three cases is similar to the church-permitted termination of an ectopic pregnancy where the pregnancy implants outside the uterus, such as in one of the woman's fallopian tubes. If not terminated, the situation would lead to her death. In this case the fertilized egg is considered under the moral principle of being an unjust aggressor, similar to why one soldier can kill an enemy soldier in battle.[28] I have no sympathy for those so rigidly against any abortion that they advocate continuation of pregnancy in the face of a mother's likely death from severe eclampsia (skyrocketing blood pressure), which is being caused by the pregnancy. The gestation period is too early for viable caesarean delivery to save both child and mother. Strengthen this case by imagining the mother having other young children at home depending on her. She needs to live. Her death, on the other hand, terminates both her and her fetus.

CODA ON OTHER EXPRESSIONS OF ETERNAL LIFE

Much in Catholicism expressing the reality of Eternal Life now, on this side of death, has gone unmentioned. My choice to express it through the lens of sacraments was selective, and even there it was further circumscribed. I've chosen only sacramental issues about which I think Catholics wonder or feel stumped and also about which my beliefs have developed over time and experience. The church's work for social justice, by which I mean the people who work for it, has gone unmentioned along with many other expressions of experiencing Eternal Life today. How does my faith view working for social justice and how do I participate in it?

I take but two examples. In 1980, Mark and Louise Zwick founded the Houston Catholic Worker home, Casa Juan Diego, named after the Aztec peasant who experienced Mary's appearing to him almost 500 years ago

---

28. The officially accepted Catholic argument justifying surgery for an entopic pregnancy, thereby terminating the fetus, is that the fallopian tube had become diseased, just as a cancerous uterus in which nidation has occurred justifies surgical removal of the uterus. Medically treating the tube is what's directly intended; loss of fetus is indirectly intended. Except for avoiding language about the fetus as an unjust aggressor, how does this explanation differ from saying an aberration in fetal development harmed the fallopian tube, and it was an aggressor against the tube's normal workings? Putting the focus back on the fertilized ovum cannot be avoided.

and addressing him in his native language, Nahuatl. She became known as Our Lady of Guadalupe. From the beginning the Casa offered hospitality to refugees from Central America's civil wars. It has expanded to offering food, clothing, shelter, and medical care to whatever poor and marginalized. The second example comes closer to me. Project Home in Philadelphia was founded by Sister of Mercy Mary Scullion in 1989 to address the homelessness of poor people living on the streets of Philadelphia. Its watchword is arresting: "None of us are home until all of us are home." Her work and that of the people who have joined her full time includes building or renovating ever more housing possibilities and finding employment and education for Philadelphia's homeless poor.

It should be clear where Eternal Life, the indwelling of the Holy Spirit, is experienced. It inhabits the Houston Catholic Workers and the tireless workers of Project Home. It drives their consciences to do what they do every day. And Eternal Life resides in the poor for whom they work. "When you did it to the least of these, you were doing it to me." How does my faith involve me in these works of social justice? Although my wife and I have not felt called to join the Catholic Worker Movement or to work at Project Home, we support both groups financially. We feel called to almsgiving. Every penny of donations goes into direct support of the poor. As for other corporal or spiritual works of mercy for us, as older church language called them, we follow the dictates of our consciences.

The concluding eighth chapter will reflect my beliefs about issues in the church that touch closer to the unique person I am, such as being a believer and having received early education in physics and mathematics. I promise only that it will be shorter than chapter seven.

CHAPTER EIGHT

Faith & Science Plus Some Unfinished Promises

*"A failure to recognize the legitimate autonomy of science...
has led many to assume that faith and science are mutually opposed."*
Gaudium et Spes, § 36, of Vatican II

The beginning portions of this chapter reflect my appreciation of the physical sciences that began in high school and continued in university. I never experienced a conflict between science and religion. As my studies turned from science to philosophy (a master's degree) to theology (a Louvain doctorate), the intersection of science and Christian faith continued to fascinate me and does so to this very day. I know that others, some Christian believers and many scientists, experience the lack of harmony between faith and science. This is not my experience. Nor is it the teaching of Vatican II. Two topics seem particularly toxic: How does belief in God square with accepting the evolution of the planet and of the human race? How does God's role as creator, regarding the *when* and *how*, square with the so-called Big Bang of scientists?

HUMAN ORIGINS

Let the words *Adam* and *Eve* represent the beginning of the human race. How are these names to be understood so as to avoid a clash over human origins between what the sciences today understand and what Catholicism teaches? Before turning to some particular questions, such as "Did the human race begin from a single mating couple as appears in the Bible?" let's locate *homo sapiens* on an understandable time scale in order to bring science into the discussion.

Our sun and the other planets making up our solar system came into existence about the same time, which was roughly 4.6 billion years ago.[1] If

1. The universe itself is calculated to have begun 13.8 billion years ago. Cosmologists calculate it by measuring the current rate of expansion of galaxies from each other and then extrapolating backwards to an initial expansion point, called conveniently the Big Bang. Back-

we describe our Earth on a scale easier to imagine, as on a 24-hour clock, our planet began at twelve midnight. When the planet cooled enough to form a crust—even today the Earth's core closest the surface is still molten—the oldest rocks came into existence at 3:45 am. The oldest form of life appeared at 4 am, and from 4 am until 1 pm single-celled organisms alone existed. Thereafter life grew more complex. The first dinosaurs didn't appear until 11 pm. Human life appeared about a minute before midnight, and some scientists fix it even closer to midnight. In brief, there was a long evolution of our planet, especially the collection of water brought by water-carrying comets and asteroids between 1 am to 3 am on the imaginary clock, the production of an atmosphere containing sufficient oxygen, and the formation of a magnetic shield to protect Earth's atmosphere from being stripped away by harmful solar particles, as happened to whatever atmosphere Mars had.

Our evolving Earth created a milieu within which human life could happen and flourish. It is to the distinction of a great Jesuit paleontologist, Teilhard de Chardin (1881–1955), to have perceived a grander plan at work: The Creator was guiding material creation to higher levels of existence, culminating in human existence and, at the very end of evolution, to Christ-filled human existence, which he named after the last letter of the Greek alphabet, the Omega Point, the end point of everything and why anything beforehand evolved at all. Most Christians call it heaven.

Chardin's faith view invites reflecting on the beginnings of *homo sapiens*, perhaps as long ago as 200,000 years, or somewhat sooner but certainly not close in time to today. Here's another question to pose to the Adam and Eve construct: Did either one of them have a belly button, that is, a navel? The question, as silly as it sounds, is simply a graphic way of asking whether the first human beings had evolved from primate parents or appeared as fully formed from the hand of their Creator, which is the picture in *Genesis*. The question holds whether people place the first humans appearing only 6,000 years ago, as most in earlier centuries did and some today still maintain it, or whether the first humans appeared 200,000 years ago. Did the first humans appear in full adult stature, or were they born originally from non-human primates and hence had navels?

Such a view of navel-less persons makes human creation by God easy to imagine, and it shelters people from the unpleasant impression that "we all descended from apes." The so-called 1925 "Scopes Monkey Trial" over the teaching of evolution in Tennessee public schools reflected this phobia. But this fundamentalist view comes with a price, as pointed out in chapter two. If taken literally, the *Genesis* children of Adam and Eve certainly underwent gestation in the womb, as did the next generation of humans, but these descendants would have come about through incest (brothers and sisters mating

ground radiation from this event, still deciphered today, is also measured.

with each other). Thankfully, Christian faith does not require this conclusion.

It seems beyond scientific doubt that the first humans did have ancestors, and they were primates. The teaching of Catholic faith that all humans, even the very first ones, arise directly from the creative power of God can be maintained, maintaining at the same time that the first humans were born from primates. Catholic faith pivots on the following issue: Human beings have souls that constitute them as human. Whence do human souls originate?

Some other questions can be added to this picture. Even if having evolved from primates and brought to a level of human life by God's creative power—infusion of the soul is the ready formula to express it—are Adam and Eve symbolic of a single mating couple or expressive of a wider range of human couples at the same time, a wider hominization to use a Chardin word? The theory of a single human couple launching the human race is termed *monogenism*.

Although the incest inference did not seem to have been discussed and solved, monogenism was the prevailing Catholic Church assumption until the second half of the twentieth century. It was operative in the teachings of the Council of Trent on Original Sin. And it renders, in a clear imaginative picture, the teaching of St. Paul: "Just as in Adam all have died, so also in Christ all will be brought to life" (1 Cor 15:22). Just as there is a singular Second Adam, Jesus, by whose life humanity became unburdened, there was a singular First Adam by whose transgression humanity became burdened. It is so easy to imagine two singular individuals, two Adams, the first causing a predicament, the second undoing it, as if each stands as a bookend to the multi-volume story of humanity.

Whereas the singularity of Jesus as the Second Adam must remain as an article of Christian faith—"by no other name are you saved" (Acts 4:12)—the existence of a singular First Adam is not similarly demanded, except in imagination. Polygenism is the term for multiple couples, multiple Adams as it were, being the source of the human race as we know it. This is the prevailing scientific perspective on human origins in the evolutionary scheme, even though there is much ongoing debate on when (200,000 years ago?) and how—the fossil record can only postulate origins, not describe them—and where (Africa's Rift Valley?) it happened. Christian faith, however, can accept the reality of polygenism by asserting that God's infusion of the human soul happened over a wider array of *hominids*;[2] the term refers to those primates closest in capacity to humans and that, not who, are the immediate

2. It is thought that hominids themselves diverged from other primate lines about 2.5 million years ago, later began walking upright and became tool makers (*homo habilis*). *Homo sapiens* emerged from hominids perhaps 200,000 years ago, moved out of Africa for Europe and Asia after 100,000 years, reaching Australia 50,000 years ago, and crossed from Siberia to North America over a land bridge when sea levels dropped dramatically during the last ice age. Human wall drawings have been found in France (Chauvet Caves) dating to 30,000 BC.

evolutionary precursors to humans. (I reserve *who* to persons.) Polygenism maintains that the breakthrough to humanization was not a unique instance for one and only one couple but rather represents multiple instances of humanizations. To the extent it can be imagined, it was like an explosion of humanness over an expanse of geography and time, a sort of Russian Spring, like the permafrost birthing a field of flowers after a barren winter.

This view, of course, entails a reformulation of the doctrine of Original Sin such as was proposed in chapter two. It is one thing to abandon the reality of a singular First Adam infecting all his progeny, which can and ought to be done, but it is another matter to toss out the doctrine of Original Sin fully, and this chapter two did not propose to do.

I wish to avoid the charge that I am rendering Christian faith subservient to scientific discoveries, however provisional and tentative and ongoing they usually are, for which fluid scientific picture I have abandoned the solidity and consistency of the church's faith tradition, even though this doctrinal tradition exhibits developments and has not always been consistent. This is not my intention, and I do not think I am doing it. Being raised, however, is the question about faith's relationship to science that has plagued Christianity's appeal for thoughtful persons, especially those of a scientific tendency. The Galileo Affair,[3] apropos whether Christian faith required a heliocentric or geocentric world, and the appearance of Darwin's 1859 book, *On the Origin of Species*, come readily to mind as prickly moments between faith and science.

Darwin's proposals about natural selection within (animal) species did not alarm John Henry Newman when Darwin's book appeared, as it did alarm most other Christian theologians. Nor did Darwin's later proposals in *Descent of Man* (1871), suggesting human evolution from primates, faze Newman's commitment to Christian teachings, even though Darwin himself was agnostic and envisioned nothing that required God's intervention. Newman had a blueprint he advocated on the sometimes contentious relationship between science and religion. It bears repeating:

> If he [the true university person] has one cardinal maxim in his philosophy, it is, that truth cannot be contrary to truth; if he has a second, it is, that truth often *seems* contrary to truth; and, if a third, it is the practical conclusion, that we must be patient with such appearances, and not to be hasty to pronounce them to be really of a more formidable character. (*Idea of a University*, 461 of the Uniform Edition)

With monogenism or polygenism vis-à-vis God's role creating humans, we are at Newman's third maxim of advice, especially where polygenism can

---

3. The Galileo controversy was the subject of one of my earliest publications while in seminary. See "The Galileo Affair," *Dominicana* 50 (1965), 258-65.

be further researched to be between human origins within a single breeding group (monophyletic polygenism) or from multiple and dispersed breeding groups (polyphyletic polygenism). It is easy to tumble over all these poly-words, but it is easier to stabilize our thinking on a cardinal principle of faith: Whoever is human now and whenever the first humans began to be human, this person, this reality addressed as a *who*, was made in God's image and was the recipient of God's breath (the *ruah* of chapter two). In language perhaps more familiar than these biblical references, this human being became human by God's infusion of the soul into the preexisting matter of a hominid.

We note with interest how the science of human origins has been undergoing developments since Darwin's day to its contemporary proposals and how the church's teaching on human origins has also been undergoing developments in its formulations, just within the twentieth century. The Catholic Church has come to accept biological evolution only slowly and with resistance. The Pontifical Biblical Commission in 1909 mandated Catholic professors to teach that the first woman was made from the first man (Denzinger § 3514), as the J account in *Genesis* describes it. But by 1950, the encyclical of Pope Pius XII, *Humani Generis*, was Catholicism's first official discussion of evolution, teaching that the human body could be the product of evolution and thus studied by science but that the human soul is caused by God alone and not by evolving material causes (§ 36).[4] Pope John Paul II, in a message to the Pontifical Academy of Sciences in 1996, observed that evolution has moved from mere hypothesis to commonly accepted theory (§ 4), but he reiterated the teaching of Pius XII that "the spiritual soul is created directly by God" (§ 5).[5] This progression in the church's position expresses Newman's first maxim that truth (scientific evidence) cannot be contrary to truth (what the church wishes to teach as a revealed message) and Newman's third maxim to have patience as convergences work themselves out.

A brief explanation is required about the papal reference to evolving material causes. Organic life appeared on our planet over three billion years ago, and for the longest time these one-celled organisms remained as such. But how, at first, was the jump from inorganic matter to organic matter achieved? A position called *vitalism* would maintain that God had to cause it, acting from without, because inorganic material causes cannot effect the "leap" to life. But scientific experiments have indicated that amino acids, the chemical constituents in all living organisms, can be synthesized from inorganic materials, with laboratory catalysts replicating early conditions of our earth (recurring lightning, radiation, an atmosphere with ammonia, etc.). It

---

4. The encyclical is available at http://www.vatican.va/content/pius-xii/en/encyclicals/documents/hf_p-xii_enc_12081950_humani-generis.html. Vatican theologians in 1950 pressed Pius XII to assert monogenism but the pope refused.

5. The text is available at http://www.pas.va/content/accademia/en/magisterium/johnpaulii/22october1996.html

is not my role or ability to unravel the supporting science but only to say that material causes and not God's special intervention can explain the evolution from non-life to life on our planet. Once one-celled life existed on earth, the evolution to higher forms of living organisms would follow more readily and from material causes inherent to the organisms and the environment.

The evolution from living organisms—primates for example—to human life is an altogether other issue. There are scientists who think that there is not much difference between hominids and the first humans. From one to the other is a rather smooth transition, not unlike Darwin's discovery of how avian species evolve by adapting to new environmental conditions. (The woodpeckers who developed long narrow beaks to grab embedded insects survived while less fitted kinds of "woodpecker cousins" died off when insects burrowed in trees more deeply.) I maintain, and so does our Catholic tradition, that the difference between being human and being anything else is as great as one can imagine. Not just intelligence but self-reflective intelligence is the new level of achievement. Not just choosing but willing to forsake on behalf of another is the new level of achievement. Not just experiences of fear or attraction or self-preservation but the experience of the demands of conscience is the new level of achievement. Between hominids and *homo sapiens* involves such a momentous leap into becoming human that mere organic material causes cannot pull it off. Therefore in this transition from hominid life to human life, God's causality is needed. It involves the infusion of the human soul. Try this personal experiment on yourself: Think of what you are holding when you hold a new-born baby. Be thinking especially of the *potential* of who you are holding.

FOUR VIEWPOINTS ON EVOLUTION

In October 2004, the School District of Dover, Pennsylvania, located about 20 miles south of Harrisburg, required the ninth-grade biology curriculum to teach Intelligent Design as the alternative to the customary way of teaching evolution. This was not an attempt to suppress evolution, such as the 1925 Scopes Trial in Tennessee tried to do. Intelligent Design accepted the fact of evolution but added some caveats. Nine parents, however, sued the School District in the U.S. District Court of Middle Pennsylvania, contending that a religious viewpoint had been injected into the curriculum. The parents won. The older curriculum was returned.

Four viewpoints on evolution can be staked out: Creationism, Evolutionism, Intelligent Design, and a fourth position, lacking a proper name, but which I believe locates where the Catholic faith should be positioned. Not all Catholics locate themselves in this fourth view. I do, and I perceive official Catholic teaching does also.

Without the word being then used, Creationism was met in chapter two. It is the viewpoint about human origins drawn directly from the Garden

Story in *Genesis*. The first eleven seemingly historical chapters of this biblical book, up to the call of Abraham, seem to attract, as if by their own gravitational force, literal-minded readers. If the cosmos is created in six days (the P Story), then God achieved everything in 144 hours. Sometimes a certain sophistication, called *Concordism*, is appended to the literal approach. Instead of six 24-hour days, God created the world within six geological epochs, but six and only six nonetheless. God created the first male, and from him came the female, and from both of them a horrible sin ensued (the J Story). But the stories need not be interpreted literally, and ought not to be, as argued in chapter two. Creationism is not really a view of evolution, except in the sense that the human race comes from that singular couple (monogenism). Otherwise, the actual Adam and Eve looked like us, spoke like us, transgressed like us, felt guilt like us, and became mortal like us.

The second approach is my coined word *evolutionism*. It carries an "ism" as an intended nuance because of its godless context. This viewpoint understands the cosmos to have been evolving almost fourteen billion years, and our planet nearly five billion years. Most adherents would claim that there is no role for God in this evolution because there is no God. A minority among them might have a deistic view of God, an uninvolved God who is bracketed out, for all intentions, when describing how the world and all life forms unfold. God merely gave everything a push into existence and stepped back.

I have little doubt that a literal advocacy of the *Genesis* picture has set evolutionism as its antagonistic counterpart. A thoughtful person committed to scientific findings might well conclude: "If these claims in *Genesis* about human origins are the truths in which belief in God entails, I simply cannot be a believer. It is all too farfetched." I would say the same for myself. I'm sure, as a youngster, that I was taught the literal Adam and Eve picture. When I began learning science during high school years, I think that I simply blocked out this picture. The more I studied evolution, the more the science made sense to me. But later, and without abandoning my esteem for science, I needed to return to the Bible with a more proper grasp of how the creation stories worked, and this I presented in chapter two. Making unwitting use of Newman's maxim but not knowing he said it, it was important for me that truth—what the sciences presented about evolution—not contradict truth—that the Bible is God's revealed word. From this point in my life, I stood for evolution but against evolutionism, because God cannot be absent from what makes the world to be the world. But how is this to happen?

One possibility is the viewpoint of Intelligent Design, even though it is not the answer for me. A small circle of biologists, uncomfortable with the agnosticism and even atheism of most of their scientific peers—biologist Michael Behe estimated that ninety percent of the elite National Academy of Scientists held these views—determined to make the case for God's role in evolution. They researched the complexities of biological processes and contended that Darwinian natural selection, with its inherent randomness, cannot explain in an intellectually satisfying manner the evolutionary transition through these complexities. A guiding hand in nature, deeper and more profound than any natural law, was needed where unbridgeable complexities were observed. Behe, for example, argued that molecular systems, such as the flagella of bacteria, appear designed because they really act that way. God designed them. Intelligent Design advocates contend that the universe, the world of nature, has a fundamental design to it, exhibited by the laws of evolution that direct the unfolding of nature. But careful scientific observation can detect gaps here and there that only the designing hand of God can bridge.

The foundations of faith in God cannot be based on this Design argument because it is like situating an argument on a house of cards that will eventually collapse, and for two reasons. The history of science is filled with instances where there had been gaps in what was scientifically knowable at the time. But later science filled the gaps with breakthrough insights. For example, after Isaac Newton's laws of gravitation and Johannes Kepler's laws of planetary motion became known, lunar and solar eclipse could be explained when earlier they could not or were attributed to divine arrangements. Filling scientific gaps by appealing to God's special intervention invites Laplace's famous response to Napoleon's question of where God figured into Laplace's book about the heavens: "I have no need of that hypothesis." Less Laplace's point be taken too far, there is one crucial exception that I mentioned earlier: Evolution's reaching the emergence of human life requires the Creator's infusion of the soul. Scientific laws come up short. The emergence of human life is indeed a gap, a leap, which exceeds natural causalities.

The second reason against the Intelligent Design position involves what I perceive as the law of cause and effect in science. It is best explained with language met earlier from Thomas Aquinas, the distinction between a primary cause and a secondary cause. Recall the illustration of a musician (primary cause) playing a melody and her violin (secondary cause) causing the melody. Earlier the distinction was applied to why prayer is worthwhile. Here I apply it to how science should be seen working.

The observations and measurements in science—the experiments—are set up to determine cause and effect relationships. This is the virus. How do you produce vaccines to engender the body's own antibodies to combat it? The entire world of science is the realm of secondary causes. Scientists do not use this phrase. They just speak of causes, and from these causes other causes are seen behind them, and so forth. The deeper that scientific exploration probes a gap or a mysterious phenomenon or whatever problem, it never leaves the realm of secondary causes and effects, because that is all there is to observe. Science cannot dig its way down to observing God in the same manner it observes material phenomena. Perceptible are only what I am calling secondary causes being met as science digs more deeply. However, for someone convinced that the universe is not its own explanation why everything exists, that person can affirm that God is the primary cause enabling all the secondary causes to be operating, following their own laws of nature.

These natural laws do not need God's special interventions to cover a puzzling gap. The world indeed depends on God's sustaining act of creating, but science, using whatever scientific methods are at its disposal, cannot discover God as the Cause of all causes or as the underlying cause to all the laws of nature. Such are the laws of evolution. This science studies. This a believer, like myself, admires. I am simply convinced that beneath all the observable and measurable evolutionary phenomena of this visible world lies the invisible world, God, this world's primary and enabling cause.

These reasons against the argument for Intelligent Design are, at the same time, expressing the fourth viewpoint on evolution, which I espouse. It provides little clarity were I to call it the Primary/Secondary Causality viewpoint, although that is what it is. It maintains the legitimate autonomy of science without the interference of theistic principles affecting observations and measurements or needing to replace them. This fourth perspective maintains the claims of faith when these are established to be commanding. For example, faith demands that being human is a gift of God, with infusion of soul, but it does not demand that the first humans lived in a blissful *prelapsarian* (pre-sinful) state before they sinned. This never happened, and neither do evolutionary scientists think so.

My admiration for scientists matches my admiration for science in general. Many are theistic, whether they be Jewish, Christian, or Muslim. Many are agnostic or atheist, but they are fair-minded men and women and do not crusade on behalf of atheism; they just do their work. Recalling Newman's third maxim, be patient with differences in matters of faith and science, and do not consider them to be "really of a more formidable character." Like titration experiments in chemistry, time is needed to sort out matters.

WHAT TO MAKE OF THE BIG BANG?

This chapter began with stating that the age of the cosmos is estimated to be about 13.8 billion years. Because the universe is expanding, the estimation of age was made by "projecting backwards" to when expansion began. This retrospective has led some to call it the *moment of creation*. If someone does not believe in God, and many scientists don't, I suppose it is understandable enough language. But it is not accurate to describe this beginning moment as creation, as if to mean there was nothing, and then there began to be something. I wish to share just enough science to make it clear that the religious understanding of creation is not undermined by what science is understanding. They are two quite different perspectives.

The galaxies in the cosmos are now accelerating away from each other, like dots on a balloon's surface that recede from each other as the balloon is inflated quickly. But it was not from a situation of nothingness that expansion of stuff began. (I use *stuff* to avoid the esoteric language Big Bang theorists use such as quarks, antiquarks, electrons, etc.).

Science doesn't have exact terminology to describe the *it* from which stuff expanded. The theorists conveniently use the language of a "point of singularity" because, conveniently, it is beyond normal scientific description and beyond the normal laws of physics. It might as well have been called a "point defying description." It is helpful to be aware that Big Bang is a theoretical model, supported indeed by plausible evidence, and that laws of physics have been stretched to their limits to depict the model. The elusive *it* is a situation of almost infinite density and unimaginable temperature that is estimated to have been 10^{40} degrees Kelvin (1 followed by forty zeroes).[6] Some describe the singularity has having infinite density, but they surely exaggerate; infinities of anything are impossible in nature.[7]

Then it explodes. My surmise is that even the word *explodes* comes from a reality closer at hand to these astrophysicists, the death of a star. Stars fuse hydrogen into helium, and the helium into heavier elements. For simplicity, think of a star burning up its hydrogen fuel. When the hydrogen is depleted and the helium has fused into an iron core, the star no longer "burns." The star then collapses under its own gravity, the core heats to billions of degrees and explodes into a supernova, shooting its materials into space, possibly to be gathered by gravitation into another star undergoing formation.[8]

This is enough Big Bang science to contrast it with what religion calls creation. The singularity point is exceedingly dense but it is not nothing. Where did *it* come from and why? How long was it there before it exploded? Why did it come to explode? Science cannot answer these questions. They lie outside the range of projecting backwards in time. These kinds of philosophical questions are sufficient to indicate that the Big Bang model is not about creation.

6. Science uses the Kelvin or Celsius (aka Centigrade) scales, not the American-used Fahrenheit. Water freezes at 273.15^0 K = 0^0 C = 32^0 F. Water boils at 373.15^0 K = 100^0 C = 212^0 F.

7. There is an easy proof from simple mathematics. The density of anything is its mass (in earth's gravity, think of weight) divided by its volume. As a constant mass gets compressed, its volume gets smaller while its density gets greater. But the density equation would reach infinity only if the volume reaches zero. If the volume were really zero, you have nothingness. Hence, affirming infinite density for what I am calling *it* is a meaningless assertion. In Newman's invisible world, the infinite grandeur of God is not a meaningless *infinite statement*. Can our minds, even in heaven, comprehend—take fully in—God's infinite grandeur? Love it, yes. Comprehend it, no. The eminent theologian, Karl Rahner, calls such divine infinity *Unbegreiflichkeit*, God's incomprehensibility, a refrain throughout his writings that echoes Thomas Aquinas.

8. Our own sun has about five billion years left of hydrogen fuel, but it won't end as an exploding supernova. It will expand into a "red giant" star, gobbling up Mercury and Venus, and making toast of Earth. Then its core will cool, and it will contract into a "white dwarf" star, eventually becoming dark. But who's around to watch?

Creation is religious language, theological language if you wish. It has to do with existence, not expansion. The focus is not on when stuff began to expand. The focus is on how stuff has being at all. (I use *stuff* to mean not just quantified matter but also radiation, energy that is real and measurable, like the microwaves heating a cup of coffee.) The focus is not on what changes into what, such as hydrogen into helium, mature stars into red giant stars, and so forth. The focus is on whether the totality of the stuff of the universe is its own explanation for its existence.

MEANING OF CREATION

These have been philosophical musings posed to the Big Bang model and unanswerable by it. But I wish to keep my musings as simple as I can as I attempt to share what I think the Catholic doctrine of creation means. My fundamental musing begins with an analogy. Pick up a book from your desk and hold it two feet higher in the air. It is suspended at this height, not by itself, but by your hand. I'll use the phrase, "it is being propped up." Moving from the image of this book to everything existing in our world, each and every thing in the cosmos is being propped up in existence, propped up from nothingness as it were, because the opposite of being in existence is nothingness. Everything, with one exception, requires being propped up because nothing brings with itself the cause of its own existence. Only God is the cause of His[9] own existence. As readily as the Bible says "God is love," the Catholic tradition of philosophy says "God is existence itself."

The book analogy helps in another manner. Some think of God's act of creating as happening "in the beginning" and then God steps back from the unfolding of creation—evolution for example—much like a watchmaker making a working watch and letting it go on working by itself. God creates but then becomes a non-interventionist. Deism is its philosophical/religious expression, among whose many adherents have been Voltaire, Benjamin Franklin, and Thomas Edison. The Christian doctrine of creation is quite different. God never stops His activity as Creator. God never stops sustaining in existence all that is. This is the real meaning of creation. God never stops propping up; otherwise, whatever is would revert to nothingness. If the hand propping up the book is removed, the book falls. But did the propping up of creation have a beginning or has it been eternal?

Creatio ex nihilo (creation out of nothingness) is a technical phrase in our Catholic tradition to describe what God does. Besides the obvious meaning that there is no pre-existing stuff God uses, a contradiction in terms anyway, I think its real meaning is what I've just explained: the understanding that

9. Recalling an earlier discussion concerning God language, God is a person but lacks gender. It is just as proper to say that God is the cause of Her own existence. English cannot express personhood without attributing gender. Masculine pronouns have become customary but they are not obligatory. By a reader's personal choice, they may be switched around.

all created realities are propped up in existence. The alternative otherwise is nothingness. However, church teaching seems to add to the phrase the notion that the propping up action of God began at a moment in the past. Before then there was nothing around, and God, not using pre-existing stuff, began creating things. This assertion troubles me because of the word *before*. It puts God's eternity in a time framework.

I introduce a second musing, in a simple enough question format: God is certainly eternal, but can his created world be likewise eternal? This possibility is not a contradiction in terms. An eternal world would not make created things equal to God. Created things would remain dependent on God's bestowal of existence. Without being divine itself, the eternal world would simply be an eternally propped up reality. But the accent of my question falls on the duration of stuff, without a beginning and without an end.

The religious question remains: Must the creation of the world as we know it have had a beginning? Does that word *nihilo* rule out an eternal world? The word *nihilo* has been met twice before now. In the six-days-of-creation story, God Creator is presented with a situation of chaos in *Gen* 1:1. Hebrew had no word for nothingness, so it uses the image of disorder. Over the six days God brings about a world of order from chaos. God is said to create *ex nihilo*, meaning "bringing order to chaos. We next met *nihilo* in the teaching of the Fourth Lateran Council (AD 1215) concerning God's "creation of spiritual creatures (angels) *ex nihilo*," that is, from nothing preexisting.

The P Creation Story begins with practically a clap of thunder: "In the beginning God created heaven and earth" (*In principio creavit Deus caelum et terram* was the Latin Bible text the Roman Catholic Church used for centuries). St. Augustine used the accepted understanding of *in principio*, meaning "when time began," as well as other reasons to argue against an eternal world that Aristotle proposed. St. Bonaventure used practically the same arguments and scripture against an eternal world proposed by the Muslim philosopher Averroes (1126-1198) and his Christian devotees at the University of Paris in the 1250s.[10] Thomas Aquinas was more circumspect. He held that a created world that was dependent on God's causality and existing eternally with its Creator is not a contradiction. Reason cannot prove it to be false. Nor can reason alone prove that the world had a beginning. It is only from revelation—he notes the *in principio* of *Gen* 1:1 and the "before the earth came into being" text of *Prv* 8:23—that Christian faith is able to assert that the world is not eternal.

Biblical scholars today would remind us that these texts are not directly

---

10. The University of Paris, in the professorship days of Bonaventure and Thomas Aquinas, had four faculties or schools: Theology, Law, Medicine and Arts (humanities, especially philosophy). The School of Arts was dominated by Aristotelean philosophers who looked to the writings of Averroes as a gifted commentator on ancient Aristotle. Their movement was called Latin Averroism. Siger of Brabant was their leading philosopher.

teaching whether the world is eternal or had a beginning. Their focus was different. The scriptural authors, like everyone else, assumed that the world had a beginning. Regarding the teaching of Lateran IV, I made the case in chapter six that its binding teaching was against the Manichean dualism of two agents of creation, a good principle and an evil principle coexisting in tension. Hence, the council's creation *ex nihilo* expression was directly addressing dualism and not the eternity of the world.

So, is it of Christian faith that our created world has a beginning? I follow Aquinas that it cannot be proven one way or the other. However, unlike him, I do not think scriptural revelation was meant to solve the issue. Where are we left?

AN EXERCISE IN IMAGINATION

To see if we can move off dead center, I invite you to undertake with me an experiment in imagination, keeping in mind the meaning of eternity discussed in chapter six. Imagine a world that had no beginning. It depends on God for its existence, and it has always been existing in propped-up dependence. God's eternity cannot experience change over time but a created world, distinct from God, can. Here's easy proof: I enjoy a prayer relationship with God who exists in eternity, in all-at-once reality. But I exist as an ever-changing reality subject to the rules of time. A world without beginning would have enjoyed the passage of time in an endless duration. The Big Bang takes you back almost fourteen billion years to a point of "singularity," indescribability, but still a *something*. Can you image anything in existence beforehand? I cannot. Furthermore, why would God create anything having eternal duration eventuating in some kind of point of singularity? What would have been the purpose? It's beyond being imagined.

Let your imagination run forward. If creation has been eternally existing, why would such a world without a start-up point have an end point? We know that our own sun is at middle age. It has five billion years to go before it cremates all the inner planets. If human life ends then, or long before then, what's the point of imagining an endless world? Will human life figure out a way to travel far elsewhere and get out of the way of a red giant star? I cannot conceive this escape possibility. We are imagining inhabitable places many light years away from earth. Light can travel that fast. We can't and won't ever be able. At some future point *homo sapiens* on Earth will stop existing. To what purpose, then, is an eternal world without people?

We are left with another invitation: Imagine how human life might end. This is harder to imagine, but at least we are imagining it with some revealed tools of faith. I think especially of the teaching on the Second Coming of the Lord, the end of history, the consummation of all things in the mystery of Christ, what Teilhard de Chardin called the Omega Point. But I cannot imagine it with any specificity. Will all human beings come to accept Jesus as Lord and Savior before the end? I doubt it although it is one way to read certain statements of Jesus. Or will the end of the world portend the rise of human evil such that "then came your day of wrath and the moment to judge the dead" (Rev 11:18). I cannot square this possibility with God's Providence and why the Incarnation happened. So, imagining how human life might end gets lost in fog.

This present world, on the other hand, is easy to imagine; it's what we experience. We experience the past in a limited sense. We have our own memories of ourselves. We experience our past in terms of the story of Jesus in the gospels. We seek a real apprehension of our Lord's life. (This is the basis of the Jesuit 30-day retreat, the so-called *Ignatian Exercises*.) We enter antiquity through good historical writing and through archeology.

But at some point the past becomes opaque and then lost in fog, too. We experience ourselves in the present moment with all the features that need not be detailed but that everyone has. And we experience the future. How so? I do not refer to soothsaying or tarot card readings or other bizarre divinations. I refer to hope. We are people who hope. We hope in our futures and in the futures of our loved ones. We hope that the world and human history will come to an end that holds out the possibility of bliss. Is this not what Christian hope desires after all? We have a right to this hope, and it cannot be taken away. Therefore, imagining an eternal world, lacking a beginning and lacking an end, staggers my imagination. The musings become unreal. My conclusion: A created world, without beginning and without end, is unreal.

IS THERE LIFE ELSEWHERE?

This question will be my final incursion into the religion and science arena because the topic draws much media attention today. An immediate precision is needed. Does "life elsewhere" mean human life elsewhere or lower forms of life existing elsewhere in the cosmos? This is the rub in the question. The interest of scientists and the curiosity of the general public concerns human life, of course. But finding evidence of any kind of extraterrestrial life is a start.

Jupiter's moon Europa, first discovered by Galileo, has become a place to start. Europa has water, which is necessary for life forms. It is thought that Europa has more water, under its icy crust, than all of Earth's oceans combined. But discovering evidence of life would require a spacecraft landing on frigid Europa (-260° F at its warmest) and looking for life next to a hydrothermal vent—Europa's core is hot—on the floor of its ocean, much like tube worms found in Earth's deepest and frigid oceans. The task is formidable. Mars is closer, and spacecraft have gone there. Mars had water once, and evidence of ice remains. The hunt for evidence of once-living organisms is going on as I write this sentence (NASA's Perseverance Rover).

The quest for *human* life elsewhere has taken two forms. One form has been to launch spacecraft into interstellar space hoping for a rendezvous with intelligent beings. NASA launched Voyager I in 1977, and its main aim was to send back data in its flyby of Jupiter and Saturn, which it did. But it had enough momentum to keep going, escaping the pull of the sun's gravity in 2012. Voyager carries messages (mathematical figures, greetings in 55 languages, music) for engaging any intelligent life out there.[11] It is on its way toward the star Gliese 455 and will enter its neighborhood in 40,000 years. This approach is, literally, a shot into darkness.

The second form of the quest is to seek a place somewhere in the cosmos where the possibility of human life could be met. The quest is assuming that the planet needs to be like the earth itself. It needs water; it would need to be near its host star for light and warmth, but not too close; and it needs to have a supportable atmosphere.

Astrophysicists, as serious minded as they are, are not without a sense of humor. They say such a planet, christened an *exoplanet*, lies in a "Goldilocks zone." NASA found such an exoplanet in 2015, just the right distance from its host star, Kepler 452, so that beings *like us* could thrive. (Kepler 452 is a mere 1400 light years away. Our fastest space craft at this time would take 25 million years to reach this Goldilocks planet!) At the current time, NASA claims to have found[12] almost 4000 exoplanets, and the discoveries keep growing.

The point of these daunting numbers allows me to introduce religion into the question by considering the conjecture of eminent British physicist Stephen Hawking before his death in 2018: "We believe that intelligent life arose spontaneously on Earth, so in an infinite universe there must be other occurrences of life." If a tiny speck in the universe, like Earth, enjoys human life, then in the vast universe of billions of stars and billions of exoplanets, there has to be human life out there. The math of probability theory predicts it. This is the mindset of many scientists, as it was the mindset of Hawking. How can there not be intelligent life elsewhere?

Let's return to that tiny speck of a humanity-covered planet called Earth. In the planet's evolution, treated above, it was recognized that life forms (one-celled organisms) could come about by natural laws but that natural evolution could not produce human life. God's infusion of the human soul—that which makes humans to image God—was necessary. Hawking, on the con-

11. The languages and music make no sense to me. Using math makes more sense for human intelligence elsewhere. The ratio of a circle to its diameter is fixed and exacting, called Pi (π). It is close to 3.1415... but the digits after the decimal point never reach an end. The Greek mathematician Archimedes (around 250 BC) was able to approximate Pi closely. The example assumes that math is a universal language of any intellect, and circles are everywhere met.

12. What does *found* mean? Exoplanets are too distant to be seen visually. The specialized Kepler Space Telescope detects ripples in the light of the host star when a sufficiently massive exoplanet passes in front of the star. NASA's new TESS satellite telescope obtains more exacting signatures (e.g., orbital period, atmosphere) of the exoplanet.

trary, would echo Pierre-Simon Laplace's "I have no need of that hypothesis" and maintain that natural laws have produced here on earth beings with intelligence. This is asserted but it has yet to be scientifically proven, and I think it cannot. On the other hand, the assertion of God's role in the creation of human souls is beyond physical proofs, at least beyond reasons that would sway scientists. My assertion of God-sourced intelligent life is a statement of faith, based on revelation, based on the *Genesis* stories at the heart of all later Israelite and Christian thinking.

So how does religion, for example, Catholic faith, respond to the question, "Is life elsewhere in the universe?" Non-human life? I think it is most probable (mathematically) that such life exists elsewhere. I've already admitted that natural laws were sufficient for its emergence on Earth. Like Newman facing the prospect of Darwin without alarm, I face life elsewhere with no alarm for my faith. Human life elsewhere? If it were so, it would have to be caused by God. Do I think this has happened? I do not. Biblical revelation never addressed life beyond Earth other than heavenly life. My reason for thinking human life, intelligent life, does not exist elsewhere is based on what the Incarnation means.

The Incarnation is the highest expression of being human. It is the being of God existing as human, something that began with Mary's conception of Jesus and continues in eternity as the glorification, or exaltation, of Christ's human nature. But the story of Jesus' human nature is the prototype story of our humanness as discussed in chapter five. Let me express it with different words. *Homo sapiens* really entails an unfolding story, and it is our story. We began from the creative hand of God, as primitive as we were long ago, by existing in God's image. We ourselves evolved, and I leave to paleoanthropologists to describe such features as increasing brain capacity. After thousands of years, we formed communities and different cultures, one of which is recounted in the Old Testament. From within it and from a woman of the Tribe of Judah came an expression of *homo sapiens* that is practically beyond grasp, where being human and being divine exist as the one person, Jesus. Our story of *homo sapiens* is now funneled through his story, and Jesus' biography has become ours: our solidarity in his life, death, and resurrection. All this reflects faith convictions, of course, and not calculated to prove matters to scientists who do not, by training, think this way unless their perceptions have been bent by God into faith assents. (See Augustine's words in footnote 3, chapter three.)

What is the upshot as it would apply to human life elsewhere? If earthly human life has achieved such possibility of grandeur because of the Incarnation, if being human cannot become more exalted, why would there be human life elsewhere if this was God's aim in creating women and men? Would this require Incarnations of God happening elsewhere in the cosmos and many times over? Such an idea seems to repel. And if Incarnation is not a replicated phenomenon, does this mean that intelligent life elsewhere is not meant for the grandeur that ours is? Such an idea also seems to repel. This is why I think there is not human (intelligent) life elsewhere.

IMAGINATION: NEGATIVE AND POSITIVE EFFECTS

I might have given the misleading impression that advocates of Creationism caused the agnosticism or atheism of scientists advocating Evolutionism. That both viewpoints are antagonistic is for sure, and this was all that I was proposing. The agnosticism and atheism prevalent among scientists have many underlying reasons, and some of them are understandable. One understandable reason was proposed long ago by Cardinal Newman, and it bears on the role of imagination working against religion.

In 1882, when Newman had already been a cardinal for three years, Anglican convert and longtime admirer William Samuel Lilly wrote him about the antipathy between religion and science and asked Newman's advice on an essay Lilly was preparing. Newman replied on the seventh of December:

> I have read your proof with the greatest pleasure, and with entire assent. Certainly there is no opposition in the respective truths of science and theology, nor do I think that an apparent opposition can be maintained, or is, by the sceptics of the day. [I am retired these days from controversies] but I will say what strikes me.
>
> First, we must grant—and it is difficult to determine how far we must go in granting—that both the Mosaic and Christian dispensations took the existing state of thought as it was, and only partially innovated on and corrected it. The instance of Divorce makes this plain as regards the Old Testament; as to the New, the first instance that occurs to me is St. Paul's simple recognition of married life in Bishops.
>
> On a far larger scale is the absence of meddling with the social and secular world. God speaks "for the elect's sake." He leaves the popular astronomy as it was. Heaven is still above, and the powers of evil below. The sun rises and sets, and at His word stops or goes back, and the firmament opens. And so with social and political science. Nothing is told us of economical laws. So from the first there has been a progress with laws of progress, to which theology has contributed little, and which now has a form and substance, powerful in itself, and independent of and far surpassing Christianity in its social aspect; for Christianity (socially considered) had a previous and more elementary office, being the binding principle of society.
>
> This primary and special office of religion men of the

world do not see, and they see only its poverty as a principle
of secular progress, and, as disciples and upholders and ser-
vants of that great scientific progress, they look on religion
and despise it....

**I consider then that it is not reason that is
against us, but imagination.** The mind, after having,
to the utter neglect of the Gospels, lived in science, experiences, on coming back to Scripture, an utter strangeness in
what it reads, which seems to it a better argument against
Revelation than any formal proof from definite facts or logical statements. "Christianity is behind the age."

I have been unable to bring out my meaning as I should
like, and am very dissatisfied with myself, but I feel what I
have been insisting on very strongly.[13]

Newman's meaning comes through clearly even though he is writing at
the age of eighty-one and is in somewhat bad health. By the late nineteenth
century, Christianity had been largely pushed aside from the intellectual life
of Europe, and it was no longer the cohesive glue of Europe as it had been
in the Middle Ages. Intellectuals became accustomed to seeing their endeav-
ors through secular optics only. It was not atheistic reasons against religion
that had made religion passé for people of science, it was their perception
of religion's unimportance for scholarly life. In his words, scientists perceived
religion's *poverty* in contributing to the advance of scientific knowledge; in
fact, they experienced religion's hostility to their investigations. Newman saw
his world and British culture becoming secularized long before other religious figures perceived it. Scientists took as a given intellectual life without
religion. They could not imagine their world otherwise, leading Newman to
say, "Imagination is against us."

On the other hand, imagination can work profitably on behalf of religion. Let Pope Leo the Great be its illustration. In a Lenten sermon he
once delivered to his flock, he began: "True reverence for the Lord's passion
means fixing the eyes of our heart on Jesus crucified and recognizing in him
our own humanity." Using imagery from *Mt* 27, to describe the effects of the
Crucifixion, he continued: "The rocks, the hearts of unbelievers, should burst
asunder. The dead, imprisoned in the tombs of their mortality, should come
forth....What is to happen to our bodies should take place in our hearts." In
a use of imagination that expressed far more strongly the truth that Christ
died so that others might live, Leo continued: "The sacred blood of Christ
has quenched the flaming sword that barred access to the tree of life [in the
Garden of Eden]." Notice how the church uses this suggestive imagery in
its Lenten prayer: "You, Lord, made the cross the tree of life; give its fruit to

13. *LD* 30:159-60, boldface added.

those reborn in baptism." Pope Leo's reference to *eyes of the heart* is nothing other than using one's imagination.

Another instance comes to mind. In the earlier chapter on prayer, I suggested that imagination played an important role in meditation, instancing the *Gospel of Luke*. The Gospel has a long journey-to-Jerusalem account from 9:51 to arrival at 18:15 where the evangelist rejoins Mark's narrative. Imagine yourself part of the pilgrimage. At one point Jesus' small troop met a crowd. Jesus began teaching them but one thing he said to the crowd shook you: "Unless you hate your father and mother, brothers and sisters, you cannot be my disciple" (14:26). Imagine yourself a little later, Jesus and you sitting apart at dusk, and you ask him about that *hating*. "Of course it doesn't mean despising; it has more to do with prioritizing," he says. "Does not Moses say, 'Honor your parents.' Or when Jacob was given Laban's two daughters as wives, he loved Rachel and the text says he hated [*s-n-h* in Hebrew] Leah. But he continued to be intimate with Leah and she conceived. Our father Jacob simply preferred Leah less. If you continue to follow me, you could be pressured by your family to quit. You will be brought to a point of preference. What life do you prefer? And this is why I added that my disciples might be asked to carry a cross, as I suspect will be asked of me. Sit here with me, quietly, as the sun goes down." This imagined scene is in the spirit of *Mk* 4:34: "privately he explained all things to his disciples."

Finally, I offer another positive use of imagination in relation to something shared earlier about the Sacrament of Reconciliation. It was there said that you do not have to go to Confession unless there is (are) mortal sin(s), but this is not the situation for most Catholics. There is for them what our tradition calls a devotional use of the Sacrament, at a frequency of their own choosing. Because there is no obligation to confess a laundry list of (venial) sins, I recommended selecting one transgression and confessing it. Bringing it into vivid remembrance, a function of imagination, increases one's sense of sorrow for having done it (the requirement of contrition) and a resolve to not repeat it (the requirement of amendment). That's all. Just verbalize it within sacramental confession, whether face to face or behind a screen. If you cannot remember the words of the Act of Contrition, that's not necessary. The contrition with which you verbalized the transgression suffices. Whether the confessor has something to say to you is quite secondary but his acknowledgement of you as a good person would be fitting. What then follows is wonderful food for imagination. The confessor verbalizes our Lord's words of absolution for you. Be imagining our Lord directing them to you, as *his* words.

THE COMMUNION OF SAINTS AND INTERCESSION

The Catholic doctrine about the Communion of Saints, an aspect of the teaching on the Mystical Body of Christ, is at the heart of prayerfully requesting saints to intercede on our behalf. It is one of the oldest and most important Catholic beliefs. At the same time, it is one of the most misunderstood because of the eternal quality of heaven. Our imagination gets in the way of thinking correctly about saints in heaven interceding for us.

Imagination portrays the doctrine in the traditional manner people think of it. St. Anthony of Padua is the patron saint for lost articles, as Mother Cabrini is for immigrants, as St. Thomas More is for lawyers, and as Mary is for almost all Catholics. In whatever year of whatever recent century someone misplaced a document, Anthony's intercession is sought to help its discovery. Your imagination pictures Anthony, in heaven, being called upon periodically to intercede with God on the distraught person's behalf. Anthony's availability seems to undergo duration in heaven; he awaits being sought, in tandem with distressing losses on earth continuing to happen over time. I am not making light of praying to St. Anthony when something's lost. I've done it myself. I only wish to say that this cannot be how it happens because a heavenly Anthony does not experience duration, waiting around for a request. Heaven means eternity, the absence of time, the absence of ongoing sequence, as discussed in chapter six. So, if praying for Anthony's intercession, or for Mary's intercession—think of how the *Hail Mary* prayer ends—is an important and true feature of Catholic life, what's involved in understanding his or her intercession?

Let me start with the conclusion and then make the case for it. God and God alone answers prayers, not the saint, even though Catholic piety tends to say that "St. Anthony answered my prayer." Protestant criticism is correct on this score. However, asking saints to intercede with God is rightly reminding ourselves that God's providence for us takes into account our solidarity with the saints and how the faithful lives of earlier saints serve for our benefit now as it did for themselves and others when they were living. I am trying to get at the benefits of solidarity. Expressed in terms of our relationship with Jesus, it is "we and Jesus," not "me and Jesus," to skirt a rule of grammar. Some Protestant traditions for whom praying to saints makes no sense stress the individualism of "Jesus and me."

The clearest first step to understand *intercession* is to begin with the Risen Jesus himself. The *Letter to Hebrews* describes him as the intercessor *par excellence*. *Hebrews*, an epistle of replacement theology, presents Jesus as replacing the Jewish priesthood and sacrificial rituals.

> We have a great high priest who has passed through [into] the heavens, Jesus, not someone unable to sympathize with our weaknesses but one who has been tested in every way we are, yet without sin. So let us approach the throne of grace to receive mercy...[He] was declared by God high priest according to the order of Melchizedek (4:14-16; 5:10).

In his lifetime Jesus did not have the priestly lineage restricted to the

Tribe of Levi. He was of the Tribe of Judah, making him a Jewish layman. Good Friday can be considered his ordination to the priesthood that he came to exercise in the eternity of Resurrection. He is High Priest, making intercession once for all in the manner of the ancient high priest and king of Salem, Melchizedek, who is never described as dying and ceasing to be priestly; hence, Jesus takes on an unending priesthood in being like him. Jesus has become the eternal intercessor before the throne of God the Father. In the words of an Easter Season prayer: "Heavenly Father, remember the death and resurrection of the Lamb slain on the cross, hear his voice as he lives forever making intercession for us."

What Jesus' intercession does not mean should be clear. He does not, again and again, bring before the "throne of grace" [bring before God the Father] our need for mercy or anything else. Even thinking that the Risen Jesus is somehow asking God the Father, time and again, something on our behalf, makes no sense, as if Christ talks to the Father repeatedly. Jesus' earthly life of "obedience unto death," as described in chapter five, is brought into the very nature of God by Jesus' Resurrection "to the right hand of the Father." It is as if Jesus the High Priest is "always" interceding for us because he is our intercession once for all and all at once. This is the only way to understand how Jesus' intercession happens in duration-less eternity.[14]

How the saints intercede for us has to be understood in similar fashion of being an all-at-once event based on what their earthly lives achieved. Jesus' role as eternal High Priest is easier to accept, it seems to me, than what I am proposing for the roles of saints, based on Newman's insight above that imagination can accustom people to envision something as true (St. Anthony waits around for requests) that, in fact, is not true.

To attempt an explanation, I wish to propose two imagined scenes, one that actually happened and one fully fictitious, both of them at the service of avoiding the imagined scene described above about asking St. Anthony of Padua to help find something. The doctrine of the Mystical Body of Christ, what St. Paul calls the head (Christ) in solidarity with bodily members (ourselves), is at the basis of two images I wish to use to explain intercession.

St. Augustine was quoted in chapter seven to show that Jesus' Ascension did not remove his ongoing presence in the church: "He did not leave heaven when he was born among us nor did he withdraw from us when he ascended into heaven." The Mystical Body of Christ is thus the church's reality in history. The doctrine of the Mystical Body describes also our solidarity with Christ in the world to come when everyone is of one body with his Headship.[15]

14. An older theology said the same thing when it spoke of Jesus, during his lifetime, winning merits for us.

15. *Proleptic* is a technical word used by biblical scholars, with rare use otherwise, to describe the anticipation of a future development as if presently accomplished. Jesus' Ascension

I return now to the two images. One of them is quite real, painfully so, and it expresses human solidarity as strongly as I can muster. On 9 April 1942, the American soldiers on Bataan Peninsula, the Philippines, surrendered to Japanese forces and were forced to walk 65 miles to prison camps. Emaciated and wounded, many soldiers could hardly walk at all. But if they fell or lagged, they were shot. Their fellow soldiers, those stronger and unwounded, propped them up. The Bataan March is an image of connectedness, of solidarity, that helped fellow soldiers to get to the end.

The second image pictures the entire earthly Mystical Body of Christ, sinners and saints of all stripes, as if everyone existed at the same moment in history—that's the unreal part—and all are marching with their Lord and Head to "Bethany" (Lk 24:50) where the Lord ascends. On this march the stronger prop up the weaker, not by means of muscles as on Bataan but by means of their virtuous lives: the sufferings of the martyrs, the steadfastness of confessors, and by whatever else saints appear to "merit" help for others. As Augustine also wrote: "And so all her members make each other's welfare their common care." *Look not on my sins but on the faith of your church* is prayed at every Mass as an expression of the connectedness of ourselves with the saints and of "help to get to the end."

What intercession of the saints does not mean was indicated in the St. Anthony of Padua story, as if Anthony awaited periodic requests. How then explain what it does mean to pray to St. Anthony, or to Mary, to intercede with God on our behalf? It is asking God, in recalling the Mass prayer, to "look on the faithful (earthly) life" of Anthony, or of Mary, with whom we exist in solidarity, when we seek their intercession. God grants what is prayed for, not the saint or even Mary. But the earthly life of saints, and especially Mary's, play a role in God's plan of Providence (the second image). I refer to their lives of faith lived out on earth (the first image), not to their influence in heaven, where living by faith has ceased.

The beauty, indeed the power, of the doctrine of intercession is our connectedness with everyone in the Mystical Body. More than matter-of-fact solidarity, it is Augustine's "all her members make each other's welfare their common care." Although all Christians benefit from solidarity with the faithful lives of saints, it is unfortunate Protestantism does not teach the doctrine of intercession. The Mystical Body doctrine is mentioned throughout St. Paul's writings; its corollary of praying to saints is not, which I think explains Protestant misgivings.

I conclude by using the example of Mary's faith and suffering, for whose help people have prayed over the centuries that she "intercede for us sinners, now and at the hour of our death." The value of her intercession comes from

---

is proleptic, that is, Jesus ascended and the church continues in history as his body, and Jesus ascended, bringing all the saved into glory with him as his body.

what she merited for all of us while she lived on earth. The most poignant expression of it, for me at least, was watching her son die and then holding the corpse in her lap. Madrid's Prado Museum is famous for its paintings by El Greco, Goya, and Velázquez but it was Rogier van der Weyden's *Descent from the Cross* that left me mesmerized after I left Spain. The fifteenth century Flemish artist gave Jesus' skin the pallor of death, and Mary's skin was the same. She was as if dead herself, slain by grief. The others at the foot of the Cross had normal looking skin. That picture convinced me that Mary is our most fitting intercessor when we approach death. She's been there! She experienced the brink.

ADDRESSING SOME EARLIER PROMISES

I begin with the Blessed Mother. I refer to her by this name because it has been a Roman Catholic way of talking about Jesus' mother for a long time.[16] My parents—this book is dedicated to them—and my maternal grandmother taught me the faith in the beginning. This was their way of talking. Praying the rosary was their way of praying. I wish to share some features of my own faith about Mary.

Ever since I began studying scripture seriously under the influence of Raymond E. Brown and some professors I had in Louvain, Mary has been the symbol of the perfect disciple. Descriptions of disciples are met throughout the gospels, and Mary is hardly mentioned. But one event is paramount. It is revealed to her that she is to mother Jesus. Set in the context of "How can this be?" and "What does this mean?" she responds with "I am God's servant. Be it done unto me according to your word" (*Lk* 1:38). At a very early age, I thought the angel Gabriel took visible shape and spoke audible words to Mary's eardrums.[17] I don't any longer but many adult Catholics do. There has been only one incarnation in history, that of Jesus. Angels don't incarnate. God's messages to us, symbolically carried in the mouths of *messengers* (aka angels), aren't physical sounds in this or that language. They are truly messages, revelations, and the recipient, the listener, must be led in faith by God to discern God's communication. I cannot describe how Mary discerned that God was communicating to her, actually inviting her, to accept a pregnancy. What I can share are St. Bernard's words describing how the plan of salvation hangs on her *fiat*, her "Be it done unto me" act of faith. (See Appendix E.) What I can further share are the words of Jesus describing true discipleship. "Blessed are those who hear the word of God and keep [accept]

16. Anglicans tend to use the phrase St. Mary the Virgin, e.g., the name of the Oxford church where Newman preached. The Orthodox in their Greek language call her the *theotokos*, the "god bearer," the Mother of God.

17. Muslims believe that the angel Jibril (Gabriel) spoke words in Arabic to Muhammad's ear, and Muhammad's subsequent recitation of them to his followers became the text of the Qur'an, an Arabic word itself meaning *recited*.

it" (Lk 11:28), which is more exalted than simply nursing Jesus at the breast.

Because Jesus' incarnation is not simply the assumption of generalized human flesh but the assumption of her flesh, there has been a tendency to preclude Mary from ever having been sullied by Original Sin. This idea precisely as such is nowhere in Scripture. Because of its scriptural absence, Mary's freedom from Original Sin is not discussed by the Fathers of the Church. The major medieval theologians, Bernard of Clairvaux and a century later St. Bonaventure and St. Thomas Aquinas, denied that Mary was conceived without Original Sin because it seemed to undermine Christ as universal Savior of every human without exception. Nevertheless the sentiment for this belief grew and spread into Catholic devotional piety. On 8 December 1854, Pope Pius IX defined the dogma of the Immaculate Conception in an infallible manner: "We declare, pronounce, and define that Mary was kept free from "all stain of Original Sin...in view of the merits of Christ" acting retroactively. The second and only other instance of papal infallible teaching was on 1 November 1950. Pius XII proclaimed the dogma of Mary's Assumption that upon death she entered heaven body and soul. (See Appendix D on levels of magisterium.)

Some comments on the dogma of the Assumption: It does not mean that she did not die. Every human being dies, even Jesus. That she entered heaven body and soul supports my belief, expressed in chapter five, that on death Jesus and we ourselves entered into glory with resurrected bodies. The dogma states that Mary's corpse did not undergo corruption, quoting meager testimony from the early church. I believe she died and resurrected without delay, just as we do. Our corpses undergo decay just as hers did.[18] Decay of a corpse does not undermine the dignity of being resurrected. On the principle that doctrines about Mary are a harbinger of understanding our destinies, I find the dogma of Mary's Assumption to be a wonderful part of Catholic faith and worthy of yearly celebration. It's what happens to us when we die.

Some comments on the Immaculate Conception: Scriptural passages on it are lacking as well as teachings of the Church Fathers. There is, however, another manner to draw inferences that are binding because scripturally *suggested*. Baptizing infants is justified by inference in this manner. Mary has been likened to being a "Second Eve" by many early Church Fathers from their meditations on the scriptures. Mary's faith and lack of sin is the counterpart to Eve's sin in the Garden. As punishments came through Eve (and Adam, of course), blessings come with Mary, the Second Eve. I believe that the retroac-

---

18. I promised I would indicate where I diverge from official Catholic teaching, and this is the riskiest. I believe the infallible dogma that Mary is "assumed into glory body and soul," as are all persons meant for resurrected bodies upon death. Pius XII adds that Mary's corpse did not experience corruption before it departed the earth, in support of which he only quotes two late seventh-century Greek writers. The Greek Orthodox Church accepts Mary's Assumption but has never insisted on an incorruptible corpse as part of its belief.

tive effects of Jesus' work of redemption can rightly apply to Mary, hence to her Immaculate Conception, drawn from the inference of being the Second Eve. This is how Cardinal Newman made the case for Mary's Immaculate Conception in the absence of clear scripture.

When I shared my faith on Original Sin and on Jesus' redemptive life, I said that redemptive healing, which I imaged as a canopy of grace, extended retroactively over every human life in the past. Without its healing effects, the "flawed" human nature everyone has, understood as the *tilt* of human freedom to selfish self-determination, would progress to ever more selfish degrees. Sinfulness would reign. Call this the "contagion of Original Sin," as church documents do, the "stain" as Pius IX did in the 1854 dogma.

The 1854 dogma described Mary's preservation from Original Sin as a unique and singular retroactive privilege. It is truly singular in its excellence but I do not believe it is unique. (I here deviate from official teaching I perceive as non-binding.) Let me run my reason *via* a clear example. The Patriarch Abraham is a saint in the Catholic Church. If this sounds novel, just read the *Letter to the Hebrews*. He's pictured a saint beyond doubt. If he was born with Original Sin in full force, it would mean he's an inveterate sinner. So, at what age in his life did Abraham cease being so evil and become the noble patriarchal figure we all acknowledge? Did he get retroactively redeemed from Original Sin when he was eight, or twelve, or twenty-one? When? My answer is that he never had to pass from being unredeemed until getting redeemed at a certain age. The answer is that he is like Mary. He was born redeemed (conceived if you will) that way. And why would others of old be unlike Abraham? What about Isaiah, "called from the womb" to be a prophet (*Is* 49:1)? Once again, a dogma about Mary is a harbinger of blessings to others. My contentions do not diminish Mary by removing unique honors. If Mary is the model of true discipleship and meant for us to replicate, why cannot her Immaculate Conception and her Assumption model the blessings God intends for us? Being the recipient of and becoming the prototype for the blessings described in the two papal dogmas carry a certain priority of excellence in her. Mary remains unsurpassed in personal dignity among the redeemed. Her role in Catholic devotions, e.g., the rosary prayer, remains fully justified.

HUMAN NATURE: HOW DOES IT STAND?

In chapter six I promised to return to the topic of human nature? Did sinfulness make it totally depraved and vitiated? On this question Catholicism and Reformation Protestantism differed. The topic is not unconnected with the above reflection on Mary's Immaculate Conception and from what condition was her human nature being preserved?

Three matters need to be kept distinct: (1) Not being stained by Original Sin, either by way of redemption-through-preservation (Immaculate

Conception) or by way of baptismal rebirth; (2) The situation of unbaptized adults and whether their human natures are totally depraved; (3) The difference between being redeemed and remaining sinless.

The first matter invites some confusion because it relies on the retroactive effects of Christ's redemptive act, an elusive concept. St. Thomas Aquinas and St. Bonaventure did not allow for it. The dogma from Pius IX applied it to Mary in a singular fashion. I saw no reason why it could not extend to everyone living earlier, using Abraham as a test case. Baptism accomplishes in the baptized the same gift of a canopy of grace to heal the "stain of Original Sin" as retroactive redemption did, the difference being that the ritual washing (or immersion) accomplishes what it symbolizes. (Recall chapter seven.)

The third matter is a distinction easy to explain. Redemption has come to me through Baptism. Essentially I am no different from anyone living before Jesus who was preserved from Original Sin. We're both redeemed. But I and others committed sins as an adult and had complete freedom to have chosen to sin or not. Although the topic is not covered by scripture, there is a tradition about Mary's perpetual sinlessness, a tradition beginning among the earliest Greek-speaking Fathers and spreading throughout the western church not long after. One could also believe that John the Baptist—his being redeemed retroactively is clearly similar to Abraham's case—remained sinless his entire life, based on *Mt* 11:11. But other great figures from the past surely sinned, such as Moses. As punishment for his sin at the waters of Meribah, he was only allowed to see the Promised Land from Mount Nebo. Being redeemed and remaining sinless are distinct issues.

The second matter is the most complicated because it assumes that Original Sin reigns among the unredeemed, both before and after Jesus's life, as unchecked misused human freedom. Adding to the complication was the difference between Catholics and Protestants at the time of the Reformation in assessing the resultant damage to human nature. Five centuries ago, neither side thought in the category of a "what if" situation, such as I proposed in chapter two.

At the Reformation, the Catholic assessment was that Original Sin *wounded* human nature but left it intact. Unbaptized persons, accordingly, retained the ability to use their minds or consciences to discern God's reality, or at least God's lure, and their wills retained the ability to choose rightly, under the assistance of grace, to repent. But intellect and will were wounded, as if beset with obstacles to their proper functioning. Consciences would be clouded but not inoperative. The Catholic tradition adopted a principle that originated earlier with Thomas Aquinas: *grace perfects nature*. He recognized that human nature was not fully corrupted and was able to perform some good actions even in its wounded condition. God's grace would perfect what the wound in nature hindered from happening readily or consistently.

The Protestant assessment, in the writings of Luther and Calvin at least, was that human nature was fully depraved under the sway of Original Sin. Original Sin rendered human nature inoperative to conceive the true and do the good. If nothing were to change, human beings with depraved natures were predestined to damnation. The only way out of this predicament was sheer divine election, bestowed on this or that person, to be counted among the saved, just has God elected Jacob over Isaac's first born son, Esau, to continue the line of inheritance. God chose Jacob to fulfill the promises to Abraham whereas Esau should have rights of the first born. Jacob was simply God's choice, and so are the persons who are predestined for salvation. They are simply God's choice. This divine arrangement better redounds to God's glory, says Calvin, than coming to salvation by the use of your human powers, even if they are perfected by grace in the opinion of Catholics.

This is not the place to delve into deeper religious controversy behind these matters.[19] It is only important to share the Catholic sense how human nature stands. It is not and never was depraved.[20] (See Appendix B on predestination that contrasts wounded nature and depraved nature, a handout I've used with Gwynedd Mercy University students to clarify the topic.)

CONCLUDING THOUGHT: ON POPES AND ON DYING

I have clear memories of every pope since Pius XII (1939–1958). The current Francis is the sixth pope to follow him, and for all of them I have had proper respect. But I have felt affection only toward Francis. Were I older then, I probably would have felt the same toward John XXIII, knowing how others did. I was entering my twenties in those days, and my affections were directed by infatuations. Francis was a different kind of pope for me from the start. His sincerity and authenticity captured my heart. Ready to speak with a prepared text before thousands of young people at the University of Santo Tomas, Manila, in 2015, he tossed aside his text and spoke from his heart, in his native Spanish, having met beforehand some of the abandoned "street children." One of them, Jun, in her tears asked, "Why is my life like this?" He spoke to the vast crowd about her question, about the role of tears, about our required solidarity with the outcasts. He replaced a prepared text about church teachings with a spontaneous reflection on compassion. I hope for our church and its needed priorities that he outlives me, although he is older, walks with a limp, and is missing a lung.

His influence on me concerns the people on the margins, the poor espe-

19. Much mutual understanding between Catholics and Lutherans has come about since the heated polemics of yesteryear. A "Joint Declaration on the Doctrine of Justification" was approved on 31 October 1999 by the Vatican's Council for Promoting Christian Unity and the Lutheran World Federation. The World Methodist Council accepted it in 2006 as did the Communion of Reformed Churches (e.g., Presbyterians) in 2017.

20. When in church I sing Amazing Grace, I recoil from the word *wretch*. "That saved a wretch like me" should in a Catholic manner run "That saved and set me free."

cially and those discriminated against. He reminds me of my sins of omission, the latter part of "what I have done and what I have failed to do" in the act of contrition. But his style of reminding me of the needs of the poor and the marginalized is not a rebuke but an invitation. He is disarming for me in the same manner I would guess Jesus was.

Francis is the first pope of that name. Almost sixteen hundred years earlier Leo was another first-of-that-name pope and preached the same message as Francis does now. "If God is love, our generosity should know no limit because God is love….No act of devotion on the part of the faithful gives God more pleasure than that which is lavished on his poor….In these acts of giving, do not fear a lack of ample means. A generous spirit is itself great wealth." We possess about 150 letters and almost 100 sermons from Leo, all of them brimming with insight and compassion. Earlier in chapter five we met Leo's decisive letter to the bishops at the Council of Chalcedon on Christ's human and divine natures existing as one divine person, God's son. I remain baffled where and how Leo learned his profound theology. There were no seminaries in those days. His letter to Chalcedon came only a decade after he was elected pope, and this was when he was about forty years old. I have an affection for Leo, too.

To these appeals from Francis and Leo for generosity toward the poor, I want to add another voice from St. Gregory Nazianzen, not a pope of course but a fourth-century Greek-speaking theologian and bishop from Cappadocia (modern Turkey). "*Blessed is he who is considerate to the needy and the poor. Let us lay hold of this blessing. Let us earn the name of being considerate. There should be no delay between your intention and your good deed. Generosity is the one thing that cannot admit of delay….Let us show mercy to those who today are lying on the ground, so that when we come to leave this world, they may receive us into eternal dwelling places.*" This is from Gregory's sermon on "Love of the Poor." Like Jesus' story about poor Lazarus and the rich man (*Lk* 16:19-31), Gregory's poor man gets to heaven first in order to welcome into heaven "those considerate to the needy."

As I near this book's conclusion, I focus on the message of Frances about the poor all around us. The notions of eternity and God's indwelling in us now have been at the heart of what I've shared about my faith in so many of Catholicism's doctrines. Eternity as the absence of the passage of time, and divine indwelling as approaching but not reaching pantheism, were meant to express a simplified faith to which I've come. Eternity and indwelling are knotty topics, to be sure. I hope I did not become too conceptual, too notional in Newman's sense, in sharing them. I've tried, but I cannot easily undo how I've been trained.

All my attempts at faith sharing would be missing the mark if we, you the reader and I, were oblivious of the poor and outcasts all around us in thinking what eternity and indwelling and anything else means. I live in a world in which Eternal Life is in me as divine indwelling. And I live in a world in which the poor and outcasts are all around me. The words of the familiar act of contrition—in what I have done and in what I have failed to do—are the test of reaching what I've called a real apprehension of these doctrines. Francis, Leo, and Gregory, the poor and the outcasts, invite examination of conscience on *what I have failed to do.*

The prospect of approaching one's death, eighteenth-century lexicographer Samuel Johnson is reputed to have said, "wonderfully concentrates the mind." Devout Anglican that he was, he might have been inspired by *Ps* 90: "Make us know the shortness of our life, so that we may gain wisdom of heart." One of the reasons I wanted to share with readers what my faith has come to mean to me is to preserve anyone from the fear of dying who might be carrying that fear.

Entering death is not without nervousness as befits anything never before experienced. But this is not the same as fright or dread. I described Purgatory as a beneficial doctrine; it was not a period of suffering of however long. God's creative action of clothing us with immortality, upon death and without delay, refashioned at the same moment whatever imperfections we carried into death. Further, I suggested that mortal sins, if one really understands what's involved in committing them, are rare and perhaps for many Catholics absent. How many, in bygone years, worried that they approached dying with still unforgiven mortal sins "on their souls" because they forgot to confess them or that their sorrow for them was not full enough?

The biggest apprehension in approaching death, I think, is that I am all alone at its doorway. Family and friends, even the priest at the bedside, are being left behind. I am told that Jesus and the saints are yonder, awaiting me. None of this relieves me of the feeling of being all alone. But what I have shared about God's indwelling, about Eternal Life being part of my identity on this side of death, gives the lie to being all alone in dying. I carry the presence of the Risen Jesus that began in Baptism, that was pledged in each Eucharist recalling the prayer of Thomas Aquinas, and that was enhanced in the faces of the poor and outcasts. "When you have helped the least of these, you were helping me." I have never really been alone in the deepest marrow of my being. This is who I am when I am dying and possessing Eternal Life already.

The end of my life, on whatever day and hour it happens, is the end of the world, too. I do not mean that world history ends when I die. My children, my grandchildren and however long the bloodline extends, have yet to live out their lives. It could be that all human life, hence history, ends with a worldwide untreatable virus, an apocalyptic pandemic. Or it could be that our planet will last five billion years more, until our sun expends its hydrogen-fusion cycle and expands into a red giant star, incinerating the inner planets. (Humans either got away, which is unlikely, or human history ended earlier when temperatures became too hot.)

From the perspective of time, such events seem in store as much as anything else. But from the perspective of eternity, into which I enter on dying, and into which the last meant-for-salvation humans enter, too, we arrive together. By definition, the world is no more. Each one of us dies into the biblical end-time, as it is called.

See you on the other side.

APPENDIX A

Louvain as Alma Mater

Louvain is my *alma mater*. Because my undergraduate years were split between LaSalle University (Pennsylvania) and Providence College (Rhode Island), I never came to see either one as fully a *nurturing mother*, to translate the Latin.[1] LaSalle's Bro. Damian Connelly and Bro. Alban Albright cultivated me into thinking like a mathematician, and Providence's Dr. Paul Van K. Thompson was the first to nurture in me, a physics major, the notion that I might have a gift for English composition. Yet it remained for Belgium's University of Louvain (*Katholieke Universiteit te Leuven* for I pursued doctoral studies in its Dutch-speaking sector) to become, as an institution, my *alma mater* in the full sense. It is to Louvain that my heart, my imagination, and my memories immediately go back when I muse about how education nurtured and fundamentally shaped me. My fellow doctoral students felt the same about the place. With immense pride and with nothing of puffery or boast, we said then and years later to ourselves, "I am a Lovaniensis." The pride had something to do with the university's being almost 600 years old and our feelings of connectedness with an illustrious past. It had something to do with Louvain's professors, each of whom was an internationally recognized scholar and was as humble as he was erudite. It had something to do with the international flair of the medieval town. Doctoral students came from all over the world. I learned more about Africa drinking a Stella Artois with friends from every side of that continent than any book ever taught me. Mostly, though, it was Jan Hendrik Walgrave, my doctoral promoter, of whom, second only to my own father, I can say: "This man shaped me more than any other man." When word of his death on 17 October 1986 arrived, it was as if a family member died. Louvain is my *alma mater*. Its sights, its sounds, its smells remain with me indelibly after almost forty years.

1. Long before the term *alma mater* was applied to colleges and universities, it described the Blessed Virgin Mary. The canticle "Alma Redemptoris Mater" originated in the eleventh century and is sung in monasteries during Advent at night prayer (Compline). The opening line, which is translated variously, was translated by Newman as "Kindly Mother of the Redeemer" in *Tracts for the Times, Tract 75*, § 1, 23. http://www.newmanreader.org/works/times/tract75/index.html.

APPENDIX B

Calvin's Doctrine of Predestination

John Calvin's predestination doctrine can be approached in one of two ways. The first is a kind of play-acting that will serve as an analogy to Calvin's teaching on "double predestination," that is to say, God decrees some for salvation and others for damnation. The second approach involves why Calvin's position is logical *if you accept his starting point*, and consequently how he differs from Catholicism.

(1) Imagine me beginning a course with you, entering the room on the first day, and saying to you, "Each one of you is so totally ignorant and irremediably dull that you will fail this course no matter how hard you try." For the analogy to work, you have to assume that my startling statement is true. Next, I say to you, "We are going to proceed with the course, but I have decided to pass you and you and you." I was pointing to three people in our class. "The rest of you will fail, as you ought, because you are going to remain too ignorant."

As I look at the three students, I ask, "Aren't I being supremely generous with a pass grade? For the rest of you, aren't I being simply just in submitting a failing grade?" A student asks me, "How did you determine who passes?" "I just decided, before I ever entered the class."

Here's the analogy. The "total depravity of human nature" corresponds to "ignorance" in my fabricated story. The class is the human race under Original Sin. God is the professor. No one can merit passing (attaining salvation). The pass grade (salvation) is purely from the prof's choice (grace, divine election, divine predetermination). Because some get passed (get saved), the prof's benevolence (God's sheer grace) is paramount. To carp or cavil against this situation is to rob the professor of his good will (rob God of His glory). Most people ought to fail the course (most people get damned); otherwise, justice is violated.

(2) If you begin with "original sin = total 100% depravity," as Calvin does, then human freedom is totally vitiated, totally *disfunctionalized*, to coin a word. You have no involvement in your salvation because you have nothing within you, in intellect or will power, that would work. The only way you are going to avoid eternal damnation is if God, from all eternity, simply picked you out and decided in His graciousness to save you. It follows logically!

The older tradition, the Catholic and Greek Orthodox tradition, also teaches that salvation is entirely from God's grace and that, on your own efforts, you cannot merit (win) it. But it also teaches that human nature has been wounded, not totally killed off, by Original Sin. It is a wounded human freedom. Without God's grace, human freedom could not, on its own, do salvation-meriting works. But if God's grace were to work within a wounded human freedom to heal it, then a redeemed sinner could say, "**I** chose to turn my life around," and also say, "Without God's **grace**, I was impotent to turn things around. It was my experience that **I** made a choice to turn things around, and **my** human freedom counted for something in being saved by **God**." If it is all by grace, but human freedom still counts nonetheless, then the other teaching of Catholics and Greek Orthodox makes logical sense. "You cannot be damned except by your own damn fault" (= freely rejecting God's gift). Calvin could never say this because he thinks my use of "I" above robs God of glory, whereas older Christianity thinks the "I" precisely gives glory to God Creator who created human freedom (the will) as a feature of being human. It's wounded freedom, but still workable freedom, that from all eternity was offered the possibility of being healed in the moment of being saved and in the redeemed life that follows.

APPENDIX C

Rome Reviews Remarriage

An assembly of 270 bishops from around the world has been meeting in Rome since Oct. 4 to discuss "The Vocation and Mission of the Family in the Church and Contemporary World." Its task is a global examination of Catholic family life, but, fair or not, many Americans and Western Europeans will measure success by whether there is some adaptation of the refusal of Holy Communion to Catholics who are divorced and civilly remarried. This prohibition is but one topic among many on the synod's table through Sunday, but in our culture, it ranks high enough to expect something other than reaffirming the status quo.

First, let's review the status quo. When two baptized persons marry and were "free" to marry (for example, not bound by a previous marriage to a still living "ex"), the man and woman enter into a sacramental marriage that is a lifelong bond and unbreakable even by the pope. It is also a civil marriage bond recognized by the state.

Let's say Alex and Beth, Catholics married for 12 years, had three children before they divorced in a civil process. The divorce does not excommunicate them from the Catholic Church, nor does it prohibit them from receiving Communion, provided a subsequent civil marriage hasn't happened. They remain as fully Catholic as anyone else.

Suppose Alex meets never-married Clare, whom he wishes to marry. Two avenues lie open to him. If he wishes his Catholic Church to perform the marriage, Alex needs to obtain an annulment, a church judicial process that, if successful, decides that his marriage to Beth lacked, from the very start of it, certain features necessary for the sacrament of marriage to have happened—though it was always a civil marriage. If Alex applies for the marriage to be examined, the investigation must contact Beth and invite her input.

Let's suppose that the process, however long, leads to a declaration of nullity of their marriage. What about the children? Are they now illegitimate? No. *Legitimate* means lawful. It is a civil term. Alex and Beth were civilly married for 12 years, and thus their children were born of "lawful wedlock." An annulment does not undo legitimacy for the children.

But what if Alex takes the second avenue open to him? He and Clare get married. (The Catholic Church considers it a civil ceremony whether performed by Clare's Protestant pastor or by a justice of the peace.) Alex attends Mass from time to time, maybe weekly. But he is not allowed to receive Communion, a most precious privilege for Catholics, because he has remarried without an annulment.

It's possible for this standoff to continue for many years because Alex values his Catholicism. But most divorcés cannot take the disconnect. They quit. It's too hard every Sunday for the divorced and remarried to observe that they are not fully part of the family.

Here is the block that the synod in Rome faces with the "Alex situation." Two reasons an accommodation cannot be made, except for advising Alex to try for an annulment, are offered.

Reason One: "You are still married to Beth in the eyes of the church; therefore, your intercourse with second wife Clare is adultery. Continuing adultery prohibits you from receiving Communion."

Stretched as it sounds, it is a reason that requires a response to get beyond the status quo. I'll make a case: *Adultery* in most cultures is a civil term, as *illegitimacy* is. Adultery involves a married person having sexual relations with someone not one's spouse. That's what it seems to mean around the world. It does not mean having sexual relations with your spouse of a second marriage. This interpretation includes Mosaic Law, where the commandment almost thunders, "Thou shalt not commit adultery." But the Mosaic Law allowed divorce, and the Israelite in a second marriage was not committing adultery.

But Jesus, one will say, overturned all that by refocusing on the primordial commandment of Genesis 2:24 concerning marriage: "That is why a man leaves his father and mother and is united to his wife, and they become one flesh." True, and it needed doing because some justifications for divorce in Jesus' day were quite lenient, such as not cooking well. Cast-off women were victimized, and Jesus demanded that this stop. Jesus wanted marriages to last. Still, he used the word *adultery* in the manner we do for dalliances outside an existing marriage. I am unaware that he or the early church called people in second marriages adulterers.

Reason Two is: "A marriage is lifelong, and you promised to keep to it. You divorced and remarried. Because you are no longer in a lifelong marriage, you cannot receive Communion." This is not so readily answered.

It's a fact that Alex and Beth broke up, and he would say, "I'm as much at fault as anyone that Beth and I didn't work out, and there's much I'm sorry for." By whom is it said, and for what reason is it said, that ruptured foreverness in and of itself precludes forever receiving Communion?

There's no doubt that the prohibiting reason has oft been repeated, but what is the precise justification making it cogent and understandable? Why can it not be overturned for pastoral reasons?

Many hope the synod can find some pastoral pathway for divorced Catholics who have remarried. People quit the Catholic Church for many reasons. But has anyone left because the church is too forgiving?

APPENDIX D

Levels of Church Pronouncements

Following is a schema that depicts the various levels of church pronouncements. Many of these pronouncements are legislated actions, called disciplinary laws. The various liturgical laws are examples: how to respond at Mass, how to receive Communion, who can serve at the altar, and so forth. Often these laws have been confused with teaching about doctrines. Priestly celibacy is not a doctrine and therefore can be changed by church decree. It is a church law that was imposed as a requirement for ordination by the Second Lateran Council of 1139 (canon 7). Disciplinary laws come readily into existence; some remain in force for a long time (e.g., Sunday Mass obligation), some get revoked (e.g., young girls can now serve on the altar), and some just fade away (e.g., head coverings in church).

Distinct from disciplinary laws are doctrines, the teachings of the church. The church's teaching role is called its *magisterium*. The biggest difference among doctrines are those that are taught in an infallible manner, called dogmas, and those doctrines that are proposed in an authoritative manner but not infallibly so. Infallibility is a Spirit-given protection from erroneous teaching when the church teaches about what God has revealed. The dogma invites the response of faith in it, on a par with "I believe in God" because the dogma represents what God has revealed, "who can neither deceive nor be deceived," in the words of an ancient formula.

There are two aspects with dogmas that are often confused and are most important. The gift of infallibility resides in the church, in the people of God, not in a personal property of the teacher(s). The infallible teachings of an Ecumenical Council show it more clearly. The bishops bring the faith of their region to the council. It is as if the faith of the universal church comes together in prayer and debate and in discernment of God's revelation, ultimately. Then the council has to teach in a *definitive* manner. Vatican II did not do this. Even when the pope is seemingly acting alone when he articulates the solemn teaching dogma, he has beforehand solicited the views of the worldwide episcopate on the doctrine being considered. There have been only two papal solemn infallible teachings, called *ex cathedra* teachings. When the First Vatican Council taught the nature of papal infallibility, it carefully said that the pope enjoys the protection of infallibility that the entire church enjoys. The pope discerns the church's mind.

The second aspect involves the difference between the "ordinary infallible magisterium" and those teachings of the magisterium that are authoritative and invite docile and respectful acceptance but are not infallible and do not demand an individual's response of faith. Both cases seem to involve the teaching of the pope and the worldwide episcopate, and there lies the confusion. If it is infallible magisterium, the teaching of pope and bishops has to clearly indicate that this teaching is to be believed with an assent of faith. Most of these teachings never had to be taught in an extraordinary manner because they were not widely denied. That's why I gave the example that Jesus resurrected. This has ever been preached and taught as a matter of faith.

Some members of the hierarchy position topics under ordinary infallible magisterium that others see as falling under non-infallible magisterium. The birth control teaching of *Humanae Vitae* is a good example, and I believe the evidence points to its non-infallible status. The teaching that women cannot be ordained priests is harder to judge. Pope John Paul II implied it fell under infallible teaching, and this was supported by Pope Benedict XVI. Whether the restriction does not change in the near term, or never, is one matter. That the exclusion is part of God's revelation is another matter, and I don't see it being so. Recall, if infallibly taught, then God must have revealed it.

Magisterium
[the teaching office of the Church]

Infallible teaching
[When God's revelation is being taught, God protects its teaching from error. Catholics give *assent of faith* to what is being taught.]

Extraordinary
aka "solemn"

[A single act of teaching of bishops, calling on God to insure the protection from error in the teaching.
The teaching is called a *dogma*.]

Ecumenical Councils
e.g., Jesus is divine, AD 325
e.g., There are 7 sacraments, AD 1547

Papal "ex-cathedra" = pope in their name
[There have only been 2 instances:
- Immaculate Conception, AD 1854
- Assumption of Mary, AD 1950]

Ordinary
[Consistent unanimous teaching of worldwide episcopate that a teaching is to be believed with the assent of faith;
  e.g., Jesus rose from the dead
  e.g., Infant Baptisms are valid
  e.g., Mary remained sinless.]

Non-infallible teaching
aka "authoritative"
aka "authentic"
[Catholics expected to give a religiously motivated submission of mind and heart, but their assent of faith to the teaching is not demanded.]
There are many different levels of non-infallible:
  e.g., artificial contraception disallowed in *Humanae Vitae*;
  e.g., only men can be ordained priests;
  e.g., the bread and wine is changed into Christ's body and blood at repeating words of Jesus at Last Supper.
  [The Orthodox Churches locate the change when the Holy Spirit is invoked.]

Disciplinary laws of church: priestly celibacy, Sunday Mass obligation, fasting laws.

Sermon of St. Bernard of Clairvaux on Mary's Annunciation*

You have heard, O Virgin, that you will conceive and bear a son. You have heard that it will not be by man but by the Holy Spirit. The angel awaits an answer; it is time for him to return to God who sent him. We, too, are waiting, O Lady, for your word of compassion. The sentence of condemnation weighs heavily upon us.

The price of our salvation is given you. We shall be set free at once if you consent. In the eternal Word of God we all came into existence, and behold, we are dying. In your brief response we are to be recreated in order to be recalled to life.

Tearful Adam with his sorrowing family begs this of you. O loving Virgin, in their exile from Paradise Abraham and David beg it. All other holy patriarchs, your own ancestors, ask it of you as they dwell in the land of death's shadows. This is what the whole earth awaits, prostrate at your feet. And this is right because on your word depends comfort for the afflicted, ransom for captives, freedom for the condemned, indeed, salvation for all Adam's offspring, the whole of your own race. Answer quickly, O Virgin....

Reply in haste to the angel, or rather, through the angel to the Lord. Answer with a word and receive the Word of God. Speak your own word, conceive the divine Word. Breathe a passing word, embrace the eternal Word.

Why do you delay? Why are you afraid? Believe, offer praise, and receive. Let humility be bold. Let modesty be confident. This is no time for virginal simplicity to forget prudence. In this matter alone, O prudent Virgin, do not fear being presumptuous. Although modest silence is pleasing, the duty to speak out is more necessary. O blessed Virgin, open your heart to faith, your lips to praise, your womb to the Creator. Behold, the desired of all nations is at your door, knocking to enter. If he passes by because of your delay, you would begin to seek him again but in sorrow, for He is the one whom your soul loves. Arise. Hasten. Open. Arise in faith, hasten in devotion, open in praise and thanksgiving.

"Behold the handmaid of the Lord; be it done unto me according to Your word!"

---

* Omnia Opera B.Bernardis, Cistercian Ed. 4:53-54

The Canonical Books of the Bible

CANON OF THE OLD TESTAMENT

1. **Torah** (aka "The Law", aka "The Five Books of Moses," aka The Pentateuch)
     Genesis ("Bereshith" = "In the Beginning")
     Exodus ("Shemoth" = "Names")
     Leviticus ("Wayiqra" = "And he called")
     Numbers ("Bemidbar" = In the wilderness")
     Deuteronomy ("Debarim" = "Words")

2. Prophets aka **Neviim**

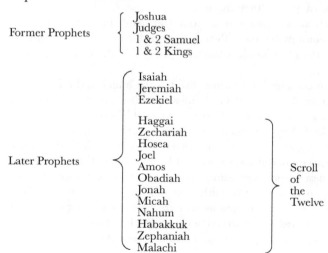

Former Prophets
$\left\{\begin{array}{l}\text{Joshua}\\\text{Judges}\\\text{1 \& 2 Samuel}\\\text{1 \& 2 Kings}\end{array}\right.$

Later Prophets
$\left\{\begin{array}{l}\text{Isaiah}\\\text{Jeremiah}\\\text{Ezekiel}\\ \\\text{Haggai}\\\text{Zechariah}\\\text{Hosea}\\\text{Joel}\\\text{Amos}\\\text{Obadiah}\\\text{Jonah}\\\text{Micah}\\\text{Nahum}\\\text{Habakkuk}\\\text{Zephaniah}\\\text{Malachi}\end{array}\right.$

Scroll of the Twelve

3. Writings aka **Kethuvim** (extra 7 of LXX in italics)

Psalms	Job	Proverbs
Ruth	Song of Songs	Ecclesiastes (aka Qoheleth)
Lamentations	Esther	Daniel
Ezra	Nehemiah	1 Chronicles
2 Chronicles	*Judith*	*Ecclesiasticus* (aka Sirach)
Baruch	*Tobiah*	*Wisdom*
1 Macabbees	*2 Macabbees*	

CANON OF THE NEW TESTAMENT

1. **gospels**	Matthew Mark Luke John
2. **historical**	Acts of Apostles
3. **apocalyptic**	Book of Revelation
4. **letters**	Romans Galatians Ephesians Philippians Colossians Titus Philemon Hebrews 1 Corinthians 2 Corinthians 1 Thessalonians 2 Thessalonians 1 Timothy 2 Timothy James Jude 1 & 2 Peter 1, 2 & 3 John